"An enjoyable read that uncovers so many fascinating anecdotes of Vancouver's rich and storied brewing history. From the turn of the century Vancouver breweries, to the amazing 1980s craft beer revival. Noelle's captivating storytelling makes it a must-read for craft beer enthusiasts and historians alike!" —TIM LAHAY, co-founder of The Barley Merchant Taproom & Kitchen

"*Brewmasters and Brewery Creek* is a thorough investigation into the history of craft beer — the main players and characters involved from Vancouver's inception to the microbrewery renaissance the city is familiar with, today. If you wish to add the texture of the days of old to your next sip of lager or ale in one of Vancouver's numerous taprooms, pick up a copy of Phillips' book. This hefty read will have you impressing friends with a plethora of historical facts that have shaped not just the industry but the city itself." —KENDALL HUNTER, author of *Beer Hiking Canadian Rockies*

"Phillips' *Brewmasters and Brewery Creek* is a compelling account of small breweries in Vancouver, from the city's birth through to present day. It shows a commitment to accuracy and research, while also displaying a true passion for beer along with a keen interest in the people behind it. It paints a vivid picture of the beer industry in the late 1800s, and I was particularly struck by the many similarities between the early days of beer in Vancouver and the current craft beer scene." —MIRELLA AMATO, craft beer consultant, and award-winning author

"Sip from your favourite local beer and dive into this informative and entertaining book that connects the early pioneer brewers who gave Brewery Creek its name with the contemporary entrepreneurs who helped make Vancouver the craft beer destination it is today." —JOE WIEBE, author of *Craft Beer Revolution*

T0348858

"Phillips expertly weaves together exhaustive archival research and interviews into a highly readable and long overdue chronicle of Vancouver's independent breweries and the enterprising personalities behind them." —MELANIE HARDBATTLE, Simon Fraser University Archives

"In depth research and analysis, graceful writing, and a great array of historical photographs make *Brewmasters and Brewery Creek* a must-read for craft beer historians and aficionados in Vancouver and across Canada." —JON C. STOTT, author of *Island Craft*

BREWMASTERS

& BREWERY CREEK

NOËLLE PHILLIPS

BREWMASTERS

& BREWERY CREEK

**A HISTORY OF CRAFT BEER IN
VANCOUVER, THEN AND NOW**

TOUCHWOOD

TouchWood Editions
touchwoodeditions.com

The information in this book is true and complete to the
best of the author's knowledge. All recommendations are made
without guarantee on the part of the author or the publisher.

Edited by Kate Kennedy
Proofread by Meg Yamamoto
Cover design by Sydney Barnes
Interior design by Sara Loos
Cover image Doering and Marstrand, Vanc. [189-?]
courtesy of the Simon Fraser University Archives; map,
courtesy of Dennis Mutter, private collection

CATALOGUING DATA AVAILABLE FROM LIBRARY AND ARCHIVES CANADA
ISBN 9781771514507 (softcover)
ISBN 9781771514514 (electronic)

TouchWood Editions acknowledges that the land on which
we live and work is within the traditional territories of the
Lkwungen (Esquimalt and Songhees), Malahat, Pacheedaht,
Scia'new, T'Sou-ke, and WSÁNEĆ (Pauquachin, Tsartlip,
Tsawout, and Tseycum) peoples.

We acknowledge the financial support of the Government of Canada
through the Canada Book Fund and the Canada Council for the Arts,
and of the Province of British Columbia through the British Columbia Arts
Council and the Book Publishing Tax Credit.

 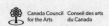 

This book was produced using FSC®-certified, acid-free
papers, processed chlorine free, and printed with soya-based inks.

Printed in Canada

28 27 26 25 24   1 2 3 4 5

This book is dedicated to the late Greg Evans, without whose meticulous research I could not have completed this project, and to the craft beer brewers of British Columbia, whose passion and skill have made the industry what it is.

TABLE OF CONTENTS

Main Street Brewing's current tasting room. (Photo courtesy of Main Street Brewing)

INTRODUCTION

I'm sitting at one of the high tables by the bar at Vancouver's Main Street Brewing, sipping a pint of their Hazy Chain IPA. The tasting room patrons and their beer flights are dwarfed by the huge space. Brightly coloured murals cover most of the walls, but one wall is left in its original 1920s brick form. "The Main Thing Is the Beer" is painted across those bricks, and above it, rafters criss-cross below the high windows. Through the front entrance, I see glimpses of Mount Pleasant's quiet suburbia: blooming trees, sidewalks, and glass-fronted condominiums. But beyond the quiet I can also hear, just a block up the road, one of Vancouver's main arteries buzzing with life and noise: the junction of Main Street and Kingsway. It feels like I'm inhabiting two very different urban spaces at once. I'm also inhabiting two different times. The building in which I'm currently enjoying my pint is over a century old. Originally built in 1920, it sits in quiet dignity among the gentrified neighbourhoods that have sprung up around it. Now creamy yellow with white trim and white-framed windows, the site began as a brewery, explored some other careers over the decades, and has returned to its roots. It takes up a good chunk of the block, claiming its place as one of the city's founding fathers.

While the site was the location of the old nineteenth-century Vancouver Brewery, Main Street Brewing's building itself didn't exist until the 1920s, when it served as the Vancouver Breweries garage.[1] This heritage structure was once a young upstart that replaced its

Main Street Brewing's current building sits on the site of the original Vancouver Brewery and was the home of the Vancouver Breweries garage in the mid-twentieth century. (Photo courtesy of Main Street Brewing)

ancestor, the original Vancouver Brewery building that sat on the corner of Scotia Street and 7th Avenue. I couldn't have found a hazy IPA there. And this brewery was less pretty. Rather than 1920s tile and plaster, this first brewery was assembled from wood, brick, and fieldstone. Instead of creamy yellow, it was dark brown. Three storeys tall with large, cross-hatched windows, it was nevertheless an impressive structure by 1888 standards.[2] The street that is now populated by folks in expensive yoga pants walking their dogs was once a dirt road crowded by horse-drawn brewery wagons that were constantly arriving and departing with kegs of lager for thirsty hotel guests in the newly incorporated City of Vancouver. Alongside the old brewery, supplying it with water and power, was a creek that issued from Tea

Swamp (now Tea Swamp Park at the corner of Sophia Street and 15th), crossing over what is now the intersection of Main and Kingsway and meandering down past Scotia and 7th until it entered False Creek, whose shores were originally at East 2nd Avenue. Although the creek was home to a tannery and some slaughterhouses, it was named for its most popular friends: the breweries.[3] Major J.S. Matthews, famed archivist for the City of Vancouver, interviewed Mrs. Elizabeth Newbury about living by Brewery Creek in the late nineteenth century. Newbury, a long-time resident of Mount Pleasant, recalled her early memories of the creek, its attachment to beer, and the vibrant life of the area: "Oh there were lots of trout in that creek, Brewery Creek I think they called it; just east of Main Street; where Doering had his brewery. Go out in the creek and catch trout for breakfast; all kinds of trout in that creek."[4]

Along the banks of the trout-filled Brewery Creek were Vancouver's first breweries, including the three storeys of brick and wood that once stood at the location of Main Street Brewing: the Vancouver Brewery, later renamed Doering & Marstrand Brewery and then Vancouver Breweries (Chapter 2 will continue that story). Brewery Creek ran across what is now Main Street and down toward the original boundary of False Creek, taking away the refuse of the tanneries and providing the most important ingredient to Vancouver's burgeoning beer industry: water. The beer industry is always about water, in one way or another. One of the most successful businessmen brewers, Charles Doering, was the first to dam the creek and use its power and resources for his own brewing systems. Jumping forward a century, one of the great early businessmen brewers of our current era, Mitch Taylor of Granville Island Brewing, built his brewery to supplement the vibrant marina community he already owned. People visiting the harbour or living at the marina quickly became the brewery's core customer base.

When the City began filling in False Creek around 1913, Brewery Creek was among the casualties, although along its old path Vancouver's breweries still stand. Where once stood the first breweries of Mount Pleasant—Vancouver Brewery, Stadler Brewery, Lion Brewery, Lansdowne Brewery, Mainland Brewery, San Francisco Brewery, Red Star Brewery, and others—are now Main Street Brewing, R&B, Brassneck, 33 Acres, Red Truck, and Electric Bicycle. Beneath my feet, as I sit at my perch in Main Street Brewing, deep underneath the well-groomed trees and glass condominiums outside the building, Brewery Creek still rushes through the city, unseen and unheard—at least, unheard by most. "Though it is now underground, Brewery Creek is still alive...you can hear it," said City Archivist Matthews.[5] So listen carefully. The water is always there. In this book, I hope you will begin to hear the water of Brewery Creek once again by reading the stories of how craft brewing became one of Vancouver's most beloved industries, both then and now.

Vancouver has been shaped by water, and it is water that makes the city's beer unique. Since the city's craft beer industry emerged around bodies of water, I'm following its lead. Local historian Bruce Macdonald describes his own developing awareness of how water created the region:

As I travelled between Annacis Island and White Rock, I could not help but realize I was living and working in the middle of a giant river delta. Suddenly it was obvious to me exactly where the delta was—all the land at sea level that was perfectly flat. The low hills were just the piles of debris left by the last glacier 12,000 years ago. We live our lives on this stage, boxed in by mile-high mountains.[6]

Water propelled—quite literally—the city's formation in the mid-nineteenth century, as sawmills sprung up along creeks and inlets and Americans, Britons, Germans, and others flooded in during the gold rush to try their luck on the banks of the Fraser River. The region's earliest pioneers knew what Vancouver's waterways could

Opposite: The original path of Brewery Creek and its first breweries. (Photo by Noëlle Phillips, with thanks to Dennis Mutter)

4

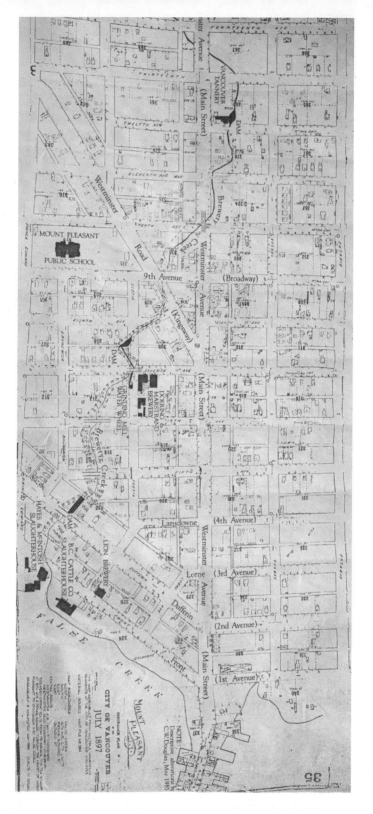

MOUNT PLEASANT
PUBLIC SCHOOL

VANCOUVER
TANNERY

DOERING &
MARSTRAND
BREWERY

GRINDING MILL
WATER WHEEL

HAYES &
McINTOSH
SLAUGHTERHOUSE

B.C. CATTLE CO.
SLAUGHTERHOUSE

LION BREWERY

Westminster Road

(Main Street)

9th Avenue   (Broadway)

(Kingsway)

(Main Street)

Lansdowne   (4th Avenue)

Lorne   (3rd Avenue)

Dufferin   (2nd Avenue)

Front

(Main Street)   (1st Avenue)

FALSE CREEK

MOUNT
PLEASANT

CITY OF VANCOUVER
JULY 1897

35

Breweries in Vancouver from 1887 to 1917. 1: Stanley Park Brewery. 2: City Brewery, Red Cross Brewery. 3: Mainland Brewery. 4: Vancouver Brewery, D&M Brewery, Vancouver Breweries. 5: Cedar Cottage Brewery. 6: Columbia Brewery. 7: Canadian Brewing and Malting. 8: Lion Brewery, Stadler Brewery. 9: San Francisco Brewery, Red Star Brewery.

do for the city's economy and their own wealth, so they bought up sawmills, dammed the creeks, and put water to work. While these activities boosted the bustling economy, they also contributed to the further marginalization of Vancouver's Indigenous population—something for which the alcohol industry more broadly was also culpable.

Most of the independent breweries that were originally built alongside Vancouver's waterways disappeared by 1917, when provincial liquor prohibition was enacted. However, contrary to my original assumptions, it wasn't actually prohibition that killed the early craft beer industry in Vancouver. It happened earlier. Prohibition just tapped the final nail into the coffin that contained the hopes and dreams of Vancouver's independent, local beer production. Don't be mistaken, however—it's not that brewing or beer disappeared. For a while, Vancouver no longer had its small, unique breweries. But, like Brewery Creek running hidden underneath the city streets, the independent brewery spirit wasn't gone, as Part II will show. In a 1998 interview, beer historian Greg Evans pointed to the early 1980s as the "renaissance of [BC] brewing," expressing gratitude that "we're returning to the kind of choices the public had before the First World War."[7] The craft brewing spirit that was alive and well in Vancouver before 1914 sparked into flame once again in 1982. This book tracks both of Vancouver's craft beer booms.

STORIES OF VANCOUVER BEER: WHAT YOU'LL FIND IN THIS BOOK

First of all, this book primarily focuses on Vancouver craft beer— Vancouver's breweries, brewers, and drinkers. While my original intent was to explore craft beer and brewing in the entire BC Lower Mainland, I swiftly realized that such a project would result in an over-whelmingly long book. It is therefore (mostly) the tales of Vancouver brewing that you'll find in these pages—not New Westminster, not Surrey, not Burnaby, not Victoria. However, that "mostly" is my caveat; I do touch upon breweries and brewers in nearby areas whose presence has influenced the craft beer scene in Vancouver. This is particularly true in Part II, which explores craft brewing after 1980. For example, Central City Brewing in Surrey helped shift consumer tastes in the region by popularizing an odd new beer style back in the early 2000s: an IPA. Dageraad Brewing in Burnaby set a new standard for experimental brewing and Belgian styles beginning in 2014. Breweries north of Vancouver, like Whistler and Howe Sound, helped beer become one of the area's tourism draws. Four Winds in Delta made people think of beer as a sophisticated drink. These and other breweries located near, but not technically in, Vancouver helped shape craft beer culture in the city itself. Moreover, they contributed to Vancouver's growing reputation as a beer destination, since "Vancouver" has long been a term that stands in for the greater Vancouver region more broadly, which has become an important player in the North American craft beer market. In his book *Craft Beer Revolution*, Joe Wiebe claims that "Vancouver has become the engine that drives craft beer in B.C.—its unique and diverse array of breweries, taphouses and bottle shops makes it now, without question, *the* craft beer destination in British Columbia, if not all of Canada."[8] He's right; Vancouver has become a craft beer hub equal to famed beer destinations like Portland and San Francisco.

This entire book is about Vancouver brewing, but it's divided into two time periods, each of which represents a thriving era of independent brewing in the city. The first half of the book tells the story of early craft beer in Vancouver: the birth, growth, and death of independent beer culture from the city's incorporation in 1886 until just after prohibition began. It also tells the smaller stories within that larger narrative, giving voice to the people whose tales have largely been lost to history. There is, unfortunately, relatively little published work on the early years of brewing in Vancouver. While authors such as William Hagelund, Allen Sneath, Greg Evans, and Bill Wilson have written important histories about this topic, these accounts sometimes conflict with one another due to the difficulty of historical sources. Moreover, Hagelund's and Sneath's books, both on early BC brewing, lack citations. This has made assessing their claims difficult. Even when authors cite their sources, however, these larger histories often sketch out brief outlines of the breweries (and the people who ran them), but provide relatively little to fill them in. This high-level approach is often necessary, especially if the book is covering a large geographical or chronological period. However, since I am focusing on Vancouver exclusively, and restricting the first part of this book to approximately 1886–1920, I have a bit more time and space to "colour in" some of those outlines. I have also had the opportunity to rectify some misunderstandings about historical events and figures. Using the work of these other historians as well as my own experience as an academic researcher, I've searched through various forms of documentation to find out more about the movers and shakers in the Vancouver beer scene. The records are sometimes sparse, but I've used the information available in census records, passenger lists, contemporary newspapers and brochures, city directories, and the Vancouver and Victoria archives to patch together a greater understanding of the lives these people led. You will find some additional details about the immigration, marriages, home life, previous employment, political activities, hobbies, and social lives of Vancouver's early brewers.

Part II jumps forward to the 1980s to tell the tale of how the city's craft beer community resurrected itself, fighting the odds to become relevant once again. A series of legislative changes gradually allowed breweries to grow on their own, to develop their own community in their own space. The brewery owners and brewmasters of this era advocated for those changes, and in doing so, they did a service to future brewery owners in the province. By interviewing brewers, brewery owners, and bottle collectors, reading memoirs, going through old business files and notes, visiting archives, and trawling through newspapers, I've developed a much deeper understanding of why craft beer became so central to Vancouver in recent decades, and why the industry hasn't fallen apart the way it did a century earlier.

A word about gender: Readers will note that much (though not all) of this book seems to focus on men. It's an unfortunate truth; the modern beer industry has been largely controlled by and marketed to men. This was not always the case, however. During much of Europe's Middle Ages, women (called alewives or brewsters) were the ones making the beer. While monks are often thought of as the brewers of the medieval period, this is only partially correct; monasteries certainly brewed in high volumes, but outside of monastic communities, women were the primary brewers. From their kitchens, they would brew beer and often sell it to their neighbours. We might even think of alewives as foreshadowing "craft" brewing while monastic breweries, with their greater access to capital and enhanced technology, were a prototype for later industrial brewing. When beer became more profitable in the later medieval period, however, women were slowly pushed out.[9] By the nineteenth century—the beginning of Vancouver's brewing history—men were fully in control of the business of beer. There were occasional exceptions, such as Mary Mueller (more on her later!), but even Mary entered the industry almost by accident, through the actions of her husband and her male business partner. As far as the records show, women were not pursuing beer as a career back then, either as brewers or as business owners. Jumping forward to the 1980s, the resurrection of craft beer in BC, we see the industry still dominated by men. Don't be mistaken; there were women in the beer industry in 1980s BC, but it wasn't that common and at first occurred almost exclusively in corporate beer. One example is Nancy More, founder of Kwantlen Polytechnic University's brewing program. More is a great supporter of the BC craft beer industry, but she has three decades of experience in "Big Beer"—Labatt and Guinness. This experience has helped her train up quality brewers who now work in craft, and there is even a brewing scholarship in her honour—one that supports women in the brewing industry. More, like other women who entered the industry in the '80s or '90s such as Shirley Warne and Lundy Dale, is well aware of how far women have come in modern craft brewing, but also how far we still have to go. The gendered and ethnic stereotypes around beer—in particular, craft beer's reputation as a white guy's drink—hold fairly true for much of Vancouver's history, but recently there has been increasing pushback, change, and desire for more equity and inclusion. This book traces the craft beer industry in Vancouver from its colonial beginnings to its post-pandemic evolution, with the awareness that we are continuing to evolve.

The very term "craft brewery" (formerly called a microbrewery) used throughout the book is somewhat contested. No universal definition exists. In the early part of this book, I use the term "independent brewery" to refer to what we might now call craft breweries. Part I ends when corporate consolidations temporarily choke out independent brewing in Vancouver, around the time of prohibition. But whether we call it craft brewing or microbrewing or independent brewing, it's always been different from the business of Big Beer. Joe Wiebe acknowledges the slippage in meaning with terms like "craft beer" and "craft brewery," whose definition shifts depending on who's talking—and where they live. He does, however, provide some general guidelines: "A craft brewery is a small-scale operation that produces less than 150,000 hL per year... The brewery must be independent, and it must be dedicated to brewing high quality beer."[10] The Canadian Craft Brewers Association states that the definition of a craft brewery varies depending on the province, but specifies that any Canadian craft brewery must have a federal brewing licence, cannot produce more than 400,000 hectolitres of beer (with most producing under 5,000), and must be independently owned. "However," they add, "this technical definition does not accurately reflect the essence of craft brewing."[11] Wiebe makes a similar assertion: "You know it [craft beer] when you taste it." In other words, while craft beer is usually assumed to be produced independently and in relatively small amounts, it has an indefinable "something" that makes it truly craft. Whether that "something" is its close connection to its community, its use of local ingredients, or its unique flavours, it's something special.

In researching the stories of these two craft beer booms, I've travelled down more research rabbit holes than I would have thought possible. As an academic, I'm used to writing about a very narrow topic and delving deep. For this project, I want to give space and time to as many breweries, brewery owners, and brewmasters as possible while still telling the overarching story of Vancouver craft beer. This means that I cannot tell the full story of each brewery that has arisen in Vancouver. In truth, I believe that each of the breweries I've encountered, past and present, has a story that could form its own book—and each of them deserves such sustained attention.

Within the space of this book, I can't do that. Instead, I hope that this will be a comprehensive but pleasurable read—one that will inflame your interest in this topic, inform, and perhaps inspire you to pursue further reading. I don't want you to feel you need to sit down at your desk to read this book—I want you to kick back in an armchair with your favourite beer.

PART I: 1886-1920

VANCOUVER BREWERY TIMELINE: PART I

(Brewery openings and other significant dates)

1886
City of
Vancouver
incorporated

1888
Vancouver Brewery;
San Francisco
Brewery;
Mainland Brewery;
Columbia Brewery

1890
Red Cross Brewery

1895

1896
Stanley Park
Brewery; Lion
Brewery

1900

1900-1901
The Vancouver
Breweries (D&M
merges with Red
Cross)

1889
Red Star Brewery;
North Arm Brewery

1887
City Brewery

1892
Doering & Marstrand
Brewing (formerly
Vancouver Brewery)

1898
Cedar Cottage
Brewery (under
Raywood);
Stadler Brewery

1902
Cedar
Cottage
Brewery
(under
Benson),
Royal
Brewing Co.
(formerly
Stanley
Park)

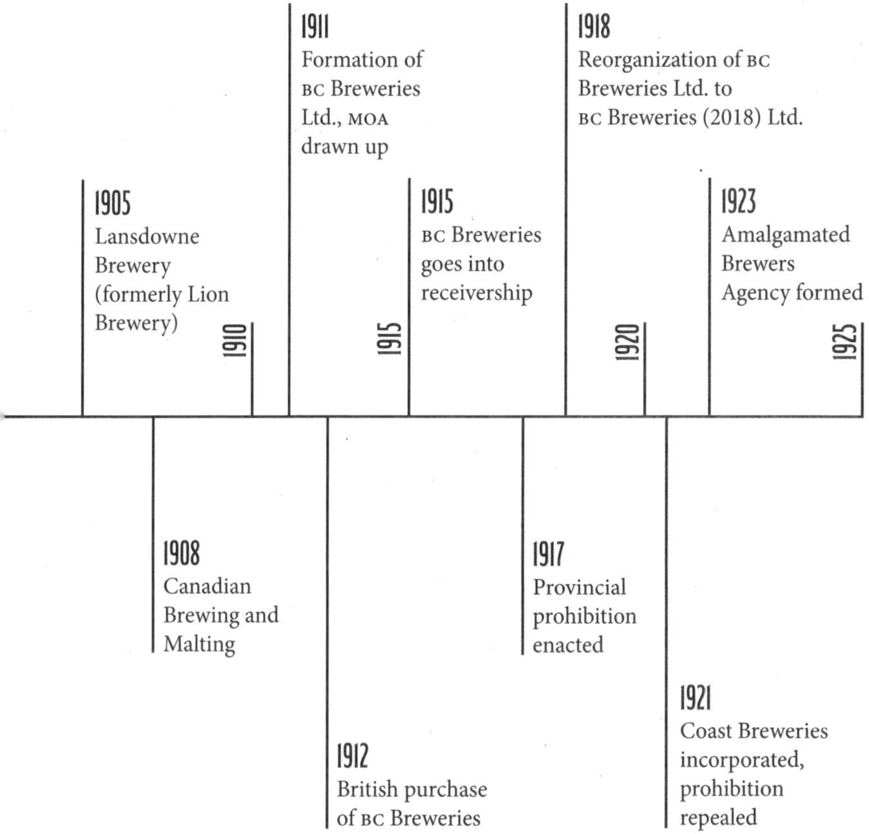

1911
Formation of
BC Breweries
Ltd., MOA
drawn up

1918
Reorganization of BC
Breweries Ltd. to
BC Breweries (2018) Ltd.

1905
Lansdowne
Brewery
(formerly Lion
Brewery)

1910

1915
BC Breweries
goes into
receivership

1915

1923
Amalgamated
Brewers
Agency formed

1920

1925

1908
Canadian
Brewing and
Malting

1917
Provincial
prohibition
enacted

1921
Coast Breweries
incorporated,
prohibition
repealed

1912
British purchase
of BC Breweries

CHAPTER 1

VANCOUVER: A CITY ON FIRE

It's hard to believe, but the first wave of craft beer fever in Vancouver spread soon after the city burned to the ground. Vancouver and its citizens are nothing if not resilient, as many years of endless rain and steep property prices have repeatedly proven. In 1936, *The Province* newspaper said much the same in its recounting of Vancouver's early years and the fire that razed it to the ground: "'I guess this marks the end of that mushroom burg of Vancouver,' remarked many a citizen of the rival community of Port Moody, while doleful prophecies were also heard in Victoria and Westminster. But inhabitants of Vancouver were made of sterner stuff."[1] They were indeed.

In the 1860s, what is now the heart of downtown Vancouver was still a collection of small cabins connected by muddy tracks, populated mostly by the workers at Stamp's Mill (later called the Hastings Sawmill Company). To the frustration of local workers, no alcohol was permitted on mill property and the nearest saloon was in New Westminster,[2] so men hoping for a drink after a long day's work didn't have many options.[3] Fortunately for them, British steamboat pilot John Deighton, popularly known in the area as Gassy Jack, had a solution. Legend has it that in 1867, with a barrel of whisky in his canoe, he paddled from New Westminster to set up a makeshift stall and sell drinks to the mill workers. At the time, he probably didn't realize that he had become the first small-business owner in what would become British Columbia's largest metropolis. Gassy Jack quickly grew his customer base and his fortune when he opened the Globe Saloon at what is now the intersection of Water and Carrall, just outside the property boundary of Stamp's Mill.[4] By 1875, four out of the ten main public buildings in Gastown were saloons—in other words, alcohol was big business.[5]

The new saloon enlivened the growing area of "Gastown" (named for Gassy Jack), where the population was quickly increasing. According to a brochure from 1891, there were only about 150 people living in the shanty town.[6] But that small population was composed of a mixture of many different cultures. The residents included not only the Indigenous people who already lived there, but former ship hands from across the world. "As a result," according to local historian Bruce Macdonald, "the millhands included people of Portuguese, Spanish, Chilean, Russian, Finnish, French, Austrian, German, Belgian, Kanakan (Native Hawaiian), Dutch, American, and Swedish origins. A list of 11 general merchants and hotel proprietors in Granville in 1882 included 2 Chinese, 2 Irishmen, 2 Scotsmen, a Black, a Polish Jew, a Frenchman, and an Englishman."[7] By 1870, Gastown was officially named the Village of Granville and consisted of just a few acres, with perhaps one hundred buildings in total.[8] However, in 1885 CPR General Manager William Van Horne announced that Granville would be the terminus destination of the new Canadian Pacific Railway.[9] This changed everything.

Bruce Macdonald describes the importance of the CPR's presence, explaining how the railway "shifted the focus of BC from an outward-looking maritime society centred in Victoria to a more inward-looking continental community centered in Vancouver."[10] Vancouver became the "Terminal City," one of the key links in the new system of transportation across Canada and the United States. With the improved transportation in the province came more immigrants. According to Macdonald's research, the non-Indigenous population of BC nearly tripled during the 1880s, reaching over 70,000. While Victoria was the biggest population hub in the early years, Vancouver/

Granville and New Westminster began to offer competition. In 1881 New Westminster had 1,500 and Granville (Vancouver) had 300–400, but by 1886 Vancouver had 2,500–3,000, then between 10,000 and 12,000 by 1890, far surpassing New Westminster's 6,000.[11]

So in the mid-1880s, Vancouver was indeed a city on fire—metaphorically. It was officially incorporated on April 6, 1886, to great acclaim. However, the city's rapid population growth in the 1880s wasn't matched by a growth in infrastructure that could support it and keep it safe. The same 1936 article from *The Province*, cited previously, describes how Vancouver looked in 1886:

> *Vancouver had no paved streets; just a half dozen planked roads and some dirt trails. Water Street was largely a trestle over a ravine; Cordova Street was Corduroy; Hastings Street with its wooden sidewalk stretched from Cambie to Westminster Avenue (now Main Street). The "Old Road" along the shore went from the maple tree [in Gastown] to Hastings Mill, Hastings Townsite, and on to the Royal City [New Westminster]. The "New Road"*

A view of Vancouver, then Granville, just one year before it was incorporated as a city. (Photo courtesy of City of Vancouver Archives, AM54-S4-: Dist P14)

was a glorified bridle track, and trailed off from Carrall Street,
squirming through the stumps to a narrow wooden bridge across
False Creek, whence it followed the present course of Kingsway
to New Westminster.[12]

The new city's wooden infrastructure combined with the CPR land clearances both increased the risk of fire. *The Province* described the new CPR townsite as "a disheveled litter of stumps and debris [with] a wild disarray of fallen trees [that] flanked Granville street on both sides, dry as tinder after days in the hot sun." Fires were regularly burning as land was being cleared, but the city's firefighting brigade was woefully inadequate. Formed just two weeks earlier, the Vancouver Volunteer Hose Company was staffed by forty volunteers whose preparation for fire entailed buckets and shovels.[13] Ocean breezes, small bush fires, dry timber, a barely-there fire department, and a wooden city: a perfect combination of elements for an inferno.

On Sunday, June 13, 1886, workers had been clearing the CPR roundhouse site in preparation for the railway. James Ross of the *Daily News* indicated that "the trees were all falled, and the fallen trees, stumps, etc, were being disposed of by burning here and there in separate heaps."[14] One of these small fires began growing, despite workers running back and forth with blankets soaked in water from False Creek in an attempt to quench it. The article from the *Daily News* explains why initially this wasn't a cause for alarm:

A few weeks ago, during a gale from the west, the city was filled
with smoke and cinders from these fires, and fire reached close
to several outlying buildings, but after some fighting danger was
averted. This, doubtless, tended to lull people into a sense of secu-
rity on Sunday. It was about two o'clock in the afternoon that the
breeze, which had been blowing from the west, BECAME A GALE.[15]

Even before this gale started up, Gallagher, the site manager, became increasingly concerned as the small outbreak resisted all efforts to contain it. He gave a prescient warning to his workers: "If the fire breaks away from the clearing, do not attempt to fight it, or you will lose your lives!"[16]

The fire did indeed break away from the clearing, forcing the workers to retreat and abandon their efforts. News of the rapidly spreading flames passed quickly around the city as folks finished church services and began preparing Sunday lunch, efforts that were quickly abandoned as they were told to gather their possessions and head for the water. CPR General Superintendent Henry Abbott learned early about the blaze, and quickly scribbled down a note that said "Good for all the pails you can find" (a note from Abbott was like cash in the shops) to the volunteers attempting to put out the flames. Pails were a staggeringly inadequate response to the flames ravaging the city's wooden sidewalks and collapsing its hotels.[17] The Vancouver Volunteer Hose Company focused mainly on moving explosive materials out of shops and homes, away from the heat. Within less than two hours, nearly the entire city was destroyed. The New Westminster's *Daily News* of June 17, 1886, described the fire's catastrophic impact: "Probably never since the days of Pompeii and Herculaneum was a town WIPED OUT OF EXISTENCE so completely and suddenly as was Vancouver on Sunday."[18] The Vancouver city directory of 1888 records that only three homes remained, and the *Vancouver·Daily World* pamphlet of 1891 describes the city as being "literally wiped out of existence...three hundred and fifty buildings were, as if in a flash, destroyed."

People from the Squamish Nation and nearby Moodyville came to offer assistance, but Vancouverites were left in shock and horror as their city collapsed around them. Mayor MacLean sent a dispatch to Prime Minister John A. Macdonald that evening: "Our city is ashes. Three thousand people homeless. Can you send us any government aid?"[19] Funds from the provincial and federal governments, as well as other cities, were quickly sent out to help the newly born city of Vancouver recover from the catastrophe.

Despite the death and destruction caused by the Great Fire, Vancouverites were eager to get back on their feet. James Ross's *Daily*

A month after the fire, Vancouver rebuilds. (Photo courtesy of City of Vancouver Archives, AM54-S4-: Str. P7.1)

News account of the fire, written just four days after the event, struck a remarkably optimistic note as it concluded:

> *Like nearly all others who had started business in the new city, however, we perceive that the fire, whatever may be its effect upon individuals, is to the city as a whole not a very serious matter, in fact it can scarcely impede the progress of Vancouver at all.*[20]

Just three days after the fire, City Council assembled, using a tent in place of a City Hall, and within five days newspapers were circulating. The 1888 city directory asserted that "within twenty months of [the city's] destruction, there now exists a city with an estimated population of 6,000 with over 1,000 houses, 40 miles of planked roads and sidewalks, a number of extensive brick warehouses...and offices, the electric light and gas works, [and] a city hall."[21] The 1891 *Daily World* pamphlet praised the "mettle of the pioneers of this city" and described the shared evening meals enjoyed by Vancouver's citizens at the Northern Hotel site on Hastings in the days after the fire. The fire brigade was also rapidly reconstructed, supplied, and funded—and enjoyed a great deal of popularity in the years following the Great Fire.

Vancouver's drinking spots were among the first businesses to open after the fire; twenty-five licensed hotels and nineteen saloons were recorded in 1886, serving enough liquor to quench all thirst in the new Terminal City. The enterprising Captain J.K. Ritchie, owner of the Tivoli Saloon, made his establishment the most desirable by offering schooners of beer for only five cents, while other saloons were charging ten or fifteen for a glass. Ritchie's "Five-Cent Beer House" quickly became a standout in the sea of saloons.[22]

But there seemed to be a shift happening—not in the interest in having places to drink and buy beer, but in the *kinds* of places. Saloons, the social hubs of settler towns in BC, were becoming increasingly debaucherous toward the end of the century. Douglas Hamilton describes the atmosphere of a BC saloon in the 1880s and '90s:

The Vancouver Volunteer Fire Brigade in their new uniforms, 1887. (Photo courtesy of City of Vancouver Archives, AM54-S4-: FD P7)

One needed no directions to find the local bar. The smell of spilled beer and tobacco smoke wafted out into the street along with boisterous voices. Refuse and filth littered the area, while drunken derelicts pawed at passersby. A gaggle of children would cluster around the unsteady, teasing them in the streets—and robbing them in the alleyways. Fights were frequent, and hotel visitors complained of noise, which usually did not let up until the festivities ended at 8 a.m. with a final "God Save the Queen."[23]

Post-fire, beer houses and saloons gradually began to decrease in numbers while hotels gained ground. Sellers of liquor, beer, or wine, whether wholesale or retail, in a saloon or a hotel, needed to apply for a licence annually. In 1886, licence records show that seventeen people applied for a saloon liquor licence, while thirty applied for a hotel liquor licence. By 1888, however, only six out of the sixty-seven liquor licences granted were for a saloon. The rest went to hotels, a shift that suggested increasing concerns about respectability in the liquor trade (drinking in a hotel was more acceptable than drinking in a saloon).[24]

Along with this interest in making drinking more socially acceptable, there was concern about the influence of non-white people in the booming alcohol business. Restricting the alcohol trade to white or white-passing people helped the appearance of respectability. Changes made to the province's 1888 Licences Act reflected this bigotry. In 1894, an amendment specified that "no licence for the sale of wines or liquors by retail shall, hereafter, be given or transferred to any person of the Chinese race in any portion of the province." The act also mandated that Japanese, Chinese, and "Indian" people were excluded from signing the petitions required for the granting of liquor licences in rural areas, and threatened forfeiture of a licence to anyone found "giv[ing] intoxicating liquor to Indians."[25] In other words, the stage was set for ensuring that the culturally diverse city of Vancouver would be increasingly controlled by its white population. And unfortunately, the beer industry would contribute to this legacy of institutionalized racism. Provincial legislation was sliding discrimination right into the legal framework and cultural foundation of Vancouver: the places where men made deals over a pint and a handshake. Saloons and hotel bars were places that men went "to drink, eat, sleep, exchange gossip, gamble, pick up the mail, find a job, cash a cheque, play cards, hear the news and sometimes even attend church."[26] Drinking spots (whether hotels or saloons) were a town's social centre. By barring Indigenous, Japanese, and Chinese people from access to these places, the province's early founders encouraged consumers to think of such spaces as naturally belonging to the white male population. These racist inclusions were eventually struck from the Licences Act, but their impact was felt for far longer.

The increase in hotels and the decrease in saloons signalled that drinking was becoming an activity that was more respectable (and more white) than it was in the early years, when an ethnically diverse crowd of mill workers living in the shanties of Gastown would guzzle whisky and beer each night at Deighton's Globe Saloon. By the 1890s and early twentieth century, the alcohol industry in Vancouver was making itself more socially acceptable—at least partially in response to the religious advocates of temperance, who were urging the government to prohibit booze altogether. And it was in this context, of a newly built city trying to make a name for itself as an international metropolis located on the nexus of Canada's railway and ports, that enterprising businessmen saw an opportunity to make money by making beer respectable—and they took it. The next few chapters tell their stories.

Charles Doering in 1890, shortly after moving to Vancouver. (Photo courtesy of BC Archives, item A-08611 141)

CHAPTER 2
VANCOUVER'S FIRST BREWERS: FIT FOR THE "FATHERLAND"

Vancouver is well supplied in the way of liquid refreshments,
there being three breweries in the city, turning out nectar fit
for the gods of the "Fatherland." —Vancouver Daily World,
September 29, 1888

Charles Doering, who relocated to Vancouver immediately after the
Great Fire, is often credited as being the city's pioneer brewer. He
actually wasn't the first—although he was close. He was probably the
wealthiest, however. By the beginning of the First World War, his net
assets were $486,400, which made him the eleventh-richest Vancouver
businessman of his era.[1] And his brewery was the largest in Vancouver
until around 1909, when beer tycoon and future rum-runner Henry
Reifel built his Canadian Brewing and Malting facility at Yew and
11th.[2] Doering certainly knew how to turn brewing into a profitable
business, but he was just one of a dynamic group of men—and one
woman—who were ambitious and gutsy enough to turn beer into a
career. As I researched their lives, I knew that Doering would be the
first thread to follow as I unravelled the tangled knot of connections
between Vancouver's earliest brewers. So we will start with him, his

brewery, and the other two breweries that started the "craft" beer industry in Vancouver.[3]

Carl Gottfried Doering (he later used Charles), born in January 1856 to factory worker Johann Doering and his wife Johanna Marie, was nineteen when he left his native city of Leipzig, Germany,[4] and sailed to North America, settling first in Colorado and eventually making his way to San Francisco. Like so many other German citizens who immigrated to the United States, Doering was an enthusiastic young man eager to make a name for himself somewhere new. It wasn't that Leipzig lacked opportunities—this was no backwater. In fact, it was one of the more influential cities in Germany at the time. Leipzig was known for its arts, culture, and book industry, all of which cemented its identity as a hub for German intelligentsia. But it wasn't just the scholarly elites and musicians that loved the city; within the remnants of its old walls, nineteenth-century Leipzig nurtured a thriving and cosmopolitan urban marketplace in which traders from across the world crossed paths and sold luxury goods to eager customers. Aspiring to the appearance of wealth and deca-dence as it competed with other urban centres in Germany, Leipzig developed luxurious gardens, built expensive promenade areas, and showcased its grand buildings.[5] When Doering visited the city with his wife Sarah Jane years later, she would praise Leipzig's beauties in letters to her mother, describing it as a place she would love to live and noting how "drinkable" their gose was (gose is a salty soured beer famous in Leipzig).[6]

Leipzig was rapidly changing during Doering's youth. Its popu-lation tripled in six decades, reaching over one hundred thousand between 1811 and 1871.[7] Competition for everything was ramping up, and wealth and reputation became even more critical. In the recollections of Doering's family, preserved in the files and memory of his great-great-grandson Dennis Mutter, Doering didn't talk about his life in Germany or why he left. However, we can speculate about how an ambitious young man from a humble family might have been feeling. In the bustling metropolis of Leipzig, the pressure to succeed must have been high. The newly settled communities of Canada's west coast offered fresh opportunities, far away from the more rigid constraints and hierarchies of Europe's ancient cities. Cities in North America were starting from the ground up and the options for an aspiring businessman were endless. There were also ample spaces for hunting and fishing, hobbies that Doering would come to enjoy. So he took the long ocean journey, moving first to Denver, Colorado, and then likely living for a while in San Francisco, a city with a thriving brewing industry.[8] Around 1881 he sailed up to Victoria with his friend (and fellow German) Benjamin Wrede.[9]

The brewing industry in Victoria was already well underway when Doering arrived in town. The first brewery had opened almost twenty-five years earlier. William Steinberger, another German immigrant, opened his brewery on the shores of Victoria's Swan Lake in 1858, and other breweries like Colonial, Phoenix, and Bavaria quickly followed. During his time in Victoria, Doering would have had the chance to see how brewing worked in Canada: how breweries were supplied with malt and hops via steamship routes between Victoria and the brewing haven of San Francisco; which men in town were the best brewers; the beers customers enjoyed the most; and who was drinking—and where. According to historian Bill Wilson and Mutter's family files, Doering managed to get a job at the Phoenix Brewery, working for Charles Gowan. He also worked as a machinist, which was his first trade.

In his early days in Victoria, he met a fellow young immigrant, Nels Nelson from Denmark, who was picking up odd jobs as a painter at the time. Shortly thereafter, Nels would graduate from painting to apprentice brewing at the Victoria Brewery, which then had been relocated to the corner of Discovery and Government in the heart of the city, and then the Nanaimo Brewery, who hired him after seeing what he could do. Little did these two men know that they would eventually both be living in the Lower Mainland, running two of the major breweries there and rising up the ranks of local politics. Nels would stay at Doering's hotel in Vancouver and Doering would give him a foot in the door of the brewing industry there. But for now, they were at the bottom of a ladder they both wanted to climb.[10]

Although he'd secured some work in a Victoria brewery, Doering's first independent foray into the booze business was as an owner of the King's Head, just the first in a long list of saloons and hotels he would eventually run. The King's Head Saloon and Boarding House on Johnson Street was opened by British immigrant William King on November 12, 1864 (the "King" in this case being not an allusion to the King of England, typical for an English pub, but to William King himself). His enthusiastic advertisements in the *Victoria Daily Chronicle* throughout that first month called residents to "Rally! Friends, Rally!!" to see his "newly arranged and fitted up house on Johnson Street" where he would serve "the best quality of food" and "Pure Liquors." The King's Head also boasted first-class sleeping accommodations for up to one hundred guests. It seemed an auspicious start. However, by September 1865, King was advertising reduced room rates, and just a few months later—one year after the grand opening—the *Chronicle*'s Classifieds section listed the business as being "sold cheap." By January 1866, it was on the auction block. Public accounts are silent until 1871, when the saloon's new proprietor, George Edward Smith, proudly advertised it as the "Naval Headquarters" (something that is repeated in later newspaper accounts). This time, the owner added "concert rooms" to the saloon's attractions. Given that the King's Head was also cited in adultery cases whose notoriety landed them in the papers, it may have been becoming a seedy spot in the growing city. It needed a facelift.

Doering saw an opportunity with the old saloon, which he purchased with his friend Bernard (also called Benjamin) Wrede. On April 13, 1883, *The British Colonist* announced that John Pabst of the King's Head Saloon transferred his licence to "Charles Darring" and "Bernard Wrede." The misspelling of their names indicates that they were likely quite new to the city and residents were unfamiliar with them, but by the time he refurbished and rebranded the saloon, Doering was a well-established resident. However, there isn't much information about what Doering and Wrede did with the saloon. What we do know is that by 1887, Doering had renovated the saloon and relaunched the business with a new partner, William White. Wrede was no longer involved with the King's Head, and instead was spending most of his time in Vancouver looking after his and Doering's interests there. A Victoria newspaper account of January 1887 described White and Doering as "two young gentlemen well and favorably known here," suggesting that reputation was a key element of making businesses work in this young city.[11] It also suggests that Doering was still spending much of his time in Victoria.

When the two partners rebranded the King's Head in 1887, they put their own spin on the saloon, calling it "The King's Head Beer Hall" and emphasizing that "beer is a specialty."[12] This may have been an intentional echo of the beer hall culture from Doering's native Saxony. They also made some bold interior decor choices, probably designed to make their new business memorable and cater to a largely male demographic (no more concert rooms!). The two partners paid for regular newspaper ads throughout 1887, each of which proudly advertised their "thoroughly renovated" saloon, "refitted in splendid style." Doering was a skilled marksman, something he proved once again just before reopening the King's Head, when he won a winter rifle-shooting contest in Saanichton.[13] A newspaper account from January 15, 1887, a month later, lauded the new version of the King's Head, proclaiming that "the [saloon] is certain to prosper." The reporter described the hunting-themed drinking hall in detail:

There are numerous beautiful deer heads to be seen adorning the walls, also bear heads, mountain goats, mountain sheep, elk, &c., all beautiful specimens of forest game. A panther destroying a fawn, in a large glass case, is very natural and worthy of inspection. A case of birds, comprising grouse, quail, pheasants, ducks, &c., the work of S. Whittaker, taxidermist, is a splendid collection.[14]

CHAS. DOERING
President Vancouver Breweries, Ltd.
Vancouver

Charles Doering was known as a skilled hunter and showed off some of his prizes in his saloon. (Printed in *British Columbians As We See 'Em*, published by the Newspaper Cartoonists Association of British Columbia in 1911)

The saloon sold local Empire Brewery beer for five cents a schooner—a very affordable price (recall the fame of Ritchie's Five-Cent Beer House in Vancouver around the same time, when other breweries were charging ten or fifteen cents per glass). A later advertisement from this same year advertised the saloon as a "wonderful museum" that "gentleman strangers visiting the city" would enjoy seeing.[15] A short reporter's note in this same issue of *The Daily Colonist* claimed that the saloon's collection of birds and forest animals was the very best in all of Victoria (one wonders how many taxidermy collections the city had on display). Other advertisements also enticed customers with promises of the finest wine, liquor, and cigars.

Despite his investment in the saloon and his popularity in the city, Doering was beginning to consider setting up in Vancouver permanently. He had been living at least part time in Vancouver (then Granville) since 1885, and passenger lists from steamships like the *Charmer* and the *Yosemite* reveal that in the late 1880s he was frequently travelling back and forth between Victoria and Vancouver, taking care of his business interests on both sides. His first step toward making his home in Vancouver permanent was taken when the newly incorporated city of Vancouver burned down on June 13, 1886—six months before Doering and White reopened the King's Head. Doering and Bernard Wrede saw an opportunity in Vancouver's post-fire collapse. The destruction of so many hotels and saloons meant that there was acute need for good food and drink in what was now the CPR's Terminal City. Wrede moved to Vancouver the day of the fire, and he and Doering quickly went to work on establishing a new hotel: the Stag & Pheasant, in another tip of the hat to Doering's hunting hobby.[16] This building actually existed before Doering took it over, according to the Mutter files and the Changing Vancouver blog (run by local historians). There was a Stag and Pheasant saloon in the same spot before the 1886 fire, and after its destruction in the blaze, Wrede and Doering opened it as a hotel just one month later. They rapidly poured money into advertising their new venture; Stag & Pheasant ads featured in many issues of the local papers, as well as the Victoria ones, which announced that Doering had purchased the hotel and "will be glad to see all his Victoria friends while in the Terminal City." One advertisement, transcribed in the Mutter family files, records Doering's announcement of his new hotel, addressed to "the General Public": "Having bought out my partner, Mr. Ben Wrede, I am now able to give my whole attention to my guests at the Stag and Pheasant ... The finest sleeping and eating accommodations in the city at most reasonable rates. I have in connection with my saloon the latest improved billiard and pool tables. Always on hand papers and periodicals of

Doering (on the right) after a successful hunting expedition at his property near Ashcroft, Hat Creek Ranch. (Photo courtesy of Dennis Mutter)

the surrounding country. Give me a call." Doering's purchase of the Gambrinus Saloon, the Atlantic Beer Hall, and the hotels Germania and Brunswick soon followed.[17] By April 1888 Doering had dissolved his partnership with White and sold his share of the King's Head, fully devoting himself to his pursuits in Vancouver.

THE BEGINNINGS OF VANCOUVER BEER: THREE LITTLE BREWERIES

Vancouver's modern craft beer neighbourhoods are haunted by the ghosts of the city's brewing origins in the late 1880s—Doering's old stomping grounds were Mount Pleasant and Brewery Creek, and he was joined there by other enterprising brewers and businessmen. This same area still holds its attractions for brewers and beer lovers alike. The largest craft brewery currently in Vancouver, Red Truck Beer Company, occupies a two-acre parcel of industrial land at Scotia Street and 1st Avenue, on the edge of Mount Pleasant. Its shiny red classic trucks—modelled off the truck that owner Mark James first used to deliver beer—and its fifties-style diner/tasting room make it instantly recognizable. During our last visit there, my husband and I abandoned any calorie counting for the day and instead enjoyed some solid diner food with our beer flights: deep-fried pickles, wings, and garlic fries. It's hard to believe, but this huge brewery, which has the capacity to produce one hundred thousand hectolitres a year (although in reality produces under fifty thousand, according to James), sits on the same site as the tiny Lion Brewery that opened in 1897, and the neighbouring brewery Lansdowne in 1906. Just a block away from these breweries, Brewery Creek once emptied into False Creek—until the 1910s, that is, when False Creek was filled in to build railroad tracks. The city took away waterways to make room for railways. A century later, the large industrial area that was once covered by the waters flowing past the entrance of Lion Brewery became the home of Red Truck.

Doering's Stag & Pheasant Hotel on Water Street. (Photo courtesy of City of Vancouver Archives, AM54-S4-: Hot P22.1)

After our snacks at Red Truck, it took us less than ten minutes to wander up the old path of Brewery Creek, now hidden somewhere under the pavement, to Brassneck Brewing on Main, and then two blocks away to Main Street Brewing at Scotia and 7th (the site of Doering's Vancouver Brewery in 1888). A quick hop across Main took us to 33 Acres Brewing (close to the location of Mainland Brewery, also in 1888), and just a few blocks north was R&B Brewing and its neighbour, Electric Bicycle Brewing. We quickly realized that during this very walkable brewery crawl, we'd need to pace ourselves—there were so many breweries in such a small area, and so much amazing Vancouver beer to try. However, this densely packed crowd of breweries that currently sit on Mount Pleasant's busy streets would be a stark contrast to the same area's nineteenth-century breweries, surrounded by quiet dirt roads, woodland, and creeks. Lion, Vancouver Brewery, San Francisco Brewery, and Mainland Brewery were some of the pioneering breweries whose spirit we can still feel at the sites of our modern-day brewery crawl.

While Mount Pleasant/Brewery Creek quickly became a desirable spot for brewing, it was actually a little place near what is now Hastings and Burrard that first inspired Vancouver's pioneering brewers. While buying and selling hotels and saloons in Vancouver during the late 1880s, Doering was also looking for suppliers of wine, liquor, cigars, and—yes—beer for his establishments. Most hotels and saloons sold beer imported from the United States or Europe, but Doering noticed a tiny business in Vancouver that was making beer locally, something that was already common in his former home of Victoria. This was City Brewery on Seaton Street, a wealthy area on modern Hastings Street known as Blueblood Alley.[18] City Brewery was established by immigrant Jan Rekab. Very little is known of Rekab himself, but the historical records often mention the fact that City was among the few breweries in BC to use steam power. City Brewery appears to be the first brewery in Vancouver proper, although James Gibson had operated his Sapperton Brewery in New Westminster since 1879. Unlike Victoria, which was teeming with breweries, Vancouver seemed just on the cusp of a growth industry. But it wouldn't be the swanky Seaton Street that would become the central locale for breweries—it would be Mount Pleasant.

Doering, with his keen business sense and his investment in hotels that needed a good beer supply, saw another opportunity in the market. He'd already seen in Victoria what a lucrative industry brewing could be, and the rapidly growing Vancouver had just one brewery in 1887. Doering noticed that fellow German immigrant Joseph Kappler had set up a brewery on Scotia and 7th in Mount Pleasant, near Brewery Creek. Not much is known of this brewery, because according to Kappler's obituary, Doering bought it shortly after its establishment and turned it into his own Vancouver Brewery.[19] Kappler would briefly brew for Doering, and then go on to open Columbia Brewery on Powell Street, in the Cedar Cove neighbourhood (more on that in the next chapter). Around the same time, German immigrant Robert Reisterer closed his City Brewery in New Westminster (no relation to Rekab's business) and in 1888 opened Mainland Brewery around 10th and Columbia, also near Brewery Creek but "quite in the bush," according to a later newspaper account. It was just a couple of blocks southwest of where 33 Acres is now. There was at least one false start; licence application records from August 1888 show that his application for the brewery's liquor licence was initially refused.[20] But he had it up and running by late September, when a local paper enthusiastically described Vancouver's three new breweries:

Vancouver is well supplied in the way of liquid refreshments, there being three breweries in the city, turning out nectar fit for the gods of the "Fatherland." The largest of these is the Vancouver Brewery, owned by Charles Doering... the company erected a most substantial building a few months ago and it is now one of the largest breweries on the Pacific Coast... [It is] of the latest and most improved ideas... The City Brewery is located on Hastings street west and faces the Inlet. It has been completed but a short

The Red Cross Brewery wagon on parade in 1894. (Photo courtesy of City of Vancouver Archives, VPD-S214-: CVA 480-210)

time, but is quickly establishing an enviable reputation for itself. It is replete with all the latest machinery for the manufacture of beer, and is rapidly working up an extensive business. The Mainland Brewery, owned by R. Reisterer, is situated on False Creek. The building is commodious and has a capacity of about 500 gallons per day. His head brewer is August Zoellmer an expert German brewmaster.[21]

Rekab ran City Brewery for only a year before English businessmen John Williams and Ernest Barker came knocking with an offer Rekab couldn't refuse.[22] Williams and Barker renovated the brewery, relocated it just down the street (closer to the CPR terminus and the wharf), added electricity, and upgraded all the brewing equipment. Around 1889 or 1890 (the exact date isn't clear) they renamed it Red Cross Brewery, apparently linking the medical Red Cross with this nutritious beer: "The red cross stands on the battlefield for help; in Vancouver it stands for pure beer [. . .] unadulterated with any of the foreign abominations that are injurious to health."[23] About ten years later more improvements would be made to allow Williams and his wife to live there comfortably.

THE RISE AND FALL OF MAINLAND BREWERY

So these were the three businesses that launched the brewing industry in Vancouver: Vancouver Brewery (run by Charles Doering), Red Cross Brewery (run by John Williams, with Ernest Barker), and Mainland Brewery (run by Robert Reisterer). However, it was really the first two that would have the most profound impact on Vancouver's beer scene. Robert Reisterer was no John Williams, and definitely no Charles Doering, and his brewery's fate is somewhat ambiguous. Public records from the time rarely mention Mainland, and it seems to have been only moderately successful—unsurprising, given that its daily capacity of 500 gallons (or 400 gallons according to the 1888 city directory) was only about one-third that of Doering's Vancouver Brewery, which produced 1,500 gallons each day, and less than half of Red Cross's 1,100. The newspaper damns Mainland by faint praise ("the building is commodious") while enthusiastically lauding its two fellow breweries, which exceeded it in popularity. The fact that no Mainland Brewery bottles have ever been found, according to collectors George and Ilene Watson, aligns with all other indications that the brewery never found a strong customer base. It may have been that its location "quite in the bush" (in the words of that newspaper story) made a successful business untenable. In April 1887, a year before he opened Mainland, Reisterer appealed to City Council for financial help opening a road to the brewery.[24] This was how much Mainland was off the beaten track—quite literally. In 1888 the city made street improvements on 10th Avenue from Westminster (now Main) to Columbia to give access to the brewery and allow its official opening. However, Mainland didn't last long.

Mainland's lack of success was probably due to Reisterer's own ambivalence about the business as well as its poor location. He was neither fully committed to his brewery in Vancouver, nor certain of what else to do and when. His City Brewery in New Westminster was only open for a short time before a fire forced him to uproot and reopen in Vancouver. Then, barely two years after setting up in Vancouver, Reisterer was advertising the brewery for rent/lease in local papers: "This first-class going concern is to let to suitable and responsible parties. Having every appliance required for the trade [brewing], it offers a splendid chance to anyone having the necessary experience."[25] It appears that he hadn't found anyone to take on the business by the following year, when the 1891 Canadian census lists him and his brewmaster August Zoellmer as brewers in Vancouver. Later the same year, he married twenty-two-year-old Clara Steinhauser, a fellow German citizen who had immigrated to New York as a teenager with her family.[26] Reisterer was ready for a new life—somewhere other than Vancouver.

He made multiple announcements about moving to Kaslo and opening a brewery there.[27] While the couple did move to Kaslo in 1893, he quickly became ill with rheumatism and malaria, which prevented him from starting a new brewery right away.[28] Stories from 1894 indicate that Reisterer and Clara may have moved back to Vancouver temporarily before returning to the Kootenays.[29] The fate of Mainland Brewery is also unclear. In Sneath's book *Brewed in Canada,* he briefly mentions that Mainland was "destroyed by fire" in 1892.[30] I could find no record of this, but it is certainly possible, given the frequency of fires in this era. It is also possible that Sneath has confused the Vancouver Mainland Brewery with Reisterer's New Westminster brewery, which did indeed burn down in a fire in the 1880s. In any case, by 1894 Charles Doering had bought up whatever was left of the brewery.[31] After recovering sufficiently from his illnesses, Reisterer eventually moved to Nelson. There, he opened Nelson Brewing Company in 1893 with John Richard Rowley. Within five years, Reisterer's wife Clara passed away and the brewery building on Mill Street burned down. However, in 1899 Reisterer rallied and started up his brewery again, this time on Latimer Street in Nelson. Sadly, by 1901 Reisterer succumbed again to respiratory problems, and passed away from pneumonia. The brewery changed hands and eventually became Kootenay Breweries Ltd. in 1928, then Interior Breweries in 1956. By 1959 it had closed. However, Nelson Brewing was resurrected nearly a century later, in 1991—at the old Latimer Street location (the same building, in fact).[32]

Mainland Brewery never achieved great brewing glory, but that may have been because Reisterer was not the kind of man likely to meet with success in Vancouver's burgeoning brewing industry. Beer historian Greg Evans describes BC's nineteenth-century immigrant brewers as well-connected and influential social climbers, rather than blue-collar workers:

Brewers were traditionally respected members of the community... Brewing's long compatibility with the gentry's style of life, based on a mutual interest in the land and its harvests, allowed brewers to overcome the built-in prejudice against businessmen rising to high social status.[33]

Evans goes on to explain how these brewers were usually businessmen who made their money by combining their brewing with related business interests that would be "an obvious adjunct to brewing," such as owning hotels or farmland. "Both brewers and investors considered brewing to be a mainstay of diverse business ventures," according to Evans.[34] Although records show that Reisterer had family members working the brewery with him,[35] he did not seem to be interested in diversifying his business ventures, nor did he seem committed to making his brewery's name known about town. It remained largely a family affair. One exception might be his going-away celebration; the city's Liederkranz (a German men's choir) hosted a surprise farewell party for him at his brewery, which was attended by thirty choir members. John Williams's Red Cross Brewery supplied some kegs of bock beer (their spring specialty), and Red Cross's new brewmaster, Henry Traeger, gave a farewell speech for Reisterer.[36] But other than this goodbye evening of beer, sandwiches, and "songs of the Fatherland," there are hardly any mentions of Reisterer in public accounts of the time, and advertisements for Mainland Brewery in the newspapers or city directories were relatively uncommon. Unlike

Red Cross, Vancouver Brewery, and Columbia, all of which pepper public documents and records with their ads, Mainland sank without making much of a ripple.

In comparison, the paths of Doering's Vancouver Brewery and Williams's Red Cross Brewery would make more than a ripple—the waves their breweries created would eventually join the oceans of Labatt and Carling O'Keefe, two of the biggest brewing corporations in Canada. This story won't take us that far into the twentieth century, but we will see what happened with these two little upstarts of 1880s Vancouver.

NEW BEGINNINGS: MARRIAGE AND A MOVE TO THE BIG CITY

1888 was a busy year for Charles Doering. He sold off his interests in the King's Head in Victoria, built Vancouver Brewery on the banks of Brewery Creek (downstream from the short-lived San Francisco Brewery, which Henry Reifel started up the same year[37]),

sold the Stag & Pheasant in Vancouver, and then on September 15 he got married in Metchosin, just outside of Victoria. He and Sarah Jane Helgesen, daughter of former Member of Parliament Hans Helgesen, said their vows in front of some of Victoria's movers and shakers, including the former mayor. The newspaper's marriage announcement signalled that Doering's new wife was

Sarah Helgesen and Doering got married in September 1888. (Photo courtesy of BC Archives, item A-08612_141)

42

The Doerings' wedding portrait, taken with their pageboys on their wedding day. (Photo courtesy of Dennis Mutter)

perhaps not going to be a conventional bride; instead of bridesmaids, which would have been expected, Sarah had three pageboys, "an innovation in marriage ceremonies that took the fancy of the company immensely. They were dressed in black velveteen suits, white ruffled vests and white stockings, and looked exceedingly handsome."[38] Sarah was a striking woman. There are few portraits of her available, but those that survive show a woman whose strong brow, intense eyes, and straight mouth convey severity. Despite that, the softness at the corners of her lips and the curly halo of hair around her head suggest a spirit of independence. This may, of course, be my own bias—my desire to understand a bit more of the woman behind the famous brewer and the MP, a woman who travelled widely but is largely voiceless in the public records. We do know that she was acquainted with the artist Emily Carr, who describes staying at the Helgesens' farm in Metchosin and listening to Sarah's "rich singing voice" when the family gathered around the piano in the evenings. Her singing was also something she was known for in adulthood, as she made frequent appearances at shows and recitals in Vancouver.

Sarah's brothers slept in the back attic room at the Helgesen farm and one of them was regularly plagued by nightmares that left him breaking his own bed in fright and shocking the rest of the household. But the family was compassionate and welcoming. Carr's description of the Helgesen farm gives us a small glimpse into the life Sarah Jane Helgesen must have had before marrying Charles Doering:

There were not then as now countless summer cottages and cabins to be rented or owned by town dwellers. If children needed a place to recuperate after illness or while parents were having a dose of hospitalization, the healthy happiness of the Helgesens' farm out in Metchosin darted into people's brains and arrangements were made. [...] The farmhouse looked right down a long straight driveway. On either side were wide grain fields. A bathing beach was within walking distance; you could hear the sea washing and washing if the wind was in the right direction. Mrs. Helgesen was a kind hostess. They had horses, cows and pigs. There were always Mary's jokes and Sara's singing.[39]

The Helgesen home was a welcoming place, a place of succour and refuge. Emily Carr's warm memories of Mrs. Helgesen and Sarah reveal something of this unique family. They were wealthy, but generous; well-connected, but also distanced from the city's crowds.

When she moved out of her family home, Sarah was comfortable spending time apart from her husband while he

Sarah Jane Helgesen. (Photo courtesy of Dennis Mutter)

Charles Doering, Beatrice Doering, and Sarah Jane Doering. (Photo courtesy of Dennis Mutter)

made business trips all over the province. Sarah frequently travelled on her own, or with their daughter Beatrice (the namesake of Doering's beloved schooner), as well as with Charles for some of the more extensive trips. The Mutter family files preserve letters from Sarah to her mother and her daughter, written while travelling abroad and referring fondly to "Daddy" (when writing to Beatrice) or "Charley" (when writing to her mother). She even lived for a while in Arizona without him, to pursue some health-care treatments, and he would travel to visit.[40] It seemed that they both lived active lives in wealth and prosperity, enjoying time away from the city as well as activities at home, such as parties, recitals, and dog shows (Sarah won a prize for Yarrow, her Great Dane, at the 1903 Vancouver Kennel Club show). One story from 1899 tells of how Sarah was leaving town for a visit and "before leaving dropped a $20 gold piece in her husband's coat pocket, laughingly telling him it would bring good luck."[41] Twenty dollars would have been more than a week's wage for a labourer at that time[42]—it wasn't a small amount of money, and yet it was a joking goodbye gift between Sarah and Charles.

Both Charles and Sarah seem to have been kind people who showed compassion for one another and those around them. Sarah served on the Working Committee for the Victorian Order of Nurses, an organization established to provide medical care to underserved people and communities,[43] and she was a member of Vancouver's Women's Exchange, which was essentially a clothing and goods consignment system. Doering, a tough and intelligent businessman, also had a soft side. His great-great-grandson Dennis Mutter learned from family members' recollections about Doering's love for animals. For example, when the horses that pulled the Vancouver Breweries' beer wagons became too old to do the job anymore, Doering gave them a comfortable retirement out at one of his ranches rather than having them put down. He loved his dogs and frequently interacted with them in the brewhouse yard. Sarah's letters also reveal a sweet, compassionate side to her husband. She refers to him bringing her flowers, selecting a special rose for her to bring to their daughter Beatrice, and spending a relaxing day at the beach in Metchosin with her when she was recovering from illness. In one memorable story, included in a letter Sarah wrote from a steamship, Doering was repeatedly on the losing end of card games because of his soft heart. Doering loved cards and played each night, often with success. However, there was a priest on board the ship who was, in Sarah's words, "the worst player I ever saw." Despite this, "Charlie takes him for a partner like the good soul he is and bets on him at other times, losing [illegible] of cigars."

Sarah died on August 2, 1906, when she was only thirty-nine. It occurred while she and Doering were travelling around Germany, visiting his home county of Saxony. She had been suffering from tuberculosis for several years, and her husband travelled around the world with her, seeking treatments. Although her passing was publicly attributed to heart failure, according to family recollections she received an unusual treatment for tuberculosis (an injection of phosphorus) that ultimately caused her death.[44] Their daughter Beatrice, who was travelling with them, wrote to her uncle to share the sad news: "Poor dear Mother suffered too much and now her troubles are over and I am sure that mother is happy. [. . .] She did not suffer when she died, she just fell asleep." The letter, which is preserved in Dennis Mutter's files, also describes Sarah's funeral service in

Seehausen, Germany—a procession accompanied by schoolchildren and others who carried a cross and sang. Beatrice placed an English flag on her mother's coffin before it was lowered into the ground. From their communications over the years, it seems that Beatrice was very close to both of her parents. When she married in 1910, it was to George Mutter, a man who worked for her father Charles at Hat Creek Ranch near Ashcroft. Doering himself remarried in 1911 to Mary Reid, a widow, but that didn't stop him from enjoying his new role as grandfather when Beatrice gave birth to her children. In the 1910s, as Doering began moving away from the brewing industry (see Chapter 5 for more of that) and into other business ventures, he spent more time on his ranch properties, often hosting friends and family. His grandchildren and the children of his friends were always welcome. For example, when Les Traeger, the son of Red Cross and Vancouver Breweries brewer Henry Traeger, became ill with pneumonia, Doering invited the boy to stay at Hat Creek Ranch, where the fresh air would do him good. All in all, Doering's move into family life back in 1888 stuck. He was very much a family man as well as a businessman, and he was generous with his time, money, and resources to those he cared about, as well as to the city in which he'd made his home.

And back in 1888 Doering wanted Vancouver to be his home—at least for the foreseeable future. After his honeymoon in San Francisco, Doering began working on getting his name known in Vancouver—not just by advertising his brewery, but by becoming involved in all

Charles Doering plays with his grandchild, Charles Doering Mutter, in 1912. (Photo courtesy of Dennis Mutter)

Charles Doering and his daughter Beatrice with her son Charles Doering Mutter in 1912. (Photo courtesy of Dennis Mutter)

aspects of civic life. Just as he had become "well and favorably known" in Victoria, he wanted to cultivate that reputation in Vancouver as well. He seemed already popular in the city at this time, judging by the response to his nuptials; when he and Sarah returned to Vancouver after their marriage and honeymoon, they hosted a "right royal reception" at their home with one hundred guests, the City Band, and late-night dancing, "mirth, and revelry."[45] Donating gifts and funds for public events, exhibits, fairs, and charity drives (either individually or through the brewery), sitting on boards and committees, and running for office all occupied Doering's time in the late 1880s and into the 1890s. He was elected alderman of the city in 1890, and became one of a socially diverse group of men who ran Vancouver: the City Council at that time was composed of a tanner, a real estate agent, a doctor, a real estate manager, a milkman, a surveyor, a sea captain, a carpenter, a stonemason, and a brewer, all led by a grocer (the mayor). Doering was well-loved, according to the July 13, 1894, issue of the *Vancouver Daily World*: "There are few men in British Columbia better known or more popular than Charley Doering... [He] is a hale fellow well met, wherever he may be." He had enough clout in the city that he could help folks get jobs in high places. For example, in 1898 he penned a letter on his brewery's letterhead to the superintendent of the Provincial Police, asking him to give his friend George Freeland a job as a police officer; Doering insisted that he would consider it a "personal favour."[46] However, despite Doering's popularity, one of his splashier gifts, made early in his career in Vancouver, didn't end up going over very well in the long term.

In 1889, Alderman Horne, the chairman of the Park Commissioners, was developing what the papers called a "zoological garden" (i.e., a zoo) in the brand-new Stanley Park. Horne was apparently so eager for animals to add to his zoo that there were noises about "expropriating"—that is, taking by legal force—any that he "had his eye on" regardless of ownership.[47] Historian Sean Kheraj identifies these years (the late 1880s and early 1890s) as the beginning of what would become the official Stanley Park Zoo. The "zoo" at this stage, however, was limited to whatever animals Horne ended up collecting. Knowing Horne's eagerness to expand his animal collection, Doering proudly presented him with a "fine bear." Doering's co-proprietor at the Atlantic Saloon, August Schwann, gave Horne a "very large monkey."[48] There were no suitable facilities for such animals so, according to Kheraj, "the wife of the first ranger tended to a captive bear and a few small local animals just outside the rangers cottage at the Coal Harbour entrance."[49] The bear was, sadly, kept in chains for the safety of the ranger's wife and the visitors to the newly formed park.

No doubt Horne was thrilled in the moment to receive such dramatic gifts for his new project. However, four years later the thrill was souring. The garden still did not have an appropriate habitat for a bear and it's likely the ranger's wife's patience with the situation was wearing thin. And there was only so much the poor bear could take! According to the *Daily News Advertiser* of February 12, 1893, "of late the bear has been rather cross and has broken the chains put on it without much trouble, and in fact caused the Ranger and the Commissioners considerable worry." When the commissioners notified Doering "that they did not want to have anything more to do with the bear as it had become a nuisance," Doering protested that he had nowhere to keep the bear himself and "was a little piqued that his donation was not sufficiently appreciated to make it worth while for the City to provide quarters for it."

There were private discussions about building a bear pit, which the Vancouver City Clerk learned (to his chagrin) would cost $200. However, according to the *Advertiser* the Park Commissioners, with the Finance Committee, had already decided on a far less expensive solution even as they were discussing the bear pit. It was a needlessly cruel solution to what was already a cruel situation: "With the consent of all parties [the commissioners and the committee], the bear was shot on Friday afternoon." The article further speculates that "it is doubtful whether the Finance Committee will gain friends" in doing this, since it was likely they could have secured the funds for a pit had they made these troubles public. Knowing Doering's love of hunting and taxidermy, it's hard to guess whether he would have been upset at his gift being so cruelly disposed of, or interested in keeping the dead bear for his own collection. In either case, the story of Doering's gift to Stanley Park is one that is tragic for the bear and illuminating for City of Vancouver politics. By 1900, however, Doering's animus had dissipated and he donated a host of songbirds to the Stanley Park aviary: two pairs of thrushes, twelve kinds of finches, a linnet, a chaffinch, and more. These were praised as being "best among the song birds of Germany" and were doubtless a safer donation option than the bear.[50]

A final note on this story: A newspaper account from 1904 confusingly announced that the bear donated by Doering had become ill, so the Park Commissioners "humanely decided to put him out of his misery." The bear is referred to as the "patriarch of the Zoo," having lived there for fourteen years.[51] The 1893 article clearly stated that the bear was put down, so it's not clear which account is correct. Either the bear's planned euthanasia was cancelled in 1893 and the paper simply misreported events, or another bear took its place afterwards and the 1904 reporter didn't realize that there were two different animals.

Doering (second from right, with a dog) and his employees near the brewery yard. (Photo courtesy of City of Vancouver Archives, AM54-S4-: Dist P18)

COMMITTING TO BEER (NOT BEARS)

As the Vancouver Brewery became increasingly successful, Doering gradually disentangled himself from commitments elsewhere, whether in politics or in other businesses. He did not become an alderman again after his service in 1890–1891, although he was elected to the Parks Board in 1906. He was devoted now to brewing, and he had planned for its success by not only building for more capacity than he immediately needed (1,500 gallons a day was ambitious at the beginning) but advertising as much as possible and making connections with Vancouver's hotels and saloons. These two strategies

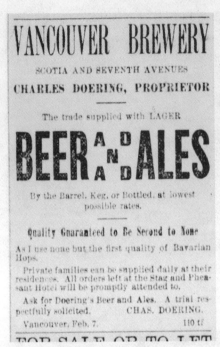

Doering's early ads boasted of the Bavarian hops he used to make authentic German lager. (*Vancouver Daily World*, February 1890)

were mutually reinforcing. His buying and selling of places such as the Stag & Pheasant, the King's Head, the Gambrinus Hotel, and the Atlantic Saloon[52] gave him the capital necessary to pay for weekly advertisements in the newspapers for years. Doering ran his hotel and saloon interests in Vancouver off the side of his desk, so to speak. He didn't own any of them for long because he became increasingly invested in the Vancouver Brewery and wanted to focus on that.[53] These businesses did, however, provide much-needed contacts.

Brewers desperately needed good relationships with hotel and saloon or tavern owners if they wanted to be successful. Hotels and bars are obviously still important funding sources for BC breweries nowadays, but a century ago they were even more so. This was because of the province's liquor laws. The 1888 Licences Act specified the conditions for retail and wholesale liquor licences, and breweries generally fell under the wholesale licence category. This allowed the proprietor to sell liquor "in quantities *not less* than two gallons in each cask or vessel" and, if in bottles, in numbers *no less* than one dozen. The act also specified that the liquor sold could not be consumed on the premises. Places where drinkers would sit down, like hotels and saloons, required a retail licence to sell in smaller quantities to individuals. The breweries were not intended to be places to gather and drink. Obtaining a retail licence, which cost twice as much money, would have required a brewery to turn itself into a saloon, essentially. In reality, law enforcement often turned a blind eye to such infractions, but if needed they could apply the law to exert pressure on a particular business.

Doering's advertisements reveal that he targeted both the individual drinker (the families who would wait for the beer wagon to drop off a box of bottles at their house) and the large businesses selling beer to an increasingly discerning consumer. The advertisements also show the appeal of lager at the time—this German-style beer was very popular, and Doering wanted to show that he had the real stuff, made with actual Bavarian hops. He used his German heritage, known to all, to market his beer as authentic—despite the fact that census records show that Doering trained as a machinist in Germany, not as a brewer.[54]

Shortly after this turn to selling authentic German lager to the people of Vancouver, Doering decided he needed a proper brewer on staff. Enter Otto Marstrand, a Danish brewmaster, who arrived in Vancouver in early 1892. Marstrand was accustomed to brewing one hundred thousand barrels a year back in Denmark, so the twenty-five

Some ladies relax together on the Doering home's veranda. The brewery warehouse is slightly visible in the background. (Photo courtesy of Dennis Mutter)

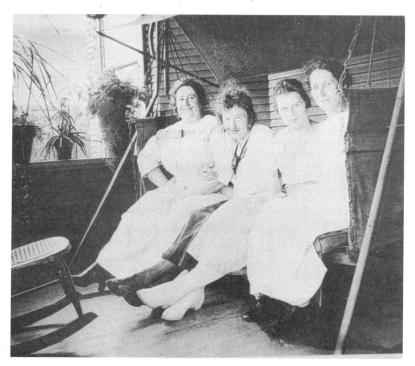

thousand barrels planned for Doering's brewery would have been no problem. On January 19, 1892, the *Vancouver Daily World* announced the newly named Doering & Marstrand Brewery as the first lager beer brewery in the province. Throughout that spring, Doering renovated and expanded his brewing facilities, adding refrigeration machinery (important for lager production), a boiler house, and a cellar, as well as new storeys (the new brewing facilities ended up being five storeys high).[55] On the same property, though not in the brewing facilities themselves, were also offices, stables, lodging for employees, and the Doering family home. Floor plans of that home, preserved in the Mutter family files, show that Doering's home on the brewery property was a comfortable two-level house with three bedrooms, a large billiards room, a solarium, parlour, sitting room, sewing room, and study, in addition to the kitchen and dining room. A large veranda out front was a good place to sit and watch the world go by.

When the new Doering & Marstrand lager was finally ready for drinking, the brewery hosted an official reopening celebration. An article in the *Daily News Advertiser* of June 24, 1892, describes the crowd of two hundred who gathered to admire the new lager-brewing facilities at the brewery, and to enjoy the free food (which had to be frequently replenished, apparently). The two business partners had even arranged for brewery-themed decor and landscaping: "The brewery yard between the office and the works was lined with beer kegs and green shrubbery, giving it a cosy appearance... [The engine room] was profusely decorated with potted and cut flowers and designs made of the beer bottles. The spacious office was also similarly bedecked with foliage plants and flowers." Lager was served and local "connoisseurs... pronounced it the equal of any manufactured on the continent." The brewery announced that Alexandra Lager would be its primary brand (along with its English Ale, Vancouver Ale, and Porter). Perhaps most interesting when we consider what craft beer culture means to us now, is how much Doering and Marstrand tried to produce everything needed for their refitted brewery "at home"—meaning, in the province. The importing of equipment

Charles Doering (right) and his employees relax outside the brewery. Brewing was a collegial industry even back then. (Photo courtesy of Simon Fraser University Archives, BC Craft Brewing History Collection, Doering and Marstrand, Vanc. [189-?])

and ingredients was slowly decreasing in popularity as Vancouver drinkers began seeking a truly local product.

After guests were toured throughout the brewing plant, the party concluded with more glasses of lager accompanied by speeches. Right before Doering and Marstrand themselves came up to say a few words, John Williams stood up to laud their brewing advances. It might have seemed an odd choice, since Williams was the owner of Doering & Marstrand Brewery's main competition: Red Cross Brewery, formerly Rekab's City Brewery. Red Cross and Doering & Marstrand Brewery were travelling parallel paths in the 1880s and 1890s. Both breweries received major technical upgrades under their new proprietors; both were run by businessmen well loved in the city; both advertised widely; both claimed lager as their specialty; and both sought ways to brew their beer with local ingredients and

Sarah Jane Doering's brother (centre) and others pose beside the bottle-washing station in Doering's brewery. (Photo courtesy of Dennis Mutter)

equipment, positioning themselves against the beers imported from the US and Europe. These two men moved in the same circles and catered to the same customers, so they probably ended up socializing as well. But Williams's speech at Doering's party may have added just a little bit of friendly competition to the occasion—just what one needs from a true "frenemy."

FRENEMIES: D&M BREWERY AND RED CROSS BREWERY

The competitive dynamic between Red Cross and Doering & Marstrand developed in the 1890s as the two breweries came to share most of the city's market for beer and ale. Just one month after Doering & Marstrand's celebratory launch of their renamed brewery and their Alexandra Lager, the *Daily News Advertiser* announced Williams and Barker's plans to make an equally popular German lager: "Seeing that the demand for lager beer in this Province was largely increasing, and that several breweries intended putting in the necessary plant, they also decided to do so...for the last fortnight they have been brewing lager beer, the first of which will be ready for the market in a month's time."[56] That summer they also hired Henry Traeger, a brewmaster from Friedewald, Germany, who had made a name for himself in San Francisco. The paper's praise for Red Cross's efforts suggested that D&M Brewery would be facing some competition: "It is doubtful whether there is a more convenient or better arranged brewery in the Province."

The newspaper followed up on this story in its issue of September 16, 1892, shortly after the first release of the Red Cross Lager. The reporter describes the lager as being "in splendid condition, clear and sparkling, and it is unanimously agreed that it would be hard to beat it." The lager also received rave reviews from the John Wieland Brewing Company in San Francisco, and Traeger was praised for his "exertions" at the mash tun. Similar to the coverage of Doering & Marstrand's party, which emphasized the local production of Doering's beer, this article ends by turning to the issue of how breweries were using local supplies: "Now that there are two breweries supplying lager beer in the City, a large amount of money that is annually sent...to the United States will be kept in circulation here, while employment will be provided for a larger number of men. All that is now wanted is a malting establishment...Good barley can be grown in this Province." The presence of two well-run breweries in Vancouver, both of which were consistently producing quality lager, was seen as a boost for other industries in the city and the province. "Drink local" was trending long before it became an Instagram hashtag.

The focus on Red Cross Brewery's local origins was a shift from its strategy in the first couple of years of its operation, which occurred during a chaotic period in John Williams's life. Williams had cheerily toasted his competition, Doering & Marstrand, in that summer gathering of 1892, but just over a year beforehand he had suffered the sudden death of his first wife. On March 30, 1891, Mrs. Williams passed away after a short thirty-six-hour battle with septicemia, leaving Williams with a two-week-old infant as well as at least one other child.[57] There was an extraordinarily large display of public mourning for Mrs. Williams when she was put to rest. Her funeral procession included over twenty carriages and the funeral was said to be one of the largest ever held in Vancouver.[58] It must have been a shocking loss for Williams, but he had invested nearly everything in his new brewery—he even lived there—so he didn't have the luxury of taking a break from business. In addition, he was in the midst of acquiring the Germania Hotel when the tragedy happened (in fact, the licence was transferred to him on April 1, the day of his wife's funeral). Over the next year and a half, he would take what had been the sleepy City Brewery and turn it into one of the most popular producers of beer in Vancouver. Two years after the death of Williams's wife, his main industry competitor, Charles Doering, would also suffer a great loss. His second child, Kathleen Mary Doering, who was born on March 15, 1893, passed away when she was just ten days old, on March 25.[59] With a young child at home (their four-year-old daughter Beatrice) and the death of an infant, Doering's and Sarah's personal life must have felt utterly upended at this time.

These tragic events did not stop business, however. Doering and Williams's breweries kept running. By 1894, they were well known in Vancouver and, judging from the frequency of their advertisements, were successful. Doering & Marstrand began boasting of using BC hops rather than Bavarian, and its beer was shipped across the province and internationally—to China, Japan, Australia, and the Sandwich Islands. Its products included their flagship Alexandria (sometimes called Alexandra) Lager, as well as English Ale, Porter, and Vancouver Ale, which was described as a non-alcoholic and "very nutritious ale...especially adapted for the use of ladies, children, or elderly people, or men not accustomed to intoxicating drinks."[60]

Doering-Marstrand Brewing Co., Ld.

ALEXANDRA LAGER, EXPORT BEER, PORTER

Our Beer is made of Malt and Hops. It is a strong and strengthening beverage, with a fine flavor, and the different kinds will suit every taste. Alexandra Lager is a strong beer, healthier than ale, which it is much like.

Our Export Beer is similar to Milwaukee beer, light, with a mild taste, and is specially adapted for ladies.

Our Porter is an excellent tonic, and particularly suited for convalescent ladies, whom it will restore to strength in a very short time.

We have put the prices down on our product to meet the public in these hard times, and we trust that the cheapened price will induce everybody to give our beer a trial.

All around, doz. qts., $1.50; doz. pts., 75c.

BOTTLES TO BE RETURNED.

Telephone 429.   Post Office: Mount Pleasant   Vancouver

A GOOD APPETIZER

Alexandra Beer is a good Spring Medicine, good to taste, easy to take, appetite creating, health upholding, content in its manufacture, special care is exercised in handling it, and every effort is made to satisfy every user. Have you ever tried

Doering & Marstrand's
Alexandra Lager
Telephone 429

D&M launched advertising campaigns that targeted an expanded demographic of drinkers. These ads are from 1897 and 1901 issues of the *Vancouver Daily World*.

This concept was later applied to their Alexandria Lager as well; an ad from 1901 described it as being suitable for weaker people (these ads often featured women) and a healthy beverage option for everyone (see the advertisements above). Other advertisements from the late 1890s and early 1900s use a similar strategy to market D&M's beer, with claims that their porter was "particularly suited to convalescent ladies" and their Export Beer was "specially adapted for ladies."[61] This new focus on women and "invalids" revealed that Doering was already thinking about how to expand the customer base for his product; he wanted beer to be seen as a drink for the whole family, not just for debauched mill workers. It may also have been a consequence of Doering's wife Sarah's health struggles. A story from 1891 refers to Sarah having to move to Victoria temporarily for health reasons, and to her recovering and returning to Vancouver. Upon her death in 1906 papers noted that she had been ill for several years.[62] According to the family records held by her great-great-grandson Dennis Mutter, she suffered from tuberculosis.

Red Cross was also recognizing the untapped market of women

Notice to Our Customers.

We, the undersigned, Lager Beer Brewers of Vancouver, hereby notify our respective customers that the price of our Bottled Lager Beer shall be, from date of this notice, as follows :--

TO THE TRADE :

Per Doz. Quart Bottles Lager Beer, - - - $1.75

Per Doz. Pint Bottles Lager Beer, - - - 1.00

Packed in Barrels containing either 6 doz.

Quarts, or 10 doz. Pints, - - - - - 11.00

(Subject to a discount of 50 cents per bbl. if paid for within 10 days from date of sale.)

TO PRIVATE CUSTOMERS :

Per Doz. Quart Bottles Lager Beer, - - - $2.00

Per Doz. Pint Bottles Lager Beer, - - - 1.25

In this price the bottles are not included.

☞ The Bottles must be Returned Free of Charge, or paid for at the rate of 25 cents per dozen.

VANCOUVER BREWERY,
DOERING & MARSTRAND.

RED CROSS BREWERY,
WILLIAMS & BARKER.

Vancouver, Aug. 1st, 1893. 14-1-3t

In August 1893, Doering and Williams attempted to take advantage of their monopoly in Vancouver's brewing industry by hiking their prices at the same time. (*Vancouver Daily World*, August 1, 1893)

and other "weaker" folks; in 1901 we see advertisements for "Red Cross porter for invalids," and in 1902 another Red Cross ad makes a crude joke that reveals the increase in female drinking habits: "Say, Jack! What makes your wife so fat? Oh! She's been buying Red Cross Porter, 75 cents a dozen up at the Gold Seal."[63] Gold Seal Liquor, located at 746 Pender Street, had a long business partnership with Red Cross; Gold Seal did their bottling, and Red Cross produced a Gold Seal Extra Lager. Red Cross's advertisements up until 1902 were far more subtle and muted than those of Doering & Marstrand, perhaps because they collaborated with Gold Seal on advertisement strategies while D&M were on their own. However, this changed when Red Cross fully joined forces with D&M.

Throughout the 1890s, the friendly competition between the two breweries became less competitive and more friendly. Greg Evans, historian of early BC breweries, describes the different strategies brewers could use to reduce market competition: "A brewer could buy out and shut down local competitors in an effort to consolidate his market share; he could retain, or even expand his market share, by operating the purchased facilities in tandem with his own plant; or, he could merge with his former competition to present a united front to the outside world."[64] Doering did the latter: he took his collegial relationship with Williams and turned it into a business partnership in order to remove his main industry competition. Doering and Williams shared a similar outlook on business, and a similar level of popularity in the city. They may also have been friends; the Victoria-Vancouver steamship passenger lists note Doering and Williams occasionally travelling together to Victoria, and in 1899, Williams's brewer, Traeger, worked with Doering on a small committee to host a party for the German citizens of Vancouver. The celebration was in honour of a German warship currently in port, and the beer served for the dignitaries was sourced from D&M, Red Cross, and Columbia (owned by another German immigrant, Joseph Kappler).[65]

As early as 1893, the two breweries were in agreement regarding pricing, and presented a united front to the city. This was quite striking; instead of competing with one another, these two breweries—the most popular in Vancouver—were essentially price-fixing, and at a price significantly higher than the previous going rate. Until then, the retail pricing for beer as advertised in the local papers was usually $0.75 per one dozen bottles. These were pint bottles—quart bottles were more expensive. The price-fixing by Red Cross and D&M raised it by two-thirds, to $1.25 per dozen. This effort was thwarted, however. By the summer of 1894, D&M had launched an advertising campaign for their new non-alcoholic Vancouver Ale at the old price of $0.75 per dozen pints, claiming its affordability for all. In winter of the same year, they began advertising their English pale ale at the new lager beer price they had fixed with Red Cross—$1.25 per dozen. The ads claimed that this ale would rival the famous import Bass. However, in 1895 they were advertising English ale and porter for only $1.00 per dozen, and by 1897 D&M was advertising all its beers at the price of $.75 per dozen pints. It seems that the market wouldn't tolerate such a drastic price hike in such a short amount of time.

The early attempt at price-fixing back in 1893 overestimated the depth of the local beer drinkers' pockets, but it was a very early hint that an amalgamation was coming. The next hint was Doering and Williams's joint attempt in the mid-1890s to enter the Victoria brewery market by purchasing partnership shares in Excelsior Brewery.

Unfortunately for them, the economy fell into a recession and they were forced to abandon those plans.[66] Excelsior didn't last long under its new owners so Doering and Williams's withdrawal was probably wise. Doering continued to promote his own brewery's brand, of course. He distributed D&M beer across the province, even sometimes delivering it himself. In May of 1899, for example, *The Province* reported that Doering would be spending several weeks in Atlin, BC, in order to "look after [his shipment of beer] and dispose of it to the hotel keepers of British Columbia's northernmost city." Then, in March of 1900, Williams's partner, Ernest Barker, sold out his interest in Red Cross to D&M. The behind-the-scenes discussions are missing from the public record, but it may have been that Williams was beginning to see amalgamation with Doering as the least stressful way to keep making money by brewing. Just one month before Barker dissolved their partnership, Williams had married his second wife, Elsie Penzer, in a quiet wedding at St. Paul's in Vancouver and then enjoyed a honeymoon in California.[67] The two of them lived in the brewery, which Elsie later recalled as "a beautifully furnished home,"[68] but running the brewery solo while living there may have been an unappealing option after twelve years in the business, especially

A photo taken near Vancouver Breweries shows Doering on the right with his daughter Beatrice and her husband George, and Henry Traeger, brewmaster for Williams and then for Doering, on the far left, with his young son Les. (Photo courtesy of Dennis Mutter)

with a new wife to care for. In addition to these stresses, city sewage was starting to leak into the Red Cross Brewery property, which of course also compromised their living space.[69] John Williams was no doubt looking for a way out of what was becoming an increasingly challenging business situation.

According to Bill Wilson, April 14, 1900, was the date that Doering & Marstrand officially amalgamated with Red Cross and renamed themselves Vancouver Breweries (not to be confused with Vancouver Brewery, which was Doering's first brewery back in 1888).[70] John Williams became the secretary and treasurer, Doering was president, and Marstrand stayed on to brew until 1906, when he returned to Denmark because of health concerns. However, newspaper accounts list Traeger, the Red Cross brewmaster, as the Vancouver Breweries brewmaster as early as 1902, so it is possible that the two men shared the position.[71] Once he started brewing for Doering, Traeger became a close friend of the family. As noted earlier, Traeger's son Les was invited to live at Doering's Hat Creek Ranch for a time when he contracted pneumonia, and Traeger and his wife would often bring their other son, Bill, to the ranch for visits. They were so close, in fact, that after Sarah died and Doering remarried, he rented his long-time family home on the brewery compound at Scotia Street to the Traegers.

D&M and Red Cross joined and became Vancouver Breweries around 1900–1901. Their new logo featured both brewery buildings. (Photo courtesy of the Thomas Fisher Rare Book Library, University of Toronto)

The amalgamation of Red Cross and D&M transformed competitors into a big family. Vancouver Breweries quickly became a well-loved part of the city. A sly introduction to the newly amalgamated brewery came in the form of a Christmas gift in 1901 to *The Province*, which described the brewery's generosity in the December 31 issue:

There is one characteristic about the people who managed the Vancouver Breweries, limited, which gains the admiration of every member of the Province staff, and that is their thoughtfulness. The arid wastes of thirst which can be found in any newspaper office were working overtime, so to speak, on Tuesday afternoon when there arrived a neat consignment of the excellent lager for which the Vancouver Breweries are famous. A veil must be drawn over the proceedings which followed, but truth compels the admission that there was not a drop of beer in the office this morning.

The big public announcement of the amalgamation, however, came in the form of a contest, which was posted in all the major newspapers in May 1902. This contest was one that, according to former alderman A.P. Horne's later recollections, John Williams had originally planned years ago for his Red Cross Brewery: "One day he [Williams] said to me, 'I'm going to give a fifty dollar prize for a good name for beer.'"[72] Williams didn't end up running the contest through Red Cross, but he suggested it to Doering after they amalgamated. The competition asked for submissions to name the new brewery's flagship beer—a beer that would become one of the most popular in the province, and that would come to embody the local character of British Columbia. The fifty-dollar contest prize was splashed across the newspapers. Wage records are difficult to come by, but the information we have from a decade later, in 1911, indicates that the average man in BC was earning $728 a year at that time, and the average woman just $439 per year.[73] Presumably wages would have been even lower in 1902, so a fifty-dollar prize could easily be equivalent to a tenth or more of one's annual salary. And all that was required to earn that pot of cash was choosing a great name for a new beer. The ad copy read as follows:

> *We, the Vancouver Breweries, Ltd (the Consolidated Doering & Marstrand and Red Cross Breweries), are about to put a new brand of Beer on the market. It is brewed by us at our breweries on the American process and is intended to compete with Beer coming into this country from outside points. We have been working on this brand for a long time—over six months. We haven't put it on sale yet, because it takes a long time for Beer to reach perfection. In about another fortnight it will have aged sufficiently to put it into a condition equal to the best light-bodied light-colored Beer brewed in the world. Then we shall put it on sale. In the meantime we want a name for it. Until we get just the name we want, we will call it "Queen Beer" to distinguish it from our "Alexandra Lager," [. . .] both beers taking their names from Queen Alexandra. Can anyone suggest some other name for the Beer? We will send our check for Fifty Dollars to the person sending us such a name as we think best for our purpose.*

After explaining the reasons for the contest, Vancouver Breweries gives some guidance for the kind of name it was looking for:

> *The name must be a short one, easily spoken, easily remembered, and appropriate. It must be a name that one would learn to say as naturally as one would say "Beer" when asking for a glass, or a bottle, or a keg of it. There is no lottery no scheme of any kind, connected with this offer. It is a pure business proposition [. . .] Every man, woman, and child in British Columbia has a chance for the money. You simply write down as many names as you like, as often as you like, and address them to The Vancouver Breweries Ltd.*

Cascade became one of Vancouver's most recognizable beer brands. Here it is being advertised on top of the Regent Hotel on East Hastings Street. (Photo courtesy of City of Vancouver Archives, AM54-S4-: LGN 999)

Finally, the beer is described in the hopes that it might inspire some excellent names:

Just a word now about the New Beer—it may assist you in selecting an appropriate name. The color is that of a delicate pale amber. It is absolutely pure and healthy and as harmless as the rippling waters of a mountain brook. It has a flavor as delicate and satisfying as it is possible to imagine. It is in fact an all-satisfying, stimulating product, equal to the best in the world. Can you give us a name for it?

The brewery received over two thousand submissions to its contest. One aspiring contestant even submitted a poem to accompany their proposed name of "Acme."[74] *The Province* published its own suggestion: Kitsalano [*sic*]. To justify its choice, it argued that "Kitsalano is euphonious, has a cool and gurgling suggestiveness and a local application."[75] However, the winner was one W.C. Green, whose beer name "Cascade" was announced as the successful entry in the June 14, 1902, edition of *The Province*. The announcement explained that the name Cascade "is

JOHN WILLIAMS
Vice-Pres. and Sec'y Vancouver Breweries, Limited
Vancouver

A cartoon of John Williams holding a glass of Cascade beer. (Printed in *British Columbians As We See 'Em*, published by the Newspaper Cartoonists Association of British Columbia in 1911)

easily spoken. It is easily remembered. It is liquid. It is full of life and vigor. It suggests coolness. It is refreshing. It is a thirst-quencher. It is as pure as a crystal. It is named after the Cascade Mountains, which gives the word a local significance—a local value. And it has a 'smack of the West.'" Doering and Williams were ahead of their time when it came to marketing strategies and buzzwords. And they knew that local could be a powerful marketing tool when it came to beer. This strategy—focusing on "local application"—wasn't used much in beer marketing again until craft beer's resurrection in the 1980s.

The strategy was successful; Cascade sold. And it sold at an increased price. While they had gradually backpedalled on the price increases attempted in the 1890s, the new Cascade beer was an opportunity to capitalize on the public's investment in the brand. Doering and Williams gambled on drinkers being willing to pay over the standard seventy-five cents per dozen, and priced Cascade at one dollar per dozen. In addition, Doering's recent marketing strategy—the focus on health and the appeal to female drinkers—was turned up in Cascade ads, which boasted "beer that is as pure and healthful as the rippling waters of a mountain brook" and claimed that it "contains only the purest and most healthful of ingredients and is a drink fit

Delivery trucks lined up outside Vancouver Breweries in 1910. (Photo courtesy of Dennis Mutter)

for the most delicate lady."[76] Cascade became Vancouver Breweries' most popular beer, even getting its own electronic signs around the city (see image on page 66). They developed a new slogan for it several years after its launch, and the "Beer Without a Peer" became a much-loved Vancouver drink.

With the consolidation of Vancouver's two biggest breweries and a new flagship beer that was selling everywhere, the city's beer market seemed to be locked down. Vancouver Breweries had capital to produce enough beer on demand and to deliver it promptly, particularly when they bought their new fleet of delivery trucks in 1910 (see image on page 68). However, a handful of other breweries emerged in the late 1890s. Of these, two made a significant impact on public life in the city. The oddball machinations of Stanley Park Brewing and Columbia Brewery would end up being an interesting foil to the smooth, professional marketing of Vancouver Breweries. These stories are told in the next two chapters.

CHAPTER 3

BORDERLAND BEER: THE STORIES BEHIND COLUMBIA BREWERY

Parallel 49 Brewery on Triumph Street in East Vancouver is crowded with happy-hour drinkers at this time of day. Overwhelmed by the huge tap list that stretches the length of the bar, I forgo a flight and instead select an old favourite: Trash Panda Hazy IPA. My husband and I sit outside on one of their sidewalk tables, guarding our rented bikes as we sip our beer (he went with one of their Pic-a-Hop IPAS). After draining my glass, I click on my phone's stopwatch and we ride our bikes up from Triumph Street to Powell just a block or two away, via Victoria Drive. We pedal leisurely through the east end of Vancouver, passing close by breweries like Andina, Storm, and Container, then cruising along the harbour and through Gastown, waving at the Alibi Room and Steamworks Brewing, then finally coast along the road beside Lost Lagoon until we arrive at Stanley Park Brewing Brewpub and Restaurant. It's about a half-hour ride from Parallel 49 to Stanley Park Brewing—and that's with modern traffic.

Our short jaunt between breweries covers just a small area of Vancouver now, but our starting and ending locations were the east and west outposts of the city 120 years ago. I would discover in the course of my research that breweries marked these borders back then as well. Within the actual borders of Vancouver, Parallel 49 is the brewery that stands farthest east, and the Stanley Park brewpub has, until very recently, been the farthest west.[1] In the 1890s, two breweries stood in nearly the same locations, but people riding between them back then would have passed only Red Cross Brewery on their journey. Columbia Brewery, established in 1888, sat near where the Princeton Hotel now stands—at the corner of Powell and Victoria, barely a block and a half from Parallel 49 Brewing's current location. Stanley Park Brewery opened just under a decade later, in 1896, on the shores of Lost Lagoon facing Stanley Park. It was essentially a renovated wood house at the end of what is now Alberni Street at Chilco, just where the old Coal Harbour bridge joined the west end of Vancouver to Stanley Park. The old Stanley Park Brewery is barely a ten-minute walk from the brewpub's new location.

These two breweries were on the edge of town and—sometimes—operated on the edges of the law as well. The slick marketing strategies and consistent branding of D&M and Red Cross weren't always features of Stanley Park and Columbia. However, like D&M and Red Cross, their owners were well known in the city. These two border breweries remind us that Vancouver really was still a city in the making—it was still the "wild west" in many ways. Finding legal loopholes, skirting the law, and taking your own revenge were all standard practices for Stanley Park and Columbia. They couldn't hold on to their businesses as increasing corporate amalgamation transformed Vancouver's beer industry, but while they lasted they were popular, unpredictable, and fiercely independent. In this chapter and the next, I hope readers will learn much more about these two breweries than has previously been told. In the sweeping historical summaries of early Vancouver brewing, the stories of Stanley Park and Columbia have long been overlooked.

COLUMBIA: THE BAD BOY OF VANCOUVER BREWERIES

In August of 1889, Walter MacDonald made a rather dramatic appearance in court, walking in with bloodied bandages wrapped around his head. Looking resentfully across at the defendants in the case, Joseph Kappler and Fred Millar[2] of Columbia Brewery, MacDonald explained to the sitting judge how he came to be there. It was a Sunday afternoon and he was enjoying a twenty-five-cent glass of beer at "Keppler's brewery," also referred to in the newspaper account as "what is known as San Francisco brewery" (more on this confusion to come). Serving beer to customers for consumption on site was illegal unless the proprietor held a liquor retail licence—and Columbia held only a wholesale licence. In addition, selling beer on a Sunday was illegal. In other words, Columbia was in trouble before the assault even occurred.

MacDonald testified that Millar, an employee at Columbia, had been serving the beer. After a full afternoon of his customers drinking, Millar came down from the upstairs rooms in the brewery with a rifle to show everyone. The small crowd, shocked, managed to wrest it away from him, and Millar quickly lost his temper. He "fetched a large shankbone...of a quadruped" which he used to beat MacDonald across the head in a fit of anger. There was some confusion on the judge's part about what a shankbone was and how it could be used as a weapon. He was on the verge of sending someone to find an anatomy book until the police chief stood up to explain exactly what a shankbone was and to allege Biblical precedent for bone-related crimes: Samson, who killed a crowd of people with the jawbone of a donkey. The judge's response, before he imposed a series of fines on the brewery via Kappler and Millar, was acerbic: "Yes, I recollect. But Samson was a much more powerful man than the prisoner [Fred Millar]."[3]

Millar and Kappler were unfortunate in being sent before this particular judge. Columbia Brewery had been open only a few months, but the judge already had strong opinions about it, which he voiced as the hearing began: "This brewery [has] already gained a reputation in this way and many disgraceful scenes have been caused by the fact that liquor was sold to Indians and others on several occasions."[4] The racist laws that prohibited anyone from giving alcohol to Indigenous people were in full force, and used to taint the reputation of any brewery, saloon, or hotel that had Indigenous patrons. During this same week Columbia Brewery was also under the city's legal magnifying glass for its proximity to a murder case that related to an Indigenous woman who frequented the brewery. It must have been a busy week for Fred Millar, who was called upon just days after the MacDonald hearing to give his testimony about Charlie McLean, who had been found dead near the Hastings Mill site after bleeding out from a gash to his wrist. A man known to overindulge and sell alcohol illegally, McLean had last been seen alive at Columbia Brewery with Kitty, an Indigenous woman with whom he lived (a scandalous state of affairs at the time). According to Millar, while McLean was with Kitty at the brewery, he himself didn't actually drink anything because he felt unwell, testimony that seemed to imply Kitty's culpability in whatever happened to her partner.[5] Another newspaper account also suggests that Kitty was untrustworthy: "The evidence adduced at the inquest... would seem to point to the fact that there must have been some foul-play... Kitty, the Indian woman with whom he co-habited, was seen with him at the Columbia Brewery on the afternoon previous to his death, but she has entirely disappeared."[6]

Despite these foreboding comments, the police located Kitty within a short time and she willingly gave her testimony. On September 4 the newspapers reported, rather anticlimactically, that the jury found insufficient evidence to prove foul play. Both Kitty and Columbia were in the clear—technically. I don't know more about Kitty, but I can say that for Columbia, its frequent proximity to events of violence and suspicion contributed to the early reputation for illegality that it was already developing. And it seems that the brewery occasionally offered some pushback against authorities. Less than a month after the unsavoury hassle of the MacDonald and McLean cases, a news-paper reported that "one of the breweries in the east end of the City" billed City Hall two dollars for the expenses of transporting "one load of drunks" home. The newspaper adds that "this would seem to be very reasonable, especially if the occupants of the wagon were well loaded themselves."[7] We cannot say with certainty that Columbia was the brewery in question, but it *was* the brewery farthest east in Vancouver and it was quite popular. Furthermore, it wouldn't be hard to imagine Joseph Kappler clapping back at the authorities, the judges and politicians who were disparaging the reputation of his new business, by getting them to pay for removing intoxicated people (and perhaps these were people who worked for City Hall) from his premises. Respectability was expensive!

AN EAST END START-UP

Joseph Kappler was still building his reputation, after all. He had only been in Canada for three years when he and Millar were dragged into court for breaking liquor laws in his new brewery (and for beating up customers). Born in Germany on September 25, 1854, to Gottfried Kappler and Magdalena Frei, he immigrated to British Columbia when he was twenty-eight. He began his new brewing career under Charles Doering, working as a brewer in 1888 for Doering's newly opened Vancouver Brewery. In fact, according to one account (cited in the previous chapter), Kappler was actually the one who first set up a brewery at Scotia and 7th, although he didn't last long as owner. Doering quickly bought him out and hired him.[8] However, Kappler advanced quickly; by late 1888 he had his brewery on Powell Street up and running. The *Vancouver Daily World's* April 4, 1889 issue cheerily announced that "Keppler & Co's brewery [later called Columbia], a little east of the Smelter, is now in full blast and turning out quantities of beer of excellent quality." Exactly *how* Kappler started his brewery is a bit fuzzy. The details of Columbia's founding aren't explained in

The early years of Columbia Brewery, circa 1892. (Photo courtesy of City of Vancouver Archives, AM54-S4-: Bu P127 N.88)

any of the brewing histories I've read, but the public accounts of the time can help us piece it together. Spoiler alert: it may be related to one of the small Vancouver breweries that rose and fell so quickly that we know almost nothing about it—the San Francisco Brewery.[9]

On March 12, 1889, newspapers published a "Notice to Creditors" regarding the San Francisco Brewery Company. This brewery, which was founded around 1887 or 1888 by the beer baron (and later rum-running) Reifel brothers of Nanaimo, was disposing of its estate and effects for the benefit of its creditors. Very little is known about San Francisco Brewery, but records show that it was located at the corner of Westminster (now Main Street) and 11th Avenue—just a few blocks south of the Vancouver Brewery but still near the banks of Brewery Creek. This is why the August 1889 accounts of Columbia's involvement in MacDonald's assault were confusing. One newspaper refers to the events as occurring in "Keppler's brewery"[10] while the same paper's story from the previous day says that it happened "at what is known as the San Francisco Brewery, situated at the east end of Powell Street."[11] The San Francisco Brewery was nowhere near Powell Street, so this was baffling. However, the confusion might be explained if we recall the San Francisco Brewery bankruptcy sale of the early spring and Kappler's opening of Columbia Brewery on Powell Street shortly afterwards. One possibility is that Kappler bought up some of the equipment and supplies from the bankrupted San Francisco Brewery to start up his own brewery in a different location. Kappler's brewery was never "known" as San Francisco Brewery, but it may have used that brewery's resources to get itself off the ground. The actual location of the San Francisco Brewery itself was shortly afterwards the site of Red Star Brewery. This brewery was run by an acquaintance of Kappler—Jacob DeWitt, another German immigrant and a member, together with Kappler, of Vancouver's Sons of Hermann club. DeWitt also worked with Doering, and in 1892 he became manager of the Germania, the Vancouver hotel Doering had recently acquired.[12] It's no wonder that newspaper reporters sometimes mixed up the brewers and their breweries!

After opening Columbia, Kappler quickly got to work making his brewery stand out from the others. He received his maltster's licence in October of 1891, which allowed him to malt his own grain in-house—unusual for a brewery at the time. Local papers announced that he was "now making his own malt and is using Lulu Island barley. So far the experiment has been a success and his venture may...add further to the growth of local industries."[13] The malthouse ended up being a resource for other breweries as well, some of which chose to buy at least some of their malt from Columbia. The brewery was also in a good location, despite its distance from the heart of the city; it made "a handy half-way house on a warm day when one is making a trip to the East End park."[14] Later in the 1890s, Kappler invested in numerous advertisements in city directories and local newspapers to present a shiny public face for his business.

Despite all these efforts, Columbia never achieved the same kind of public respectability that Doering's brewery did, although it did seem to be popular. Part of the problem may have been its location, rather than any fault of its owners. As noted above, Columbia made a good "halfway house" for trips out of town. In the 1890s, according to an anonymous quotation recorded in George and Ilene Watson's *Pioneer Breweries of British Columbia,* "there were no street cars east of Victoria Drive, people attending the races, etc had to walk from the end street car there and back. Sometimes there was quite a host of them, and when the day was sunny and hot they all made a dash for Columbia Brewery."[15] However, this location, in a less populated and less regulated area of the city, and in close proximity to Tar Flat, also made it potentially more dangerous. Tar Flat was technically a residential area, but the residences were mostly shacks and tents. Homelessness was rampant. According to Lani Russwurm, a local Vancouver historian, the papers first refer to the area as Tar Flat in 1899, when police arrested C. Haultgreen there for breaking into and vandalizing cabins:

> *Most of the attention Tar Flat received in the papers was for petty criminal activity, often coupled with calls for its destruction. Newspapers characterized Tar Flat in the harshest terms: "resort of evil-doers," "that unsavory suburb," "that vile section of the city," "rendezvous of the outlaw and thief," and "a cancer that can only spread its malignant growth" are some examples. Serious drinkers were attracted to Tar Flat by its proximity to the Columbia Brewery, a popular watering hole about where the McDonald's is today at Powell and Wall Streets.*[16]

Columbia's location in a disreputable area didn't help its reputation. (Photo courtesy of City of Vancouver Archives, Map 384, Sheet 38 [Goad's Atlas])

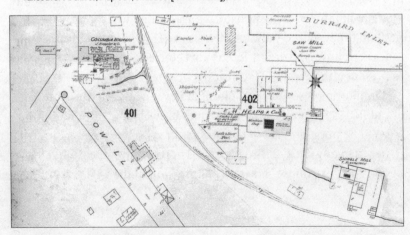

Many of Columbia's neighbours—and its regular drinkers—would have been residents of this impoverished and marginalized area. One couldn't assume one's own safety, even in the middle of the day. The *Weekly News-Advertiser* of April 30, 1890, for example, recounts how Peter Miller, driving Columbia's beer wagon to deliver ale in the area, was shot at three times from a window by a woman named Sadie Clark, who was apparently intoxicated and had a "fierce and unrestrainable temper."

Columbia was also known for illegally serving alcohol to patrons (more on that later in this chapter), and it therefore attracted disreputable customers. In their meeting of April 18, 1902, the city's Board of Licence Commissioners called for the chief of police to address "reports that there was a great deal of Sunday drunkenness connected with an East End brewery."[17] This brewery could only be Columbia, which by then had established a reputation for serving illegally (too much, and on the wrong day) and turning a blind eye to criminal activity. The *Daily News Advertiser* of October 8, 1909, describes how "four vagrants" who were sleeping in a dugout beside the brewery chose their location "because they heard they could get a good big drink" before passing out, and there is more than one newspaper account about known criminals frequenting the brewery.

In March of 1898, a notorious murder happened near Columbia. John Bray from Toronto was walking along the train tracks toward "the brewery, near Hastings" with two acquaintances. When they were already a mile and a half outside of the city and approaching the brewery, one of his companions asked Bray if he could spare twenty-five cents for beer. When Bray offered to buy all the beer for the evening, the "friends" attacked and shot him. This didn't kill him immediately; he wandered around alone for a period of time before finding shelter in a little shack, where he died.[18]

The tragic violence in the neighbourhood wasn't due to the brewery itself. Some of Columbia's wild reputation, however, was attributable to Joseph Kappler's response to the area's notoriety as well as his loose and easy way of doing things—how he behaved, who he hired, how much everyone drank. Kappler seems to have been an unusual sort of man. Unlike most of the other major brewers in early Vancouver, he never married—at least, there is no record of it. The Canadian census of 1901 lists him as being a forty-six-year-old single man lodging in the home of Andrew and Mary Mueller[19] (ages fifty-two and forty, respectively), along with their son William (nineteen) and daughters Emma (seventeen) and Mary (fifteen). His early life seems to have been dedicated to music, and in Vancouver he was known not just for his brewing but for his operatic singing. One account of the 1893 Leiderkranz Ball in Vancouver—an event celebrating the German population of the city—describes how "Mr. Joseph Kappler gave a Tyrolese joddling [yodelling] song in costume in his well-known style, winning hearty applause. He was obliged to appear again in response to an encore."[20] Kappler sang, laughed, danced, and brewed—and was known for his cheery and extroverted personality, perfect for a brewery owner.

The Muellers, like Kappler, were also from Germany. Census and marriage records indicate that they immigrated to the United States separately, married in Streator, Illinois, then moved to Vancouver in 1883 (pre-incorporation) to become one of its pioneer couples. It is not clear when Kappler moved in with the Muellers, but it seems that they all lived together in the brewery and ran it co-operatively, so it likely happened as soon as he established the business. While the lodging officially belonged to the Muellers since at least 1894, the business itself was Kappler's, who co-owned it with Emil Gerhauser, another brewer, in the early 1890s. However, even though the Muellers' names were not legally tied to the business until the early 1900s, they owned the building and ran the brewery with him. Calvert Simson, the storekeeper at the Hastings Sawmill, recalled how Mary Mueller would call on the hotels in Gastown and take their orders, then Andrew would deliver the goods in a horse-drawn wagon. Apparently he used to "go asleep on the seat and the horse took him home." This may have been due to Andrew's drinking problems; Simson claims that "when he [Andrew] went to bed at night he always had a jug of beer at his side in case he woke up thirsty at night. He smelled of beer when he perspired."[21] Both owners and employees lived at the brewery. Some of their workers were known for problematic behaviour, such as Anton Staden, who was charged in 1893 for being "drunk and incapable" but let off with a slap on the wrist. The close proximity of employers with employees, combined with Kappler's sometimes impetuous actions and Mary Mueller's temper, resulted in some explosive moments that brought the brewery into court again and again.

MARY MUELLER: VANCOUVER'S FIRST FEMALE BREWERY MANAGER

Mary Mueller is of particular interest for anyone investigating the history of Columbia Brewery, since she eventually took over ownership after both Kappler and her husband died.[22] Before she was left in charge, she worked on what appeared to be equal footing with the two men, judging from the stories told about her. She and her husband seemed to have a real affection for one another, and public accounts of the couple suggest a solid bond. On a summer's day in 1903, a man named James Gordon was in the brewery with friends. According to city directories, Gordon was a long-term resident of the Badminton Hotel on Howe and Dunsmuir—a place that was generally respectable, hosting conventions and offering family-friendly accommodations. After drinking for a while at the brewery, he began to be abusive, targeting Mary Mueller and spouting insults at her. In a rather dramatic response, Mary's husband grabbed a sickle and brandished it at Gordon to defend his wife.[23] In another instance of Mr. Mueller's affection for his wife, accounts of a 1905 fire at the brewery highlighted his soft heart and courage: the papers reported that he ran back into the flames to save Mary's little poodle.[24] Just two months after this catastrophe (the poodle was saved, but $10,000 worth of damage was done to the brewery), the couple celebrated their twenty-fifth wedding anniversary in a party at home with their family.

While the public saw her husband as usually stolid and slow to anger (as well as slow to forgive), the tales about Mary indicate that she was fiery and unafraid—good qualities for someone living and working in that area of town, but also traits that got her into trouble. From what we can assess through US and Canadian census, immigration, and marital records, Mary was born on New Year's Eve of 1860 in Magdeburg, Germany, to Frederick and Sophia Leseman (maiden name Richard), a farming family. She travelled to New York in steerage on the steamship *Oder*, arriving one month before her twenty-first birthday. Unlike Clara Reisterer, Sarah Jane Doering, or Elsie Williams, this brewery owner's wife did not grow up with many middle-class comforts. She could take care of herself, which was a benefit to anyone starting up a rough-and-tumble brewery. In July 1901, for example, she was driving the brewery wagon when she saw a panicked runaway horse dragging a half-disconnected cart behind it, with a young man caught in the harness and receiving a hard battering around the head. Mary was able to stop the runaway horse and assist the boy, who was injured but survived.[25] However, Mary's quick wit and temper sometimes got the better of her. One incident early in Columbia Brewery's tenure on the east side memorably illustrates that side of Mary's character.[26]

On March 31, 1891, one day after the sudden death of John Williams's wife down at the Red Cross Brewery, a popular fish and game dealer known as Dutch Bill[27] came into Columbia Brewery to collect some items he had left there. Mary, who was in charge of keeping house then, was waiting for him; she had heard about town that he'd called her a name and spread some gossip about her, and she was ready to take her revenge. When he arrived, she "administered a horsewhipping which left an ugly scar across his face, blackened an eye, and left him covered with bruises." Another report says that "she gave him a severe licking with a whip. She smashed one end of the whip, then continued hitting him with the butt end." According to Dutch Bill's testimony in court, Kappler held him down for the whipping and "applauded the deed"—although Kappler "stoutly denied" the charge. As a fish and game dealer, Dutch Bill was probably not a slight or weak man, so Mary must have had prodigious strength in order to carry out her punishment.

Mary and Kappler were brought into court and the case was heard by Judge Hallett, who fined Mary fifty dollars "with the option of one month's imprisonment for chastising Dutch Billy." Charges against Kappler were dropped, probably to Mary's chagrin. She immediately appealed her conviction, no doubt feeling that her actions were justified. She was fortunate enough to be heard by Justice McCreight, a quiet, reserved, eminently non-political judge who had been the province's first premier back in 1871. McCreight had been reviewing the decisions made by Judge Hallett since the beginning of the year and when Mary submitted her appeal, McCreight was open to hearing it. According to a student of McCreight's life, "the use of the expression 'I think' was apparently typical of McCreight's judgments and his extreme regard for the truth... a favourite expression of the judge's, especially when presiding at criminal trials was 'my conscience is troubling me'... he hesitated to express himself with any certainty until he had studied all the legal decisions."[28] Mary's conviction of "inflicting grievous bodily harm with a horsewhip upon a certain unnamed information [*sic*]" was reversed: "The Court found the conviction to be bad on all the points raised in the counsel for the appellant, Mr. Louis P. Eckstein, and remarked the frequency of convictions from the same police court of a similar untenable nature."[29] Mary's was among the twenty-two convictions by Hallett that McCreight quashed that summer.

COLUMBIA BREWERY: COME FOR THE BEER, STAY FOR THE BRAWLS

The Dutch Bill fiasco had barely faded from memory when, just over a month later, Columbia Brewery was in the public eye once again.[30] John Balfour-Ker, a well-respected member of the Vancouver Institute, an organization that hosted philosophical debates, poetry readings, and other cultural events, testified to a frightening experience he had near the brewery. He was walking past the Hastings townsite near Columbia to look at a piece of property for sale. By the time he was done, it was dark and he had a lengthy walk back to the city. Balfour-Ker was a gentle person, a thoughtful and well-read intellectual known for his "able and happy manner" and his engaging lectures on topics ranging from Wordsworth to economic policy to the new technology of telephones.[31] Walking through a rough area of town late at night wasn't his usual practice, so he kept his revolver strapped to his waist. He was undisruptive as he walked past Columbia Brewery, so he was shocked when two or three wolfhounds came rushing out "barking loudly, and seeming to be unusually vicious." Not used to handling a gun, he nevertheless took a wild shot at one of the dogs when it lunged at him, causing all of them to retreat back to the brewery.

Balfour-Ker was breathing a sigh of relief when he heard a whole pack of dogs come running again at him from the brewery, men shouting behind them. He wasn't particularly athletic, but in desperation he broke into a run and managed to scramble up a fence. Emil Miller, a large, muscled German man who worked at the brewery,[32] along with Joseph Kappler, who had heard Balfour-Ker's shot, joined the dogs and called up to the frightened man. "He called me some vile names and threatened to kill me if I did not come down and give up my revolver," Balfour-Ker testified of Miller. Kappler apparently stood behind and observed. Balfour-Ker told Miller to call off the dogs, and was threatened again in response. Finally Miller called off the dogs and the men confiscated Balfour-Ker's revolver. Balfour-Ker suggested going to the police to resolve the issue formally, but Miller and Kappler refused. Kappler's statements the next day were casually unrepentant, and Miller insisted that their actions were justified and the dogs weren't an issue: "We have been bothered around here with men who come and steal our things; I didn't know who he was." This response is a stark contrast to how another Vancouver brewer handled a similar situation. When Charles Doering's business partner Otto

Marstrand heard that Doering's dogs (left loose while Doering was out of town) had attacked someone, he assured authorities that action would be taken: "He was sure when Mr. Doering learned of the vicious tendences of his dogs, he would consent to have them destroyed."[33] Miller dismissed any such concern about his animals. The dogs, Miller laughed, weren't kept at the brewery for nothing. I can't help wondering if Balfour-Ker's recent advocacy for non-prohibition of liquor may have been shaken by this experience with the city's most notorious brewery.[34]

Newspapers published numerous stories over the years about other violent events occurring at or around the brewery. Of course, the papers covered human interest stories involving all of Vancouver's breweries, but the "wild west" events at Columbia were an outlier. One Saturday, for example, Kappler had friends over to the brewery. As they were drinking and chatting about their hunting prowess, Kappler thought it would be a perfect opportunity to show his gun to his companions. Upon handling the weapon, one of the men accidentally shot Kappler through the arm.[35] The doctor found the bullet flattened out on the bone. In another incident, Mueller and Kappler got into a heated argument about, of all things, a tub of water that was stored up near the ceiling for use in a fire. Kappler thought it wasn't secured properly and blamed Mueller, which enraged him. In the dispute, Mueller stabbed Kappler twice in the side, penetrating his lung. The initial newspaper accounts were doubtful of Kappler's survival, so serious was the injury (although a week later he was reported as being on his feet again). The reporter offered his own take: "Kappler is the soul of good humor and whatever bad temper he gets into passes away like a flash. Mueller, on the other hand, is phlegmatic and is slow both in anger and in good humor."[36] He was also a heavy drinker, as noted earlier, and this may have contributed to his "phlegmatic" reputation. Mueller's stolidly unchanging disposition didn't seem to be in action when he attempted to escape after this altercation—a rash decision supported by his friends, George Stummer and Henry Domino, who rowed Mueller all the way to Ladner. It didn't take long before he was caught, however, and arrested. Fortunately for Mueller, Kappler wasn't interested in actually pressing charges—in this case, it seems that the newspaper's assessment of the brewer's happy disposition was essentially correct.[37]

The problems around Columbia continued after the 1890s. In one case in 1900, a known criminal called "Liverpool Shortie" (real name Flynn) got into a knife fight either in or beside the brewery. Someone at Columbia called the police "when the knife was still cutting the air" to report that Flynn was lying bleeding on the tracks outside the brewery.[38] In May of the following year, there were reports of young men drinking "several glasses of refreshing beer . . . in the vicinity of Columbia Brewery." As the drunkenness increased, they got into some trouble with a large rubber hose and one of the men was hit so hard that his leg broke. The brewery was also the victim of theft on multiple occasions, from beer to kegs to chickens. In December of 1901, Bob Rhodes stole two chickens from the brewery right before they were destined for Mary's Chinese New Year feast. Both chickens were brought into court to convict him. In 1902, some boat thieves took refuge in the brewery, but were tracked down by police constable Colin Campbell.[39]

Perhaps the most memorable theft was in 1904, when repeat offender William Rutt from the Tar Flat area, a man known as Billy the Rat, broke into the brewery with a friend on a Sunday night. They'd already visited that afternoon, but returned later under cover of darkness, hoping for more drinks. They stayed for several hours, drinking Columbia's lager and its xxx Porter (the more Xs, the higher the alcohol content), until they had "lowered the level in the 10,000 gallon vat several inches." Before they left, they filled a sack with several dozen bottles of beer. Rather than bringing the stolen goods to his own house, Billy and his friend, both intoxicated, snuck into his neighbour's place and stuffed one of his mattresses full of bottles. Then, according to *The Province*, "Billy's friend got into bed with the owner of the house . . . When Mr. Fredericks [the owner] awoke in the night he found his guests, and they hospitably asked him to drink beer. Mr. Fredericks would not, and now he is glad."[40] Mrs. Mueller and Mr. Fredericks were the primary witnesses in court against Billy "and they told hard stories." Mary Mueller was a woman with a reputation for temper and Mr. Fredericks was a Black man living in the slum area of Vancouver, but judging from the tone of the newspaper, both were respectable enough to provide credible testimony in court. Columbia was a bit rough, but was well loved by many Vancouverites.

This affection for Columbia Brewery was reflected in the *Daily World*'s support for the ad campaign that Kappler launched in the late 1890s, when he placed advertisements for his brewery in the city directories[41] and local newspapers. This may have been an attempt to shine up the brewery's reputation a bit. One ad that ran frequently was for a new, unique German beer he was selling—one that might tap into the same customer base that purchased Red Cross Brewery's seasonal bock beer each spring. This was Culmbacher, a now nearly extinct beer style originating in Kulmbach, Germany. By the mid-nineteenth century, with boatloads of German immigrants arriving on the shores of the US and Canada, Culmbacher became popular in breweries across the continent.

According to Michael Stein, "the original, Old World Kulmbacher was a dark beer. It had a pronounced malt flavor and a sweetish taste. For American brewers, it had Bavarian characteristics, in that it was brewed along the lines of a Bavarian Lager, with

William Rutt, a.k.a. Billy the Rat, made a daring theft at Columbia but bungled it after drinking too much. (Photo courtesy of City of Vancouver Archives, VPD S714-: CVA 480-456)

a strong starting gravity" (and we know from Billy the Rat's escapades that Columbia brewed high-alcohol beers in its facility).[42] Kappler's new ad, which ran in the *Vancouver Daily World* throughout the same year as his ads in the city directory (1899), boasted that the brewery "is now turning out a magnificent sample of Culmbacher Lager. Experience, good material, and a complete plant combine to make this the finest beer in British Columbia. TRY IT AND BE CONVINCED."[43]

This challenge was endorsed by a July 1899 write-up in the *Daily World*, which called Culmbacher lager "a choice brew" and praised the technological advancement of the brewery itself. It promised readers that "a visit to the brewery will convince anyone that no requisite to the making of good beer has been overlooked. Joseph Kappler, the manager, has had plenty of experience and gives close personal attention to the whole process…Culmbacher lager is a beverage calculated to delight connoisseurs." The write-up placed Columbia among the breweries producing high-quality German beer for the Germans in Vancouver who knew what good beer tasted like. German beer in Vancouver started with lager around

Columbia Brewery in 1909. (Photo courtesy of City of Vancouver Archives, Am54-S4-: Bu P728)

1890, but within ten years was branching out into specialty styles like bock, which Red Cross released seasonally, and Culmbacher— styles that would remind German-origin drinkers of their homeland. This turn to a German specialty at the end of the century stands in contrast to what Vancouver Breweries did with Cascade just two years later, which was to cultivate a beer brand that reflected Vancouver. Perhaps Kappler's frequent involvement in (and sometimes leadership of) German clubs and musical groups over the years encouraged him to market his product to the Vancouver demographic he most often encountered, and the one he trusted: German immigrants.

CRISES AT COLUMBIA

Kappler's cheery nature and desire to see everyone around him happy caused him to close his eyes to some of the truly troubled people who worked for him. The case of Fritz Herzberg, a man Mary hired to be the brewery's distribution agent in Steveston in the summer of 1896 and who also lodged at the brewery with them, was a tragic example.[44] Herzberg had Bright's disease, now called nephritis, which caused kidney inflammation. On his doctor's orders, he stopped drinking in an effort to extend his lifespan. Once sober, he commented to friends that if he ever drank again he would shoot himself, so when he returned intoxicated to the brewery on a Tuesday afternoon after his employment contract had been terminated, both Kappler and Mary Mueller knew it wasn't a good sign. Throughout that afternoon, both Kappler and Herzberg were in and out of the brewery, with Mary repeatedly trying to get Kappler to join them when Herzberg was present. Herzberg was playing with a revolver, and frequently referred to a rifle he owned that he could shoot with his big toe if needed. He started burning some of his financial and land-ownership records in the hearth fire, claiming that he didn't need them anymore. According to Mary's court testimony, he was not just implying but explicitly stating that he planned self-harm. When she asked him to give her his gun, he refused. "I was anxious about it," Mary testified, "because of his burning the papers and his having told me before that he would kill himself if he ever got drunk again... I sent the boy to tell Mr. Kappler that Fred [Fritz] was going to shoot himself because when I felt the revolver [in his pocket] he said that he was going to shoot himself tonight."

When Mary finally got the two men to sit down with her, with no guns out, she said to Kappler, "Joe, what did you think, Fred [Fritz] wants to shoot himself." Kappler laughed in response and insisted that men who talk about such an act rarely carry it out. Herzberg replied, "Joe, do not take me for a coward. I mean it." Kappler lightheartedly suggested that Herzberg show him the gun and said that he'd bet it wasn't even loaded. That got Herzberg's back up, and he pointed the gun at Kappler, insisting that no one—not Kappler, not even ten men—could take that gun away from him, and anyone who tried had better be careful. Herzberg then suggested that they should all have a drink together—even though, as Mary noted in her testimony, he himself had never consumed alcohol in the brewery before. She believed it meant he wanted to "die happy." Mary continues her account of what happened after that:

We each had a glass of beer and then Herzberg started to sing. Kappler sang with him. Herzberg said, "I will die anyway tonight and let us have another song." They sang Tyrolese echo songs [a form of German yodelling]. I thought that if he commenced singing the morbid thoughts might leave his mind. After the singing Mr. Kappler again asked Herzberg to show the revolver. I said, "Do not pull it out, I do not want any shooting in the house." Herzberg said, "I would not make any dirt in your house Mrs. Muller, I have too much respect for you." I went to Emil Gerhauser's room in the brewery and told him that Herzberg— Fred—wanted to shoot himself. Gerhauser laughed and said that he had said that a hundred times before.

The evening continued in this same pattern, with Herzberg giving clear signs of his intention—giving Mary a four-dollar watch chain, tabulating what he owed to others and what they owed him but saying there would never be payment, repeatedly saying goodbye—and Kappler and Gerhauser laughing off Mary's concern. More beer was consumed, some brought in by Kappler and some by Herzberg. There was more singing, and more clinking of glasses. In between, Herzberg would make assertions that he'd soon be gone but that he was not "crazy": "I have my full senses and I do not want anyone to think I was crazy," he told Kappler and Mary.

As the evening progressed, Mary decided enough was enough: "Herzberg came up to me and wanted to shake hands again. I would not shake hands with him, and told him that if he would not stop his foolish nonsense I would go at once to Heaps and telephone for a policeman." She left the brewery and was about to walk toward Heaps when a freight train passed, forcing her to wait. Then Kappler and Herzberg exited the brewery. Herzberg said he was going into town, and Kappler offered to give him a ride in the wagon: "Wait a bit and I will hitch up the team and go with you." Kappler then briskly made off toward the stable to get the horses. However, in the Vancouver dusk Mary could see Herzberg going in the opposite direction. The train had just finished passing and by then Herzberg was out of her line of vision. A sudden gunshot rang through the air.

Kappler shouted to Herzberg, "What are you shooting in the air for?" But Mary knew what had happened. She ran to Gerhauser's room before even seeing the body and told him that Herzberg had turned his gun on himself. Getting a lantern, they hastened outside to where they'd heard the shot and found Herzberg "lying on his back, with his legs crossed, his arms lying parallel with his body and the revolver lying across the breast. Gerhauser took hold of his hand and said that he was dead." Kappler rapidly hitched up his team to go get the police, and Mary and Gerhauser stood watch over Herzberg's body. Night had fully fallen by then, and it was a chill fall evening, so according to Mary they briefly went into the house for a cape and a pipe, and at that moment the policemen arrived.

Up until the very end, when he asked why Herzberg was shooting in the air, Kappler blinded himself to the possibility that his former employee was experiencing a very real crisis. A similar dynamic may have occurred with Emil Gerhauser, Columbia's first brewer and the man who guarded Herzberg's body with Mary while they waited for the police. After working for Kappler for a number of years, he went to San Francisco in 1898 with cash from his brother in hand, possibly to do some prospecting (something he'd attempted before, albeit unsuccessfully). When he returned with only $500 of the $1,500 given to him, he went to the Sapperton Brewery, which was owned by Nels Nelson by then.[45] However, shortly afterwards he sent an "urgent message" to Kappler "to come and take him away from them [Sapperton]. His request was complied with." After staying at Columbia for several days, he went to visit a friend at the Doering & Marstrand Brewery. This friend, not identified by the papers, believed that Gerhauser "had something on his mind. When leaving, he said, 'Well, if you do not see me any more you will know what has happened to me.'"[46] The newspaper account concludes by stating that Gerhauser's family and friends had seen no trace of him, and I could not find reference to him in the city directories I could access from after 1899. Kappler seems to have truly cared for his employees, which is why he tried to cheer up Herzberg and why he left to "rescue" Gerhauser from Sapperton when Gerhauser was in some sort of crisis. However, he didn't always know how to respond appropriately to serious problems that arose. It seemed Kappler laughed off Herzberg's mental health crisis and the attack on Balfour-Ker by Columbia's dogs. It is likely he also didn't make much of an attempt to stop Mary's illegal sales of beer, a habit that brought them into court multiple times. He loved people and took joy in life, but he avoided dealing with some critical issues.

KAPPLER'S DEATH: A NEW ERA FOR COLUMBIA

Joseph Kappler died in 1904, when he was just in his late forties. His death was due to a heart condition from which he had long suffered. Knowing of this condition, he mused to friends that doctors should examine his heart when he died, so that they could learn more about the disease that killed him. He put this specification in his will, and the post-mortem examination was duly completed. Physicians discovered that one side of his heart was considerably enlarged and so hardened it was like stone, while the other side was completely normal.[47] We can hope that this knowledge contributed something to medicine, in honour of Kappler's wishes. His funeral was well attended, and wreaths and flowers were left by his fellow brewers, including Doering, Williams, Marstrand, and Thorson (of North Arm Brewery), and the German clubs in which he was involved, such as the Sons of Hermann and the Eagles. The Muellers posted a letter of thanks in the newspaper to all the people who attended Kappler's funeral and donated tributes.[48]

After Kappler's death, the legal status of Columbia becomes a bit fuzzy. It was referred to as being owned "by the Miller & Kappler estate" and it seems to be run for at least the next year or two by Mr. and Mrs. Mueller together. A large Seattle company—kept anonymous in public accounts—visited Vancouver in April of 1905 with the hope of either building a new brewery in North Vancouver or buying out and expanding Columbia Brewery.[49] This does not appear to have gone through, because two years later, *The Province* announced that the brewery, which "was owned" by Mrs. Mueller, had been sold for $35,000 to a Vancouver company, which also took a lease on the nearby Heaps property with views to expanding the brewery. At this point, one would assume that the corporate takeover would occur and the Muellers would disappear from the scene. Wrong.

After this sale, there is no more mention of the company that purchased the brewery. Instead, all accounts of the brewery are about Mrs. Mueller, usually named as either the owner or the proprietor.

One newspaper refers to the brewery as reverting to Mr. Mueller after Kappler died, but goes on to describe how it was Mrs. Mueller who ran the business, with seven staff under her, with her "capable directing mind." There is no mention of Mr. Mueller, nor is there mention of him in any future stories, so he may have died not long after their anniversary party in early 1906.[50]

Bill Wilson's directory of BC breweries identifies "A. Mueller & Co" as proprietor from 1904 to 1910 (this was probably the company name, and seems to have been run by Mary), Mrs. Mary Mueller from 1910 to 1911, then "(Andrew) Mueller" from 1911 to 1912.[51] It may have been that Mary returned to using her husband's name as a front for the business, especially after she had a history of being fined, but newspaper accounts from 1911 to 1912 still name her as the owner (more on this below).

Indeed, most of the stories about Columbia from after Kappler's death are about Mary Mueller getting fined and trying to get out of it. In two cases, she attempted to use contemporary debates about Dominion (i.e., federal) licensing versus provincial and municipal licensing to wiggle out of allegations that she was selling beer illegally.[52] In the first case, a customer claimed, "I bought a gallon, and with my friends drank it in the brewery." This was illegal under Mrs. Mueller's wholesale licence. In court she readily admitted that she had no retail licence, "though she held a Dominion and a city wholesale licence," which should be enough. The judge's response was that Mrs. Mueller "ought to know that the wholesale license doesn't permit you to sell in smaller quantities than two gallons."[53] Mrs. Mueller paid the seventy-five-dollar fine, only to use the same defence again six months later, when she was fined for illegal beer sales during a party her brewer, Louie Frisch, hosted at the brewery in August 1907.[54] Her lawyer asserted that the bylaw restrictions applied to wholesale licences but not to brewery licences, which fell under the Dominion Licences Act of 1888. Mary further bolstered her case by insisting that she had never actually sold the beer—just produced it. Since it was Frisch's party, she was just giving beer out to guests for free.

Witnesses at the gathering contradicted her: one said that Mary's daughter Emma Mueller had come to ask him whether he wanted a quart or a half-gallon of beer, and when he chose the half-gallon, Emma accepted the fifty cents he paid her and passed the cash to her mother. Other witnesses said much the same. Emma Mueller, a Mrs. Schulte, and the brewer Frisch all corroborated Mary's story that the beer was given out and that neither Mary nor Emma accepted any money for serving it. However, given that Emma was Mary's daughter, Mrs. Schulte was her close friend (a divorcee, she'd married her second husband in a ceremony held at Mary's house several years earlier), and Frisch was her employee, one might question the veracity of their testimony. In addition, Mary had been charged with the same infraction just two months earlier, in June 1907. According to the paper's account of the hearing, "one witness swore that he had gone into the kitchen of the brewery and asked for a drink of beer...her daughter brought him a quart of beer for which he paid fifteen cents...the witness said that [the beer] was not up to much as it had made him sick after drinking it."[55] The judge had little patience for Mary's repeated infractions, and little regard for her witnesses: he fined her one hundred dollars on the spot.

Columbia Brewery ultimately closed down not because of Mary's insistence on skirting the law, but because of the power of Vancouver's water—and more specifically, a foolish decision that City Hall made about that water. On the evening of November 2, 1908, the heavy clouds that had been lying low over the city—typical for the season—opened up, releasing torrents of rain into the streets and streams. Capilano and Seymour creeks began rising, flooding adjacent areas and washing away telephone poles that maintained communication between North Vancouver and the south side of the inlet. Throughout Vancouver, from the West End to the East End, in Fairview and Mount Pleasant, water began to rush. Culverts that had been dug for directing excess rainwater failed to control them. The unsurfaced brand-new sewer recently constructed near the famous Woodward's department store at Hastings and Abbott soon collapsed under the weight of the rain, and around 3:00 AM Woodward's lone night watchman was shocked to hear a crash and see water pouring forcefully into the basement, rising up to three or four feet. More rushed in as the fire trucks tried to pump it out. The city engineer was bombarded by calls throughout the day: "Every five minutes I have had to answer a telephone complaint of sewers backing up, surface drains blocked or basement drains failing to work," he told a reporter.[56]

To make this situation worse for Columbia, the brewery was already suffering from a flooding event several months earlier. During the spring of 1908, City Hall discussed what to do about the blocking of two natural waterways that had flowed through the property of Mr. Heaps, a former alderman. The blocking was done to "suit a private individual," and Alderman Morton later implied that there might be some backroom deals done at City Hall—perhaps for the former alderman himself. The water used to flow under the CPR track, but when it was blocked it had to redirect. That redirection "nearly washed away the Columbia Brewery, undermining the engine room and playing havoc generally."[57] The Council disagreed on whether to reopen the waterways or dig better culverts under the CPR tracks, but I could find no record of a decision being made.

Fast-forward from April 1908 to November 1908. After recovering her business from the earlier flooding, Mary Mueller must have been horrified to see what was happening in the early hours of November 3. According to the *Daily News Advertiser* of November 4, "the people in the brewery awoke yesterday morning to find the engine surrounded by six feet of water, and a regular river running through the lower part of the establishment." On November 6, further details were released, as the reporter described barrels and other items floating through the engine room, brewery machinery fully submerged, and the boiler's foundations completely washed away by flood waters. Mary announced that she would be suing the City for $10,000 worth of damage. Over the next two years, the case dragged on, with additional damages added for other flooding that was due to the City's incompetence. By December 1910 *The Province* announced

Despite the brewery's struggles, it featured on a postcard in 1909. Note the attribution to Andrew Mueller as owner, although it is unclear whether he was alive at this point. (Photo courtesy of City of Vancouver Archives, AM1052 P-2520)

that Mary Muller, "owner of the Vancouver Brewery [*sic*]," was now bringing two damage actions, worth a total of $25,000, against the City. In the liquor licence register for 1910, "Columbia Brewery" is written down and then crossed out in red, suggesting they may have attempted to restart the business but decided against it. Almost a year later, in November 1911, the brewery flooded yet again—four feet of water submerged most of the basement. However, by that point the brewery hadn't been in use for over two years, so additional damages were minimal. By January 1912, "an arrangement had been made between the city solicitor and Mrs. Mueller, owner of the Columbia

Brewery property," for the City to make a new culvert from Powell Street in exchange for Mrs. Mueller waiving all her damage claims. Mary agreed, and Columbia did not open again.

Columbia's closure marked the end of independent brewing in Vancouver for a long time (see Chapter 5 for the story of how the breweries amalgamated). It was the final holdout, and along with the furor over the potential opening of a new brewery in south Vancouver (a movement that fell through), it was the subject of various temperance-oriented societies' anger. The Christian Endeavor Society included the prevention of Columbia's reopening in the list of "moral reforms" they had accomplished in 1909 and 1910 (these reforms also included stopping the sale of fruit and candy in Stanley Park on Sundays).[58] Their effort to take credit for the brewery's closure certainly testifies to Columbia's gritty reputation, but it rings false in the face of what we know. The City's poor handling of infrastructure and property development left Columbia, along with many other properties, vulnerable to the destructive power of Vancouver's rainwaters. After multiple floodings and equipment collapses, Mary had run out of capital to keep the business going.

Back to the question of ownership. It remains unclear when Mary's husband Andrew died, but it was before 1916, since in that year Henderson's Vancouver city directory lists her as a widow. The provincial vital statistics records have so far turned up nothing, but it seems likely that he died closer to 1907. The city directories during the decade between 1907 and 1916 are very inconsistent in their records of his presence. In 1908 and 1909 he is listed as proprietor of Columbia Brewery, then in 1910 Mary is listed as proprietor and Andrew is not listed at all (although his son William is included as an employee). In 1911 Mary is referred to as proprietor of the brewery, but Andrew is listed simply as living at Columbia's location (1973 Powell). In 1912, Andrew is listed as being "of Columbia Lager Beer Brewery." In 1913 only their daughter Emma Mueller is listed as living there, and neither Mary nor Andrew appear. In 1915 Andrew is listed, and in 1916 Mary is identified as his widow. Whatever the reason for these inconsistencies, all evidence indicates that Mary was the one in charge of running the brewery regardless of the name on the business and Andrew had definitely passed away by 1915 or (likely) earlier.

On July 24, 1919, Mary Mueller, then fifty-eight, married forty-nine-year-old Clarence Brownlee at Holy Trinity Church in Vancouver. They remained married until Clarence's death in 1940. Mary and Andrew's son William died in 1926, but their daughters Marie and Emma (married names Wilder and Hanna, respectively) lived until the mid-1960s. Mary herself passed away in October of 1951. A *Vancouver Sun* article about her from one year before reveals a woman who remained active and vital into her nineties. The story describes her as a woman who loved life:

> *Still able to read a newspaper without glasses, she takes an active interest in the news and follows the [horse] racing news carefully. An active horsewoman in her earlier years, she drove and loved fine horses, although the etiquette of her day prevented her the pleasure of horseback riding. [. . .] "Mother loved racing and was a born gambler," says [her daughter] Mrs. Hanna. "She looked forward to the pne every year." Mrs. Brownlee has no special formula for her long life and hopes to see 1961 ushered in. She takes an optimistic view of world conditions. "I've seen so much trouble and war that I don't worry," she says, "and things always seem to get better in spite of everything."*[59]

Mary's daughter Emma, quoted above, often helped her mother in the brewery and would eventually travel to Germany on her own to visit friends. Although she married, she never had children and was survived only by her nephew Frederick Dittbeiner, since her siblings Marie and William predeceased her. However, there is another interesting possibility for the young, pre-married Emma, one that leads us to our next brewery. According to William Hagelund's *House of Suds*, a woman named Emma Mueller was the brewmaster for Royal

Brewing Company, the firm that took over Stanley Park Brewery around 1903. Hagelund claims that Emma was the niece of "Fred" Hose (the name elsewhere is "Frank"), who owned Royal Brewing. Unfortunately, no source is given for any of this information so it cannot be corroborated. If this is the Emma Mueller who was also Mary's daughter, she would have been in her early twenties while Royal Brewing was operational, and it seems very unlikely that she, as a young woman, would have been a brewmaster at this point in a very male-dominated industry. I asked Bill Wilson, author of *Beer Barons of BC*, if he had heard of anything regarding Emma Mueller brewing for Royal, and he had not. He did, however, suggest that she may have worked in the brewery. This seems a possibility, given Emma's involvement with the running of Columbia Brewery as attested in the accounts of Mary's court cases (handling money, serving beer, and probably cleaning and bottle-washing).

Whether Emma of Columbia Brewery spent extra hours working at Stanley Park Brewery across town may never be confirmed. However, we do know that Vancouver's easternmost brewery had its own drama and a rather rocky road business-wise. Stanley Park Brewery has its own tale to tell.

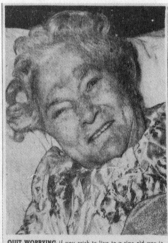

QUIT WORRYING if you wish to live to a ripe old age is the advice of Mrs. Mary Brownlee, 1764 West Eighth, who celebrates her 91st birthday New Year's Eve. Good food is also part of her longevity recipe.

Mary was featured in a *Vancouver Sun* story on December 30, 1951, when she was about to celebrate her ninety-first birthday.

CHAPTER 4

THE STANLEY PARK BREWERY: ENGLISH ALES IN A LAGER CITY

It was the spring of 1891. Just two weeks after he'd presided over the trial of Columbia Brewery's Mary Mueller, who had horsewhipped Dutch Bill in her brewery, Judge Hallett had an equally stubborn lawbreaker sitting in his courtroom—one who would eventually come to know Mary as a colleague in the brewing industry, and possibly her daughter Emma too. At the time, Frank Foubert was a well-known Vancouver hotel keeper. A few years later he would establish the Stanley Park Brewery beside Lost Lagoon at the western edge of Vancouver—a city's length away from Columbia on the east. But for now he was a busy man with little time for government bureaucracy. T.J. Wilson, the unfortunate enumerator for the 1891 census in Vancouver, knocked repeatedly on Foubert's door with his forms and his questions, only to be rejected each time. Foubert dismissed Wilson's entreaties: "I have no time to be bothered by answering all these questions. I don't see why they're being asked." Wilson even explained the legal consequences of such refusal, to no effect. Judge Hallett listened to the testimony of both Foubert (who reiterated his earlier position) and Wilson, and promptly fined Foubert ten dollars, commenting that "it was the first case of the kind that had come before him, and he hoped it was the last." By the time the next census rolled around, Foubert decided it would take less time to complete it than to contest it. He reported a salary of $2,000 per year and listed his origins as French and his profession as "Brewer." Hallett wasn't bothered by this census refuser again, and Foubert paid his fine accordingly.[1]

Foubert was indeed selling beer in 1901, but he wasn't technically a brewer—nor was he French, for that matter (he was from Ontario, although likely of French descent). "Brewer" was just one more title he'd taken on over the years as he scraped together some business success using good instincts and charisma. After labouring as a clearing contractor for the CPR as he journeyed across Canada, he arrived in Vancouver in 1888, an energetic thirty-six-year-old single man, ready to work at whatever he could. The 1888 directory still lists him as a clearing contractor, but by 1889 he was owner of the Charles Hotel, then the Arlington Hotel the following year. In 1892 he transferred his licence for the Arlington to Anna Schmidt, and he was well on his way to building and opening the Clarence Hotel. Advertisements from January 1893 boast the new Clarence Hotel as "the very best on the Pacific Coast," with electric lighting, new furnishings, modern conveniences, and "the very best of wines, liquors and cigars." While establishing his hotel empire, Foubert also worked as a butcher on Hastings Street, as a dray man (a cart or carriage driver), and as a liquor importer.[2] While juggling these multiple jobs in the 1890s, he married twenty-nine-year-old Charlotte Atkins, who gave birth to their children Ethel and William in the next few years. Their housemaid, Isabella Ferguson, helped Charlotte with the home and the children while Frank kept busy with his different enterprises across Vancouver.

Foubert's work in both hotels and liquor imports gave him a sense of what Vancouverites liked to drink and how he might find a place in the alcohol industry. He began by selling beer made by the large Canadian beer corporations, Labatt's and Carling's,[3] but by the summer of 1895 he'd found an unfilled niche: English-style ales. By then the city was awash with the German lagers sold by Red Cross and

Doering & Marstrand, who largely catered to a German-origin demographic, but Foubert was thinking about what Vancouver's English immigrants would like to imbibe. Although "lagers were very much the prevailing taste" at the time,[4] with one early historian estimating the Vancouver region's beer offerings to be fully 96 percent lager,[5] Foubert did everything he could to energize a market for English beer. Advertisements for the Clarence that summer revealed Foubert's new focus: "English ale on draught at lager beer price, where you can get the pewter pints or the jug and glasses, Old Country style, and English ale."[6] The Clarence would later be the first retailer of Stanley Park Brewery's ale and porter—a hotel/brewery partnership in the style of Charles Doering's Vancouver Brewery and his Stag & Pheasant.

And Stanley Park Brewery was just over the horizon when Foubert began advertising English ales on tap at the Clarence in 1895. Stanley Park itself had officially opened on September 27, 1888, and two weeks later Jessie Simpson MacKay purchased the property across the water, facing the new park, for $1,000. MacKay and her husband, Scottish immigrant George Grant MacKay, built a two-storey house on their new property, which is where the end of Chilco Street is now. Upon the house's completion in 1889, MacKay was appointed chairman of the Vancouver Parks Board, which was charged with regulating Stanley Park—the view he took in every day from his new home. MacKay continued purchasing properties around BC, and particularly in the North Vancouver area, where he built the first Capilano Suspension Bridge (he owned both sides of the canyon). He earned the name "The Laird of Capilano" before his premature death in 1893, after which his son acquired his holdings. Following his son's death in 1896, their home and property went back to the Law Union and Crown Fire & Life Insurance Company of London, which held the mortgage.

Frank Foubert knew a good deal when he saw it. A property within spitting distance of the popular new Vancouver park would be an ideal place for a new business. He contacted the London insurance company that held the title and managed to acquire the property and

The MacKay property and house (soon to be renovated into a brewery). This photo was taken in 1889 from Stanley Park, facing the south side of the inlet. (Photo courtesy of City of Vancouver Archives, AM54-S4-: St Pk Pl15)

the house on it for $2,000 in 1896. He had big plans to turn it into a brewery. With his regular involvement in civic activities, Foubert was also doubtless aware of the new electric railway line (a streetcar) that was going to be built in 1897. In 1895, City Council, in the midst of excitement about new electric conveniences of all sorts, had approved the existing streetcar line for extension all the way up to the bridge leading into Stanley Park—a location that would drop passengers off at the brewery's entrance.[7] People flocking to Stanley Park for picnics and entertainment could slake their thirst by stopping by the brewery to pick up some beer or ginger ale to take with them.

THE BUSINESSMAN FINDS A BREWMASTER

Because he was nothing if not a smart businessman, Foubert kept his hotel interest in the Clarence until 1899, by which time his brewery was well established. But in order to get the fledgling business off the ground, he needed to take a few important steps. The first was to renovate the 2.5-storey MacKay home into something that could be used for brewing. Bill Wilson, in his history of the brewery, reviews

Goad's 1901 City of Vancouver insurance map to see how the property was transformed: "The second floor was used as a bottling room, while the basement was used for general storage and hop storage purposes, leaving the main floor for brewing."[8] It wasn't as extensive as Doering's brewery, but it would do. The next step was to find someone who could brew—and brew well. Foubert, much like his fellow Vancouver businessman Charles Doering, called himself a brewer though he did none of the brewing himself. He knew when to delegate.

The account of Stanley Park Brewery's opening in the July 17, 1896, edition of the *Vancouver Semi-Weekly World* referred to Foubert hiring an experienced English brewmaster named Robert Day, a man whose name is in the 1897 Henderson directory but disappears afterwards. In email correspondence with me, historian Bill Wilson speculated that Robert Day must have been a very short-lived employee, possibly lasting only a few months at the brewery before Foubert hired the man who was the brewmaster for almost the entirety of Stanley Park Brewery's existence through multiple owners: John Dyke. What other historians have learned about Dyke has largely been informed by an article his granddaughter Rosamond Greer wrote for the Summer 1993 issue of the *British Columbia Historical News*. I was fortunate enough to have met Rosamond's son Hugh Greer, and through him I gained access to various family documents. Using this information as well as Rosamond's original 1993 article, I can now provide a more detailed portrait of John Dyke, the brewmaster for the original Stanley Park Brewery.[9] Dyke's life, and his role in the changing fortunes of Stanley Park Brewery, reveals how human weakness and bad luck can frustrate the ambitions of even the most skilled individual. In the accounts of him written by his children and grandchildren, we also see traces of an imperfect but touching love story between two people who each wanted something different for their lives.

John Dyke was born in England in 1845, the youngest of six children. Living in the shadow of his successful brother Edward, who was a private school headmaster and wealthy landowner, John struggled to find consistent work. Things didn't improve much after he married

JOHN 1845
m. Martha Mather

John Dyke in his younger years (left), and John (middle) and his wife Martha in their later years.
(Photos courtesy of Hugh Greer)

Martha Mather, the daughter of an engineer and the "spoiled darling" of her family, according to John's daughter Kathleen: "My father was a Master Brewer and was considered quite a good 'catch,' but he possessed neither the personality nor the ability to hold a position or run a business, and he failed in one venture after another. He took his family from town to town in search of a livelihood, so that the ten[10] children born to the family were nearly all born in different towns." Edward tried to help John capitalize on his brewing skills by setting him up as brewmaster at the Eagle Brewery in Dublin, but this did not last long; according to his daughter Winifred, he "blew it, and became bankrupt for the second time." At last, exasperated, Edward encouraged his brother to seek work in Canada. The children were living with various caretakers and schools, John and Martha having at that time (in the words of one of his grandchildren) a "cuckoo-like readiness to deposit [their children] in any nest available." Martha took on the position of a "Lady's Nurse" in Ireland, and in 1893 John sailed to Canada on his own.

For several years he worked as a farm labourer in what the family documents describe as the "wilds of Canada," desperately trying to find something in the brewing trade but having no success. "There seemed to be no opening for him in his trade as a brewer," Kathleen's account reads, "for the favorite beer of the country was Lager and he had no knowledge of brewing that type—in fact he had an extreme disdain of it." John's love of ale and disdain for lager would be to his benefit when he met Frank Foubert several years later, but in the early 1890s it put him at a disadvantage. When he arrived in the Vancouver region he settled on farming again, on the advice of his brother. He purchased a twenty-acre lot in Port Haney that was already cleared and included a log house, apple trees, and a hayfield. Without even a cart at first, he was forced to take his apples miles to the market in a wheelbarrow.

Eventually, in gradual "installments," Martha and the children sailed across the Atlantic to join John on the farm in Port Haney. Kathleen recalls how difficult farm life was for her mother, who had never experienced the kind of menial labour required of her in her new position as a farmer's wife. The beds had fleas, the floors were covered in dirt, and she had to learn to do proper baking. Without a doctor nearby, Martha also took on the role of nurse for her children, stitching deep wounds and even setting broken bones. The summers were particularly brutal, Kathleen explains, since Martha "suffered intensely from mosquito bites, so much so that her features were almost unrecognizable and she could not open her eyes. The poison finally spread through her system and she was obliged to take to her bed." Kathleen praised her mother's fortitude, but it all became too much—the fleas, the mosquitoes, the dirt, the pain. After two years, Martha insisted John find proper work as a brewer in the booming nearby city of Vancouver.

The timing was perfect. This was the late 1890s and Frank Foubert was looking for a good brewer of English ale (not lager!) to get his new brewery up and running. The Dyke/Greer family documents do not mention "Stanley Park Brewery" by name, but instead refer to John as becoming brewmaster of a brewery near Lost Lagoon, in Coal Harbour. Dyke's product was praised by Foubert in ads over the next several years, and when the brewery was leased and then sold in 1902 and 1903, due to Foubert's ill health, Dyke apparently stayed on as brewmaster. His sons helped as bottle-washers. However, his attempt to incorporate "Stanley Park Brewing Co." in order to buy the brewery out from under other interested parties around 1902 led to some trouble for him, which I will get into later in the chapter. Dyke's ambitions to become the owner of a successful brewery were thwarted once again, and he was sued by his competitors. Sadly, after about 1903 it is likely that he never worked as a brewer again.[11]

Accounts of the family from the Dyke/Greer documents indicate that Martha and John became increasingly unhappy after he lost his job at the brewery, with Martha becoming "a nervous as well as a physical wreck" who constantly nagged, and John developing a "terrible temper." Eventually they separated, and Martha stayed in the family house on Comox Street with the children who were still living at home. She developed what was then diagnosed as "acute melancholia," a condition that we'd probably now call clinical depression, and one afternoon attempted to take her own life. Her youngest daughter Phyllis found her and immediately sought help, actions that saved her mother's life. In that moment of crisis, Phyllis—who was encouraged to drop out of school at twelve because she was supposedly not smart enough—showed the intelligence and initiative that foreshadowed the strong woman she would grow into. She became an adventurous mountaineer and was the first person to build a cabin on Mount Garibaldi; in fact, one of the Garibaldi peaks, Phyllis's Engine, is named after her.[12] However, she did not have the power to make things better for her mother. Martha was eventually institutionalized and isolated due to her worsening depression.

While Martha declined in mental health, John seemed to be improving, despite the resentment and anger he felt at losing his position and his much-loved career. He eventually moved in with Kathleen and her husband; happily, his temper mellowed and he became gentler as he aged. Kathleen says that he was "quiet, uncomplaining and helpful" in his later years, even stepping in as caregiver for her infant daughter Rosamond. John also began to visit with his estranged wife in the institution where she was housed, "and they seemed to recapture much of their earlier affection for each other. [Martha] wept bitterly at the news of his death." Rosamond had warm memories of John Dyke as well:

Although he had displayed a terrible temper at times (one of the reasons he could not hold a job or get along with his family), I remember him as a very kind Grandfather. He always had a treat in his pocket for me when he came home from a trip into town... When he died he was 89 years of age and I was 9. We had been good friends, and I was heartbroken.

The resentment and temper that John showed to his wife and children when he was younger seemed to have dissipated over the years. His tenderness to Martha in the late stages of her mental illness and the warmth and care he showed to his daughter and granddaughter suggest that he was eventually able to move beyond his anger at losing his career. We might speculate that he found a new sense of purpose, one that didn't rely on his ability to brew.

John Dyke's daughter Kathleen Fiddes (left) and granddaughter Rosamond Greer. (Photos courtesy of Hugh Greer)

STIFF COMPETITION: MAKING STANLEY PARK STAND OUT

While Dyke was still with the brewery in the late 1890s and early 1900s, he and Foubert were of one mind about what they should sell: traditional English ale. This plan to make English ale in a lager town was somewhat risky, but necessary if Foubert wanted his brewery to make its mark on Vancouver. Stanley Park Brewery needed to find its own niche, and English beer seemed to be it. Foubert did everything he could to make Stanley Park Brewery a household name, from advertising campaigns to public events to donations—and possibly even some under-the-table deals. From 1896 until he leased it to a new owner in 1902, Foubert was the face of Stanley Park Brewery and made sure everyone had heard about it.

The brewery officially opened in the summer of 1896, with Robert Day briefly serving as brewmaster before John Dyke stepped in. At this time, Vancouverites were flocking to Doering & Marstrand Brewery and Red Cross Brewery for their newly refined lager beer, which was being sold as fast as they could make it. Foubert had identified ale as the gap in the market, which is how the *Vancouver Semi-Weekly World* framed his story on July 17 of that year. After emphasizing the importance of "keeping the dollars at home" and supporting local industry, the paper proudly announced the intro-duction of a new brewery "that will manufacture ale after the English style. There are many who prefer this to the lighter lager and much of it is now imported." Doering's and Williams's breweries target-ed Vancouver's German immigrants who were tired of having to pay extra for imported beer from their homeland, and Foubert was doing the same thing—for the English. The story went on to praise Foubert's reputation in Vancouver and the quality and modernity of his thousand-gallon brewhouse: "Everything is of the latest improved style." Also like the advertisements for German lager, this introduc-tion to Stanley Park's English ale focused on the beer's nutritious, masculine elements—praising Foubert's beer as a drink that would keep you strong, healthy, and eminently English: "Though [the beer] was new it nevertheless had that wholesome body and rich full flavor that characterizes English ale. It is of the kind that with the aid of beef has made Englishmen so brawny, there being as much, if not more, nourishment than stimulant." Foubert's facilities for the convenience of cyclists and pedestrians made the brewery an excellent adjunct to a day wandering in the nearby Stanley Park, and the reporter concluded by estimating that the brewery will be "a benefit to the city as a whole."

Foubert began advertising Stanley Park's beer in Vancouver (and eventually Victoria) newspapers, initially offering English ale and stout for sale at fifty cents per gallon via the agents Weeks & Robson or

A detail from an anonymous 1897 painting of the Stanley Park entrance and brewery. (Photo courtesy of City of Vancouver Archives, AM 1562: 72-574)

at Foubert's hotel, the Clarence. These ads did not yet have any visuals (Foubert added images several years later), but many ended with the all-capitalized phrase "TRY IT," an enjoinder that was Foubert's way of pulling customers away from the two big lager breweries that held the market. It may also have been his way of competing with one style of Doering & Marstrand advertisement from a year or two earlier. In these ads, which were admittedly less common than their lager ads, D&M advertised their non-alcoholic Vancouver Ale along with "OUR ENGLISH ALE & PORTER." The phrase "TRY IT" appears in the middle of the advertisement. The Vancouver Ale and the English Ale weren't D&M's popular products—but they were attempting to get more drinkers to buy them. Foubert used the same strategy, placing very similar advertisements in the 1899 Vancouver city directory, boasting of the English ale and porter sold at his brewery and emphasizing that "Family trade" was a specialty. Occasionally he tried different marketing moves to see if he could find success some other way. In a 1901 edition of *The Province* under the "Lost" section of the Classifieds, he placed an ad saying: "MY THIRST, AFTER DRINKING Stanley Park ale, $1.75 per dozen quarts." The joke was amusing, and the price was competitive—D&M had been selling their ale for two dollars per

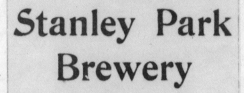

Stanley Park Brewery

Bear in mind that Stanley Park Ale and Stout are the best in the market. Also English Ginger Beer delivered to any part of the city free of charge, in quarts, pints, 5 and 10 gallon kegs.

TRY IT.

F. FOUBERT,

Tel. 261 and 263.   .Proprietor
P. O. Box 234   6-1m

Vancouver Daily World, April 1897.

THURSDAY, JUNE 13 1895

OUR VANCOUVER ALE

A non-intoxicating Table Beer, especially adapted for nursing mothers, children and everybody in need of a refreshing, healthy and nourishing Beverage.   NOW READY

The price is $1.00 a keg (C.O.D.) containing 4 imp. gallons, in bottle 75c. per dozen qts. TRY IT.

OUR ENGLISH ALE & PORTER

Are well known and need no further recommendation.—Connoisseurs have pronounced our Ale to be as fine an Ale as can be bought anywhere.

Price in kegs, 4 imp. gallons $2.25,
"   "   8 "   " $4.00,
in bottles per doz. qts. $2.00, per doz. pts. $1.00

CASH ON DELIVERY,   Bottles to be returned free of charge

Doering & Marstrand Brewing Co.

Mount Pleasant

Daily News Advertiser, June 1895.

dozen quarts for years by this point (prices per pint were half as much, as the ad below demonstrates).

In brewing and selling English-style beer, Foubert was finding a market niche *and* tapping into a powerful emotional current of the time: patriotism. Although Vancouver was inhabited by both German and English immigrants, and there was a strong German community in the city, the province was still called *British* Columbia. There was growing support of the province's—and the country's—British identity. This became more pronounced a decade later, as Vancouver became a more staunchly British city, despite its friendliness with Germany and German culture. In fact, according to historian Margaret Ormsby, out of all areas of Canada in the late nineteenth century, British Columbia had the greatest "martial ardour" and the most "enthusiastic endorsement of the British cause."[13] By 1911, Britain and America were the top two countries from which Canadian residents had emigrated.[14]

Foubert's appeal to English ale was well before the onset of the First World War and the explosion of anti-German sentiment in the city. His marketing strategy didn't grow out of a backlash against German immigrants and German culture, but instead was a point of connection with Vancouver's British identity: its role as part of the powerful British empire. To further use this emotional pull, Foubert had his brewery participate in various military-oriented events. For example, Stanley Park Brewery donated twenty-eight gallons of ale and eight dozen bottles of ginger beer to the city's "Battery Smoker," a military social event involving smoking, drinking, and dancing. Labatt, with its vastly greater financial resources, donated nine casks of ale, or approximately one hundred gallons (if the cask was a regular-sized British firkin). Not to be outdone by his wealthier competitor, Foubert also, "with his usual generosity, sent a man to help the boys tap barrels...the boys would have been short-handed, as not everyone knows how to do it."[15] Another time, Foubert donated two kegs of beer "to the Drill shed on Saturday to refresh the soldier boys after their somewhat tedious parade."[16] The drill shed was on the former site of the Imperial Opera House on West Pender, and this was where the city's Fifth Regiment (described in the following paragraph) practised drill and other military exercises. It was apparently none too impressive, but it served its purpose.

One of the brewery's most memorable patriotic activities was its involvement in a war re-enactment that took place in Stanley Park for the Dominion Day celebrations of 1899. Several years earlier, Vancouver had formed its first artillery company, the Vancouver No. 5 Battery, followed soon by a second, and both were then combined to form the Second Battalion, Fifth Regiment, Canadian Artillery (Victoria was home to the First Battalion).[17] The newly commissioned officers in the Fifth Regiment "were all of British birth or descent," creating a "cultural uniformity" that held a "special appeal for those who prided themselves on their British heritage."[18] According to Lieutenant Colonel T.O. Townley, the leader of the regiment and future mayor of Vancouver, the inspecting officer judged the Fifth Regiment to be "as smart a body of men as any in Canada"—a point of pride for the city, who welcomed their new British-descended militia happily.[19] With the First Battalion in Victoria and the Second Battalion in Vancouver, and military fandom growing, the cities began hosting sham battles both on the mainland and on the Island, usually on a patriotic holiday. For example, on Victoria Day in 1895, militias from Vancouver and Victoria joined together to defend Beacon Hill Park against the Esquimalt Bluejackets (members of the Royal Navy). Similar skirmishes were scheduled in Vancouver and over the border as well, to the enthusiastic applause of local crowds.

This was the context of the Battle for Stanley Park during the Vancouver Dominion Day celebrations of 1899. Troops from Victoria and Esquimalt came to the mainland to join the Second Battalion and an extensive battle was organized. The newspaper account is confusing on some points,[20] but it seems that the navy men from Esquimalt—the Bluejackets—acted as "guerillas" who took possession of Brockton woods and Deadman's Island, "defying all attempts to dislodge them." According to the "war" correspondent tasked to cover the event, troop leaders—the actual leaders of the First and Second Battalions, Major L.R. Johnson and Colonel Gregory—received communication about the Bluejackets' plans to (horrors!) take over Stanley Park Brewery, which was south of the Coal Harbour bridge. Their goal was to leave their fortress on the island and seize control of the brewery. As the Bluejackets advanced, the reporter, watching from his post on a nearby boat, hyperbolically described the bullets flying and the men who were prepared to die: "Undaunted by the fierce rattle of bullets about them, the thirsty invaders [the Bluejackets] came trooping on. The waters of the harbor leaped and sparkled as thousands of harmless bullets found watery graves." In the meantime, Gregory's men—the First Battalion from Victoria—were standing guard over the brewery on the other side of the bridge, ready for "the thirsty and hungry guerillas" when they made their attack. The bridge battle lasted an hour, and apparently the First

Battalion was set to blow up the bridge when the Bluejackets surrendered. The terms of surrender were conditional upon Stanley Park Brewery's co-operation: "The leader of the invaders demanded that two wagon-loads of beer be sent to his famishing followers and he would lay down all arms and peacefully evacuate all points of vantage... including a shady spot in the Stanley woods where beer bottles could be tapped easily and comfortably." In the end, the two armies "mingled together and attested the splendid quality of the Stanley Park Brewery and tested their capacities. It was a glorious and bloodless victory, and the brewery is saved!"

I could find no records indicating why Stanley Park Brewery was chosen for such a central role in this mock battle. However, Foubert liked to keep himself and his businesses front and centre in Vancouver's civic life, so he may well have suggested it. Two weeks earlier, Foubert was included in a list of corporate and individual donors to the 1899 Dominion Day festivities (he chipped in ten dollars, and the highest corporate donation was twenty-five dollars). He may have offered an additional, non-monetary donation of beer in exchange for his brewery being the setting for the Dominion Day battle. While we won't know for sure how it came about, what is certain is that Stanley Park Brewery received a lot of publicity that day. The newspaper correspondent reported that ten thousand spectators were watching the battle over the brewery with "thrilling interest." It's hard to buy that kind of advertising!

Other unique advertising campaigns that Foubert launched also invite questions about Foubert's role behind the scenes. The first was newspaper ads in 1899 and 1900 that referred to the *American Journal of Health* or physicians more generally recommending Stanley Park beer for its nutritious qualities. Foubert launched this campaign after a Dr. James Thompson published an article titled "Is Ale-Drinking Healthy?" in the *American Journal of Health*. I could not locate an original version of this article, or even the journal itself, but the *Daily News Advertiser* quotes the article directly:

It is not the intent of the writer to commend all ale or stout, but is his twofold purpose to fasten the thought in the mind of the reader that some ale is strictly pure and that any such is very beneficial in its use. A sample of the ale and stout brewed by F. Foubert of Stanley Park Brewery, Vancouver, BC, Canada, was tested by our chemist a few days ago, and we use it to illustrate our position on the subject. The most careful analysis failed to reveal even a hint of adulteration in this beverage, and with no fear of having our statement refuted by any person whose technical knowledge qualifies him to give an opinion upon the subject, we may say most emphatically that this ale or stout, on account of its purity, has a great hygienic value.[21]

It is difficult to speculate upon why this doctor chose Stanley Park beer to test, and why his praise of the ale is so heightened. We might guess that Foubert had a hand in the situation, but nothing can be confirmed. It is clear, however, that Foubert used this endorsement to his full advantage, advertising his beer's healthy qualities in the immediate aftermath of the article and for years later. His efforts in the early 1900s to prove that beer was healthy aligned with similar campaigns by Vancouver Breweries (the merged Red Cross/D&M brewery). The temperance movement was growing at the time, and alcohol producers and retailers were attempting to polish their products' reputation.

In 1900, Joseph Elwood Miller, the collector of Inland Revenue, conducted several tests on Stanley Park Brewery's ale, comparing it point by point with Bass ale, one of the most popular imported English beers. Miller's tests concluded that the alcohol content of the two ales was identical, while Stanley Park had a higher grain bill

Opposite top and middle: These ads are both from a 1902 issue of *The Province*. They strongly assert the physical benefits of Stanley Park ale.

Opposite bottom: This ad from an 1899 issue of *The Province* boasts of physicians' support for Stanley Park beer. Stanley Park was unusual among Vancouver breweries in producing an early IPA— an "India Ale" (erroneously spelled "Iudia" here). It's likely that Foubert chose this style because Labatt had had great success with it, and he'd previously been an importer of Labatt products.

Tel 361
P. O. Box 234

Equal to

Bass' Bitter Ales.

That is not only what we say about our ale, but it is certified to by official analysis.

And why not?

We have an English brewer of long experience brewing ale on the famous Burton system, using only the finest malt, choicest hops and the purest Capilano water.

Prime October brewing:

5-GAL KEGS **$2**
10-GAL. KEGS **4**

Bottled Ale and Stout:
QUARTS. PER DOZ. **$1.75**
PINTS, PER DOZ .. .. **.90**

(Bottles allowed for if returned —quarts, 25c doz; pints, 10c doz.)

STANLEY PARK
Brewery,

Near foot of Georgia St.

This 1901 ad from *The Province* boasts of the Stanley Park/Bass comparison and highlights the importance of the brewery's English brewmaster.

than Bass. According to *The Province*, "the test showed conclusively that the Stanley Park is as pure and strong an ale as even the famous Bass, and it has at the same time what connoisseurs call more 'body' to it." Miller's testing supposedly proved what Foubert had always claimed: that his local ale was equal to the more expensive imported beers.[22] Now, the reason Miller tested the beer at all was most likely because Inland Revenue collected excise tax on liquor, and factors such as alcohol content would need to be established. It's not clear, however, why Miller would have compared the ale to Bass, or why he chose Stanley Park ale to make such a comparison. Like Foubert, Miller was a long-time resident of Vancouver and was very involved in civic events and organizations. It is certainly possible—likely, even—that they became acquainted simply because they occupied similar social circles. Mutual back-scratching was (and is) common practice in local politics and polite society. Indeed, Miller was present at the brewery during its opening week and testified to the papers that "the plant, though small, is very complete."[23] Whatever the reason for Miller's tests, Foubert ran with it: many of the brewery's newspaper advertisements over the next couple of years described Stanley Park beer as "equal to Bass" and its status as "certified by official analysis." John Dyke's status as an experienced English brewer also added to the brewery's credibility when lined up beside the English imports offered by Bass.

POWER STRUGGLES

The good PR Stanley Park Brewery garnered from the praise of Miller and American physicians, as well as the publicity it enjoyed via its contribution to city events, may have increased the brewery's visibility to the public, but it didn't solve Foubert's health problems. In late 1901, his ill health forced him to make some hard decisions about his businesses, and how many he could handle. Newspaper accounts from early 1902 indicate that Foubert was planning to build a new hotel at the corner of Pender and Howe, so this may have been the impetus for him to let his brewing business go. News soon spread that Foubert wanted to sell. In the hopes of acquiring it, two companies quickly incorporated in early 1902: Royal Brewing Company Limited and Stanley Park Brewing Company Limited. Royal Brewing Co. was owned by a small group of Vancouver businessmen, including John Benson (owner of the small and remote Cedar Cottage Brewery), William and Frank Robertson (insurance brokers), E. Fenwick Smith (bookkeeper and solicitor for the Robertsons), and William McKinnon.[24] Shareholders in Stanley Park Brewing Co. Ltd. were John Dyke (brewmaster), Harold Martin Henderson (City treasurer), R.L. Leigh-Spencer (mining broker and property agent), Thomas Spencer (machinist, unrelated to Leigh-Spencer), and J. Bowden (engineer).[25]

Stanley Park Brewing Co. Ltd. was an odd bunch, especially when compared with the politically savvy businessmen of Royal Brewing Co. It almost sounds like the beginning of a joke: a brewmaster, a City treasurer, a mining broker, a machinist, and an engineer walk into a brewery. It wasn't clear that any of them really knew how to take control of the business—John Dyke had certainly proven his inability to do so numerous times in his past, however skilfully he could brew the beer. To add to their odd qualities, one of their group was a woman: R.L. Leigh-Spencer was Rosa Leigh Leigh-Spencer, a mining broker and real estate agent living in Vancouver. Leigh-Spencer negotiated large and expensive land deals, ran a real estate rental agency, and—according to the *Napa Journal* of June 4, 1897—advised women on investment. Originally from England, she had also lived in Toronto, Nanaimo, California, and New Westminster before settling in Vancouver. Ads for her professional services were all over the city's newspapers, and she was known for her love of animals; she was often seen driving a team of Shetland ponies down Granville Street, and she frequently showed dogs and horses. She was even included in the 1911 edition of *Who's Who in Western Canada*. A 1952 issue of the *Vancouver News-Herald* recounts Leigh-Spencer's unconventionality: "Generously built, she wore mannish tweed and was a law unto herself in an effeminate age. Playing croquet at a garden party…she noticed that very gracious hostess, Mrs. McKinnon, staring at her through her lorgnette as she smoked a cigarette. Promptly, Miss Leigh-Spencer brought a small telescope out of her pocket and stared straight back."[26] One can't help but wonder if the Mrs. McKinnon at this particular party was the spouse of the William

Rosa Leigh Leigh-Spencer (right) walking her dogs with Mr. E.R. Ricketts. (Photo courtesy of City of Vancouver Archives, AM54-S4-2-: CVA 371-1803)

McKinnon who was a shareholder of Stanley Park Brewing Co.'s competition—Royal Brewing Co. Either way, the tension at that party must have been high but it seems Leigh-Spencer didn't care much. John Dyke seemed to be leading the charge, but given her business experience, Leigh-Spencer was responsible for the legal paperwork involved in the formation of Stanley Park Brewing Co. and its efforts to acquire the brewery. She was listed as trustee on the early 1902 advertisements that invited investors. These advertisements, which ran in the March and April issues of *The Province* that year, show the ambition of the newly incorporated company. The ad leads with "GREAT CHANCE FOR INVESTORS" and explains that "the Stanley Park Brewery Company Limited has been incorporated for the purpose of taking over the business of the Stanley Park Brewery." It offers shares at one-hundred dollars each and promises dividends from the start. The ad concludes by explaining that Frank Foubert "is retiring from the business on account of ill-health." The advertisement implies that the corporate takeover was a given. The name of the company is almost exactly the same as the brewery's name (which would lead to confusion among consumers), and the mention of Foubert at the end suggests that he was handing over the reins to the new company. This impression was reinforced by a short write-up in *The Province* of March 12, 1902. This write-up seems like a short business report, but in fact may have been something that the Stanley Park Brewing Co. paid for (or the reporter simply misunderstood the situation):

STANLEY PARK BREWERY: *Mr. Frank Foubert, proprietor of the Stanley Park Brewery, is retiring from business owing to ill-health, and the business has been incorporated under the name of the Stanley Park Brewing Company Limited. Sixty shares in the company are open to the public for investment at the par value of $100 each. Particulars of the new company may be learned from Miss R.L. Leigh-Spencer.*

This announcement assumes that the new company had already taken over the brewery business, with the implicit approval of Foubert himself. The language is misleading: it says the business (i.e., the brewery) *has been incorporated* as a new company. However, although Stanley Park Brewing Co. was indeed incorporated as a company, it had not acquired Stanley Park Brewery at that point—and never did.

Neither Stanley Park Brewing Co. nor Royal Brewing was successful in obtaining the brewery in 1902. Instead, Foubert decided to lease it to Hose & Allan, wine and spirit merchants and founders of the Gold Seal Liquor Company. It was an interesting choice; Gold Seal had long worked with and bottled Red Cross beer, and by 1901 Red Cross's owner John Williams was a major shareholder in the company. So Foubert was essentially leasing his brewery to his own competition.[27] John Dyke was kept on as brewmaster in order to ensure quality control. The announcement of the change in operations assured Vancouverites that the "high standards of quality attained by the Stanley Park ale and stout will be maintained under the new management."[28] Immediately afterwards, advertisements for Stanley Park beer included Gold Seal as the retailer. Gold Seal amplified the focus on the beer's healthy qualities, with ads that boasted of Stanley Park ale's ability to invigorate and strengthen drinkers.

A year later, in 1903, *The Province* announced that the Royal Brewing Co. had purchased Stanley Park Brewery from Frank Hose, although Foubert still owned the land.[29] Either Hose changed his lease to a purchase before that date, or the reporter had inaccurate information about who owned the brewery before Royal's purchase of it. In any case, John Benson's Royal Brewing Co. was the successful company in the contest to take over Stanley Park Brewery, buying the brewery business outright and leasing the property.[30] Benson had been running his own Cedar Cottage Brewery outside the city limits since about 1901, when he purchased it from North Arm Brewery's founder George Raywood.[31] Located at what is now 1404 Kingsway, Cedar Cottage Brewery was away from the heart of the city and was also restricted by its aged technology. A water tower was placed up in

Cedar Cottage Brewery in 1902. (Photo courtesy of City of Vancouver Archives, AM54-S4-: Dist P69)

a fir tree, and water for brewing was pumped by hand from Gibson Creek. Benson describes Gibson Creek, like Brewery Creek, as full of life—there were so many salmon and trout that you could spear them with a pitchfork, apparently.[32] Another interview of Benson indicates that there was also a well from which they pumped, and their main technology was that pump and the water tower. Moving their brewing operation to the Stanley Park Brewery was a welcome change, even though they had to source their water from the city pipes rather than the creek.[33]

But John Dyke and Stanley Park Brewing Co. weren't ready to give up. It seems that Dyke may have been let go at this time because John Benson, a brewer himself, now owned the brewery.[34] Too many brewmasters spoil the beer, right? Dyke wasn't giving up on his brewing dreams though. At the end of March 1903, either immediately before or after Royal's purchase of the brewery, Dyke placed several ads in the Classifieds section of *The Province*: "Employment wanted by late brewer at Stanley Park Brewery, or correspondence with party willing to invest." It appears that Dyke was out of work once Royal took over operations, but he hadn't abandoned his plans of running a successful company through the Stanley Park Brewing Co. Ltd. However, Dyke's daughter's assessment of her father as "having neither the personality nor the ability to hold a position or run a business" held true. The actions he took at this time were neither wise nor profitable. The ads themselves indicated his inexperience and uncertainty, as they suggested he either wanted a brewing job *or* wanted money from investors—two very different propositions. Whatever else Dyke did, he got on the bad side of his old employer, Frank Hose, who issued a writ of $210 against him one month after these ads were placed. Dyke disputed it, but the outcome is unknown. From then on, we have no more records of Dyke actually brewing anywhere, although he is listed in directories as a brewer until 1912. His children were well-reputed in the city by that time, with one news story referring to his son Fred as a "prominent Vancouver man" and praising his son Sidney for his achievements as a Rhodes Scholar. Dyke was working in the sawmills by then, and in 1914 a mill accident required a partial amputation of his hand.[35] Shortly after that time, Dyke moved out of the family home and his wife Martha's mental health degenerated, as described earlier in this chapter. He never achieved his dream of owning his own brewery, although he tried. His final years, until his death in 1933, were in the company of his daughter and her family, when he seemed—at last—to enjoy his life.

After Royal Brewing Company's purchase of the brewery in April 1903, its fate becomes foggy. Foubert died two months later, at the age of fifty, disrupting his new liquor import business and his plans for a new hotel. His death also left his wife Charlotte to continue collecting lease money for the property (not for the business) from Royal. Advertisements for the brewery completely stopped after Royal's purchase; the only thing advertised for Stanley Park Brewery after April 1903 was brewers' grains for sale in the Classifieds. Royal Brewing occasionally placed small text-only ads listing their Crown Ale and Stout for sale in wooden bottles or patent tap jars, and Gold Seal (the liquor merchants) advertised both Royal and Stanley Park beers among their available tipples for purchase. It appears that Royal was preserving at least some of the Stanley Park brand, although it wasn't building anything with it.

Stanley Park Brewing did crop up on its own one more time after that sale. A month after Royal acquired full control over Stanley Park Brewing, the latter was accused of illegally selling beer on a Sunday.[36] Interestingly, the brewery's defence lawyer, Osborne Plunkett, was on committees and boards with J.E. Miller, the Inland Revenue collector who tested Stanley Park beer and compared it to Bass, very much to the favour of the former. It certainly seems that Foubert made some friends in high places. However, despite Plunkett's efforts to launch a defence, the brewery ended up pleading guilty to the illegal selling and paying a fifteen-dollar fine. The brewery limped along for the next several years—newspapers mention a Mr. Gartley managing it, and the sad tale of Walter Travis, a sales representative of the brewery who took his own life on a business trip in 1906.[37] City Archivist J.S. Matthews also records an interview with Vancouver Parks Board Chairman Rowe Holland, who recalled a sailor named Louis Wicker who was a childminder of preteen boys (he'd take them sailing) and a caretaker of "the old brewery" in 1904 or 1905, from which he'd take beer as part of his wage. On his sailing trips with his young charges, he'd boil the beer until they were "lulled into a deep slumber" and then spend the evening drinking "can after can of this nectar." In the morning, they'd all go swimming in Howe Sound. It's not clear from Holland's account how active the brewery was at this time, but it seems it did have kegs of beer in storage. It was also still making occasional donations to events.

By 1909 the liquor licence registry notes that Royal Brewing Co. was out of business. The registry also reveals that liquor wholesale licence fees had doubled in just three years, from $125 to $250, so keeping the brewery alive may have been financially untenable. Royal's/Stanley Park's reduced activity came to a halt in 1908, when the City of Vancouver purchased the property on which the brewery was located. Benson refers to this action as "expropriation" in his interview with Matthews, but it seems that it was a simple property flipping deal. The City was interested in purchasing the parcels of land—including that of Stanley Park Brewery—along Coal Harbour, with the intent of making it "a beauty spot." The newspapers indicated that Charlotte Foubert had offered it for $15,000 earlier, but the City was unable to purchase it "at that time" (the year is not clarified). At this point, in the spring of 1908, several neighbouring property owners had already agreed to sell at the City's offering price, but Charlotte Foubert was not among them. Instead, she brought in the well-known and savvy businessman Jake Grauer to help with the negotiations. She sold the property to him for $16,000 ($1,000 more than she would have made from the earlier offer to the City), and the next day Grauer sold it to the City—which was now desperate—for $23,000. Although the brewery was listed as being a business until 1909, it didn't have a liquor licence and it wasn't doing much for that final year after Grauer's sale.[38] Brewers' grains and lost pets from the brewery were still listed in the Classifieds for 1909, so there was still activity of some sort, but it can't have been much. In 1910, the City's engineer was instructed to tear down "the old Stanley Park Brewery site" and clear it.[39]

The gradual fading of what had been such an energetic brewery in Vancouver has no climactic ending, just a series of ownership changes that resulted in the brewery being run apathetically rather than enthusiastically. John Benson, the de facto leader of Royal Brewing, moved back to live in his old Cedar Cottage Brewery property in 1907, which was perhaps a reflection of his increasing distance from Royal's business. Under his leadership, Stanley Park Brewery disappeared from the Vancouver scene, with the only clue that it was still producing beer being the sale of brewers' grains in the Classifieds and an occasional listing of Stanley Park ale for sale via Gold Seal's shops. However, this forgotten brewery was revived with new life in the twenty-first century, when its brand was purchased by the Mark Anthony Group's Turning Point Brewery in 2005, with the first brew released in 2009—exactly a century after the original Stanley Park Brewing collapsed. Six years later, the Stanley Park Brewing brand, via Turning Point, was acquired by Labatt—the massive Canadian brand that Frank Foubert originally put his tiny brewery up against, offering an India pale ale to rival Labatt's popular version of the style. And of course, at that point Labatt itself had already been acquired by Anheuser-Busch InBev (a.k.a. Budweiser), the corporate juggernaut that controls most of the global beer market. Stanley Park Brewing's path from craft to corporate is one that we'll see echoed multiple times in Vancouver's breweries both then and now—starting with the corporate mergers that eventually erased Doering and Williams's hugely successful craft brewery. But that's for the next chapter.

Resurrecting the story of the original Stanley Park Brewery is an important counterbalance to the modern corporatization of the Stanley Park Brewing brand. Stanley Park Brewing's real history is, to my mind at least, more interesting and more human than the creation of its brand under Turning Point a century later. City Archivist Matthews also felt passionate about recovering such lost histories. On July 2, 1948, Vancouver businessman W.C. Ditmars sent Matthews a sketch of a beer jug he had unearthed. It belonged to Royal Brewing Company, which used the Stanley Park Brewery and owned the branding. Matthews sent a letter back the same day, eagerly requesting that Ditmars send him the jug and explaining his passion for finding and reconstructing Vancouver's history. In a letter kept in the City of Vancouver Archives, AM54-S23-2 (Royal Brewing Co. Ltd), he says:

*There is no harm in asking you for it. If a young man wishes to marry a maiden, the best thing for him to do is to ask her; she cannot eat him raw [sic] for it; the worst she can do to him is say "*NO*" out loud, and stamp her foot... reflect, please, I ask in the name of those who have gone; those here now, and those coming in the long years before Vancouver. What people do not understand is that in order to have this material available—five minutes after your letter came we were preparing the answer—it is necessary to* WORK. *I rose from my desk at home last night just after midnight; I was at it again this morning at 6 a.m. We* *prepare scores and scores of things which, possibly, may never be asked for, so we prepare the whole lot... And so it goes, day after day, and the City Archives is still struggling with the indifferent, the negligent, and the fool.*

It's in large part thanks to Matthews's labour that we have so many details about the early Vancouver brewing industry. I'm not sure if he ever received the Royal Brewing beer jug, but his passion for ensuring that old stories survive to be passed down to later generations is one that I hope this book honours. The disappearance of independent brewing in the wave of corporate consolidations, as described in the following chapter, doesn't have to mean that those breweries' stories disappear as well.

CHAPTER 5
THE DISAPPEARANCE OF CRAFT: ONLY THE LARGE SURVIVE

This book tells the stories of craft breweries and the people behind them—breweries that are independent producers of local beer and not owned by a large corporation. As we saw at the end of Chapter 4, many independent breweries end up becoming part of the corporate monolith. And as the second part of this book will explore, the corporate monoliths can sometimes provide valuable information to craft brewers. Those blurred boundaries interest me: What happens when craft goes too big, or too small? What are the different ways craft breweries thrive—or die? The parameters of governmental regulation had (and have) a massive impact on any brewery's success, as many tales from Vancouver's early breweries have shown. And the biggest, hardest-hitting governmental regulation was provincial prohibition, enacted in 1917.[1] There's no doubt that prohibition was one factor that led to corporate breweries monopolizing the industry in BC for most of the twentieth century. However, it wasn't the only factor.

The years before prohibition were a time of corporate consolidation, during which the wealthy businessmen running the breweries had far more power than the actual brewmasters, most of whom had little to no ownership stake (think of poor John Dyke). These businessmen held all the cards in the brewing industry and small, independent breweries had no chance. The growth of corporate beer just before prohibition primed the province for six decades of corporate monopolies in brewing. In this chapter I'll provide a glimpse into what was happening in the Vancouver beer scene shortly before prohibition, from the tiny breweries lost to history, to the corporate giants that began to form after 1910. Prohibition wasn't the death of craft beer—but it certainly helped put it in the ground.

THE LITTLE GUYS

There were several small Vancouver breweries that opened but then sank with hardly a trace between about 1888 and 1910. For most of these, we have very little to no information, even if they operated for years. However, I think it's important to acknowledge their presence in the city's early years of brewing. Perhaps future historians will unearth more about them.[2] So let's lift a glass to the Vancouver breweries lost to history.

Lion Brewery

Established in 1897, this brewery was located at 286 Front Street (1st and Scotia), the same location Stadler Brewery would occupy in 1899—and then Red Truck Beer Company in 2015. No names are on record as being associated with this brewery, but it was under ten minutes from Doering's brewery and close to where Brewery Creek emptied into False Creek. Unfortunately, such close proximity to Vancouver's main brewery usually meant a quick downfall for smaller breweries (Lansdowne, Red Star, San Francisco, and Stadler, for example).

North Arm Brewery

This brewery is referred to both as North Arm and as Reywood/Raywood (North Arm is the area—North Arm Road, now Fraser—and Reywood/Raywood refers to owner George Raywood). This seems confusing to the modern eye—giving a brewery two names and vacillating between them—but it was not uncommon at the time. For example, Doering's brewery (either Vancouver Brewery or Doering & Marstrand) was often referred to as the Alexandra Brewery because it produced Alexandra Lager. North Arm Brewery was located at North Arm Road, a relatively remote area, and as such it experienced frequent bear appearances and attacks.[3]

The dates of North Arm's operation are confusing and the evidence provided by historians isn't always consistent. The Watsons' *Pioneer Breweries of British Columbia* says that a "Reywood Brewery" was in operation from 1897 to 1910, and owned by George Raywood & Co. However, Sneath's *Brewed in Canada* claims that George Raywood and Charles Thorson operated a "North Arm Brewery" from 1898 to 1907. Bill Wilson's *Beer Barons of BC* lists North Arm as being open under the ownership of George Raywood from 1889 to 1898, with a Benjamin L. Wood as proprietor from 1894 to 1895. It's a bit of a strange pattern but makes more sense when we look closely. The brewery certainly existed in the late 1880s but it burned to the ground in 1891. Though Raywood had insurance, the process of rebuilding would have been extensive. Perhaps because of this, later that year Raywood left and spent several months in Europe.[4] He wouldn't have been able to get the brewery back up and running until 1892, which is when his partner Benjamin Wood got his brewer's licence (see below). Perhaps Raywood took another hiatus in 1894 and let Wood run things, before taking control of the brewery again around 1895. Such stops and starts may have misled some into thinking that the brewery wasn't in business until the late 1890s.

Newspaper accounts from those years bear out Wilson's proposed dates more than Sneath's or the Watsons'. The *Vancouver Daily World* of November 28, 1888, announced that "Mr. Raywood" was constructing a new brewery on North Arm Road. Four years later, on April 2, 1892, the *Daily World* stated that a "B.L. Woods of the North Arm Brewery" was granted a brewer's licence. These are among several other newspaper accounts that corroborate Wilson's version of North Arm's history. When Sneath says that George

Raywood and Charles Thorson opened North Arm in 1898, he may have mistaken Thorson's joining (and eventually taking over) the existing business with Thorson and Raywood actually *starting* the business. What seems to have happened is that Thorson, who had been brewing for Doering & Marstrand around 1896, started brewing for Raywood's brewery in about 1898. Around this same time, Raywood started up Cedar Cottage Brewery (see "Cedar Cottage Brewery" on page 134) and Thorson took over more of the business at North Arm. Newspaper stories about North Arm from the early 1900s refer to Thorson as the proprietor and brewer and indicate that the brewery had been operating for about fifteen years,[5] which again would put North Arm's founding squarely within Wilson's time frame. Sneath's closure date of 1907 may be correct, however. In December 1907, a short article refers to applications for "proposed hotels at the North Arm Brewery." This odd turn of phrase suggests that the brewery may no longer have been functioning, but if so, its closure was probably recent (or they would have referred to it as the old North Arm Brewery property, as was standard reporting practice with the Stanley Park Brewery and Red Cross Brewery properties when they became defunct).[6]

My last observation about North Arm is how poor its delivery system was early on (at least, judging from the accounts below). There are very few stories about North Arm in the papers, but two of those occurred in the summer of 1890 when its delivery wagon had two major accidents within ten days. The first accident happened on July 19, when the horses drawing the brewery wagon "concluded to run away and they made it interesting for people on the street for some time." As the horses tore around the corner of Cordova and Richards, the wagon tipped over and an empty cask and bottles rolled out onto the road (but no beer was lost, thankfully). The wagon disconnected but the tongue and whiffletree (the swinging bar that attaches the horses' harness to the wagon) stayed with the horses as they continued on their adventure until they were caught on Water Street. Then, on July 29, the horses drawing the North Arm delivery wagon again took off, this time down Hastings Street. The paper reports that "the driver held on very pluckily" despite being dragged for fifty yards, and finally managed to stop them near the post office. A defective whiffletree was to blame, according to the paper. North Arm acquired some free publicity—for that week, at least![7]

Lansdowne Brewery

Mr. A. Hasenfratz of Nanaimo opened this brewery in 1906 at almost the same location as Lion and Stadler—288 Front Street.

Red Star Brewery

This brewery was open from 1889 to 1891 at 11th and Main. It was owned and operated by Jacob DeWitt. A Eugene DeWitt is listed as a salesman for the brewery.

San Francisco Brewery

This brewery was opened in 1888 by Henry Reifel, the wealthy German brewer who established Union Brewing in Nanaimo. Since Reifel and his brother had acquired much of their brewing experience during their years in San Francisco, they named their new Vancouver brewery after their old home. It was located near Main and 11th, not far from Doering's brewery, and in the same location as its successor, Red Star. The competition may have proved too much, though, because the brewery closed its doors in 1889 and sold off its assets. As discussed in Chapter 3, Columbia Brewery's owner Joseph Kappler may have bought some of this equipment to start Columbia, which opened two months after San Francisco closed.

Stadler Brewery

August Stadler opened this brewery in 1899 in Lion Brewery's former location at 286 Front Street. Unfortunately, like Lion, it closed within about a year. Stadler opened several breweries around the province, and perhaps felt that the market competition in Vancouver was too keen. He seemed to have better luck in Nelson and Trail, where he opened the Castle Brewery and the Milwaukee Brewery respectively.

Cedar Cottage Brewery (Raywood Brewery)
Cedar Cottage Brewery was located on the southeast corner of Kingsway and Knight. Back then, it was a wooded and remote area. After he either left or closed North Arm Brewery in 1898 (see "North Arm Brewery" on page 130), George Raywood opened Cedar Cottage Brewery that same year. His brewer, Charles Thorson, joined him but is also on record as brewing at (and perhaps running) North Arm. It isn't clear how he divided his time between the two businesses.

Around 1902 or 1903, John Benson and his company, Royal Brewing, purchased Cedar Cottage Brewery. They had plans to take over Stanley Park Brewery as well. However, Raywood apparently regretted his decision to sell, and later in 1903 he attempted to regain possession of Cedar Cottage. Royal Brewing Company issued a writ

The former Cedar Cottage Brewery building, with John Benson pictured in front. (Photo courtesy of City of Vancouver Archives, AM 54 – S4 -: Dist P68)

and notice of motion for a restraining order against Raywood that they brought before a judge on September 31, 1903.[8]

THE BIG GUYS: CORPORATE CONSOLIDATION

The merger of Red Cross and Doering & Marstrand (described in Chapter 2) foreshadowed much larger amalgamations that would change the beer scene in Vancouver—and in British Columbia as a whole. BC wasn't alone in this, however. Corporate consolidations were happening across Canada.[9] In 1909, a huge brewery merger in Quebec increased chatter about what would happen here. BC newspapers reported that all of Quebec's breweries were merging as "one huge concern" under the leadership of Charles Hosmer. The papers anticipated, rather shockingly, that this amalgamation "may later be extended to take in all the breweries in Canada."[10] While such a massive consolidation did not come to pass, it nevertheless indicated what the general public was anticipating from the brewing industry in the years before the First World War and prohibition. Breweries on the Island and the mainland were already moving from private ownership to incorporation,[11] but bigger corporate consolidations were coming.

For those on the ground in the 1900s, corporate brewery mergers at first seemed the most cost-effective and economically productive way to go. Increased taxation was placing heavy pressure on small brewers, often driving them out of business. In 1906, Royal Brewing Co. appealed to Vancouver City Council to reduce brewery licence fees from $600 to $250.[12] The $600 was a heavy financial burden to bear, especially since breweries already had to pay for Dominion brewing licences from the federal government. Royal Brewing Co. argued that these fees and the new taxes had been "very hard" on brewers and "would crowd some firms out of business. Some [breweries] are now doing only a business of $50 per month."[13] Council rejected Royal's appeals, and small breweries continued to suffer. It was thought that joining breweries under one management, acquiring investors, and profit sharing would benefit both brewery owners and investors—not to mention local industry as a whole.

As brewery mergers began to increase in the late 1900s and early 1910s, they became the subject of more public discussion. One reporter praised mergers, wondering why a consolidation of BC's major breweries hadn't happened yet. "Larger mergers," he wrote, "instead of creating a monopoly, immediately set other people thinking that the market must be a good one and, in this way, bring about competition within a comparatively short time."[14] However, behind the scenes, the businessmen negotiating these deals had a different idea of what corporate mergers would do. A letter of August 11, 1909, written jointly by John Mahrer, managing director of Union Brewing, and Frank Stillman Barnard, investor and former trustee of Victoria-Phoenix Brewing Company, reveals some of their motivations. Mahrer and Barnard were writing to an unknown addressee (someone who owned a brewery) regarding "the sale of the B.C. Breweries."[15] This is likely in reference to the first planned brewery consolidation under a holding company. The writers say that such an amalgamation "of all the competitors under one management will add further to the prosperity of the business—*which will monopolize the trade*—and the price of the article can easily be advanced $1.00 a barrel, thus increasing the profits to about $230,000 a year" (emphasis mine). Monopolizing the brewing industry and fixing prices was front of mind for those organizing these mergers, despite the optimistic view from the outside. And indeed, monopolies are exactly what happened in the following decades.

THE FIRST MERGER: BC BREWERIES LTD.

The first rumours of big brewery mergers—far bigger than partnerships like Red Cross and Doering & Marstrand, or Victoria Brewery and Phoenix Brewery—were swirling in British Columbia by 1907. Word had spread about Doering's plan "to arrange a scheme for the amalgamation of the breweries on the British Columbia coast. The object is to unite under one management all the breweries of Vancouver, New Westminster, Victoria, and Nanaimo."[16] Change was definitely in the air. Vancouver Breweries was growing, and even though they'd already built an $8,000 addition in 1903,[17] Doering received a building licence in 1908 to add even more manufacturing space (at this point the brewery was taking up almost an entire city block). In 1909 there were reports of Henry Reifel, proprietor of the large and successful Union Brewing in Nanaimo, trying once again to start up a brewery in Vancouver. But this time, unlike his first efforts in the 1890s with the short-lived San Francisco Brewery, he was coming prepared. Newspapers reported that Reifel was planning to build "a large brewery in Vancouver and enter into active competition with the mainland breweries of the city... [He has] on several occasions informed friends that his company contemplated entering the business in Vancouver."[18] Indeed, by 1910, Reifel, who had already incorporated his new brewery, the Canadian Brewing and Malting Company (CBM), had obtained his local liquor and building licences and was ready to move the brewery into Vancouver. His new brewing facility, which was large and impressive, was built at Yew and 11th.[19] However, it turned out that he wasn't going to be in competition with Vancouver Breweries at all: he was going to be joining with them.

At the same time that Reifel was moving CBM into his new space, the consolidation process for BC Breweries Limited was beginning. In late 1910, Doering moved brewing operations from Vancouver Breweries' original location at Scotia and 7th to Reifel's CBM brewery at Yew and 11th. It's not clear how this worked out in practicality—whether Reifel's and Doering's respective businesses each had their own section of the brewery, or they were simply brewing together since they were on the point of joining. On February 20, 1911, a holding company called BC Breweries Limited formed to hold the assets of Union Brewing (Reifel's Nanaimo brewery), Vancouver Breweries, and CBM. In May of 1911, Pilsener Brewing of Cumberland was added. The offices of BC Breweries were set up at Vancouver

Breweries' previous building—263 7th Street—but the actual brewing continued at Reifel's CBM location.[20]

BC Breweries was the first of several holding companies that ended up controlling the brewing industry in the province and eventually the country. While its formation was met with enthusiasm by some, there was resistance as well. The August 11, 1909, joint letter from Mahrer and Barnard (cited previously) proposed several options for BC Breweries' success on the stock market. Different options were on the table because, according to Mahrer and Barnard, the English ownership question was a sticky one for Canadians, and on the other side of the pond, the British were not very invested in Canadian breweries:

> *What I most fear in London is that "breweries" are in bad odour. While Canadian and BC flotations are fashionable the securities of Home Breweries are a drug[21] on the market. Cape and American breweries stink in the nostrils of the victims. New Zealand breweries are in better shape. But altogether I should be of the opinion that the public are not likely to take to any breweries. Your friend [a London contact] may be able to assure us on this point, and if the time is opportune we might, jointly with him and his friends, accomplish something. [. . .] When we get satisfactory assurances from your friends, I will get all figures from the concerns in Vancouver and Victoria and proceed with you to London prepared to place before them a businesslike and attractive proposal.*

From this letter, it appears that both men saw British opposition to Canadian or "home" breweries as the main hurdle to overcome in consolidating BC Breweries and opening it to investment. However, Mahrer and Barnard's suggestion of an "Alternative Proposal" indicates that making the holding company Canadian might help avoid problematic entanglements with English politics:

An Alternative Proposal: Owing to the unpopularity among City men of Lloyd George's [British chancellor of the exchequer] Finance Bill I understand that many of the companies registered in England contemplate incorporating in Canada and the Colonies [. . .] Therefore it may be found advisable to incorporate and register the amalgamated BC Breweries here, rather than to bring out an English company.

There was also local, BC resistance to the merger, which was revealed in a private letter that Barnard wrote to Mahrer the following day (August 12, 1909):

I must say, however, that if more new, and opposition, breweries are threatened, as per enclosed clipping from "Colonist," it is useless to try to effect a sale. Nothing is more likely to kill our scheme to amalgamate and sell than the prospect of opposition to the new Company. You should keep the opposition Vancouver brewery in the background at present, or else have an understanding that if a sale is made to English investors that work won't proceed.[22]

The accompanying clipping did not survive with the letter. However, on the same day Barnard wrote this letter, the *Daily British Colonist* published a short blurb about Reifel's new brewery in Vancouver: "Backed by Nanaimo capital, a brewery...is to be immediately erected in Vancouver...by J. Reiffel, who conducted the negotiations for the property on behalf of the promoting syndicate. It is estimated that the buildings and the plant will involve an expenditure of between $175,000 and $200,000." Given the timing, this may have been the story that Barnard attached to his letter. The projected cost of Reifel's new brewery suggests that his investors had deep pockets; the Bank of Canada inflation calculator estimates that $200,000 in 1914 (the nearest year available) would be worth $5,090,000 in 2022 currency.[23] Reifel was going to spend over $5 million in today's dollars on a new brewery.

We can only speculate about whether this blurb about Reifel is what Barnard was referring to in his letter, and what it might mean. John Mahrer was the managing director of Reifel's Union Brewing, which was under BC Breweries, so we can assume he participated in the discussions about the amalgamation. However, it's not clear how much he knew about Reifel's Canadian Brewing and Malting Co. The *Colonist* clipping indicates that Reifel had an extraordinary amount of capital available for this brewery via his Nanaimo investors, and it's therefore likely that the "promoting syndicate" referred to was a BC-based company, not a British one. At this time Doering was president of BC Breweries, and Mahrer and Barnard were obviously involved at some level. Was Barnard concerned that Reifel, the company's manager, wouldn't keep Canadian Brewing and Malting under the holding company if it was sold to a British syndicate? If Reifel was already in business with Nanaimo-based investors, perhaps it was Canadian Brewing and Malting—the newest brewery in Vancouver—to which Barnard's letter referred: "if more new, and opposition, breweries are threatened..." A separate news story reports that as late as September 1912, Reifel was on the verge of closing a deal for BC Breweries with an American syndicate.[24] Whatever the case, it is clear that at least one Vancouver brewery was unhappy with the prospect currently on the table—that BC Breweries Ltd. would be purchased by a British-backed holding company. And it seems that Barnard and Mahrer were among those who wanted to lock down a deal. Whether Reifel was equally invested at this stage is less clear. Reifel's later conflicts with Doering and Williams might be explained, in part at least, if it was Reifel who was resistant to the British acquisition while Doering and Williams accepted it.

Regardless of the challenges and opposition to the British acquisition, the sale took place on November 1, 1912. *The Province* announced it with enthusiasm, emphasizing the successful flotation of the new company on the London Stock Exchange and highlighting how things were already going well. It even made the news in the papers of Washington and Oregon. However, for regular citizens of Vancouver it didn't make much of a difference. The beer that had been brewed at the Yew Street location for several years was still branded "BC Breweries." The day after the sale, *The Province*'s joke page included a comment about such brewery mergers: "The only interest the ultimate consumer has in a brewery merger is the effects it will have on the height of the collar [i.e., foam or head] in the glass of his favorite beverage."

Top: An ad from the February 11, 1913, edition of the *Vancouver Sun* links Heidelberg to Canadian Brewing and Malting. Bottom: An ad from the May 12, 1913, edition of the *Vancouver Daily World* links it to BC Breweries.

Over the next several years, under the auspices of BC Breweries, Vancouver Breweries and Canadian Brewing and Malting brewed out of Reifel's facility; they dominated the industry in Vancouver. Reifel's plant was expanded in 1913 at an expense of approximately $300,000, giving it a storage capacity of about twenty-seven thousand barrels.[25] BC Breweries had several brands under its label, including Heidelberg, Cascade, UBC Bohemian,[26] and BC Export. Most of its Vancouver advertisements were for Cascade or Heidelberg—the flagship beers of Vancouver Breweries and Canadian Brewing and Malting, respectively. These two breweries kept their own distinct brands under BC Breweries, with their own style and focus. Sometimes advertisements would present a beer as a product of BC Breweries, and sometimes as a product of an individual brewery; the two images on page 141 give an example of each. In the first image, Heidelberg is produced by Canadian Brewing and Malting, and in the second it's produced by BC Breweries. Both claims are true.

In my admittedly anecdotal review of beer advertisements in Vancouver between 1912 and 1917, I found that the ads in which beer was attributed to BC Breweries (the larger corporation) tended, on average, to be more general and neutral than those in which the beer was attributed to Vancouver Breweries or Canadian Brewing and Malting (individual breweries)—even though the beer and the ads were all produced by the same company. The images on page 141 show what I mean. In the bottom ad, BC Breweries' Heidelberg beer is represented as always the same, always consistent, "always clean, mild and delicious." Nothing too strong or memorable. The version of Heidelberg in the Canadian Brewing and Malting ad is more emotionally compelling and evocative, inviting us to imagine flavours and feelings. In the BC Breweries ad for Heidelberg, we see an image of crisp, neutral beer—an image that Molson, Budweiser, and other big beer corporations used as their standby for the rest of the century. This version of beer was what 1980s beer pioneer Frank Appleton was rejecting in the short manifesto he published in the 1978 issue of *Harrowsmith* magazine: "The new beer ... must not offend anyone, anywhere. Corporate beer is not too heavy, not too bitter, not too alcoholic, not too malty, not too yeasty, and not too gassy. In other words, corporate beer reduces every characteristic that makes beer beer."[27]

BC Breweries Ltd., in this form anyway, didn't end up lasting very long. According to Bill Wilson's research, the company "had major operating problems" and Doering and Williams "reported irregular bookkeeping and improper company filings with the Registrar of Companies."[28] Problems were already evident in January 1915, when BC Breweries had to defer paying interest on its mortgage bonds. By the fall of 1916, the strong possibility of prohibition was looming and investors with holdings in the alcohol industry were panicking. BC Breweries' bondholders were petitioning the government because they had been guaranteed that their financial interests would be protected in the event of prohibition—but it looked like this protection was going to fall through the cracks.[29] A London finance column titled "The Financier and Bullionist" was republished in British Columbia

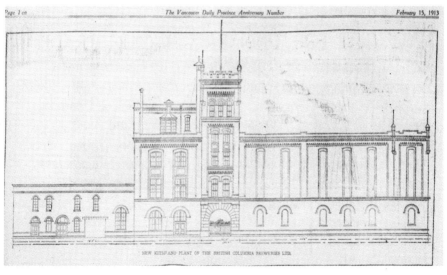

NEW KITSILANO PLANT OF THE BRITISH COLUMBIA BREWERIES LTD.

A drawing of Reifel's large new brewery on Yew and 11th, taken from page 50 of the February 15, 1913, issue of *The Province*.

to draw attention to the dire investment situation prohibition would create. The author argued that the possibility of prohibition

> *is of more than academic concern... the interests of at least one enterprise in which British capital is employed will be gravely prejudiced [if prohibition happens]... We refer to the British Columbia Breweries, over $2,500,000 of whose six per cent 20-year first mortgage gold bonds, offered for public subscription in London in October 1912, are now outstanding... It is no exaggeration to say that if the Prohibition Act comes into operation in its present form the whole of that capital will be lost, and the people who subscribed to it will be victimized through the direct instrumentality of the British Columbia government.*[30]

At this point, according to the *National Post,* BC Breweries controlled "all the important breweries in British Columbia," except for two Victoria breweries, as well as fifty to sixty licensed premises in Vancouver. They had an extraordinary amount of influence, so their imminent collapse was a big deal.

Due to a combination of financial mismanagement and market panic, BC Breweries was in trouble. Between 1915 and 1917 it was in receivership and under the management of Sam Prenter, and by 1918 it was dissolved and reorganized under the name "British Columbia Breweries (1918) Ltd.," then, after 1923, "Brewers and Distillers of Vancouver." Henry Reifel was president until 1933, but Williams and Doering had completely cut ties by 1915, when Reifel was listed as the manager of Vancouver Breweries as well as BC Breweries. There were some ugly legal struggles between Doering and Reifel in the aftermath, apparently surrounding how money had been managed between the pre-1912 BC Breweries and Vancouver Breweries. They eventually settled out of court.[31] By that time, Reifel wanted to proceed with growing his brewing and distilling empire, and Doering and Williams were fully involved in their hotel and land ownership concerns. BC Breweries was now Reifel's baby. Through a complicated series of mergers and acquisitions over the next several decades, what began as BC Breweries Ltd. would eventually become Carling O'Keefe, one of the largest brewing corporations in Canada. Carling O'Keefe would eventually be acquired by Molson Coors.[32] All roads lead to Big Beer.

SUBSEQUENT MERGERS, CONSOLIDATIONS, AND PARTNERSHIPS

The consolidation of BC Breweries Ltd. was the largest and most influential brewery merger in British Columbia during the first two decades of the twentieth century. Because this book focuses on the world of independent breweries, it doesn't explore these complex mid-century amalgamations. After prohibition, the world of BC beer belonged to the corporate giants. However, contextual information about what happened after BC Breweries' collapse and resurrection can illuminate how the later consolidations established the macro beer industry—an industry that craft brewers would chip away at, beginning in the 1980s. Two major early mergers or partnerships that occurred after BC Breweries were the Coast Breweries and the Amalgamated Brewers Agency of BC. In addition, beer- and distilling-related industry organizations such as the BC Brewers and the BC Bottlers Association formed, often with Henry Reifel's involvement. These organizations did not involve mergers or legal acquisitions; they were simply meetings of brewery and distillery owners to discuss various industry-related issues. However, they built relationships between industry insiders that would have influenced how and whether legal consolidations proceeded.

Coast Breweries Ltd.
In 1911, Robert Fiddes and John McLennan, businessmen and fellow members of the Vancouver Conservative Club, together drew up a memorandum of association for their proposed holding company,

Coast Breweries. The MOA, in its length and level of detail, suggested that the men had high ambitions for their company. It wasn't just brewing in which they wished to invest; they were also interested in water resources, electricity, and shipping.[33] However, the company didn't get incorporated immediately. For the next ten years, Fiddes ran hotels, was secretary to the King David Masonic Lodge, and kept involved in local politics. It wasn't until 1921 that Coast Breweries was officially incorporated. At first, Coast Breweries only held the merged company Victoria-Phoenix Brewing, one of whose trustees (Frank Stillman Barnard) had been very interested in the possibilities of the BC Breweries merger.

By 1928, Coast Breweries had added Silver Spring Brewery (of Victoria), Rainier Brewing (of Kamloops), and Westminster Brewery (of New Westminster) to its holdings. According to its prospectus, the goal of Fiddes's company was to optimize the profits of all the breweries: "By amalgamating the operations of these companies a very substantial saving in freight and overhead expenses will be effected."[34] The huge ambitions of the original MOA seem to have dimmed by this point. However, the company was growing. In the 1930s some American breweries joined the fold. In 1954, however, the picture changed: Coast Breweries was renamed Lucky Lager Breweries, and then purchased by Labatt shortly after, in 1957.[35]

One final note on Coast Breweries, a detail that I've not found mentioned in any other history of Vancouver brewing: there appears to be a connection between Coast Breweries' founder Robert Fiddes and the earlier Vancouver brewing scene. In 1922, one year after Fiddes finally incorporated Coast Breweries, John Dyke's daughter Kathleen married a carpenter called William Findlay Fiddes. On the marriage certificate, a Robert Fiddes of West Vancouver is listed as witness. We know from the original Coast Breweries MOA that the Coast Breweries' Robert lived at 1859 Pendrell Street—an address in the West End of Vancouver—and according to city directories he remained at that residence for years afterwards. The Robert Fiddes who married Laura Johnstone in Vancouver in 1913 had his brother

William Fiddes as a witness. Fiddes was an unusual last name (I could find only eleven listed for all of British Columbia in 1911), so it seems likely that John Dyke's daughter married the brother of Coast Breweries' founder. And that means that John Dyke ended up living with Robert Fiddes's brother, since Dyke moved in with Kathleen's family in the 1920s. Such intersections of family and business were common enough; for example, Joseph Loewen, owner of Victoria Brewery, became father-in-law to Frank Stillman Barnard (the same Barnard who wrote the letters above regarding BC Breweries). Barnard, in turn, became a company trustee when Phoenix and Victoria Brewery merged in 1893. Perhaps Dyke got to experience more of the brewing industry in his old age, as he watched some of the Coast Breweries activity from behind the scenes.

Amalgamated Brewers Agency of BC

This is an odd and rather elusive organization. At first glance at the records, the ABA seems to be a holding company similar to BC Breweries or Coast Breweries, but in reality they were a group of breweries that worked with the government to fix prices and control distribution. They were, in other words, a cartel. The agreement was worked out by Attorney General Alexander Malcolm Manson with the input of Henry Reifel in the early 1920s, when Manson was trying to control Reifel's bootlegging of liquor into clubs. Under their memorandum of association, dated 1923, the breweries involved would each be guaranteed a percentage of sales to the government, and the government would buy most of its beer from those breweries. Breweries could only sell their product through the ABA (which itself had a deal with the government), and profits would be shared "according to the percentages herein set out."[36] The breweries that joined the ABA were already part of BC Breweries or Coast Breweries, but since ABA wasn't a holding company there was no conflict: Phoenix-Victoria, Silver Spring, Vancouver Breweries, Westminster Brewery, and Rainier Brewing.

While an R. Samet occasionally made an appearance in newspapers as the head of ABA, often trying to present breweries as respectable and good for the community,[37] it was Henry Reifel who truly ran it. Conveniently, he was also president of BC Breweries and of BC Breweries' most powerful member, Vancouver Breweries.[38] A decade after the formation of ABA, both Samet and Reifel would be criminally charged for liquor trafficking,[39] so they were clearly both involved in the ABA's illegal activities. The collusion between the government and the ABA didn't go unnoticed; there were reports of bribes being accepted by Liquor Control Board employees, for example. Fake permits, illegal kickbacks, and in general "the grossest kind of fraud" characterized the provincial government's relationship with the ABA. Reifel and the Attorney General had to work together to conceal the deceit and keep the profits coming.[40]

◆

When it comes to beer history in Vancouver and in BC more generally, the bulk of the twentieth century is dominated by the narratives of corporate beer: Carling O'Keefe, Budweiser, Molson, Labatt, and a few others. BC Breweries, Coast Breweries, and other brewery amalgamations all eventually came under the control of one of the corporate beer giants. The stories of these holding companies and what became of them—not to mention the shady practices of the ABA—could be their own book.[41] These were powerful companies with powerful men leading them, about which much has been written. There's far less, however, written about the smaller, independent breweries that struggled to be successful, and that's why this book skips over the next few decades, picking up in the late 1970s and early 1980s, when consumers and brewers alike were becoming frustrated with corporate beer and ready for a change—any change. Vancouver played a huge role in bringing this new version of beer—craft? microbrew?—to western Canada.

PART II: 1980-2023

VANCOUVER/LOWER MAINLAND BREWERY TIMELINE: PART II

(Brewery* openings and other significant dates)

1982
Horseshoe
Bay Brewery

1987
Shaftebury Brewing

2000
Brewpubs
permitted to
distribute off
premises

1984
Granville
Island Brewing

1995
Russell
Brewing

2005
Red Truck
Beer

1980 | 1985 | 1986 EXPO | 1990 | 2005 | 2010

1986
Steveston
Brewing

1997
R&B Brewing

2012
Callister;
Parallel
49;
Powell

1994
Storm Brewing;
Yaletown Brewing;
Sailor Hagar's
Brewpub

2003
Central City
Brewing

1983
Bryant Brewery;
Mountain Ale Co.

*Not all breweries are included. Please see Appendices 1 and 2 for spreadsheets listing all early Vancouver breweries and all Lower Mainland breweries from 1982 to 2024.

2013
Tasting room legislation enacted

2016
Faculty; Field House; Luppolo; Parkside; Trading Post

2020
Superflux; Barnside; Farmhouse

2015
Twin Sails; Dogwood; Foamers' Folly; Off the Rail; Old Abbey Ales

2018
Electric Bicycle; Northpaw

2022
Shaketown; Brewing August; Brave

PANDEMIC

2014
Main Street; Strange Fellows; Steel & Oak; White Rock Beach Beer; Yellow Dog; Bomber; Dageraad; Four Winds; Moody Ales

2019
House of Funk; Slow Hand; Wildeye; Container; Another Beer Co.; Camp; Farm Country; Five Roads; Tinhouse

2013
Brassneck; 33 Acres

2017
East Van; 3 Dogs; Mariner; Andina; Smugglers Trail; Beere

2021
Locality; Studio

CHAPTER 6

THE RETURN OF CRAFT: A POT-SMOKING HIPPIE, AN ENGLISH GENTLEMAN, AND HORSESHOE BAY BREWERY

It was June 1978, and British Columbia was entering a hot, dry summer. Vancouver locals were looking forward to a respite from the rain as they enjoyed some cold beer by the water. However, the summer was destined to be dry in more ways than one. During the spring, the 1,500 Lower Mainland employees of what were by now, after decades of corporate consolidations, the "Big Three" of Canadian brewing—Carling O'Keefe, Molson, and Labatt—had been in unsuccessful contract renewal talks. Rumours of a beer strike were in the air and the entire BC beer industry felt unsettled. Then, on June 8, the Vancouver factories of Carling, Molson, and Labatt locked out all their employees, leaving them picketing on the streets. As the corporate employers struggled to make the beer themselves, taps at pubs and bars were drained and liquor store shelves across the Lower Mainland emptied out. Beer became like gold dust. People rushed for the border, businesses went through legal hoops to bring American beer to their customers, and some people even tried bootlegging Budweiser into Canada on their pleasure boats.

The lockouts lasted for four painful months, costing the BC economy an estimated $50 million in layoffs and lost profits, and costing Canadian beer its reputation; post-lockout, 58 percent of British Columbians surveyed said that they'd now come to prefer American beer.[1] By 1980, there were only forty breweries across Canada—a record low—and thirty-two were controlled by the Big Three.[2] Beer looked like a dying industry. But it was actually on the cusp of change, thanks to a few forward-thinking, beer-loving men: Frank Appleton, John Mitchell, Mitch Taylor, and Bill Harvey. The path these men took into brewing would change the face of the industry and resurrect Vancouver's independent breweries. This chapter and the next explore the stories of these new-generation BC beer pioneers.

Six years before the big lockout of '78, trained English brewmaster Frank Appleton had already firmly rejected Canadian corporate beer. An employee of Carling O'Keefe (formerly just O'Keefe) for years, Appleton became increasingly frustrated with the series of corporate mergers the company underwent and their cheap, automated version of what he considered real brewing. His expertise deserved more. So when, in 1972, they announced the closure of the O'Keefe plant and the move to Carling, he dramatically quit his job:

> I wrote a scathing letter to the president and posted copies on the notice boards in both plants. They were soon taken down and shredded by management, but not soon enough: a number of copies were circulated "underground" by junior staff and workers. I walked out, thinking I would never return to the brewing business again.[3]

Appleton had purchased twenty acres of untouched land in the Kootenays, so after slamming the door at Carling O'Keefe, he began homesteading his new property—felling trees, building a house, learning to garden. By the mid-1970s, he was picking up writing contracts for various magazines and newspapers. He spent his time working his own land and writing about local issues. And because beer is deeply tied to land and to community, it wasn't long before the beverage of the gods made its way into his life once again.

Just a couple of months before the brewery lockout of 1978, Appleton was working on an article for the country living magazine *Harrowsmith* titled "The Underground Brewmaster." The sense of subversion Appleton expressed in this piece has, in fact, characterized much of the craft beer industry for the past forty years, and it's a big part of craft beer's appeal. The article was published just as the beer lockout started and became famous among homebrewers, would-be craft brewery owners, and beer aficionados across the country. It expressed everything that was wrong with the control that dead-eyed corporate greed exerted over beer. It also condemned what beer had become under the Big Three: technological advances had turned beer into an anonymous corporate product that had little flavour and required no skill to produce. "In times past," Appleton wrote in his manifesto, "the brewmaster was an all-powerful figure. This man [the O'Keefe head brewer]—after 10 years' training in the art and science of brewing—now held down a job that consisted only of filling out endless forms and preparing tedious budgets for the head office in Toronto."[4]

Appleton's article gave a voice to the growing group of people who felt frustrated and angry at how disappointing beer had become. He wasn't actually advocating for craft breweries (or microbreweries, as they were first known) at this point. The article was intended to encourage people to make their own beer, which Appleton insisted was doable for pretty much everyone, and to reject corporate beer with its low-quality blandness. Keep in mind that Appleton's powerful words were circulating just as the Big Three were locking out their employees, grasping for more money, and leaving British Columbians dry for four months:

More aggravating than the cost of the stuff, to my mind, is the lack of any alternative to the blandness of present-day beers. The drive for super-efficiency has wreaked havoc among North

American breweries... The stage has been reached where all the big breweries are making virtually the same product, with different names and labels. Accompanying this trend is a shift in power from the hands of the brewmaster to the marketing, accounting and advertising men... Like tasteless white bread and the universal cardboard hamburger, the new beer is produced for the tasteless common denominator. It must not offend anyone, anywhere. Corporate beer is not too heavy, not too bitter, not too alcoholic, not too malty, not too yeasty and not too gassy. In other words, corporate beer reduces every characteristic that makes beer beer.[5]

As Appleton wrote those words in his rural Kootenay home, hundreds of miles away Vancouverites were starved for beer—any beer—and anger was growing at BC's corporate beer overlords. Something needed to change.

THE ODD COUPLE: MITCHELL AND APPLETON

It was 1981. The meeting with Allan Gould, manager of the BC Liquor Control Board, had been going for forty minutes but John Mitchell hadn't stopped pacing the office floor. Beer was on his mind. The British expat was recently back from a trip to England with his wife Jenny, where he had become galvanized by England's Campaign for Real Ale and saddened by the loss of neighbourhood pubs in his home country. He had also seen the dismal beer offerings in BC and anticipated the embarrassment the province would experience once the world arrived for Expo 86 and they were served "rubbish."[6] He called BC a "beer desert." Gould sat watching in bemusement as Mitchell paced. This carpenter and chef—born in Singapore, raised in a boys' school in England, and now settled in West Vancouver—had big plans, but Gould wasn't sure he could pull them off. However, he was willing to hear him out. "I own a pub out in Horseshoe Bay—the

Troller," said Mitchell, gesturing to his pub co-owner, Dave Patrick, who was also in the meeting. "And I want to start a brewery there. I want to make my own beer—good beer. I want to turn the Troller into a brewpub." Gould thought it through, smoking at his desk as Mitchell paced and finally said, "Well, I can't think of a reason to say no!"[7] Gould was quick to advise Mitchell, however, that he would need approval from the minister of Consumer and Corporate Affairs, Peter Hyndman, before anything could be put in motion. And after that, he'd need the District of West Vancouver to give their stamp of approval. At the time, provincial regulations prohibited brewery owners from having an establishment that sold beer to consumers and municipalities had strict zoning guidelines for alcohol production, so legal and policy changes would need to happen. Gould and Hyndman were the first people who needed to be convinced.

John Mitchell wasn't quite ready to send a formal proposal to Hyndman, but Gould was the first step—or almost the first step. Mitchell was trained as a chef and had fifteen years of hospitality experience at the Sylvia Hotel in Vancouver. Two years earlier, in 1979, Mitchell and his wife Jenny had purchased the Troller Pub in West Vancouver together with their business partners, Don Wilson and Dave Patrick. It was a decent deal because it was, in Jenny's recollection, a dump. "It was such a mess, we had to clean it up," she remembers. "And it was full of heavy drinkers—John didn't like that." Mitchell wanted a different sort of clientele, patrons who would value quality beer and weren't just looking to get drunk on whatever was available. He knew Expo 86 was coming and he was, as he emphasized to Gould and later to Hyndman, embarrassed by the recent brewery strikes and the "rubbish that we call beer" that would be served to visitors from across the globe in just a few years' time. "You can't have a country without good beer," he would insist. However, to Mitchell's chagrin, provincial liquor laws of the time forced him to sell beer from one of the Big Three. The Troller was a pub "tied" to Molson[8] (this is where the term "tied house" comes from). As he worked to turn the dingy building into a cozy brewpub that felt like those in England,

Mitchell imagined what it would be like to offer real, quality beer to his patrons—to not feel embarrassed at the drink he was selling. He would chat with some of the customers at the Troller about his dream, asking for advice and input. "I'd love to open a brewery, to make my own beer," Mitchell said to one of his regulars one day, a man named Roger Cross. By coincidence, Cross had recently read Appleton's "Underground Brewmaster" article, and he enthused to Mitchell about Appleton's ideas and qualifications. "You need to go see him," Cross insisted.[9]

The next day, Frank Appleton answered his phone and heard an unknown English-accented voice ask for him. John Mitchell had gotten his number from *Harrowsmith*. "I read your article and was wondering if you could help me," Mitchell asked. "I want to make a beautiful beer, a beer with character, like some you can still find in England. We've just been back there, and real ale is making a comeback."[10] Appleton agreed to meet, but only if Mitchell would come to him—he was not interested in making the 600-kilometre drive back to the big city. So John and Jenny got out their BC map book and the next day, on July 28, 1981, they made the trek out to the Kootenays. Appleton describes Mitchell arriving at his house bearing gifts: lots of British food and (of course!) beer to share. Appleton was used to unlabelled homebrew, but Mitchell had brought high-end English ale, "dressed up in a fancy package, all British flags, crowns and stuff."[11] The plan, at least for the Mitchells, was to talk about beer in the evening, and then prepare to celebrate the royal wedding the next morning—Charles and Diana were getting married on July 29, at 5:00 AM Pacific time. After a convivial dinner—with plenty of beer and Scotch—John and Jenny set up sleeping bags in the living room to prepare for their early start. The sounds of the pipe organ as Diana walked down the aisle roused Appleton from his slumber the next day. With a raging hangover, he stumbled into the living room to see John and Jenny drinking tea in their sleeping bags and watching the procession. Appleton grumbled and went back to bed. It was the beginning of a long, interesting, and sometimes vexatious friendship. The pot-smoking hippie and the English gentleman made a strange pair. Once Charles and Diana were married off, Appleton and Mitchell got into the details of what Mitchell wanted to do. Mitchell knew the kind of beer he wanted to make—something like Fuller's London Pride—and Appleton knew how to reverse-engineer a recipe as long as he could taste the beer. After a few days in the Kootenays, they'd managed to put together a proposal to present to Hyndman.[12] With Appleton's knowledge of the beer industry and its politics (not to mention brewing equipment) and Mitchell's experience in hospitality, they had a combined expertise that made for a strong proposal. However, Appleton still felt uncertain about its success. "Good luck with it," he said to Mitchell, who was planning to take the proposal directly to Hyndman, "but don't be surprised if you don't hear back from them this year. And don't be surprised if their answer is no."[13] Nevertheless, Appleton joined John and Jenny Mitchell at their home in Vancouver so he could start assembling a brewhouse while Mitchell began working the political and legal side.[14]

BARRIERS TO BEER: CLEARING THE HURDLES

Peter Hyndman, a thirty-something Socred MLA and former lawyer, was new to his cabinet post of minister of Consumer and Corporate Affairs when he received Mitchell and Appleton's brewpub proposal in 1981. The year before, he'd quit his job in a law office to show that he was ready for more responsibility as an MLA; he was ambitious and wanted a cabinet position under Premier Bill Bennett. As one of only six MLAs not in cabinet, he was feeling left out. His first step on the ladder to success was his appointment as deputy whip, a position that earned him the nickname Bam-Bam. Some men might get huffy at that, but Hyndman embraced it with a laugh. He was known for having a kind of levity about the political process. According to one account, during a childish and heated debate among his colleagues in the legislature, Hyndman scribbled down the following message on foolscap paper and sent it flying as a paper airplane up into the press gallery: "Last 30 minutes a good example of what may appear boring as Hell, but to a student of this floor, is a fascinating exercise to watch. Are you having an exciting time?!!? Hyndman."[15] In January 1981, he was at last appointed to the provincial cabinet. However, he didn't lose his sense of humour. After a column about Hyndman's possible legalization of beer and wine advertisements on radio and TV, in which the writer referenced the fictional Canadian icons Bob and Doug McKenzie, Hyndman sent him a note: "Your column raises some good points. However, it is surprising that you would cite the example of Bob and Doug McKenzie to back your argument. They are the only broadcasters who have not, like written me a letter about this, eh?"[16] When questioned about his qualifications to run the ministry responsible for booze, Hyndman often laughed and said he was a beer drinker, so that gave him enough experience. Previous political leaders in BC, like Bill Bennett's father, were teetotallers and not particularly friendly to the alcohol industry, so Hyndman was showing the public that there was a new generation of leaders in charge—ones who would not be so Victorian in their attitudes to alcohol. Some people liked this. Others did not. Hyndman had been given a particularly challenging portfolio.

By August 1981, when Mitchell brought his cottage brewery proposal to Hyndman, the minister was putting all his energy into managing the challenges of his new position. He wanted to make an impact as minister, so he made some strong decisions early on—and not all of these went well for him. One of those decisions was to reduce governmental overreach and improve market competition by deregulating beer prices.[17] It didn't work. In response to the deregulation, the Big Three raised their prices the same amount, at the same time—and they did it repeatedly. This price-fixing angered Hyndman, who, after the first instance, convened a meeting with the CEOs of Molson, Labatt, and Carling O'Keefe to demand an explanation. After the meeting, the CEOs filed out of Hyndman's office right past

Vancouver Sun reporter Der Hoi-Yin, ignoring her questions about the outcome. Hyndman, however, stopped and chatted. "Well," he said, "I told them that I was most unhappy with their response to the expected pricing differences and if they couldn't do better, they may find themselves getting competition from elsewhere."[18] And what did that mean, the reporter wondered. Hyndman clarified. It turned out that Hyndman had already read Mitchell's proposal and was planning to use it as leverage. He mentioned to the Big Three CEOs that he had received an application from a man who wanted to make his own beer and serve it at his pub in Horseshoe Bay—and that he was inclined to approve that application. One of the CEOs responded flippantly: "We're not worried—if we thought *that* was a good idea, we would have done it ourselves."[19] Graham Freeman of Labatt said that they "knew it's not going to work."[20] Famous last words for breweries that, years later, would imitate craft breweries with their own "crafty" beer brands like Shock Top and Blue Moon.

Mitchell remained in contact with Gould and Hyndman as he waited anxiously for official word on his proposal. In a letter he wrote to Gould in October 1981, he indicated that he had provided Hyndman with "additional information to add to our original proposal" and he included a copy for Gould as well. With this same letter he also sent Gould a book that "puts our case rather well," encouraging him to read Chapter 5 in particular. He concluded the letter by emphasizing that he'd like to meet with Gould again soon.[21] While there's no record of what book Mitchell sent Gould, or what supplementary information he added to his proposal, it's clear that Mitchell was very good at maintaining relationships and keeping himself top of mind with people who mattered. The old cliché "The squeaky wheel gets the grease" might apply here. And it worked.

Hyndman's public remarks about Mitchell's proposal, even before it was approved, were positive. "Personally, I'm intrigued by the idea and I'm certainly not going to dismiss it out of hand," he said to *The Province* on September 30, 1981. Everyone knew that this possibility was now out there—that there might be some alternative to the big beer that was dominating the industry. What if pub owners could actually make and sell their own beer?! Anticipation was in the air, even outside of the country. One letter Mitchell received in November 1981 was from a Gordon William Hardwick in England, whose Canadian grandparents had sent him a newspaper clipping about the potential cottage brewery in West Vancouver. Hardwick expressed his enthusiasm for the project, and even provided an abbreviated resumé of his own experience as a chemical engineer should Mitchell need more staff at his new brewpub.[22] For now, however, Appleton was the brewer and would train Mitchell to take over when he was ready. Appleton lived with the Mitchells at their home in Copper Cove during this time and kept busy that fall building the brewhouse out of old dairy equipment and playing with recipes for their inaugural ale. Jenny Mitchell recalls John trying to find the perfect yeast during this recipe-building process. He had asked for yeast from Molson and Carling O'Keefe, but both had said no. However, the brewery that created John's model for the perfect beer— Fuller's London Pride—said yes. He ended up bringing malt back from England along with the Fuller's yeast and a special strain from the National Yeast Institute (the yeast regularly used throughout

Mitchell and Appleton finally receive their licence. (Photo courtesy of John Ohler)

Mitchell's time brewing at Horseshoe Bay remains a secret). Then it was up to Appleton to work his magic.

When John, Jenny, and Frank finally got the good news about the government approving their brewpub, in November 1981, it was third- or fourth-hand, via someone coming in to the pub and telling them. Hyndman had emerged from a meeting and announced it to the reporters nearby. One of the pub's patrons was listening to CBC that afternoon and heard the news. They immediately rushed into the Troller to tell the Mitchells, who were thrilled. Mitchell headed straight to the offices of the Liquor Control and Licensing Branch. His opening remarks, according to Appleton's account, were, "So, gentlemen, I hear we're getting our licence?" They were indeed. The papers were signed, legal requirements adjusted, and Mitchell and Appleton completed the brewhouse—at a total cost of about $70,000, according to Appleton.[23]

There were a few more legislative hurdles to jump at the municipal level, however; the District of West Vancouver would need to amend the zoning bylaw to permit a cottage brewery to operate in a Marine Zone 3 area (the section of Sewell's Marina where the brewery was built). Peter Hyndman was among those who sent in a letter of support to the public hearings on the topic and there was generally a warm reception to the possibility. After public hearings on February 1 and 15, 1982, Council approved the rezoning with only one councillor, Diane Hutchinson, voting against it. However, despite the support, the District was still very careful about the changes. The definition of "Cottage Brewery" specified that the business should be "not more than 1,000 square feet" and that its production of beer could not exceed an average of 400 gallons a week. It also prohibited the sale of beer on the premises—which meant that the kegs would have to be transported over to the Troller Pub, since Horseshoe Bay Brewery was a separate property. Finally, Council also determined that a "Cottage Brewery" in this Marine Zone could only be used at 6695 Nelson Avenue (the brewery's address) and not in any other Marine Zone.[24] Legally, the brewery needed to have a separate address from

Top: Jenny Mitchell (right), her brother Michael Coigley, and his wife Sylvia in front of the Troller Pub, where John sold his Horseshoe Bay Brewery ale. (Photo courtesy of John Ohler)

Bottom: Frank Appleton in the middle of a brew day at their new brewery. (Photo courtesy of John Ohler)

the pub in which its beer was served and could not sell its product anywhere else. These legal restrictions hamstrung brewpubs for years but were eventually lifted thanks to industry lobbying.

OPEN FOR BUSINESS!

After all the hoops they had to jump through, Mitchell and Appleton were excited to start pouring Bay Ale (their London Pride clone) for customers at the Troller Pub. On June 17, 1982, the pub was packed with people eager to try the new beer made right next door. Appleton and Mitchell were down in the cellar, tapping the very first keg. To the chagrin of both, the beer they poured was hazy and flat. A cask-conditioned ale will not be as carbonated as your standard macro beer, but it should have *some* carbonation. Appleton describes his heart sinking when he realized the problems. However, they quickly found a solution: after a slight increase in both temperature and CO_2 top pressure, the beer poured slightly clearer and with a nice foamy head. "You've done it, my boy! You've done it!" Mitchell exclaimed to Appleton as they danced around the cellar. "Let's put it on tap right now and see how it goes."[25] It was now 9:00 PM and they were ready to serve. They sold out that night, and almost every night afterwards. Customers were buying Bay Ale twice as often as they bought the domestic "big beer" on tap at the Troller. After all, Bay Ale was $1.70 a pint versus $2.00 for Carling's Pilsner—and it tasted better!

However, its popularity became a problem; customers were coming from long distances (one even came from Los Angeles!) to try Bay Ale, and on some nights the kegs were empty by 6:00 PM. One solution they came up with was to restrict sales on low traffic days. "Under this scheme, we don't sell Bay Ale on Mondays and Tuesdays," said Mitchell's business partner David Patrick at the time. "We sell seven kegs on Wednesdays and Thursdays and eight kegs on Fridays and Saturdays."[26] Trained English brewmaster Robin Wright visited the brewery a couple of weeks after the first keg was tapped, and reviewed

John Mitchell (right) toasts with a glass of his Horseshoe Bay Brewery ale. (Photo courtesy of John Ohler)

Bay Ale with an expert's palate. Wright's praise of Appleton's product garnered even more attention for Mitchell's new brewery and the potential of good beer for British Columbia.[27] An official "coming out party" for Bay Ale was held on July 6, with various dignitaries (including Allan Gould) in attendance to enjoy hors d'oeuvres and ale as they watched the keg being wheeled out.

After a month of bustling business, Appleton left to go back to his home in the Kootenays. Mitchell continued running the brewery on his own and trained up an assistant brewer to help him manage. Mitchell's success at brewing was striking—mainly because he'd hardly done any brewing at all before meeting Appleton. In remembering the years before they opened the brewery, Jenny says Mitchell would

Opposite: John Mitchell and Frank Appleton worked hard together in the brewery's first month to make sure everything was in line for continued success. Appleton left after a month to go back home to the Kootenays and Mitchell continued on as the brewmaster. (Photos courtesy of John Ohler)

make a batch of homebrew now and then, but always from a kit. She recounts one instance in which he brought some of his beer-kit homebrews into the kitchen and most of the bottles exploded. After this fiasco they put a sleeping bag over the bottles and John drilled holes in the lids. However, despite that inauspicious start, Mitchell was a fast learner and Appleton was a good teacher. Mitchell did the first brews at both Spinnakers and Howe Sound, two of his later endeavours. He even taught his daughter Louise to brew on her school holidays, although she was too young to actually enter the pub. Everyone he taught received a lesson in very traditional brewing—no shortcuts. His apprentice David Bruce-Thomas (more on him in a moment) recalls Mitchell refusing to use hop pellets, instead picking up truckfuls of fresh whole cone hops from hop farms in Chilliwack.

Horseshoe Bay Brewery made a huge impact on the craft beer industry in Vancouver and in British Columbia—even the whole country—more broadly, but in its first iteration it didn't last long. In September of 1982, shortly after the brewery started serving its ale at Troller Pub, Paul Hadfield of Victoria was watching with keen interest. Hadfield, who had been an architect but suffered from the housing crash at the time, was seeking a new career opportunity. He wanted to do in Victoria what John Mitchell had done in West Vancouver. Mitchell had just returned to Vancouver from a trip to the UK, where he was sourcing better brewing equipment and sampling British beers, and Hadfield got in touch. He, Mitchell, and several homebrewers met up one chilly evening in October 1982 for a bottle-share in the Dunbar home of Lou Curnick, a prolific homebrewer and wine and spirits agent with a passion for British-style ales. Curnick had fashioned his basement into an unofficial English pub, which he called the Pickled Onion, and which became the site for "real ale" fans to gather. Everyone brought beers they made or beers they loved. Mitchell alone brought about fourteen bottles of English ale. In my interview with him, Hadfield described this evening as a "light-bulb moment...there was such a phenomenal range of flavours in these beers that didn't exist in the BC marketplace. Some of the best beer in the room was made by homebrewers!" On that evening, he decided that bitter was the beer he'd pursue—he wanted to start an English pub and serve cask-conditioned English bitter. Not only that, but he wanted Mitchell to take the lead. Mitchell agreed, in part because tensions were growing between him and his business partners in terms of his influence in the pub versus the brewery. His wife Jenny recalls Mitchell feeling that Wilson and Patrick were keeping him out of the pub and trying to make that space their domain, while he stayed in the brewhouse. It wasn't what he wanted.

So in 1983 Mitchell sold his share of the brewery to his partners. He and Jenny moved to Victoria and had launched Spinnakers Brewpub by 1984 (a move that Jenny was not thrilled about—she loved their home in Vancouver). In 1996, Mitchell helped establish Howe Sound Brewing in Squamish.[28] Appleton continued boosting the beer industry as well, travelling extensively to help brewers set up brewing systems, sometimes working with Mitchell while he did so. He was involved with Swans, Hoyne, and Spinnakers in Victoria, Yaletown in Vancouver, Howe Sound in Squamish, High Mountain Brewhouse in Whistler, Tin Whistle in Penticton, Deschutes in

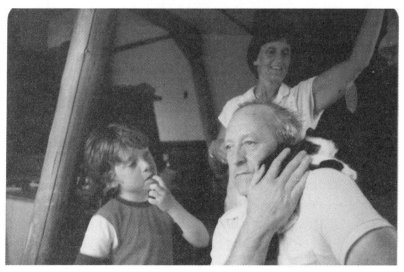

Even the busy John Mitchell needed a break! Here, he takes a quiet moment with a kitten. His wife Jenny is behind him. (Photo courtesy of John Ohler)

Oregon, Humboldt in California, and Ninkasi Ale House in Lyon, France. And there were more.

In between his big projects, Mitchell continued advising and assisting breweries and brewing students up until his death in 2019. For example, he was integral to the launch of Shaftebury Brewing, as Chapter 8 details, and even after the opening of Horseshoe Bay Brewery he continued lobbying for legal and taxation changes for years—changes that benefited the province's beer and wine industry. This was complicated, dull, and often invisible work, but it was critically important to the success of small breweries in BC. And Mitchell also maintained the relationships he built along the way. Peter Hyndman, Mitchell's advocate in government, lost his cabinet position shortly after Mitchell's brewery got up and running. Mitchell sent him a letter of encouragement after that occurred, expressing his sympathy: "I am very sorry to see you go. Although we have not met I feel indebted to you for your constructive and helpful leadership in making our dream a reality…I hope in the future that your creative initiative can continue to help us all." In his response, Hyndman wrote:

I have always been so enthusiastic and proud of the fine work you and your associates have done that your recent letter meant a very great deal to me. Thank you so much for sending along your kind sentiments. The decision to give you the "green light" will rank as one of my favourites; I have quietly been into your Pub from time to time and have been thoroughly impressed by the atmosphere and the product.[29]

Hyndman may have fallen from grace, but he remained gracious to the man who had tenaciously pursued his dream of bringing "Real Ale" to British Columbia. Both Hyndman and Gould were known to visit Troller Pub and imbibe Mitchell's ale, and Mitchell continued to express gratitude for both of them in his later conversations about how his brewery got started.

Years later, in 2009, John Mitchell paid a visit to the original site of the Horseshoe Bay Brewery. In this photo, he is accompanied by Mirella Amato, craft beer consultant and award-winning author. (Photo courtesy of Mirella Amato)

THE AFTERLIFE OF HORSESHOE BAY BREWERY[30]

Once John Mitchell sold his share of Horseshoe Bay Brewery back to his business partners and headed to Victoria to launch Spinnakers, the little cottage brewery seemed to run out of steam as far as press coverage was concerned. Articles praising Mitchell, Appleton, and Horseshoe Bay usually do not extend past 1984—as if the brewery simple faded out of existence.[31] However, this isn't how Horseshoe Bay Brewery ended.

After Mitchell's departure, Wilson and Patrick kept things going for a little while but then the story gets a bit fuzzy. Sneath's *Brewed in Canada* briefly alludes to the brewery's continuation past 1984: "A few years later, the Horseshoe Bay Brewery was reopened at a new location by David Bruce-Thomas who operated the business until it finally closed in 1997." Oddly, the timeline in the book's appendix lists Horseshoe Bay Brewing as closing in 1999, not 1997, when it was acquired by the Coquihalla and Bowen Island Brewing Company. This larger brewing operation bought out both Horseshoe Bay and Whistler Brewing that year, closing Horseshoe Bay but keeping Whistler running and eventually merging it with other breweries.[32]

As will be discussed briefly in Chapter 7 and evident here, Sneath's dates and details are not always consistent, and his summary of Bruce-Thomas's reopening of Horseshoe Bay is sometimes contradicted by Bruce-Thomas's own account. While Sneath's brief description of the brewery's relaunch indicates no relationship between David Bruce-Thomas and John Mitchell, it turns out that Bruce-Thomas had been working closely with Mitchell since the brewery opened, and that both Mitchell and Appleton contributed to its continuance. Horseshoe Bay Brewery had a post-Mitchell afterlife that many beer fans have forgotten about.

While Mitchell and Appleton were busy brewing their first batches of beer, nineteen-year-old Bruce-Thomas was clearing plates and cleaning ashtrays in the Troller Pub, which was just a few minutes' walk across the marina from the brewery. A general errand boy and helper, Bruce-Thomas was sometimes sent over to the brewery to help clean kegs as business started picking up. As he cleaned, he was invited to observe the brewing and even taste the beer. His first taste of cask-conditioned ale was a shock to a young man used to mass-market American lager: It wasn't cold! It wasn't heavily carbonated! Was this even beer? Mitchell and Appleton were quick to educate him. "I remember John and Frank talking about chill haze—the protein gets cold and it clouds up, and when it warms up it gets clear," Bruce-Thomas recalled. "But no one wants to drink warm beer! That was the battle. John didn't want to put it in the fridge, so the first ones were served from right behind the counter." But he learned—and he learned quickly. It started small, with Bruce-Thomas helping monitor the mash. Mitchell would call him over: "Hey, Dave, I'm just mashing in—can you finish it while I deal with this?" Within a year, Mitchell had full trust in Bruce-Thomas and the young apprentice was brewing nearly 50 percent of the brewery's beer while still working as a tow-truck driver. "I didn't know anything," he laughed. "I had no interest in beer; it was a job to me. It was an interesting process, just hanging around and watching it."

However, Bruce-Thomas's disinterest quickly turned to more passionate investment. He soon began debating Mitchell about the type of yeast they should use (Mitchell had the final say, of course, and it remains cloaked in secrecy). He recalls how Mitchell used the German hop variety Tettnanger at the end of the boil (for flavour) in their English-style Bay Ale, although a different hop variety was used at the beginning for bittering. By the time Mitchell had sold off his part of the business and left for Spinnakers, Bruce-Thomas was fully into brewing. Don Wilson and Dave Patrick, Mitchell's former partners, hunted around for a professional brewmaster, but such a person was a rarity back in the mid-1980s. Bruce-Thomas was already right there—and he knew the equipment and the brewing process. The partners kept him on as brewmaster (a title with which he remains uncomfortable since he never received formal training) until they decided to dismantle the brewery altogether. Knowing that

The front window of the newly reopened Horseshoe Bay Brewing Company. (Photo courtesy of David Bruce-Thomas)

David Bruce-Thomas (right) and brewing equipment manufacturer Ed Ripley with the newly recovered equipment in the Horseshoe Bay Brewing Company brewhouse. (Photo courtesy of David Bruce-Thomas)

their lease was up in several years, they wanted to secure as much profit as possible from the pub—and the brewery was eating into that. Around 1986 they shuttered the brewery and towed the equipment to the scrapyard for destruction. And that was that.[33]

Or was it? Once the brewery was shuttered and he was out of a job, Bruce-Thomas walked down to the pub to pick up his severance cheque. After that, he stopped by Dan Sewell's office (of Sewell's Marina) and casually asked whether Patrick and Wilson had secured or put any legal controls on the brewery building itself. They hadn't. On the spot, Bruce-Thomas gave Sewell his $2,000 severance cheque and asked him to hold the building for six months until he could scrape together the funds to lease it. Sewell agreed.

After leaving Sewell's office, Bruce-Thomas visited several local establishments to figure out whether there was a local market for beer. His contacts included Troll's Restaurant (a different establishment from the Troller Pub) and Yaya's Oyster Bar, both of which committed to buying his ale should the brewery reopen. He then figured out how to get the brewing equipment back. After making a convincing business pitch to his mother, Bruce-Thomas managed to scrape together enough money—he believes it was around $6,000—to buy back the brewing equipment from the scrapyard before it was destroyed. He used his own tow truck to haul it back to the Nelson Avenue location. Contrary to the version published in Sneath's book, he did not reopen in a new location—although the brewery *was* relocated several years later.

A few months later, in the spring of 1988, Bruce-Thomas had secured a lease on the building, and the equipment was ready to be reinstalled. He phoned John Mitchell over in Victoria and told him all about it. "Are you interested in helping me put the brewery back together?" Bruce-Thomas asked his former boss. Mitchell was soon back in West Vancouver to help out. The day he arrived, Mitchell asked Bruce-Thomas what the plan was. He responded with a grin: "We're going to open the brewery building and sit in there by the front window and wait for Don and Dave to walk by."

The reopening plans precipitated a conflict. In the belief that Bruce-Thomas shouldn't be able to lease the building or obtain a brewery licence, Wilson and Patrick brought in lawyers. Legally, however, Bruce-Thomas's case held up. He then applied to West Vancouver Council, which approved his desired microbrewery licence—the kind of licence that would allow him to distribute like most craft brewery licences we see today. Horseshoe Bay Brewery was thus resurrected under a slightly different name: Horseshoe Bay Brewing Company, with Bruce-Thomas as both owner and brewer. His first sales went to Troll's Restaurant and Yaya's Oyster Bar, both of which became customers for years. Bruce-Thomas recalls regularly delivering 200 gallons of his special "Yaya's Oyster Ale" to Yaya's, where he had installed a 200-gallon tank. He'd pump a full batch of beer directly from the transport tank, which was mounted in a pickup truck trailer, into the tank at Yaya's, which he would clean himself each time. At Troll's Restaurant, Bruce-Thomas could be found rolling kegs across the floor to where they'd be hooked up to draft lines. The owners of those restaurants—Alex von Kleist and Gary Troll—were always supportive of Bruce-Thomas's aspirations to keep the brewery going.

Bay brew returns

HORSESHOE BAY brewmaster David Bruce-Thomas holds aloft a sample of the test-run ale for his first production brew, which is scheduled to start flowing from Horseshoe Bay restaurant taps April 1. Bruce-Thomas will initially produce custom ales for Ya Ya's Oyster Bar and Troll's Fish and Chip Restaurant from his Horseshoe Bay Brewing Co. Ltd. The brewery, dedicated to brewing British-style ales with no chemical additives, was established by Bruce-Thomas after the Troller Pub's Horseshoe Brewery was closed last September. See story on page 3.

NEWS photo Neil Lucente

Top: David Bruce-Thomas makes headlines in the *North Shore News* with the newly opened Horseshoe Bay Brewing Company. (Photo courtesy of North Shore News)

Bottom: The beer tank Bruce-Thomas made for Yaya's Oyster Bar, one of his first clients. (Photo courtesy of David Bruce-Thomas)

This was encouraging for a young entrepreneur, especially given the financial pressure.

Despite the challenges, Bruce-Thomas certainly had his successes. With his father's help, he developed a consistent brand identity for Horseshoe Bay Brewing's products, creating labels and selling their beer—including Bay Ale, Raspberry Ale, Pale Ale, Nut Brown Ale, and seasonal ales—to restaurants and bars across the Lower Mainland. His father, David Sr., did much of the advertising and graphic design work, while his mother, Josephine, worked in the brewery. John Mitchell and Frank Appleton both stopped by to visit and provide advice. Bruce-Thomas also had a mutually supportive relationship with Tim Wittig and Paul Beaton of the newly opened Shaftebury Brewing, which is where craft beer pioneers like Iain Hill of Strange Fellows first got their start (see Chapters 8 and 9 for more on this).

In addition to supplying beer to the locals, Horseshoe Bay also sold ten pallets of beer to Japan (a one-time deal arranged by David Sr.) and regularly sold beer to Western Family Foods, where it was used in their Caesar's Shandy—a drink that could be sold in grocery stores because it was below 0.5 percent ABV. The cash from these

Bruce-Thomas (right) and a colleague toast at the new brewery. (Photo courtesy of David Bruce-Thomas)

Welcome to Ya Ya's Oyster Bar & Ale House

~ Brewers of Traditional Real Ale ~

Ya Ya's is proud to serve you Traditional Real Ale, brewed especially for our restaurant by the Horseshoe Bay Brewing Company Ltd.

Ya Ya's Oyster Ale is a carefully blended combination of the Best British Barley Malt, Home Grown Western Hops and Fresh Mountain Water from the peaks around you.

Oyster Ale is first gently fermented, then transferred into holding tanks at the brewery. When the time is *just right* the ale is carried to our restaurant by the Horseshoe Bay Brewing Company custom built Ale-Transporter.

After the brew arrives it is carefully conditioned, right here in the restaurant, until it reaches the perfect age and temperature for Traditional Real Ale.

Then - *and only then* - will we allow it to be served ...

CHEERS!

An ad for the special craft beer sold at Yaya's Oyster Bar. (Photo courtesy of David Bruce-Thomas)

ventures helped keep the business going. As the brewery continued pumping out the beer, Bruce-Thomas expanded his workforce, hiring brewers and delivery drivers. Early IPA innovator Bill Herdman brewed at Horseshoe Bay before he established his own brewery, Tall Ship Ales. According to an interview with *What's Brewing*, Herdman felt that he was more invested in Horseshoe Bay Brewing's history than the owners were.[34] However, it's clear that Bruce-Thomas also was deeply attached to the brewery's legacy. It seemed that each man held the brewery in high regard; they simply had different approaches to running it.

When Bruce-Thomas acquired a partner, John Allen, in the early 1990s, he realized that the cost of running Horseshoe Bay was cutting into profits, making the business largely untenable. The sales to Japan and Western Family had kept them financially afloat for a while, but it wasn't enough. Bruce-Thomas's lack of involvement once Allen became the majority investor meant that he had little recollection, when we spoke, of the brewery's later business details, but *What's Brewing* and BCBeer.ca both indicate that Horseshoe Bay stopped bottling in

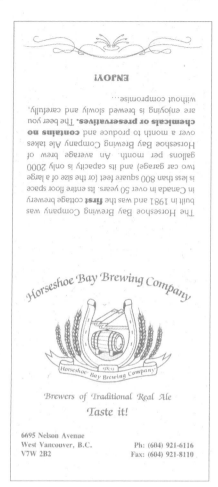

ENJOY!

The Horseshoe Bay Brewing Company was built in 1981 and was the **first** cottage brewery in Canada in over 50 years. Its entire floor space is less than 800 square feet (or the size of a large two car garage) and its capacity is only 2000 gallons per month. An average brew of Horseshoe Bay Brewing Company Ale takes over a month to produce and **contains no chemicals or preservatives**. The beer you are enjoying is brewed slowly and carefully, without compromise...

Horseshoe Bay Brewing Company

Brewers of Traditional Real Ale

Taste it!

6695 Nelson Avenue
West Vancouver, B.C.
V7W 2B2

Ph: (604) 921-6116
Fax: (604) 921-8110

A restaurant table brochure advertising Horseshoe Bay Brewing Company. This was part of Bruce-Thomas's efforts to make a name for his brewery. (Photo courtesy of David Bruce-Thomas)

1995, selling only draft beer after that. Things were going downhill. Bruce-Thomas recalls a day around 1996 when he simply left his key, locked the brewery door, and never returned. Horseshoe Bay Brewing limped along a little while longer under Allen until, according to Sneath's book, it was acquired by the Coquihalla and Bowen Island Brewing Company in 1999 and closed for good shortly after.

Horseshoe Bay Brewing still has a presence in the beer community. Rebecca Kneen and Brian MacIsaac of Crannog Ales managed to obtain Horseshoe Bay's brewing equipment after its closure, and they've used it ever since. Kneen shared with me that John Mitchell visited after they installed the equipment and gifted her his traditional malt sieve, which is used to assess the coarseness of the ground malt before brewing (the way malt is ground can make a big difference in how well the brew goes). In addition, in 2023 David Bruce-Thomas reacquired the rights to the name "Horseshoe Bay Brewing Company" via the BC Business Registry. Who knows—maybe there will be a new Bay Ale in the future?

Left: Rebecca Kneen of Crannog Ales stands beside Mitchell's original brewing equipment, which now has a home in her brewery.

Right: Kneen displays the malt sieve that John Mitchell gave to Crannog Ales.

THE LEGACY OF JOHN MITCHELL AND FRANK APPLETON, POST-HORSESHOE BAY

As the years progressed, Mitchell's and Appleton's influence on the craft beer industry would become even more evident. Mitchell continued to advocate for shifts in governmental policy, lobbying the provincial legislators to rectify the tax inequities experienced by breweries and wineries, even submitting a long report to the government. It was, according to his good friend and business associate John Ohler, a risky move at the time. However, it contributed to important changes that made it possible for smaller breweries to get started. The tax and other financial and legal barriers were nothing to the Big Three, but they prevented independent owners of smaller businesses from entering the market. Mitchell knew this had to change. Ohler is proud of Mitchell's legacy: "Canadians who enjoy craft beer are really indebted to John

Mitchell and the sacrifices he made." However, he adds, "It's important to know why he did what he did. It wasn't about money or commerce, and it wasn't about recognition. It was about entrepreneurial fairness and our ability as a society to have choice."³⁵ Healthy market competition, consumer choice, and quality products: these were priorities for Mitchell, and they've helped to build BC's beer industry.

He became famous among brewery owners, and always recognizable with his lanky frame, traditional flat cap, and ever-present thermometer tucked into his jacket pocket, ready to test beer temperatures. Once when Ohler and Mitchell were in Penticton, they walked past Bad Tattoo Brewing at about nine in the morning and Mitchell's curiosity was piqued. He went up to the side windows and pressed his face against the glass so he could see into the darkened interior. He just wanted a glimpse of whatever brewing equipment they were using. One of the owners saw this shifty fellow trying to spy on his establishment and yelled out, "Hey! What are you doing?" However, when

he approached the two men he realized that he was in the presence of *the* John Mitchell. He literally bowed down on the sidewalk in a humorous but sincere gesture of admiration for the beer pioneer, and brought him

John Mitchell in 2009, posing by a door at Spinnakers that he had constructed himself. According to Paul Hadfield, this door was Mitchell's custom construction, designed to allow access to the grain loft, which was located above the brewhouse. The measurements were specifically formulated to accommodate the pallets of grain. (Photo courtesy of Mirella Amato) inside for a private tour. That night, Joe Wiebe (author of *Craft Beer Revolution* and content manager of the BC Ale Trail) was giving a talk on the history of BC craft beer, and Ohler and Mitchell were in the audience. As they listened to Wiebe's talk, Mitchell chuckled to Ohler, "I really did start something, didn't I?"[36]

Mitchell spent years consulting for other breweries, including Shaftebury and Howe Sound, but he also followed his colleague Frank Appleton in becoming a teacher in the field, passing on his brewing knowledge to others. Iain Hill, founder of Strange Fellows Brewing and pupil of both Appleton and Mitchell back in the early '90s, recalls Mitchell as being "a real sweetheart."[37] In his later years, Mitchell would give guest lectures to students of Kwantlen Polytechnic University's Brewing and Brewery Operations Diploma, a program designed by former long-time Labatt brewer and executive Nancy More. He would emphasize the important things about quality beer: cask conditioning, the right temperature (not too cold!), mash time, and using whole hops rather than pellets. According to KPU students as well as Ohler, Mitchell had little patience for "cheating" on a good brew. Serving beer at anything higher than four degrees? Don't do it! Taking too long with a mash-in? You're wasting time! Using some CO_2 pressure to get beer into the line even if you're also using a cask? Nope! Pelletized hops? Not nearly as good as the whole cone! He was well known—and well loved—for these strong opinions, even if brewers couldn't always follow them to the letter. Mitchell would wander through a brewery with his thermometer in his pocket, checking details and making sure things were being done right. "He liked doing things the old-fashioned way," according to Ohler. Sierra Nevada Pale Ale remained his favourite beer for his whole life—a testament to Mitchell's love of simplicity and tradition. In his later years, he was thrilled to see the number of BC breweries skyrocket and to taste the quality of their beer. "Here's to BC craft beer," Mitchell said in a farewell toast to the brewing industry when he realized his health was failing. "Jolly good luck to the lot of you, and I hope you'll have a howling success. Cheers!" He passed away just a few months later.[38]

Kristy Isaak, professional brewer and former KPU brewing student, has warm recollections of Mitchell speaking to her and her KPU cohort. He began his talk by insisting on standing on his own, despite his family pressuring him to sit down. He shared how things used to be—how incredibly difficult it was to get government support in the early '80s, and the challenges posed by all the bureaucratic red tape. But brewing beer correctly was something he was passionate about, and he wanted students to show that passion as well. Isaak recalls him saying, "There seems to be a notion out there that making craft beer is an easy labour of love—and it's not." He wanted to make sure the new generation of brewers weren't starry-eyed fantasists, but instead left the program well educated about the history of craft beer in BC and the reality of what goes into making quality beer. "He left quite an impression!" Isaak laughs. One moment that stood out for the students was when Mitchell held up Frank Appleton's book, *Brewing Revolution,* and asked, "Who's read this?" His copy was dog-eared and full of Post-it notes. At least 70 percent of his audience, a group containing the nerdiest of the beer nerds, shot their hands eagerly into the air. "Load of crap, all of it," Mitchell responded, then put the book down and said no more about it.

Frank Appleton had his own legacy in the BC craft beer industry—and the craft beer industry in the United States as well. I've listed just some of the breweries and brewpubs he helped to establish, but he did more than order equipment and install brewing systems. His attitude toward brewing touched everything he did and affected everyone he worked with. Sean Hoyne, a long-time friend and protege of Appleton, emphasizes that his mentor deeply believed in the science of brewing and had great respect for each step in the process. To rush through any stage for the sake of expediency or to cut corners on ingredients was anathema to him. Appleton's high standards for the scientific elements of brewing were what stuck with Hoyne when he set up his own brewery. Hoyne Brewing has a comprehensive laboratory and three lab technicians to ensure their beer meets Hoyne's standards—standards he developed from working with Frank Appleton. He recalls first meeting

Appleton in 1989, when he (Hoyne) was a homebrewer applying for a brewing position at Buckerfield's Brewery in Victoria, which is connected to Swan's Brewpub. When he walked in for his interview, he brought his resumé and a six-pack of his homebrewed beers. After a brief greeting, Appleton nodded at the six-pack: "What do you have there?" Hoyne was incredibly nervous to show this master brewer his beer, he recalls. But he got past his fear and Appleton popped the first bottle as they began the interview. After a few questions and a few sips, Appleton looked at the bottle, looked at Hoyne, and said, "This beer's quite good! Did you bring along a recipe for these?" Hoyne pulled out his recipes and watched in apprehension as Appleton perused them. "Well, let's try another one!" he finally said.

Appleton and Hoyne ended up going through the whole six-pack during that interview, and the conversation meandered from beer and brewing to literature. It turns out both shared a love of Shakespeare, but differed in their opinions on James Joyce: "I don't know how many books I have just on *Ulysses* itself," laughs Hoyne. "It's too many. But I got to talking about *Ulysses* and Frank's eyes started glazing over." Appleton had other literary passions. Warmed from several home-brews and some passionate discussion about poetry and literary value, Appleton asked Hoyne to wait while he rushed up to his room to get a book. He brought down a volume by Don Marquis called *Archy and Mehitabel*, a collection of oddball poems originally published in the 1920s. With great pleasure and dramatic flair, Appleton read several of the poems aloud. Hoyne was so caught by the strange, silly poems that later on he tracked down his own copy of the book (and he still has it). After hearing Hoyne's story, I came across this volume at a used bookstore in London and had to add it to my collection. In reflecting on Appleton's love of unusual poetry, Hoyne emphasized that Appleton's scientific mind didn't prevent him from enjoying the creative, the strange, or the satirical. He spent his retirement years writing an opera about Francis Rattenbury (the architect who designed the BC Parliament Buildings and was later murdered with a mallet) and playing in a garage rock band.[39]

Appleton, as Hoyne and others are quick to acknowledge, sometimes rubbed people the wrong way. He said exactly what he meant and wasn't particularly concerned with sugar-coating hard truths or cloaking them in diplomacy. John Mitchell could also be very straightforward, but his style was still quite different from Appleton's. And anyone who knew them is aware that Mitchell's relationship to Appleton was a complicated one. They lived together and worked together, yet their personalities were wildly divergent. Appleton was, in Mitchell's words, a pot-smoking hippie,[40] and Mitchell was a proper English gentleman. Mitchell was often frustrated that he and Appleton were seen as business partners in opening Horseshoe Bay, when in fact he had hired Appleton for his brewing knowledge. It was Mitchell who was the business owner and the one who had managed to slash through the legal and policy red tape. For his part, Appleton often disregarded public perception and simply did what he enjoyed—which was making beer of the highest quality he could. As the years passed, Mitchell's and Appleton's paths crossed periodically—they would sometimes work on the same brewery together—but the friendship was somewhat strained through time and distance. However, judging from the accounts of those who knew and loved them, they never lost respect for one another.

One particular story illustrates this point. Shortly before Mitchell's passing in 2019, John Ohler and John Mitchell took a road trip around

BC to visit different breweries and see the sights. They happened to be passing near Appleton's house in the Kootenays, and Mitchell wanted to extend a gesture of friendship—an instinct very typical of him throughout his life. He decided to buy Appleton a cake. In the past, Mitchell did a great deal of free labour at Appleton's house, and he always arrived

John Mitchell and Frank Appleton at the Great Canadian Beer Festival in 2009. (Photo courtesy of Mirella Amato)

with a cake in hand. So they picked up a cake and went to see Frank. Unfortunately, he wasn't there. They sat waiting for a little while, and finally decided just to leave the cake on the doorstep. Appleton would know who had left it.[41]

Mitchell knew he owed a lot to Appleton, and Appleton knew he owed a lot to Mitchell. They may have clashed over the years, but they had, underneath it all, a deep affection and respect for one another. The BC craft beer industry has paid tribute to both of them by brewing beers in their name: Appleton's Finest British Ale by Hoyne Brewing, and the John Mitchell Signature Cascadian Dark Ale brewed in collaboration with Russell Brewing and the students of KPU's brewing program. The Mitchell beer was a special 2022 release, with funds going toward a brewing school scholarship in Mitchell's name, while the Appleton ale is one of Hoyne's core lineup and offered year-round. Hoyne points out that the label art, which is styled like a medieval manuscript page, was designed to honour his and Appleton's shared love of literature, as discovered in that first interview back in 1989. These two men—the hippie and the gentleman—did more for BC beer than many craft brewery patrons will ever know.

I don't know whether Appleton contacted Mitchell after finding that cake when he arrived home, but it seems he still had warm feelings about his old friend. Mitchell passed away in 2019, shortly after that trip, and a celebration of his life was held in Vancouver. Appleton was invited but sent his regrets; he was quite ill himself and unable to travel the 600 kilometres to attend. He did, however, send a note for inclusion in the memorial: "John was my great friend for over 30 years. His passing was a sad day for me. He was the man with the idea... Really a wonderful person, the best 'front man' the craft beer movement needed at just the right time. I will miss him."[42]

Opposite top: John Mitchell's long-time friend John Ohler and Mitchell's widow Jenny pose with some John Mitchell memorabilia. (Photo courtesy of John Ohler)

Opposite bottom right: The Cascadian Dark Ale made by Russell Brewing and the KPU brewing program in honour of John Mitchell. (Photo courtesy of Brian K. Smith)

Opposite bottom left: Hoyne Brewing's Appleton's Finest British Ale, a tribute to Frank Appleton. (Photo courtesy of Sean Hoyne)

A TRUE
FIRST

Two years later, John Mitchell changed the brewing industry forever when he opened Spinnakers, the first brew pub in North America.

CHAPTER 7
GRANVILLE ISLAND BREWING AND THE BUSINESS OF BC BEER

Granville Island is currently one of the top tourist destinations in Vancouver and you're lucky if you can snag a parking spot there on a Saturday. Its colourful mix of artisan shops, restaurants, and play areas is a far cry from what these spaces looked like in the early 1970s, however. Back then, Granville Island was a dark, unappealing industrial area that was "little more than a collection of corrugated tin shacks, surrounded on all sides by increasingly decrepit sawmills."[1] Its transformation into the community hub it is today owes much to the two ambitious businessmen who established one of BC's most influential microbreweries in the heart of this area: Granville Island Brewing.

In the early '70s, friends Mitch Taylor and Bill Harvey quit their reliable jobs in banking and oil to join forces in pursuing their entrepreneurial passions. Recognizing the untapped potential of Granville Island and False Creek, they established a marina along with space for retail businesses that, with the support of the Canada Mortgage and Housing Corporation, ultimately boosted the area's overall revitalization. However, soon the two partners were itching to start a business that was truly their own, moving beyond renovating buildings and renting space. Both men had read Frank Appleton's *Harrowsmith* article and were inspired. Maybe a small brewery was the way into the Vancouver market! The idea was on paper by 1980—but it wasn't until 1984, two years after Mitchell's Horseshoe Bay Brewery opened, that Granville Island Brewing welcomed its first customers. While Horseshoe Bay was the first business to make and sell craft beer in Canada, however, Granville Island was one of the first in BC that could brew beer *and* distribute it outside of a single location.[2] It was a watershed moment for the craft brewing industry. But let's go back in time a bit.

DREAMING OF POSSIBILITIES

Mitch Taylor grew up in a poor farming community in Manitoba. He recalls being only seven years old when he was sent on a train, accompanied by his older brother, 400 miles away from his parents to live with a foster family that could offer him schooling and work. Through a hard-scrabble childhood supported by a kind foster family, he built resilience and tenacity that prepared him for the challenges of entrepreneurship.[3]

Taylor had a successful career during the 1960s and 1970s with Imperial Oil, working his way up the corporate ladder in the company's Vancouver, Toronto, and Kamloops locations. A life in Vancouver gradually became his ambition; after his wife Anne got a full-time job teaching English at a Vancouver high school, they decided to make their permanent home there (even if that meant some commuting for Taylor). Working for the oil company was starting to pale in comparison with the possibilities offered by owning his own business. His good friend Bill Harvey was in a similar situation. He had a solid job with Royal Bank, but his true passion was in entrepreneurship. After months of research and many conversations, Harvey and Taylor settled on a plan for success in Vancouver: build a new marina, with all the amenities, in False Creek.[4] At the time, False Creek was "incredibly forlorn," according to Taylor. "It smelled like a cesspool and looked like one too."[5] It was neglected and unappealing—which made it more affordable. However, if the marina plan looked like it wouldn't work out, they had a Plan B: developing a real estate hub on nearby Granville Island, which was then owned by the chemical company Monsanto. Like False Creek, Granville Island was also a bit of an eyesore around 1970. No one was going there. And no one wanted to.

Well, it turned out that both Plan A and Plan B were possible—so why choose? Harvey and Taylor had a plan for success. This was not pie-in-the-sky dreaming: numbers were crunched, research was done, governments and organizations were lobbied. "I'm a businessman and I approach things from a yellow spreadsheet perspective: what I need, what I've got, what I need to acquire," said Taylor, recalling those early days.[6] Marathon Realty approved their proposal for False Creek Marina west of the Cambie Street bridge, an area that consisted of "mudflats, railway, and industrial detritus" that would be transformed into "a new-built 25,000 square foot building complete housing a major restaurant, several boat dealers, a boat repair shop, a ship's chandlery shop, and a coffee shop" as well as the marina itself.[7] At the same time, they purchased from Monsanto four buildings making up 40,000 square feet of retail space on Granville Island. Today, that much space on Granville Island would cost a small fortune, but the area's state of dilapidation and neglect back in the early '70s meant that they could buy those 40,000 square feet for what now seems like pocket change: $18,000. In those four buildings, they planned a large restaurant space facing the water, plus office and shop spaces for about twenty to thirty tenants.

In 1973, after getting funding in place and completing renovation of all four buildings, Taylor and Harvey proudly opened Creekhouse Industries on Granville Island. The Creekhouse restaurant, located in a former brewing and distilling facility, was the main attraction at this point. Owner and chef Costas Syskakis served up whole suckling pigs and other unusual fare to entice customers to what had been a dark and unappealing area of town. Syskakis didn't end up running

Mitch Taylor (left) and Bill Harvey outside their offices at Creekhouse Industries. (Photo courtesy of Mitchell Taylor)

the restaurant for long, but the opening made a bit of a splash in the newspapers, partly for the unusual food and partly for the strange location. It was really "off the beaten track," according to one reporter. Another wondered whether the Creekhouse's success might be compromised by the remote setting: "Now, if somebody could only figure out a way to get people into the area—some signs pointing the way would help."[8]

This state of affairs didn't last for long. As anchor tenants were established and smaller spaces rented out, Granville Island became a destination for tourists and locals alike. The land itself was owned by the National Harbours Board, which hadn't done much of anything with it, but shortly after Creekhouse opened, land ownership was transferred to the Canada Mortgage and Housing Corporation. The CMHC quickly poured money into the area, transforming it "into a combination urban park, artist colony, and upscale public market offering fresh produce year round."[9] With improved infrastructure on all levels, designed by DIALOG architecture Granville Island quickly became "a people place."[10] By the early 1980s, an estimated six million people were visiting annually. However, Taylor and Harvey didn't have their own business there yet. They were co-owners of the retail spaces and rented them out to entrepreneurs who wanted to set up shops and restaurants on the island, but they had no passion project of their own—and they wanted one.

Like John and Jenny Mitchell, Mitch Taylor and his wife Anne travelled to Germany in the late '70s and early '80s. As they visited beer gardens, pubs, and breweries, trying the beer and the food, they realized that this was what Vancouver was really missing: good beer. A brewery had always been in the back of Taylor's mind, since both he and Harvey were beer fans and one of their renovated buildings had once been a brewery, but now it was something that seemed like a real possibility. They already had property on the island, and they knew people liked going there. "Why not build something there, take advantage of the fact that people are already coming there?" Taylor recalls of the decision he and Harvey made. Frank Appleton's *Harrowsmith* article, which had inspired John Mitchell's creation of Horseshoe Bay Brewery, reinforced their instincts. By 1980 they had decided a brewery was their next project.

"UNPRECEDENTED": PLANNING BC'S FIRST MICROBREWERY

First, the partners needed to convince the Granville Island Trust that this was a good idea. Moreover, they needed money. Taylor managed to fund part of the business with his own capital, but they brought in others, in the form of limited partnership shares. Taylor and Harvey also did their market research. Microbreweries—as craft breweries were then known—were still unprecedented in Canada, but they had a strong presence elsewhere. The two partners visited countless microbreweries in the United States, Europe, and South America, travelling across the globe to taste beer and view production facilities.[11] Taylor also consulted with his friends in the industry, including Paul Shipman of Redhook Ales and Fritz Maytag of Anchor Steam Brewing in California. He even stayed at Maytag's home and visited Anchor Steam in person to see how the brewery was set up. They received advice on beer production and packaging from Coors when they were down in Colorado. The Big Three did know how to make and market beer, so why not use that knowledge?

When Horseshoe Bay Brewery opened in 1982, Harvey visited to check out the brewery and the beer, even though he and Taylor were going to be attempting something different:

We wanted to move beyond the service-oriented brewpub model—kegs brewed for in-house consumption in a single establishment—to build a substantial product company: a craft brewery that barrelled and bottled beer, built a brand, distributed a premium product to numerous bars and restaurants, and established a retail presence both on-site and in government liquor stores.[12]

While Horseshoe Bay was the first to produce and sell craft beer in Canada, it could only sell its ale via the Troller Pub. Granville Island Brewing would be producing beer and distributing it around the province. Both breweries were "firsts" in their own way. "I do want to acknowledge and give kudos to John Mitchell with his Horseshoe Bay Brewing who started the CAMRA [Campaign for Real Ale] movement here in Canada selling real ale at their Troller Pub. They were the first," Taylor affirmed in a 2014 speech he gave for Granville Island Brewing's thirtieth anniversary. In a discussion with me, he reiterated this point: "John deserves that credit. And he was a real beer guy—I'm more of a business guy. In so much of craft brewing afterwards the passion for beer drove how the businesses operated. I did it the other way around: the passion for business drove the beer model."[13]

The legality of their endeavour was another hurdle that the partners had to clear before they could really get to work on their new project—something else they had in common with John Mitchell. At the time, provincial and federal liquor laws were "draconian," in Taylor's view. No liquor sales on Sunday, unless you were serving in a restaurant with food. You could have a brewery, but you couldn't sell on the premises. You couldn't serve beer unless you had a pub, and you couldn't serve beer without food. This was why Mitchell's Horseshoe Bay Brewery had to be located on a separate property from the pub, but could only be sold in the pub. "We had a beautiful premises on Granville Island," Taylor recalls. "We needed to sell our beer there. That was our only hope of getting our foot in the marketplace. We didn't want to have just draft beer, just a pub. We wanted bottles, merchandising, marketing. We wanted to build a brand we could sell." The government was initially supportive of a brewery licence for their facility on Granville Island, but insisted that they follow all the laws currently in place. This would make business untenable for a small brewery.[14]

Using his political contacts in Victoria, Taylor decided to be the squeaky wheel in search of some grease. He made visits and phone calls to various bureaucrats and politicians. While he doesn't have written records of these interactions, he remembers that many legislators were persuaded to pursue changes to the liquor licensing system because Expo 86 was looming on the horizon. The stringent liquor legislation made it difficult to import good beer, to make and serve microbrew beer, and to purchase liquor seven days a week—and all of these issues would make Canada look like a backwater compared with European countries. Taylor made sure that provincial and federal politicians knew about the risk of ignoring these issues. "You guys are gonna look really silly when the chancellor of Germany comes here for Expo and wants a beer on Sunday but can't get it," he insisted to them.[15]

Taylor's lobbying was successful. The laws that had previously forced BC breweries to sell their beer only through a government-licensed liquor store or restaurant were amended to allow a new category of brewing licence: the microbrewery. This was different from Horseshoe Bay Brewing, which was licensed as a brewpub. They also acquired a retail licence that permitted liquor sales in their retail store seven days a week—a huge coup for them at the time, when no other BC stores were permitted to sell liquor on Sundays.[16] Taylor also lobbied politicians at the federal level in order to get the federal Excise Tax Act amended to allow the brewery to sell on site without the ridiculous runaround required by the existing tax laws. Because the law required tax to be collected after the beer was made but before it was sold, the beer could not be sold in the same place it was produced (the idea was that there must be a time-out for tax calculation and collection between production and sale). This law meant that Granville Island Brewing staff would have to "take the beer out of the back door of the brewery, go around to the front on a public street or road and then return the goods to the store."[17] Ridiculous. Taylor recalls that "our first set of drawings could not have a door from the brewery to the retail store to keep the brewer from cheating [on the excise calculation]...I think that rule went back to Prohibition days when the moonshine guy might just harm the tax man if he came snooping around his private property trying to collect taxes, so the tax man collected it at the gate."[18] Fortunately, Taylor's connections to the federal Liberal Party helped the wheels of bureaucracy move, and an amendment to the excise tax was passed by a vote in Parliament, which Taylor watched on TV with pride.

He had lobbied Prime Minister John Turner directly to get that public road requirement axed so Granville Island Brewing could have a proper retail store on site.[19]

A final element that Taylor and Harvey needed to consider before finding a brewmaster and launching their business was what their beer would look like. Well, not the beer itself, but its presentation. At that time, the Big Three breweries (what Taylor calls "Ubiquitous Beer") sold their product in dark brown stubby bottles, and these breweries monopolized access to that packaging. Taylor and Harvey wanted something different for their beer—something that would immediately distinguish their product

A Budweiser stubby-style bottle and the new Granville Island style pictured on the opposite page (Photo by @benoitb, iStock).

GRANVILLE ISLAND BREWING
VANCOUVER, CANADA

(Photo courtesy of Mitchell Taylor)

from that of the Big Three. They decided on "elegant long necked bottles" that would be "sold with both a marketing flair and a concerted effort to educate and convert consumers."[20] This bottle style is commonplace now, but back then it was a different story. Harvey and Taylor based their bottle prototype, which they had specially created for the brewery, on retro bottles from the 1950s that were modernized for a new era. Granville Island Brewing partner Larry Sherwood saw the bottle style and label as another consumer draw (and later craft breweries know this very well): "And if they don't drink beer themselves, the package is attractive enough to take home…as a souvenir," he said. A reporter at the time described the label as "eye-catching," "with a vivid, jagged gold, blue and green logo…The tall, slender-necked brown bottles, reminiscent of the 1950s, have a bright, busy label [that] shows the brewery's cream and green building on the island, set against a stylized Vancouver skyline."[21]

Granville Island Brewing's beer would need to be priced higher, Taylor and Harvey realized, not just because of ingredients and a smaller-scale production, but because of that premium packaging. On average, GIB beer would cost 30 percent more than Budweiser or Molson, but its pricing would reflect its higher value to an increasingly discerning consumer. Analyses of Granville Island Brewing's strategy by students and faculty at UBC's Faculty of Commerce indicate that the premium pricing model worked in the brewery's favour; these analyses showed that beer consumers are very brand loyal and their behaviour is generally not affected by price increases. GIB's early strategy of appealing to a "discerning taste market" solidified their brand's place in the provincial beer market, and their appeal spread to a wider consumer base in the following years.[22]

PAIRING THE BREWMASTER WITH THE BUSINESSMEN

After the logistical and legal foundations were in place, Taylor and Harvey were ready to begin building the business itself—which meant making key decisions about beer and brewing. Taylor knew that he wasn't a "beer guy" in the model of John Mitchell, who was an enthusiastic CAMRA advocate, or Frank Appleton, with his world-renowned brewing expertise. He wasn't foolish enough to pretend to a skill he didn't have, or to hire an amateur, particularly when he had so much money invested. "We knew we had to be different and we wanted to be very high quality," said Taylor. "We knew that we had only one chance to convince our public that they should pay a 30% premium for our beer."[23] With his business acumen, he evaluated what the Vancouver market needed and how to meet that need. The first question was: What kind of beer should his new brewery produce? He and Harvey knew that Horseshoe Bay was selling ale (an English style of beer), likely because the CAMRA movement had drawn more attention to ale as beer aficionados rejected the dull lagers the Big Three were making. However, Taylor figured that also meant that there was a gap in the market for high-quality European lager—the kind of lager he and Anne had enjoyed in their travels to Germany. And if he wanted to make one that was distinct from Molson, Labatt, and Carling O'Keefe's offerings, he needed to do something different from what they were doing. The first step was building a brewing facility in which good lager could be made (it's a bit more complicated than ale brewing). Taylor's friend Robert McKecknie, a UBC professor of engineering, helped on that end. The brewhouse was constructed in England with equipment from Germany and then shipped to Vancouver for installation. The next step—equally important—was finding the right brewmaster.

Taylor may not have been the "beer guy" but he wasn't going to let just anyone into his brewery to make his beer. After placing ads in several German beer publications, he assembled a candidate list and flew to Germany to interview them. With a promise of a work visa and a full-time job as brewmaster, Rainer Kallahne joined the Granville Island team. Kallahne, a brewer certified by the Berlin Institute of Technology, was previously brewmaster for Koepf Brewery in Aalen, Bavaria. Before accepting the job, he thought carefully about what it required and what he could do for this start-up North American brewery. While Kallahne was still in Germany, Taylor sent him water samples from Vancouver so he could test them in his lab and determine what quality of beer he could make with it. "The water was soft, soft, soft, perfect for brewing beer!" Kallahne had exclaimed.[24] When he arrived in Vancouver, he was ready to show the New World some Old World beer. In setting up his office, he rejected the sleek modern furniture the company had purchased, and instead used a very old and worn wooden desk and chair that had been in his family for generations and that he'd shipped all the way from Germany. He'd also brought with him an old German ceramic beer dispenser. This

was soon put to use serving samples of beer to customers in the retail store.

Kallahne definitely had his opinions about what worked and what didn't, and he was committed to tradition—particularly brewing tradition. He was a passionate adherent of the *Reinheitsgebot*, the Bavarian beer purity law of 1516. Granville Island Brewing adopted the *Reinheitsgebot* as a core principle of its operation, but Taylor did

Kallahne's German beer dispenser, used in the brewery shop to serve samples to customers. (Photo courtesy of Mitchell Taylor)

Left: Certification from Germany proving that Granville Island's lager adheres to the standards of the 1516 German purity law. (Photo courtesy of Mitchell Taylor)

Right: Mitch Taylor and his brewmaster Rainer Kallahne drinking beer together in Germany. (Photo courtesy of Mitchell Taylor)

find Kallahne's stubborn adherence to traditional brewing practices frustrating at times. One example was Kallahne's refusal to use carbon dioxide from an external source (instead they recaptured the CO_2 produced during the brewing process, per German tradition). Taylor didn't understand how it made a difference to the consumer's experience of tasting the lager, and tried to persuade the brewer to cut that corner in the name of expediency. However, Kallahne stuck to his standards and Taylor accepted it.

Taylor's respect for his brewmaster's authority highlighted an important difference between the culture of the "Big Three" and the culture of the newly emerging microbreweries in 1980s Vancouver. In his *Harrowsmith* piece, Frank Appleton had lamented that the modern day brewmaster—someone who should be a creator, an innovator—had become a paper-pushing accountant, just ticking boxes. This attitude toward the brewmaster's role was evident even in smaller breweries when a corporate owner wielded control. One example was Whistler Brewing, established in 1988 by Gerry Hieter, a man passionate about beer. While trying to launch his business, Hieter found himself and his four partners—a group that included a brewer and a brewer's accountant—running short on funds and in danger of having to give up on their brewery dreams. "We were hopeless; we couldn't raise the money," he told me.[25] A financial saviour came in the form of Rob Mingay, a businessman and investor who called up Hieter when he heard about the business. He promised to fund the brewery, and Hieter sold him the name for one dollar. With that funding, however, also came Mingay's authority over the business. Several newspaper accounts from the time, as well as Sneath's book *Brewed in Canada*, erroneously claim that Whistler Brewing was Mingay's brainchild and that Mingay wrote the business plan and started it up, but in reality it was Gerry Hieter who did that (incorrectly named "Jenny Hieter" in Sneath's timeline of breweries, but not included in Sneath's actual account of Whistler Brewing's history).[26] Mingay did end up taking the position of president and assuming full control over the brewery, however, and making decisions that pushed Hieter out. Mingay insisted that they should not hire a brewer who was certified by one of the brewing schools or technical institutes. Instead, he wanted someone with just a bit of brewing experience who would simply follow instructions—right down to where to go in the brewhouse and the order of a brew day. No creativity, no room to experiment with brews or perfect a recipe. Mingay simply wanted the head brewer to press the correct buttons in the correct order and make the beer the exact same way each time. It wasn't in the spirit of craft brewing as Hieter knew it, and it wasn't what Mitch Taylor was looking for when he hired Rainer Kallahne.

Taylor's respect for Kallahne's expertise shaped the brewery's business structure, management plans, and public presentation. GIB's earliest organizational chart, dated to January 1984, shows the general manager and the brewmaster as equivalent authorities in the company structure, with only the board of directors above them.[27] The job descriptions clearly show the brewery's priorities. The GM's job was to "make available to the general public a truly outstanding beer and at the same time run a harmonious and efficient plant producing maximum profits for its owners over a long time frame." However, for Taylor and Harvey, profit was linked to quality. The business plan further specifies that "the GM jointly with the brewmaster must seek to attain the highest possible standards for a non-pasteurized Bavarian-style beer brewed from traditional natural ingredients. There shall be no compromises for quality." The brewmaster's authority in the company structure was one protection they used for quality assurance:

> The <u>brewmaster</u> is responsible for the production and quality of the beer. He has the final say in all matters relating to quality (see item 3) and has the unique ability to report directly to the board of directors to ensure that this objective must never be compromised.

Taylor recalls one or two uncomfortable situations in which staff members challenged Kallahne's authority in the brewery and Taylor supported Kallahne. Even today, he insists that choosing a good brewmaster was one of the most important decisions he made, and one that contributed to Granville Island Brewing's success.

STARTING OUT

On June 9, 1984, the Granville Island Brewing retail store opened its doors to the public. Kallahne had been brewing for several months, and cases of bottled Island Lager—the brewery's first product—were stacked up in the store. Four-packs and eight-packs, a size chosen to stand out in a beer market of six-packs and dozens, lined the shelves. Beer was on tap at the front, ready to be served to customers in sample sizes (since, legally, the brewery couldn't sell beer to drink on site other than as samples). As soon as the doors opened, people crowded in, eager to see what this new "microbrewery" thing was all about. Taylor and Harvey had invited friends and family, members of the press, business associates, and representatives from local restaurants and pubs, but there were many others who showed up

202

Top: Mitch Taylor and Bill Harvey prepare to light a cannon for the brewery's opening-day celebrations. (Photo courtesy of Mitchell Taylor)

Bottom: The brewery's retail shop being prepared shortly before opening. (Photo courtesy of Mitchell Taylor)

Mitch Taylor's 1936 Ford, used as the brewery's delivery truck. (Photo courtesy of Mitchell Taylor)

just to see what was going on. There were so many people that they actually had to close down the street outside in order to accommodate the crowd. A small cannon was placed out on the roadway and Taylor and Harvey set it off with a bang when it was time to begin the speeches. Taylor's treasured 1936 Ford pickup, which became the brewery's famous delivery truck, was out front as well. Taylor recalls the feeling of that day: "the crush of the well fueled crowds, the noise and the euphoria of everyone involved."[28] They ended up selling 265 cases of Island Lager out the front door of their store on opening day, and an additional 50 cases to businesses around Granville Island.

Granville Island Brewing was a very small operation when they first opened, as many newspapers pointed out. One writer praised the brewery for providing a "new and eminently civilized variety in the ordinary man's drink," but emphasized that Granville Island Brewing was "not a name to set Canada's Big Three suds moguls shaking in their corporate shoes."[29] There were about six to eight staff members (including the brewmaster and general manager) and six partners. Seven licensed outlets on Granville Island itself were the first places to commit to selling their beer in 1984—hard to believe,

Mitch Taylor making a sale at the newly opened brewery store. (Photo courtesy of Mitchell Taylor)

since Granville Island beer was in five hundred restaurants and one hundred liquor stores by 1987! However, it didn't take long for the brewery to become big news in the city. In July 1984 they nearly ran out of beer, and in August they did—within eleven days. Island Lager was an immediate hit in Vancouver. Kallahne had developed the recipe carefully, using Canadian malt and German hops, and ensured that the beer met the standards of the *Reinheitsgebot,* the Bavarian purity law of 1516. According to one reviewer, "it has more flavor than the pop beers, a touch of sharpness that the fans of imported beers will appreciate, more hops and other good things that make you think less of huge stainless steel vats and chemical additives and more of the old brewmaster's art."[30] Another writer reported that drinkers "thought [Island Lager] was more bitter than North American beer, and fresher, fuller, more aromatic," and yet another rated it as high as Mitchell's Bay Ale and said it was "one of the nicest bottled beers around—anywhere . . . it's dark with a full, bitter flavour.[31] It even earned the praise of Bill Herdman, another early beer pioneer whose Tall Ship Ales pushed beer style boundaries in the '90s. He remembers his first taste of Granville Island Lager: "That beer was amazing. It was a shocking beer." Their pilsner, he recalls, "had an intense bitterness, and a full body; it was a real sandwich of a beer."[32] Gary Lohin, another craft beer giant from the '90s, remembers that pilsner as having a level of bitterness that the general public wasn't used to.[33] In a conversation during March 2023, Gerry Hieter told me that Granville Island's original lager was the best lager ever produced in British Columbia. High praise, indeed, coming from someone with long experience in the industry. Granville Island Brewing introduced European tastes to Vancouver.

With the popularity of Island Lager, seven licensees on Granville Island quickly became nine, and within a year the beer-oriented restaurant Fogg N' Suds had put Island Lager on tap. Taylor was good friends with the owners, Gerry Kierans and Paul Carino, who opened Fogg N' Suds the same year as the brewery. Kierans and Carino made a name for their establishment by turning it into an early prototype of later craft beer taphouses and brewpubs like Yaletown Brewing, St. Augustine's, or the Alibi Room. Fogg N' Suds offered up to 160 different beers in its tap rotations, which was an extraordinary variety for the time. In fact, it claimed to have the largest selection of beers in Canada and became the place to drink for those who liked import or other unusual beers. Indeed, Fogg N' Suds was so trendy in the mid-'80s that it epitomized the newly defined "yuppie" consumer culture. One insert column in a *Province* article about Kitsilano gave readers a humorous list of ways to spot a yuppie in 1985 Vancouver:

If you want to know what's trendy in Vancouver these days, just ask anyone from Kitsilano—or anyone who looks like they are.

- *Kits residents know that mousse is not a dessert but a hair-styling potion.*
- *They drive BMWs.*
- *They drink imported beer, usually American, at the Fogg N' Suds.*

The list, which continues on, is clearly meant to be entertaining, but it gives us a glimpse into how cutting-edge "fancy" beer was at the time. Shaftebury Brewing, when it opened in 1987, embraced the yuppie label: "We're a downtown beer," according to co-founder Paul Beaton, "a yuppie beer."[34] When Granville Island Brewing managed to get a tap at Fogg N' Suds, they boosted their own visibility and they began to take their place at the forefront of a new cultural movement. And like Shaftebury, they embraced it. "A big part of our market is younger people," said Bill Harvey at the time. "We're trendy!"[35]

Granville Island Brewing's first few years of business were an exciting time for the brewery owners—and for Vancouver beer fans. Taylor knew most of the big restaurants in the city, and he owned one himself (Ondine's in the False Creek Marina). He and his sales staff would be out making contacts and socializing on a regular basis over lunches and dinners in Vancouver's best places. Getting Granville Island beer on taps at restaurants required some charm and some convincing—and Taylor taught his staff how to do both. If faced with a "Nope, not interested!" when knocking on the door of a restaurant or pub with their pitch for Island Lager, the sales reps would invite the establishment's staff to come down to the tasting room and try the beer. In fact, GIB ended up hosting numerous informal parties this way. Getting the staff who actually served beer to come to the brewery was an effective way to convince them that Island Lager would sell. They would drink the beer, chat with the brewmaster, learn about pouring techniques and proper glassware, and learn the difference between a traditional German lager and a mass-produced

Brewmaster Rainer Kallahne cleans up after a brew day. (Photo courtesy of Mitchell Taylor)

North American lager. It was education—but education that generated enthusiasm. These educational tasting events became even more relevant when GIB began producing additional styles, such as Island Lite (a low-ABV lager to compete with the likes of Bud Light), Granville Island Bock, Granville Island Marzen, and Lord Granville Pale Ale. Most Canadian consumers weren't familiar with these beers, something that could work either for or against the brewery. GIB turned it into an opportunity to educate and expand their consumer base—to bring more drinkers into the world of microbreweries.

Taylor also developed strong relationships with his staff and with the local community in these first few years. Friday nights became an informal time of socializing at the brewery, even though back in those days there was no tasting room and they couldn't sell beer to drink on site (although they *could* give samples). Taylor's wife Anne would often stop by, drinking water because she was allergic to hops but nevertheless enjoying a catch-up with the brewery team. Taylor also opened the brewery to the Vancouver Porsche club. A German-focused group, the Porsche Club was attracted to Granville Island Brewing's focus on traditional German-style brewing and they were happy to support the fledgling business. Taylor would open the back of the building for the club's meetings. Sometimes there were over one hundred people there, he recalls, with Porsches parked all around and in the entrance of the brewhouse. In thanks, the club gave Taylor a one-day race-driving course. Participants could use their own car if they wished. Taylor chose to use his Mercedes, and had a great day on the track, putting 180 miles on his vehicle in just a few hours and wrecking his brakes. He called Anne on his way home, telling her everything about his race day on his brand-new car phone. "It took up half the trunk," he chuckled while remembering the day.[36]

STRUGGLING TO SUCCEED

Despite the brewery's popularity, it faced huge financial challenges in those early years. Some of these were directly due to the Big Three macro breweries throwing up roadblocks that would hinder the progress of the tiny upstart. For example, to make their unique packaging—those retro-style bottles—fiscally viable, Granville Island Brewing had to collect all its empties from its retailers, wash them, and reuse them. Taylor recalls how Molson, Labatt, and Carling O'Keefe would have their contractors collect *all* the empties from restaurants and pubs, but then would crush Granville Island's because they were a different style and not useful to them (and because they knew that this would put the new microbrewery at further disadvantage). There was also the case of Molson sales reps who were spreading rumours that Granville Island's beer had off-flavours and would make people sick. Rather than trying to convince all his licensees that these reps were lying, Taylor went straight to the source. He recalls bringing some of his beer to Molson's headquarters and asking them to test it.

He also said the rumours needed to stop, or he would be taking legal action. They tested it, found it to be perfectly fine, and agreed to back off. In fact, Molson would later do regular quality testing for Granville Island Brewing in their own lab, since the microbrewery was limited in its space and resources.[37] Taylor turned an antagonistic moment into an opportunity. Little did he know that eventually Molson would end up owning the microbrewery that it had tried to destroy.

The money challenges went deeper than these spiteful sabotage attempts by the Big Three. However, that wasn't obvious from the outside. From its opening day, Granville Island Brewing was incredibly popular with Vancouverites. Brewery tours were given every hour, and they'd sell all the beer they made. All evidence seemed to indicate that Taylor and Harvey should be rolling in cash. Microbrewery sales in general were steadily increasing across the province, and Granville Island Brewing's own sales were nearly doubling by the year: 2,500 hectolitres (hL) sold in 1984, 4,500 in 1985, and 8,000 in 1986. Between 1984 and 1986 they invested more money in order to expand capacity to 6,500 hL, but they were still not able to match the huge consumer demand for their product. In 1987 their goal was to expand incrementally, according to demand, up to a maximum capacity of approximately 28,000 hL—a huge jump from their original size, but still a limit.[38] Neither Taylor nor Harvey was interested in turning GIB into a huge brewery. "I believe there is an optimum size for a small brewery," Harvey proclaimed in 1985, "and I believe that when Granville Island Brewery has reached that optimum size we have to stop. Otherwise this thing will self-destruct. If it starts to grow into a big brewery it will destroy itself."[39] Similarly, Taylor wanted to run a small company—not become a cog in the wheel of a huge corporate machine that would ignore his original objective of producing high-quality traditional German lagers for Vancouver's beer drinkers.[40]

Despite its impressive sales numbers, the microbrewery was losing money. In its first year of operation, it lost $670,000.[41] The capital required to start up a brewery was significant, and making that money back would take time. Indeed, it wasn't until the first quarter of 1988 that the brewery made its first profits: $5,995. It doesn't seem like much, but it was a big jump from the first quarter of 1987, in which they *lost* $22,884. "We're a perfect example of how difficult it is," Taylor told the *Vancouver Sun* in July 1989. "Well-run, well-financed with superior marketing thrust, selling everything we make, and still we're having trouble making money." In 1985, a year after opening, GIB began contract brewing for Pasadena Brewing in California—the first international contract brewing agreement between the US and Canada.[42] By 1986, they were exporting their lager for sale down in California. Every step was taken to increase the available funds, with the exception of cutting corners on the brewing side. These tough early years were why Taylor had plans from the very beginning to take the brewery public and acquire funds via investment. His strategy in 1985 was to "ask the limited partners [of GIB] to approve a reverse takeover plan in which Quantum Energy Corp., a shell company listed on the VSE [Vancouver Stock Exchange], 'takes over' the limited partnership. The limited partners would end up with control of the company, which would then be used as a vehicle to raise funds." The idea was that the corporation would acquire other companies connected to the distribution or manufacturing of its beer.[43] As soon as news spread that this was happening, Quantum's shares jumped 400 percent.[44] By the middle of 1985, Granville Island Brewing was a publicly traded company.

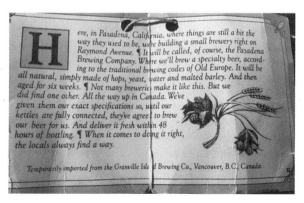

ere, in Pasadena, California, where things are still a bit the way they used to be, we're building a small brewery right on Raymond Avenue. It will be called, of course, the Pasadena Brewing Company. Where we'll brew a specialty beer, according to the traditional brewing codes of Old Europe. It will be all natural, simply made of hops, yeast, water and malted barley. And then aged for six weeks. Not many breweries make it like this. But we did find one other. All the way up in Canada. We've given them our exact specifications so, until our kettles are fully connected, they've agreed to brew our beer for us. And deliver it fresh within 48 hours of bottling. When it comes to doing it right, the locals always find a way.

Temporarily imported from the Granville Island Brewing Co., Vancouver, B.C., Canada.

A label from Pasadena Brewing Co., for which GIB was contract brewing for a short period of time. (Photo courtesy of Mitchell Taylor)

But this wasn't enough to make the brewery turn a profit. While Quantum's shares went up, when the company became GIB on the VSE, traders began to short it, forcing Taylor to buy his own stock back in order to shore it up. The price went from $2.40 a share to $0.20. It was a rough go; "I was naive," Taylor admitted.[45] Even with its first profitable quarter in 1988, Taylor knew that something needed to change if the business was going to make it. In his memoir, he considers why this successful brewery wasn't making money:

> *There were two big problems I had not been able to overcome. Problem one was that our volume was constrained by the six week aging cycle of the lager beer. The obvious solution was to expand the storage or aging capacity. That required more capital investment. Initially raising money had been easy because it was such a novel idea [. . .] In reality, raising even the second round [of investment] was difficult, because investors now wanted to see a profitable financial statement before putting in additional capital.*[46]

There are some parallels between the position in which Granville Island Brewing found itself in 1988 and the situation of Chicago's Goose Island Beer Company back in 2010. Like GIB, Goose Island had become very popular, selling all their beer and trail-blazing new paths in the growing craft beer industry. But Goose Island's success was also potentially its downfall, according to writer Josh Noel: "Times were good at Goose Island. They couldn't make enough beer! But they were also dire. *They couldn't make enough beer.*" The little family-run brewery simply didn't have the capital to produce beer at the rate their licensees demanded. They were losing taps and rushing through batches, which resulted in production errors. These, in turn, resulted in beer that needed to be dumped, and restaurants and bars dropping their Goose Island taps. "We have to do something," brewery founder John Hall told his management team at the time. And in 2011 they discovered what that something was: selling Goose Island to Anheuser-Busch, the corporate beer behemoth that produced Budweiser. The brewery was

Granville Island Brewing had a solid customer base that loved their beer, but the business still struggled to be profitable. Here, customers are trying beer after a tour of the brewery. (Photo courtesy of Mitchell Taylor)

publicly castigated for "selling out" but in reality, they had few options if they wanted to remain financially viable.[47]

Back in the 1980s, Taylor may have felt a bit like John Hall did in the 2010s. He was in charge of a popular and thriving brewery, hardly able to keep up with demand, but making very little profit. The Quantum reverse takeover hadn't generated the funding required, so he was still hamstrung by the challenges of making lager production profitable. Without profit, they couldn't get more investment, but without more investment, they couldn't make a profit. As Frank Appleton put it, "GIB's problems stemmed from its great success."[48] They were in a Catch-22. A potential deal with Australian Corporate Holdings in 1987, a takeover that would have funded the brewery but brought it under a different corporate umbrella, fell through at the last minute when Taylor realized his potential Australian business partners weren't being honest. The company claimed to have a profitable brewery and winery in Australia, an assertion confirmed by an engineering report from SNC-Lavalin, which the Vancouver Stock Exchange accepted as proof that the company's assets were legitimate. Things were positioned for the Aussies' $1 million investment in GIB. However, Taylor had some nagging doubts—and his wife Anne and two daughters expressed their apprehensions even more clearly: "They thought [the Australian partners] were flimflammers," Taylor recalls.[49] A trip to Australia to see the brewery and winery in person proved them right: the supposedly profitable brewing business was in fact "a jumble of tanks and pipes that could only with great imagination have been the parts of a brewery…Game over."[50]

The deal that finally worked for Taylor was a sale to International Potter Distilling in 1989. The company already owned Calona Wines and Pacific Western Brewery, and was therefore well equipped to continue the work of brewing Granville Island beer at their facility in the Okanagan. "They had two things I wanted," Taylor said in an early interview. "Expansion capital and a distribution network…They looked like a company that was going somewhere."[51] A share exchange agreement was completed, and Mitch Taylor went from being the primary shareholder of GIB to a 10 percent shareholder of Potter's, where he became vice-president of sales and marketing. The bigger umbrella company that owned GIB, Potter's, and Calona Wines would soon become Cascadia Brands, headed by Ian Tostenson. In his new position, Taylor was now a smaller part of a much bigger company. His statement to the press at the time suggested a sunny outlook about the takeover: "The association with Potter's gives us access to capital and other resources that will enable us to rapidly and profitably develop the company," he told *The Province* in March 1989, shortly before the deal was completed. And indeed, it seemed that this takeover was the only way to make the brewery financially viable. But behind the scenes, Taylor wasn't feeling quite so positive. Under the authority of a much larger company, he was no longer the sole decision maker. More importantly, to his mind, the brewing wasn't happening on site under the direction of his German brewmaster. Beer production was controlled by the brewer at Pacific Western instead. "This was the slippery slope of the commercialization of Granville Island Brewing," Taylor recalls.[52] In a magazine interview shortly after the sale, he admitted how quickly he regretted his decision: "I thought it was the best decision at the time, but I certainly wouldn't do it again."[53]

With the sale to Potter's, the atmosphere at GIB changed. Some of their original employees left, including their brewmaster, Rainer Kallahne, and several salespeople. Unionized truckers took over delivery, reducing delivery frequency (no more evenings and weekends) and causing some restaurants to cancel their Granville Island Brewing accounts. "Service went to hell," Taylor lamented. Most of the brewing and all of the bottling was eventually moved to the Kelowna facilities and the final product began to taste more like Molson or Budweiser, according to Taylor. He was increasingly unhappy in his decreased role: "I lost control of operations at Granville Island Brewery and could not do anything but look on in dismay as the integrity of the beer declined... I was not a very happy guy and the same could be said for many of our original partners and employees. Our sparkle had dimmed and I had lost my passion."[54] The president of Potter's at the time, Ian Tostenson, acknowledged that Taylor's complaints were accurate; the new Granville Island Brewing was nowhere close to Taylor's original vision. In his interview with me, Taylor enthused about the excitement of working in craft beer in those early days—the wheeling and dealing with government, the growing public investment in good beer, the community that quickly developed. "I wish I could have stayed in the brewing business," he admitted. "It's an exciting industry. The 185 breweries currently in the Lower Mainland show that this was a good idea!"

The sale to Potter's was the beginning of GIB's slide from "craft" to "craft-ish" to "not really craft anymore." In 1992, Molson brewer Mark Simpson was hired as Granville Island's new brewmaster. With the changes in structure and practice, Mitch Taylor eventually parted ways with Granville Island Brewing. By 1994-1995, Taylor was back in the marina business full-time and Granville Island Brewing, Potter's, and Calona Wines were all under the newly formed Cascadia Brands headed by Tostenson. Within a decade, Cascadia became a subsidiary of the wine conglomerate Andrew Peller Ltd. There were layers upon layers of corporate ownership—very different from Taylor's early vision of a small (micro, craft) brewery. The definition of "craft" has always been somewhat fraught, as this book's introduction explains. The Canadian Craft Brewers Association specifies that a brewery claiming to be craft cannot have a large alcohol company as a majority shareholder—in other words, it must be independent. However, GIB was still considered a craft brewery at this time, despite its assimilation under larger corporate overlords (perhaps because there was no Canadian Craft Brewers Association yet). By 1997, GIB held 35 percent of the BC microbrew market and was itching for more. At this time, Tostenson proudly announced the company's rebranding of its core lineup to reflect various Vancouver landmarks, reinforcing that Granville Island was indeed local and community-oriented— that it wasn't "Big Beer." Island Bock became Brockton Black Lager, named after Stanley Park's Brockton Oval. Granville Island Light became Kitsilano Light. Anniversary Amber Ale became Gastown Amber Ale.[55] Two new beers were released as well: a blonde ale and a honey lager, the latter of which would become one of the brewery's top-selling core brands. Tostenson also splashed out on a $2 million renovation of the brewery and its premises, "including designer clothing racks with shirts, caps, and the like attesting to their wearers' expertise in regional beer drinking."[56] Granville Island Brewing was still the microbrewery to beat and still seen as local.

A second rebranding in 2002, after new brewmaster Vern Lambourne was hired and Mark Simpson left for new pursuits, was designed to reach a slightly older demographic, drinkers who wanted a more mature, cultivated drink. Up-and-coming craft breweries like Storm, Shaftebury, Tree, and Russell, along with brewpubs like Sailor Hagar's and Yaletown (discussed in Chapter 9), had "reposition[ed] [Granville Island Brewing] as the staid old brand," according to GIB's marketing manager, John Trotter. They were no longer trendy, the way they were in the '80s. However, they chose to embrace their "senior" status rather than try to play with the young bucks.[57] Adman Bill Downie described what the brewery's new tag line, "Tastefully evolved," meant:

> *The campaign is an insight into the male psyche. Guys go through different stages in their beer life. You drink beer for chuggability... but you get to a point in your beer life when you actually want to taste what you are drinking. "Tastefully evolved" talks to how much you've evolved as a person.*[58]

Advertisements that ran in the *Vancouver Sun* illustrate the new angle. In two examples, a Granville Island Brewing bottle cap is pictured on the left and the face of a male Vancouver bartender is on the right, facing the viewer. A scrolling sentence connects the two images: "Since my resume made it to a second page" and "Since making rent didn't involve returning empties." "Tastefully evolved" is in small font at the bottom. The idea is that Granville Island beer is for men who have grown up.

The flattening of BC beer sales in the early 2000s, combined with the novelty and appeal of the newer breweries, prompted the redesign, which focused on "local faces" (the bartenders in the ads) and a new, mature stage of adulthood. Of course, this rebranding did not "evolve" far enough to include women in its target demographic. The whole campaign was, according to Downie, about the male psyche—not unusual for breweries at the time, but nonetheless painfully indicative of how far the brewing industry still had to go.

In late 2009, newspapers announced that Molson Coors was going to purchase Granville Island Brewing via its subsidiary, Ontario's Creemore Springs Brewing. Creemore Springs had opened in Ontario in 1987 and was sold to Molson Coors in 2005. Molson's planned purchase of GIB seemed unexpected after the interview given by Granville's sales and marketing director at the brewery's twenty-fifth anniversary celebration just a few short months before.

217

Walter Cosman, in the spring of 2009, proudly reasserted Granville Island Brewing's independent status, despite their ownership by a large winery, and stated that "the secret to surviving in a world of large corporate brewers is to avoid trying to emulate them."[59] The subsequent Molson sale announcement seemed to suggest that the brewery's attitude had changed from "Be as different as you can" to "If you can't beat 'em, join 'em." In early 2010, as the sales agreement was being worked out, the BC Craft Brewers Guild asked Granville Island Brewing to withdraw their guild membership. Barry Benson, guild executive and owner of R&B Brewing, explained that they weren't exactly kicking Granville Island out—more like inviting them to depart voluntarily: "I wouldn't say 'gave them the boot.' But they didn't fit in any more. We had a dialogue."[60]

Despite its sale to Molson Coors and its departure from the BC Craft Brewers Guild, Granville Island Brewing was, for years afterwards, still treated like a craft brewery. It sponsored local events and participated in local craft beer festivals and competitions. Gerry Hieter, who co-founded the Great Canadian Beer Festival and helped run it from its beginnings in 1993 up until 2018, recalls that Granville Island Brewing was always welcome at the festival, even when it wasn't technically a craft brewery. The brewery's long-time, consistent support of such local events had earned Hieter's loyalty. "Regardless of how much grief I got, I allowed them to participate," he says.[61] However, Granville Island Brewing's continued success in the 2010s, even with the Molson Coors sale, was also partially due to its brewmaster, Vern Lambourne, who took over at the original GIB location after Mark Simpson's departure in 2001. Lambourne realized he had a passion for beer while on a working holiday in the UK, during which he learned to brew small-batch ales at three different brewpubs. Back home in Canada, he got a job at Steamworks, one of BC's most successful brewpubs, and then helped open Big River Brewpub in Richmond. When he was hired at Granville Island in 2001, he came in with a craft beer mindset. While the big batches were brewed in Kelowna, Lambourne kept making unique small-batch beers at the Granville Island location. Beer tastings, dinner pairings, and competition brews were all on the menu. Some have attributed the GIB brand's survival post-Molson to the decision to keep that original brewhouse on the island,[62] but credit must also be given to Lambourne for maintaining high standards for Granville Island's small batches and special releases, standards that kept the brewery from becoming completely swallowed up in corporate mediocrity. And when Lambourne opened Parkside Brewery in 2016, he showed what he could do when not constrained by layers of corporate ownership. His last brew at Granville Island, before leaving for Parkside, was a small batch of an old style, the classic brown ale: Brass Knuckles American Brown Ale.

The gap Lambourne left after his departure in 2015 was filled by another craft brewer, Kevin Emms. Emms came to GIB from Deep Cove Brewers and Distillers and Coal Harbour Brewing, both of which were new start-ups when he brewed there. Like Lambourne, Emms had a small-batch, independent brewing background that was an asset to Granville Island. In 2015, five years into Molson Coors ownership, Granville Island Brewing's beers hadn't slid into what Taylor called the "Ubiquitous Beer" model; instead, they occupied "a middle ground between [Molson] Canadian and [Labatt] Blue at one end of the scale and hardcore craft double IPAs at the other."[63] Emms continued what Lambourne had started, maintaining a lineup of unique, small-batch local beers at the original Granville Island brewhouse. He's currently the brewmaster at the newest craft brewery in Surrey—WayBack Brewing, a small and nostalgic brewery that produces classic styles.

Granville Island's most recent rebranding happened in 2022, under a new head brewer (Robert Hagey) and in the aftermath of the pandemic. The global agency BrandOpus designed the rebrand with an eye to returning Granville Island Brewing to its local roots:

At Granville Island, adventure is never too far away, and this is embodied in the new identity with an illustrated depiction of the brewery on one side, and the experiences around the corner, on the other. The identity flexes across the range to allow the personality and attitude of each brew to come through. Each name and illustration is inspired by a well-known area throughout B.C., areas that locals know and love. From Kitsilano Juicy IPA to False Creek Peach Sour, each place as unique as the beer style it inspired.[64]

This was the strategy GIB used very early on, so it has proven its worth. With the rebranding, the brewery is even returning to selling their original beer: Island Lager.

Granville Island Brewing today is not the same craft brewery that Mitch Taylor and Bill Harvey launched in 1984 with their German brewmaster and just six employees. However, it has been an important trailblazer for Vancouver craft breweries. Craft beer pioneer Gerry Hieter has praised the work of GIB and Mitch Taylor: "Mitch advanced the cause of every craft brewery of the time with his lengthy negotiations with the BC Liquor Distribution Branch."[65] I know I'm not alone in having fond memories of some Granville Island Brewing standbys from years ago, like the Cypress Honey Lager or the Lions Winter Ale. To this day, the brewery remains active in the community and popular at liquor stores. As I draft this chapter, I plan to attend an upcoming drag brunch at their tasting room. So even if you don't care for Granville Island Brewing beers now, I encourage you to raise your pint (or your flight) to them next time you visit your favourite craft brewery. They did a lot to get the Vancouver craft beer scene to where it is today.[66]

CHAPTER 8
MICROBREW REVOLUTION: STRUGGLES, SUCCESSES, AND SHAFTEBURY BREWING

In the mid-1980s, four young men were struggling to make a living in Vancouver's West Point Grey neighbourhood. All were living in very temporary accommodations (a car, an illegal laneway house, the homes of family or friends) and all were working at Trimble's Cafe, a small mom-and-pop restaurant around Trimble and West 10th that eventually became Earl's Place. Tim Wittig, Paul Beaton, Richard Jaffray, and Scott Morison became fast friends as they spent long hours waiting tables at Trimble's, then Earl's Place; however, while they were surviving on servers' wages, they were dreaming about far bigger possibilities for their lives. And all of them managed to make those dreams a reality, which in turn changed the face of Vancouver's food and drink scene. Scott and Richard started the Cactus Club. Later, Scott founded Browns Socialhouse. And Tim and Paul joined forces to establish Shaftebury Brewing, a beloved Vancouver microbrewery and the only 1980s microbrewery start-up, aside from Granville Island Brewing, that achieved long-term success.

Shaftebury Brewing is no longer a Vancouver craft brewery; it was sold in 1999 to Sleeman, and then in 2014 to Fireweed Brewing Corporation of Kelowna (Fireweed also owns Tree Brewing). However, it is still remembered fondly by long-time local beer drinkers, many of whom saw Shaftebury as their introduction to craft beer. Those who played the oddball niche sport of Ultimate Frisbee in early 1990s Vancouver, for example, recall bringing bottles of Shaftebury or Granville Island beer to practices rather than Molson or Budweiser. Like Ultimate, craft beer was proudly resistant to the mainstream.[1] Shaftebury Brewing, which was located close to where Parallel 49 Brewing is now, and around the corner from the nineteenth-century Columbia Brewing, was an important early contributor to the growth of Vancouver's unique craft beer culture.

VANCOUVER'S BEERVOLUTION: THE FORGOTTEN START-UPS

Vancouver in the mid-'80s was an exciting place to be: Expo 86 had raised the city's profile to new heights, built out its infrastructure, and turned it into a prime west coast tourism destination. Its rapid growth in population and popularity coincided with the expansion of the craft beer industry up and down the Pacific coast. Pioneering American craft breweries like Anchor Steam, Sierra Nevada, New Albion, Redhook, Deschutes, and others were revealing as well as creating a hidden demographic of passionate beer drinkers—people who wanted to support high-quality, local beer over the mass-produced industrial lager. One province over, Big Rock Brewery had opened in Calgary in 1985, and to the west, on Vancouver Island, Spinnakers Brewpub and Island Pacific Brewing were making waves.

In Vancouver, Granville Island and Horseshoe Bay Brewing Company were piquing consumer interest, as was the introduction of what would eventually be called taprooms, such as Fogg N' Suds (discussed in Chapter 7). A spokesman for the local chapter of the Campaign for Real Ale, Chris Sagris, proudly told *The Province* in 1985: "People are starting to ask to see a beer list rather than a wine list when they go out now." Craft beer seemed a market ripe for harvest in Vancouver and the Lower Mainland. Unfortunately, brewing was still a tough industry, and most of the craft breweries that emerged in the greater Vancouver region during this decade are no longer remembered. Among these early start-ups, it was only Shaftebury that had a lasting effect on Vancouver craft beer. However, Shaftebury's forgotten fellows, regardless of their short stints on the scene, reveal the new enthusiasm for craft beer that was swiftly developing in Vancouver and its surrounding municipalities. Before I tell Shaftebury's story, these early breweries deserve acknowledgement.

Mountain Ale Co.—Surrey

Inspired by Horseshoe Bay Brewing and his own experience drinking real ale back in England, British expat realtor Charlie Spruce partnered with Ralph Berezan to launch Mountain Ale Co., the second microbrewery in BC back in 1983. Spruce was passionate about beer and excited about the possibilities of making his own, especially after he saw what John Mitchell had done with Horseshoe Bay. However, neither Spruce nor Berezan was a brewer, so they brought Frank Appleton on board to set them up at their chosen location in north Surrey, not far from where Bear Creek Park is now. Their brewmaster, Roger Thirkell, was trained by Appleton and supplied with his recipes. "I left the brewing to someone who knew what they were doing!" Berezan laughs, remembering those early days.[2]

Sadly, however, Spruce passed away from cancer mere months before the brewery's doors opened. His wife Joanne stepped in, and she and Berezan ended up running Mountain Ale together, sometimes with the help of Berezan's brother Leo. In 1983, they launched Mountain Premium Ale and Mountain Malt—"a light-coloured ale and a dark-coloured ale," as Berezan recalls it. Saturday mornings they would open at 11:00 AM and immediately start pouring pints for local homebrewers who would stop by. In fact, homebrewers were a major part of their customer base. It was Surrey in the 1980s—there wasn't the same kind of interest in craft beer that was starting to emerge in Vancouver. Most bars and restaurants were hesitant to give up a Molson or Labatt's tap for a Mountain Ale tap, but sometimes

Frank Appleton joins Mountain Ale Co. owners at Ponderosa Pub to toast the brewery's opening. (Photo of *The Columbian* newspaper clipping provided by Ralph Berezan)

the pubs supporting English soccer teams would be willing to put Mountain Ale on draft. To pitch their product outside the Lower Mainland, Berezan recruited his friend Marty Peacock, who owned a small airplane. They would load up his plane with kegs and bring them to pubs in Victoria and Kamloops, hoping for some regular customers.

They quickly ran into trouble trying to make brewing profitable. Hoping to sell bottled beer, Berezan purchased a bottling machine that did more harm than good. He remembers that one night, the machine started breaking every third bottle (he called his brother over to watch the chaos). In addition, the taxes on breweries in the early 1980s were so prohibitive that they acquired an export licence and began selling their ale in Washington and Oregon, delivered by Leo. They had the homebrewers coming to taste the beer, but they couldn't sell it at the brewery, and it was proving hard to sell elsewhere in BC.

Lower Mainland drinkers just didn't seem interested enough in Mountain Ale to keep it going. The first pub to serve their beer was North Delta's Ponderosa Pub, whose expat Brit customers flocked to try the new beer on its opening day—August 24, 1983. They sold three kegs in three hours, charging $2.30 per pint (sixty cents more than what John Mitchell was charging for his Bay Ale the year before). However, the pub's owner, Gordon Cartright, was hedging his bets;

he said he'd "wait to see if the ale's popularity holds."[3] He was right to be cautious, since there were mixed reviews of the beer's quality. *Province* reporter Bob Chamberlain, in announcing the brewery's opening, favourably compared their brown ale (either Mountain Malt or Mountain Ale) to Newcastle Brown Ale, an English classic.[4] However, a couple of years later beer reviewer Damian Inwood wrote, "This nut-brown ale is not for me," in an article for *The Province*. "My notes describe it as 'black swill, like watery Guinness with an odd, burnt taste. Like a strange dark medicine.'" The Mountain Premium Ale was better, but still didn't impress him that much: "[Mountain Premium] is much more acceptable to my taste buds. It's light brown, cloudy, and a little thin, but has a nice flavor. A vast improvement over its darker brother."[5] Tim Vandergrift, formerly of Fraser Mills Fermentation and now of Canadian Craft Tours, recalls beer-filled nights at a Coquitlam bar where "Make mine a Mountain!" (one of Mountain Ale's slogans[6]) was a common refrain. He also remembers that the beer wasn't always the best, although whether the problem was poor draft lines or rushed production is a question to be answered. Regardless, "it had a mighty salient effect on digestion!" according to Vandergrift.

In 1984 and 1985, Berezan and Spruce were running newspaper ads seeking an "active partner with capital for expansion" to help fund the brewery, since the provincial taxes shouldered by small breweries were destroying them: "It costs about double for breweries like ours to produce our product than it does for the major companies like Molson," Berezan said.[7] However, they eventually realized they needed to, in Berezan's words, "stop the bleeding." They just weren't profitable. An Alberta company expressed interest in putting in an offer, although with the caveat that they did not negotiate without a bottle of whisky. Leo Berezan went out to obtain the required whisky, and over a few drams they sold the brewery for $350,000. Berezan eventually established the Berezan Hospitality Group, which remains a successful and active company to this day, managing a popular chain of private liquor stores.[8]

Steveston Brewing—Richmond

When Frank and Helen Malek moved to Richmond from Cairo in 1969, they hadn't initially planned to open a brewery. They were running a combination grocery store, deli, and beer bottle depot in Steveston until a brewery rep suggested that they use their facilities to brew beer. In an interview with *Equity Magazine* in 1988, Frank Malek recalls that the process to set up the business was quick; he asked for an application form in 1985 and by 1986 he was approved to set up a brewery. While it was commonly referred to as Steveston Brewing Company, the actual company listed on the stock market was Canadian Heritage, a publicly owned brewing company. Malek made four beers—pilsner, ale, lager, and light beer—and brewed with malt extract rather than whole grain. This drew critique from Malek's fellow brewery owners, including Shaftebury, whose draft business plan refers to Steveston's products: "Since they forgo the traditional brewing process in order to use concentrates imported from Scotland, the lager and ale they produce are of inferior quality."[9] Mitch Taylor of Granville Island Brewing remembers Malek as "a nice guy" but also indicates that brewing with extract "was considered a second-class way to make beer at the time."[10] Frank Appleton insisted that malt extract is no substitute for whole grain in brewing: "No extract beer I've ever met tasted exactly like the ground-malt mash original. This is because of the excessive heat treatment the wort endures in evaporating it to a syrup. It changes the biochemical makeup of the wort, the flavour dynamic."[11] Regardless of criticism from fellow beer industry folks, Malek stood by his choice.

At its busiest, Malek's brewery bottled about 1,500 cases of beer a week; 80 percent went to government liquor stores, and 20 percent was sold at the retail store attached to his plant. His primary seller was Steveston Heritage, an unpasteurized pilsner. Despite the odd brewing set-up (more bottling plant than traditional brewery) and lack of whole grain production, Malek emphasized what he saw as the benefits of his product: beer that undergoes triple filtration and has no additives or chemicals. "We've taken British-type beer and suited it to Canadian tastes. And smoothness is the key," he stated.[12] The use of malt extract over whole grain was still decried by beer purists, but Malek stuck to his position. However, despite best intentions, by 1989 the brewery was in receivership and owed the Royal Bank of Canada approximately $200,000.[13]

Bryant Brewery—Maple Ridge

Bryant Brewery opened in 1983 in Maple Ridge with just two full-time employees, one of whom was Drew Simpson. The brewery made a lager (with Hallertau hops, to give it a slightly different flavour profile from Canadian lagers) and an ale, both of which were on tap at about six pubs in the Lower Mainland. Bryant's Bullfrog Bitter, however, received public praise from beer critic Damian Inwood, with the caveat that it came second to John Mitchell's ESB.[14]

However, like Mountain Ale Co., Bryant couldn't maintain a local customer base and ended up exporting some of its product to Washington. By 1984 it had been acquired by Minstral Resources through a share swap agreement, and in 1986 the Bryant Brewery's brewing equipment was sold in a distress auction.

The Survivor: Shaftebury Brewing

Of the small-scale start-up breweries that emerged in the 1980s, Shaftebury Brewing was the only one that survived long-term (with the exception of Granville Island Brewing, discussed in the previous chapter, which was organized and established more carefully than many breweries at the time). Shaftebury wasn't launched by an experienced entrepreneur, nor was its beer brewed by a certified brewmaster from Germany. Shaftebury was very much a grassroots operation, which presented its own challenges and charms. Tim Wittig and Paul Beaton were university kids working as waiters when they brainstormed their brewery idea, yet somehow they made it a Vancouver icon. It even earned praise from the legendary Frank Appleton, who called Shaftebury "one of the early successes in the microbrewery scene of Vancouver."[15]

From working as a server with his three friends and living in an illegal laneway house to running the successful mortgage lender Capital Direct, Tim Wittig has been smart and ambitious in his career moves—big or small. He's not averse to hard work, and it showed in his ability to turn Shaftebury Brewing into a success when breweries around him were failing. He did so by partnering with Paul Beaton, a man who is now apparently elusive to all. Wittig hasn't been in touch with him for years, and last heard that he had moved to the US Virgin Islands. However, Wittig was happy to meet with me and chat about his brewing days. A compact, energetic man, he greeted me with a friendly smile, showed me around his office, and shared with me some of his story over lunch.[16]

Wittig doesn't consider himself a beer expert—but he's always enjoyed beer. He recalls his years growing up in Kitchener-Waterloo, when he would sneak cheap beer from his dad. "I grew up stealing my dad's [Carling] Black Label in the stubbies. We'd take two to three bottles out of his case of twenty-four, so he wouldn't notice." Wittig was not the first in the family to enter the beer industry; his father

Left: Tim Wittig and the author at his Capital Direct office in 2022.

Right: Tim Wittig at his office in 2022. (Photos by Noëlle Phillips)

had worked for Blue Top Brewery in Kitchener in the 1930s, helping to deliver beer and ice to households. He recalls that his father's specific job was to use big pincers to move ice from the truck and into the houses receiving the beer delivery.

Wittig continued his enjoyment of beer when he moved to Vancouver for university in the early '80s, following his brother's relocation there. He took a joint honours in history and political science, but he wasn't really serious about his studies. "We kind of majored in beer drinking," he admits with a laugh. "But I was drinking the slop—the industrial brew." When he began looking for work in Vancouver, his brother took him out onto the back porch of his home on West 8th and pointed across the laneway at Trimble's restaurant. "That's where you want to get a job," he told him. Wittig took his advice, and soon met the other young men introduced in this chapter's opening: Paul Beaton, Richard Jaffray, and Scott Morison. When Jaffray and Morison paired up to open their own restaurant (efforts that would eventually result in the Cactus Club), Beaton and Wittig were inspired. They had become roommates after renovating Wittig's brother's laneway garage into a livable home space, so they had plenty of time together to brainstorm and figure out how they could stop being servers and start being entrepreneurs.

It was 1985 by then, and Expo 86 was just around the corner. They wanted something off the ground before the world came to Vancouver's doorstep. The first thing they considered was a whitewater rafting company in Boston Bar—an idea that they eventually dismissed as too dangerous. They kept spitballing but nothing felt right. One day, however, inspiration struck. While Beaton was working across the alley at the restaurant, Wittig was at home in their tiny garage house watching a TV show about Seattle's Pyramid Brewery. "It was just two guys and honestly, they looked like hippies," Wittig remembers. "They had a small brewery that was set up in the hills." Later that day he insisted to Beaton that they should go down and visit the brewery and talk to the owners. So they did. It was a six-hour road trip, and Wittig recalls being surprised by the low quality of the business. "It was a joke," he says. "They only had one beer—this cloudy wheat beer—and they were selling everything they made! They had sixty accounts between Seattle and Portland." The bar was so low for breweries and the demand so high, at least in that area, that even what appeared to the roommates to be a subpar business was succeeding. "We thought breweries had to be a monster! Labatt's, Molson," Wittig says. "We had no idea someone could actually start a brewery that small. We were completely floored."

Their discovery of craft breweries spurred more research, and their introduction to the man who had started the BC craft beer craze. "The more we researched, the more we realized that a critical thing had occurred," says Wittig. "John Mitchell had taken his business plan to the guys in Victoria to start the first brewpub." Wittig and Beaton traced Mitchell's path to brewing success, from the bureaucratic hurdles he'd cleared to open Horseshoe Bay to his success with Spinnakers. "That's when we came along and met him," enthuses Wittig. "We figured that micros were allowed now. There were a few around the province that followed in John's footsteps quickly, but they had all gone broke." These were the breweries noted above, which opened and closed within a few years in the mid-1980s. Wittig and Beaton visited all of them—and more.

When Wittig and Beaton met up with Mitchell, they shared with him their plans. They wanted to open a brewery that would make British-style ales, different from the German lagers of Granville Island. They had tasted the ales at Horseshoe Bay and Spinnakers, and they liked them. They also noticed that they were hard to find; as their draft business plan put it, "of the major breweries in the province, only one ale is being produced."[17] However, they needed to tweak their ales for Canadian tastes: Canadians liked their cold, fizzy beer, but British ales tended to be warmer and flatter. They decided they'd "Canadianize" British ales—pump up the CO_2 and turn down the tank temperatures. They also wanted their beer to be marketed as healthier than corporate beers: "Our microbrewery will be producing a natural, preservative-free beer geared for today's more health conscious market.

Our unpasteurized product will be an English-style ale."[18] Mitchell agreed to help them launch the business, and he brought over Brad McQuhae, an early brewer at Spinnakers and important contributor to the brewing equipment industry, to help. Mitchell and McQuhae introduced them to the basics of the brewing business—how to brew, equipment specs—and guided them in drawing up an official business plan. Neither Wittig nor Beaton had done such a thing before, and they had no money—they were both still servers. They came up with a budget of $150,000 and crossed their fingers that someone would give them some cash. Their parents weren't rich, but they co-signed bank loans for half the budget. However, they still needed another $75,000, and additional bank loans weren't an option. They ended up getting in touch with a Colin Gumbert who worked for BC Development Corporation, a government-funded entity that helped small business start-ups. Gumbert was the person who decided which projects received money, and to Wittig and Beaton's relief, he approved their funding request. Half of that $75,000 from BCDC was interest-free, and the other half was at a low interest rate, which put the new business partners in an advantageous position from the start.

Once the finances were in place, they needed to find a suitable brewing location. Wittig and Beaton began driving around Vancouver, looking for potential sites that met the main criteria—a long drainage system and a sump, according to Mitchell's advice. They noticed one potential candidate being built at 1973 Pandora Street, near Victoria Drive, an area that was low-rise industrial and well suited to something like a brewery. The sign out front identified the property owner: businessman and developer Leon Menkis. Despite the reputation many developers in Vancouver now have, Menkis was a generous and well-loved Vancouver icon; he was a member of the Jewish community and financial supporter of the Jewish Museum and Archives of BC, while also stepping in as Vancouver's own special Santa Claus, renting office and rental space to the Lower Mainland Christmas Bureau charity for half the market value. He even paid for all necessary renovations out of his own pocket.[19] Wittig remembers that when they first met, Menkis was dressed sloppily, with his shirt unbuttoned, but he'd later see him driving around in a fancy car. "He was always just such a nice guy," Wittig says. Menkis, being the good guy he was, rented his new building to these two young unknowns. Because the building was still under construction, they rushed to get a sump to install before the cement went down. "The sump we got was about the size of Texas—and we needed to make a hole for this thing to go into!" Wittig laughs.

The partners rented a jackhammer and got to work, drilling down into the packed dirt in circles. Wittig remembers the construction workers standing there waiting for them, checking their watches because they needed to finish the cement flooring. Menkis brought in a case of beer for the workers to drink while they watched the two young men. At last, the hole was dug and the tank lowered in. And from that point, after the floor and walls were up, Wittig and Beaton did the majority of the interior work themselves with the guidance of Wittig's brother and Brad McQuhae's father. Two fermenters and four brite tanks comprised their initial brewing set-up, in which they planned to brew a dark and a mild to start.

Naming the brewery was another hurdle to clear in the business set-up process. They knew they wanted to make British ales, so they'd need a British name. When a Scottish friend was visiting, they asked his advice. He wrote eight different names on a piece of paper (Wittig remembers "Shaftesbury" and "Cotswolds"). "Shaftesbury" stuck with them, but since they knew they were going to make Canadian versions of British ales, they dropped the second s and named their brewery "Shaftebury." Later on, one elderly lady told Wittig that she loved their beer but that they misspelled Shaftesbury. "I got a kick out of it," Wittig laughs. In the following years they went to Munich for Oktoberfest to try the beer and source brewing equipment, and they always stopped at a Shaftesbury Pub in London while waiting for a connecting flight to Germany. Once he'd heard about their brewery and its name, the publican supplied them with free beer until they had to head back to the airport.

While the brewery property was coming together, the pair went out to hunt for equipment. Wittig remembers picking up bits and pieces from breweries around the province that had gone defunct, even buying equipment from out of someone's garage in one case. Shaftebury archival materials include a list of items they were planning to source from other breweries, with equipment listed under each brewery. For example, the "Equipment from North Island Brewing that can be used by Shaftebury brewing" list included the coffee maker, toilet, keg bungs, CO_2 bottles, and various pieces of lab equipment.[20] Once everything was installed in the brewhouse, Mitchell and McQuhae taught Wittig and Beaton how to operate the brewing equipment, make the beer, serve it properly, and sanitize, sanitize, sanitize. "It was like cooking on a grand scale while keeping everything incredibly clean," Wittig says. "We had never seen the brewing process before. The whole thing was brand new to us, but it was really cool trying to figure it out. I liked that whirlpool centrifuge!" Because they were keeping things simple and brewing just two beers, Mitchell provided basic recipes. For the grain bill, he ordered the specialty malt from England and the base malt from the prairies. As with Horseshoe Bay, the yeast came from England as well. The hops were shipped from Washington. To optimize the English flavour of these recipes, Wittig and Beaton were taught how to adjust Vancouver's water with brewing salts to imitate the famed Burton-on-Trent water. After two weeks of intensive brewing instruction, Mitchell and McQuhae left and Wittig and Beaton were on their own.

By this time, it was the summer of 1987. They had started the financial grunt work a year earlier, in March of 1986, and the whole thing had at last come together. In August 1987 they sold a total of seven kegs—their first brews. However, there was a lot to learn still. Their first two beers were the cream ale[21] and the bitter. There's really no beer more English than a traditional bitter, but Canadian drinkers did not know what to do with that name.[22] "The bitter did *not* go over at the beginning!" Wittig sighs, shaking his head and laughing. The cream ale, however, was immediately a hit. Wittig credits Beaton with the marketing instinct that led them to misname a beer so successfully. As Beaton and Wittig knew, Shaftebury's cream ale was not actually a cream ale. Cream ale, while there are regionally different definitions, is somewhere between a lager and an ale, similar to a Kölsch. The original Shaftebury Cream Ale was essentially a dark mild; a full-bodied, slightly sweet, malt-forward beer. This was confirmed by the famous beer writer Michael Jackson in his *Beer Companion*: "I would also deem to be a dark mild the malty, nutty brew curiously launched as a Cream Ale by the Shaftebury Brewery in Vancouver, Canada."[23] Beaton just thought that cream ale had such a nice sound to it—like something you'd want to drink. And people definitely wanted to drink it. Wittig recalls that Jackson, despite his quibbles with the name, visited Shaftebury in person and downed three pints of beer (at least one was the cream ale) before heading to his next stop. It became so popular that when Barry Benson, former brewer at Shaftebury, opened R&B Brewing with Rick Dellow, he knew at

once that he wanted to make a cream ale that tasted like Shaftebury's. And thus the award-winning Raven Cream Ale—still a core beer at R&B—was born. Shaftebury also influenced Russell Brewing in Surrey, which opened in 1995. Beer writer Joe Wiebe praises Russell's Cream Ale as "an example of what I call the 'Vancouver Cream Ale,' a dark version of the style that was first brewed by Shaftebury in the late 1980s."[24]

For the first six months, the brewery was operating on a shoestring budget. They would buy used Grolsch bottles (the flip-caps), remove labels, sterilize them, and use them to provide samples to restaurants and pubs. Wittig and Beaton knew business owners would want to

The Shaftebury Cream Ale. (Photo courtesy of SFU Archives, BC Beer History Archive, Dave Smith fonds, item F-314-5-4-0-26-3)

taste the beer before putting it on tap, and they really needed some draft lines in order to make money. Their branding was done at home by friends rather than by an advertising agency. Wittig's brother, an artist, drew their first logo, a cheery English barman, in response to Wittig and Beaton's prompt: "Can you make a funny brewer guy stealing a pint of beer off some barrels?" Wittig's former roommate, Rita, painted it on a piece of plywood in their backyard. But even with these cost-cutting measures, the margins were still far too tight; Wittig's brother had to lend them an additional $12,500 before Christmas of 1987, and both sets of parents were starting to get pretty worried. Their homes had been leveraged to finance the brewery. Wittig's brother and father persuaded Beaton's father to hold on and give them a bit more time. Beaton and Wittig sat down and took a good look at how they were running things—and decided to make some changes. Up until then, there had been no clear division of labour or specific roles for either of the partners; they were both just kind of doing everything. Instead of continuing that chaos, they opted to specialize. Wittig would do sales and deliveries and Beaton would take on the brewery work. This worked: in January 1988, they sold one hundred kegs, and for each of the next ten years they had 100 percent annual growth.

For the first year and a half, it was just Wittig and Beaton running everything in the brewery, then they hired a brewery worker through a governmental wage subsidy program for the next year and a half. By that time, they had paid off their bank loans and were able to hire sales and delivery people. Their beer was becoming popular; people would stop by and ask for brewery tours. They were also making connections in the brewing community. They enjoyed a mutually supportive relationship with David Bruce-Thomas, John Mitchell's assistant brewer at the original Horseshoe Bay Brewery and the new owner of the brewery when Mitchell left.[25] And they often had conversations about brewing with Shirley Warne, who was eager to get into the industry. Wittig recalls her stopping by to chat about brewing—these were the days when she'd just moved to Vancouver from Toronto, where she'd brewed at Amsterdam Brewing, and before she became the first brewer at Steamworks. "She had a million questions!" he laughs.

James Walton, the founder of Storm Brewing, recalls how effective Shaftebury's marketing strategies were. From Beaton's reinterpretation of the cream ale style to the British nostalgia that pervaded the name itself and the logo, they had something that appealed to Vancouverites who wanted good beer. Walton remembers their seasonal Christmas beer, called the Wet Coast Winter Ale: "That Christmas beer was so popular—people would book a keg of that six months in advance. That showed me that people wanted richer, stronger beer."[26] Wittig remembers that Christmas ale as well, since it was their only seasonal beer. "That was a really weird recipe that included blackstrap molasses, brown sugar, all these things that we normally wouldn't put in our beer," he says. "The least it came out to was 8.7 percent ABV, the most was 12.4 percent." He recalls that they had to ration the kegs because the ale would sell out so quickly; everyone knew about it and wanted it. But this boom in popularity wasn't due to paid advertising; their marketing didn't extend much beyond that cozy logo of the English barman and talk around town. By 1990, locals were calling their beer "the best produced in BC," a reputation that spread by word of mouth rather than traditional advertising.[27]

In the first couple of years, as they were becoming profitable, Wittig and Beaton focused on providing two main beers to their licensees: the cream ale and a honey pale ale, knowing that restaurants and pubs would want a light and a dark. The honey pale used Kidd Bros. honey and was a smooth, sweet tipple that immediately took off, coinciding with the popular honey

Shaftebury's Wet Coast Winter Ale. (Photo courtesy of SFU Archives, BC Beer History Archive, Dave Smith fonds, item F-314-5-4-0-26-6)

brown lagers made by Sleeman's and Okanagan Spring around the same time. With profits increasing every year after the first two, Shaftebury was buzzing. They eventually expanded to include seven salespeople and a delivery driver, and they had to move into the space next door because they were getting bigger. They ran the brewery twenty-four hours a day, seven days a week, and demand was exceeding what they could actually make. This was what prompted their decision to relocate the brewery to a larger facility in Delta around 1995. By then, according to a price list from that time, Shaftebury's core lineup was composed of four beers: the Cream Ale, the Rainforest Amber Ale, the ESB, and the Honey Pale Ale. It seems that the ESB (Extra Special Bitter), which had been shelved early on because of consumer response to the word "bitter," was enjoying some renewed popularity. It was also the most expensive of the four, priced at $150.50 per 50-litre keg versus $145, $144, and $147 for the others. At the new Delta facility, which was set up by Brad McQuhae, they could make sufficient quantities of all four beers with no problem. This new brewery was six times the size of their original; while they were doing 30 kegs per batch at their Pandora brewhouse, in Delta they could do 180 kegs. They also bought a bottling line from Germany and increased their retail output.

Shortly after their ten-year anniversary, Wittig and Beaton were realizing that the craft beer scene had changed. It was the era of quality craft beer brewpubs, like Yaletown, Dix, and Sailor Hagar's, and up-and-coming craft breweries, like Russell, Storm, and R&B. They had opened Shaftebury because they were passionate about owning their own business, making some money, and having fun. However, they hadn't started it out of a passion for beer and brewing. With enthusiastic brewing experts like Iain Hill, James Walton, Shirley Warne, and others now entering the scene, Wittig and Beaton knew that their version of Shaftebury couldn't compete. They had made some efforts to expand and keep up, even producing a lager when they had been making only ales before,[28] but they knew that their margins would quickly tighten if they stuck around. So when Big

Beer came knocking, they knew that they would sell, despite their early denials of the acquisition rumours that had been swirling for a couple of years.[29] Molson, Labatt, and Sleeman were all interested. After all, at the time Shaftebury was the third-largest craft brewery out of the twenty in BC (by volume).[30] Wittig and Beaton ended up choosing Sleeman, which had just bought Okanagan Spring. It was clear, however, that Sleeman was not interested in the brewery itself, but in the draft market that Shaftebury had established.[31] Sleeman just wanted to appropriate the Shaftebury brand for themselves while disposing of the actual brewery. Wittig claims that after the sale happened, Shaftebury Cream was never brewed again, because Sleeman's "Shaftebury Coastal Cream" is actually a lager ("they were making lagers masquerading as ales!").

After the sale was finalized, Wittig and Beaton were looking forward to beginning new business ventures—and post-sale, they were well equipped to do so. The price they'd received for Shaftebury was an estimated $10 million—a far cry from their $150,000 initial investment.[32] However, Beaton also made a statement at the time that reveals their sense of loss at letting their little brewery go: "It makes me sad because I never envisioned selling this business. Running Shaftebury has been a dream, a fairy tale and a party." But then he added, "Then again, I used to live in a blue Dodge Dart in an alleyway; things do change."[33] Vancouver's little upstart microbrewery was now owned by the big boys. Production moved to Vernon, and the Delta plant was no longer used.

While Shaftebury continues as a brand today, it is not the Shaftebury created by Tim Wittig and Paul Beaton. Their success was a magical combination of luck, strategy, charisma, and connections. When they launched their brewery, there were no import beers allowed on draft at pubs and restaurants. This meant that there was a niche market for locally produced ales that would quench the thirst of those who enjoyed English beer. The ban on import taps was in place until 1994; Wittig says "that seven-year window was golden for Shaftebury." People who were looking for import beers turned to

Shaftebury instead (and sometimes Granville Island). But it wasn't sheer luck. They maintained beer quality by hiring brewers with homebrew experience and biology or food science degrees—people like Iain Hill, Gerry Hieter, Michael Stewart, and Barry Benson, who ended up shaping the Vancouver craft beer community. "They knew how to keep the beer clean!" Wittig asserts—and anyone who has made beer knows that this is one of the most important rules of brewing. They also connected with the local community and hired salespeople who could do the same. And they made beers that sounded good and reached a broad demographic of drinkers. Their famous cream ale is the best example: "If you tell people it's creamy and they taste it, they'll visualize the creaminess. We had as many women drinking that beer as men," says Wittig. This was surprising to him in a time when many people erroneously saw beer as a man's drink and not suited to the female palate.

If the same Shaftebury that opened in 1986 tried to enter the brewery market now, it wouldn't get very far. But time and context make all the difference. Almost all the brewers and owners I interviewed for this book believe that Shaftebury was influential in expanding Vancouver's craft beer palate and training Vancouver's craft brewers. According to Ken Beattie, the director of the BC Craft Brewers Guild, Shaftebury helped to "create taste" in the nascent craft beer community.[34] Together with Granville Island Brewing, Shaftebury changed what we expect from beer and planted the seeds for a new, quirky community of beer lovers.

CHAPTER 9

THE NEW GENERATION OF BREWMASTERS: VANCOUVER CRAFT BEER IN THE 1990S AND EARLY 2000S

By the 1990s, craft beer had a small but tenacious foothold in BC, particularly in Vancouver and Victoria. Horseshoe Bay Brewery, Granville Island Brewing, and Shaftebury Brewing had introduced high-quality, traditionally made craft beer to the province. CAMRA (the Campaign for Real Ale Society) members Gerry Hieter and John Rowling started BC's first craft beer festival in 1993—initially called the Victoria Microbrewery Festival, but soon renamed the Great Canadian Beer Festival. Stuart Derdeyn, writer of *The Province*'s "Beer Hunter" column during the 1990s, recalls that Victoria's GCBF had a huge influence on the craft beer industry in Vancouver during this time; through providing a space to share ideas, beer styles, and business plans, the GCBF helped to consolidate a true craft beer community. And at the time, that community was a small but vibrant group of beer lovers who were excited about the potential of craft beer, even if the general public wasn't quite there yet. "It was a pretty lonely time back then, in terms of what was available," Derdeyn remembers. "It was a big deal when something came along that was really good."[1] However, despite the limitations of beer in the early

'90s, things shifted rapidly as more breweries and brewpubs opened throughout the decade.

As the craft beer industry took root in Vancouver, it needed not just its foundational members—the Shafteburys and Granville Islands—but new growth as well. On the west coast, the '90s embrace of grunge and an anti-corporate aesthetic revealed a rejection of conventional expectations of success and beauty. The "anti-corporate" ethos of early craft beer fit well into Vancouver at this time, where weird, non-mainstream sports like Ultimate Frisbee were emerging as alternatives to hockey or soccer and where beers like Shaftebury Cream Ale were being chosen over Budweiser. When R&B Brewing's Barry Benson and several Vancouver Ultimate Frisbee players told me how the Ultimate teams would stop by R&B in the mid-1990s to fill up milk cartons with beer (often for free) before heading out to play, it struck me as beautifully anti-corporate, pro-community, and wholly true to the era.[2]

The breweries and brewpubs that emerged in the decade between the mid-1990s and the mid-2000s solidified the growing Vancouver craft beer community and shaped expectations for the industry. The *What's Brewing* "Class of '94" thirtieth anniversary issue describes the brewers of this era as "a new generation who had learned their skills both as homebrewers and on the job at 1980s-era breweries" but who "broke away" from the movement for traditional beer that Horseshoe Bay and Granville Island had launched. Instead, these new brewers "followed the trends coming from the increasingly hops-centric Northwest USA, experimented with stronger UK and Belgian beer styles, and pushed the limits of brewing long before the craft beer audience was ready to support them."[3] It was the age of brewpubs—what Joe Wiebe called the "brewpub boom"[4]: Yaletown, Steamworks, Big River, Dix, Big Ridge, and others opened in greater Vancouver during this period, as did a handful of foundational new breweries, including R&B, Storm, Central City, and Red Truck. Now that the three solid 1980s breweries had established the foundation of this new industry, the 1990s breweries had a bit of room to play and to expand. Craft beer had been accepted as good beer—but now people wondered how good it could get. The work of this next generation of Vancouver brewmasters and brewery owners showed the city what they could do. Their efforts set the stage for the true explosion of craft breweries that would happen in the 2010s.[5]

The tight-knit brewing community that formed in the 1990s and extended into the early 2000s meant that owners and brewers in Vancouver were frequently moving from one brewery to another in a small, messy Venn diagram of beer connections in which everyone knew everyone else. Brewer Tony Dewald describes the community in a way that likely resonates with others from that time: "Until about 2012 there were so few people involved. I probably knew the first name of every craft beer drinker in Vancouver! It felt like it, anyway."[6] If you worked in Vancouver craft beer back in the 1990s or 2000s, you probably had an impact on multiple breweries and brewpubs—not just your primary business. Taking a cue from Nigel Springthorpe when he opened the Alibi Room in 2006 and listed beers with their brewmaster,[7] this chapter tracks the Vancouver beer industry of this era by person rather than by brewery. While I regret that I can't tell the story of every Vancouver brewer or beer insider from these two decades, I hope that this chapter will illuminate some key figures who shaped the industry.

Iain Hill

Iain Hill was in quality control at Shaftebury Brewing before becoming a brewer there. He quickly earned a reputation and was hired by Mark James to brew at and set up Yaletown Brewing, Dix Brewpub, Big Ridge Brewing, High Mountain Brewhouse, and Avalon/Taylor's Crossing Brewpub. Arguably his greatest brewing achievement is the establishment of Strange Fellows Brewing, an award-winning brewery in East Vancouver.

"The smell was awful!" Iain Hill and I are sitting in the taproom of his brewery, Strange Fellows, and he's recalling the distasteful walk to his first brewing job, at Shaftebury Brewing's plant on Pandora.

The neighbourhood was also home to a chicken butchering facility. "In the summer it was so hot and uncomfortable. Crows and seagulls were picking up bits of flesh and bone, and occasionally there'd be flesh and bone dropping from the sky. It was a very strange area."[8] It was an odorous part of town and the job wouldn't make him a millionaire, but Iain Hill knew he was at the bottom of a ladder he wanted to climb: craft brewing.

A biochemistry graduate from the University of Victoria, Hill had a background in science that ended up being his ticket into the craft brewing industry. He had homebrewed before, using Charlie Papazian's *The Complete Joy of Homebrewing* as his guide, and even worked at Broadway Brewing, a homebrew supplies shop. But it wasn't his homebrewing experience that led him to Shaftebury—it was his scientific acumen. He started at Shaftebury in 1993 as a quality control manager, a field related to food biotechnology rather than brewing specifically. Around that time, Barry Benson (later the "B" of R&B Brewing) was working for Newlands, the brewing equipment company, and crossed paths with Hill while consulting for microbrewery set-ups. Benson helped him with some of the technical aspects of beer quality testing. Hill was good at his job, but not particularly passionate about it—and if you've met Iain Hill, you know he runs on passion. Quality control checks gave him a foot in the door, but he wanted to brew the beer, not test it. To accomplish his goal, he volunteered for the worst brewing shift available at Shaftebury: Friday nights. He remembers that his first beers were the Cream Ale, the London Porter, and the very sweet Christmas Ale. This was his world for the next year and a half: quality control for most of the week and brewing on Friday nights when no one else wanted to.[9]

Around this time, Hill heard through the grapevine about a businessman who was trying to start up a brewpub that made and served its own craft beer. The person in question was Mark James, a long-time Vancouver entrepreneur (more on him in a moment). Hill contacted James about his plans and asked if he might be needing a brewer. He did; when James opened up his Yaletown Brewing in 1993, on the advice of Frank Appleton he offered the job of head brewer to Iain Hill. Shirley Warne, a brewer from Ontario who was looking for opportunities in BC, also applied for the Yaletown job, but was unsuccessful. This may have been fortunate for the city, since she went on to be the first brewer at another major Vancouver brewpub: Steamworks, which opened in Gastown not long after. However, Yaletown was the gatecrasher: it was the first of several brewpubs[10] that provided invaluable exposure for craft beer and boosted its popularity in the city.

After seeing what he had done with Swan's Brewpub in Victoria, James brought Frank Appleton on board to design Yaletown's brewing set-up, train Hill on the equipment, and establish its recipes. To save time and effort, Appleton called up Chris Johnson, the head brewer at Swan's, and asked for the recipes. He and Hill then adjusted and renamed the recipes for use at Yaletown: they had a Mainland Lager, Northern Light Lager, Red Brick Bitter, Frank's Nut Brown Ale, Double Dome Stout, and the Indian Arm Pale Ale.[11] Soon, however, Hill's creativity took over and he began to develop his own

Iain Hill pours a beer at Yaletown Brewing. (Photo courtesy of Mirella Amato)

recipes, sometimes making more interesting and daring beers than other brewers at the time. His Brick and Beam IPA and Hill's Special Wheat were two standouts; at the time, hardly any breweries were making wheat beers *or* IPAS. He'd been influenced by a trip to Belgium in 1996, when he had tried Belgian ales made with the wild yeast Brettanomyces. When he got home, he bought some Brett from an American lab, brewed it up and added cherries, and entered it in the Brewmaster Festival at the Plaza of Nations in Vancouver.[12]

Hill's brewing creativity continued to grow. Soon he was able to cultivate his own strain of Brett from a bottle of Orval rather than ordering it from a lab. His unique take on brewing and beer ingredients surprised and delighted the "old guard" of craft brewing, including Frank Appleton, the person who set him up at Yaletown. In Appleton's memoir, he recollects one of the unusual beers Hill created early on:

> *One day when I walked into Yaletown Brewing, he had a surprise for me: "Try this!" he said. The foamy, opalescent beer that surged gleefully up in the tall glass was not only replete with aromas of berries and a whiff of Belgian yeast, it was pink!*
>
> *"Raspberry hefeweizen!" said Iain.*
>
> *I thought, This is great because I would not have brewed a beer like this. Fruit beers are not to my palate, and I wouldn't have believed in it, risked it, had faith that such a product would sell—which are, of course, exactly the reasons you would never see a beer like this coming from one of the big breweries.*[13]

Appleton recognized when something was good even if it wasn't quite "to his palate," as he put it. And he was right about Hill's pink beer; it was counter to all mainstream expectations of beer, but it sold well, and people came back for more. Hill recalls him as being "kind of crotchety" but also very straightforward. Appleton's strong opinions, like those of Mitchell, were born out of years of expertise.

As Mark James opened additional brewpubs, Hill took on a leadership role, hiring and training brewers for each location—Whistler,

North Vancouver, Surrey, and Vancouver. The brewers who worked at these brewpubs would go on to brew for Dead Frog, Trading Post, Old Abbey Ales, Tofino Brewing, Longwood, 33 Acres, Shaketown, and more.[14] Yaletown remained Hill's primary location, but his influence as brewer extended across the Mark James Group brewpubs and the Lower Mainland more generally.

Hill is now known for his very successful brewery Strange Fellows, located in East Van (lately nicknamed "Yeast Van" because of its high concentration of breweries), an artistic, industrial area of Vancouver that seems a natural fit for him. But back in the '90s, he was trying to cultivate a beer community in Yaletown, where the brewpub was located. In the late '80s and early '90s, Yaletown was light industrial—very different from the high-end neighbourhoods we see there today. Hill recalls foil-covered windows and lots of metal- and woodworking shops in the area, with a sports-loving clientele patronizing the brewpub before and after games at Rogers Arena. He wanted to make it a beer-centric place but it was really more of a sports bar rather than a craft beer hub. "I was a round peg in a square hole," he admits. "[Yaletown] wasn't my business, and I struggled with how the owners wanted to run it. I do think I contributed to the business, though, because I made decent beer when there was a lack of decent beer." Hill's pink beer was far from his only creative beer at Yaletown, despite the difficulty of finding an audience for them. He became known for the Belgian styles he'd create, such as the Grand Cru that he served at the Great Canadian Beer Festival in 1997. Beer writer Stuart Derdeyn praised Hill's skills, stating that under his leadership, Yaletown was "continuing to lead the pack in Belgian styles."[15]

Hill notes that atmosphere can really affect the beer experience, so the sports-bar-like vibe of Yaletown Brewing led to sports-bar-like expectations for the beer. IPAs didn't do well at Yaletown, although Hill knew they were on the rise. He recalls how later on, his creative beers would be hugely successful if served at the Alibi Room but then would bomb if served at Yaletown Brewing. This was happening even as Yaletown itself became more high-end and the brewpub became a hot spot for minor celebrity sightings, including the likes of Adam Sandler, Howie Mandel, and an assortment of Canucks players. Celeb hangouts don't often overlap much with beer nerd hangouts. The beer community needed beer-centric spaces to help craft beer—and craft beer tastes—grow, and Yaletown wasn't the perfect fit for that, despite its important role in supporting and selling craft beer. Another Mark James brewpub, Dix, would end up being the perfect space for Vancouver craft beer nerds. And for Hill, his own brewery would give him all the opportunities for innovation that he craved. It was at Strange Fellows, which he opened in the mid-2010s craft beer boom, that Hill hit his stride as a craft beer creator and entrepreneur (more on that in Chapter 10).

James Walton

James Walton founded Storm Brewing after developing his skills as a homebrewer (and achieving an education in the sciences) and has had no official employment with other breweries as far as I know. However, Storm frequently makes collaborative brews and Walton's support of the BC craft beer community has been invaluable and long-standing.

James Walton's labour of love, Storm Brewing, sits modestly on an industrial stretch of Commercial Drive, just a couple of blocks from Powell Street. A passerby could be forgiven for thinking it's simply an old, graffiti-covered warehouse. However, although Storm looks like a warehouse on the outside and a chaotic garage on the inside, it is one of the longest-running craft breweries in British Columbia. It started in 1994, just one year after Iain Hill became the brewmaster at the new Yaletown Brewing. Storm has delivered the unconventional and the unexpected from the beginning, making beers that align with the mad scientist reputation of its founder and brewmaster, James Walton.[16] He is an incredibly busy man who is passionate about what he does and full of ideas for what to do in the future. As I sat down with him on a rickety metal stool just outside the garage doors, I could sense his dynamic energy—the energy that has kept Storm Brewing a vibrant part of Vancouver's beer community for nearly twenty years.

In my mind, Walton is 50 percent scientist, 50 percent artist, 50 percent entrepreneur, and 100 percent independent thinker (I'm no mathematician, but that sounds about right). In our conversation,[17] he remembered childhood aspirations to own his own business, much like his father, who owned and managed a horse ranch. In 1986, with a biochem degree from UBC and a deep knowledge of mycology (the study of fungi, which includes mushrooms and yeasts), Walton started his own mushroom farm. It didn't last too long, and he soon moved into the pharmaceutical industry. Those nine-to-five jobs were good experiences, he acknowledges; they gave him management and technology skills that he otherwise wouldn't have had after finishing his degree. But they weren't what he wanted to do.

He had been homebrewing since he was fifteen, when he would use barley meant for his parents' horses and try to sprout, roast, and mash it (it didn't turn out too well, but his friends still drank it).[18] During

and after his time at UBC he would do road trips into the United States to taste beers and check out breweries. He was impressed by how good beer could taste and believed BC needed to step up its craft beer game. Where were the risky, weird, interesting BC beers? He felt he could do a better job of craft brew-

James Walton having fun on the job. (Photo courtesy of James Walton/ Storm Brewing)

ing right there in

James Walton and his unique mash tun back in the 1990s. (Photo courtesy of James Walton/Storm Brewing)

his backyard. And that is almost what he did. After a visit to the first location of the long-running East Van restaurant Café Deux Soleils, with its mismatched chairs, linoleum-covered tables, and hearty, delicious breakfast fare, Walton thought to himself, "I don't have to spend a million dollars on a fancy brewhouse or equipment! *They* didn't!" With this realization inspiring him, he spent months hunting down old pieces of equipment—a soup tank here, a yogourt mixer there—and soon he had a mash tun and some fermentation tanks ready for use, sitting in his yard until he was able to install them in the Commercial Drive location. Apparently "his East Side neighbours thought he was building a boat."[19]

For the first couple of years of business, "it was really rough," Walton admits. "I'm not an outgoing schmoozy person, I'm more technical." Walton is unabashed about his steampunk look and fearless sense of innovation, but he's not salesy or, in his words, schmoozy. With no tasting room at the time, all sales were on draft, and he counts himself fortunate to have obtained twenty accounts in the first few months thanks to a supportive restaurant community. Walton eventually hired Jon Larson, a talented salesperson, to manage accounts, leaving Walton to perfect his craft. Larson was responsible for selling the mad scientist brewer and what he brewed, which wasn't always an easy task. "In marketing books about starting your own brewery, they always said to start with a light beer," Walton says. "I didn't do that. I did something unique, because I figured there were lots of pale ales around already." His first beer was the Red Sky Altbier, something he had brewed over thirty times as a homebrewer. It was a complicated recipe, with four different malts, five different hops, and extra lagering time required. Another early beer he tried was a light black stout that was similar to Guinness. It didn't resonate with customers; people who wanted Guinness would order a Guinness, not an unknown stout trying to be *like* Guinness. He decided to follow his own intuition and brew a beer that he would like: a big, bold stout. "I like rich, heavy beers, so that's why I make them," he says. This revised stout eventually became one of Storm's core beers, the Black Plague Stout.

Two of his earliest and most supportive accounts were the iconic Indian restaurant Vij's, which opened just three days after Storm, and Railway Club, whose owner Steve Forsyth would open Off the Rail Brewing in 2015. Walton recalls pushing beer boundaries in those first years and trying unsuccessfully to convince Forsyth to sell a new dry-hopped beer at his restaurant: "I brought him this brilliant beer that I'd wanted to make for a long time. But it was dry-hopped so there were some hop chunks floating in it. Steve would *not* take it! He said, 'There's no way we can sell this!'" A dry-hopped beer is now common as rain in Vancouver, although the extra fibre is perhaps less so. In any case, Walton was ahead of the curve when it came to beer styles. He was interested in brewing a true IPA early on, after noticing how Alexander Keith's was marketing its "IPA." Customers were drinking it, without realizing what a real IPA could be.[20] However, Bill Herdman's Tall Ship Ales in Squamish was the only other brewery making an IPA at the time, "and he didn't want to step on their toes."[21] Eventually he released his Hurricane IPA, which is still part of his core beer lineup. But he kept having to explain to his customers, even if they loved the product, that his beer wouldn't be perfectly clear because he didn't filter it—something that was unheard of at the time. Apparently one of his accounts called to chastise him about this after a year of drinking slightly hazy beer: "We must have given you $10,000 worth of business. You should be able to buy a filter by now."[22]

Thanks in large part to Iain Hill, Walton also began exploring sour beers far earlier than most breweries, way back in 1996. According to Joe Wiebe's profile of Walton, Hill "encouraged him to re-pitch some yeast cultures from leftover spoiled beer in kegs. The last of this sour Lambic, aged for twelve years in oak casks, was released in 2010 and won accolades."[23] Tony Dewald remembers Walton making lambics when he, Dewald, was working there in the early 2000s. "Making lambic, it was so unusual back then!" he remembers. "Anything was possible. I had such a good time there."[24] Having tried one of Storm's lambics—the King Rattus Blackberry Lambic, brewed in 2017 for the brewery's twenty-fifth anniversary in 2019—I can confirm that Walton knows how to use yeast to create magic.

Walton's wild beers draw all sorts of craft beer fans to Storm's garage doors nowadays, partly out of curiosity and partly due to Walton's reputation in the industry. Dewald describes him as having "no peer...He is one of the best people in the industry."[25] Craft beer industry insiders have some fun Storm memories (hot-tub parties in the mash tun, for one) and they always have a kind word to say about Walton. His generosity and creativity are widely admired. I don't think I'd try a Turkey Dinner IPA or Cinnamon Toast Crunch Ale if anyone else had made them. But Walton showed this level of daring even in his early years. He recalls that around 2000 he made a

Left: Storm's Cinnamon Toast Crunch Ale, made in collaboration with Old Abbey Ales.

Right: James Walton in 2022 with his brewing equipment. (Photos by Noëlle Phillips)

line of medicinal beers, many of which had some sort of sexual health component: a UTI beer, an echinacea stout, and a sex tonic beer aptly named "Stiff Breeze." The 2003 Great Canadian Beer Festival program describes Stiff Breeze as "a stout based tonic to counter brewers droop. Stiff Breeze Ale is 'Doctor' Walton's secret blend of herbs and botanicals to arouse…your senses, and it tastes good too!"[26] Walton gives credit to CAMRA and the Great Canadian Beer Festival for promoting craft breweries' products and expanding his customer base. "There was a sea change in people's attitudes towards beers," he says. "And I never cared that much about making money. I just wanted to feel happy about my job. Having people who respected my work was really great." He emphasizes that changing public attitudes toward beer and expanding the public palate can never be done by just one brewery—it's due to the efforts of the whole community of brewers, restaurateurs, publicans, and of course, customers.

Barry Benson

Barry Benson worked at Shaftebury Brewing and his business partner Rick Dellow worked as a chemist for Granville Island Brewing before they founded R&B Brewing in 1997. Benson and Dellow also worked for Newlands, installing brewing equipment and training brewers at various BC craft breweries, including Granville Island Brewing, Steamworks Brewing, and Russell Brewing.

Barry Benson raises a glass in the R&B tasting room. (Photo by Noëlle Phillips)

Barry Benson and I are sitting down together over beers at the R&B Brewing taproom. Benson is no longer co-owner of R&B, which he founded with Rick Dellow in 1997, but he remains deeply involved in the business and is clearly passionate about R&B and its history.[27] His warm demeanour with me, a relative newcomer when it comes to the timeline of BC craft beer, is appreciated but also not unexpected. He's known as a friendly and generous person, and has been the main voice and face of R&B for years. But it wasn't at R&B that he got his start; Benson's history in beer goes further back.

Benson was working at Molson when he met his future business partner Rick Dellow (another co-worker was Bill Hagelund, who wrote the beer history book *House of Suds*). They were well suited to the beer industry: Benson had a food sciences degree from BCIT and later studied brewing at Chicago's Siebel Institute, and Dellow had a brewing certification from Heriot-Watt University in Scotland.[28] They both eventually realized that they wanted to pursue brewing apart from Big Beer. This isn't to say that Benson disparages the presence of the larger beer corporations in the beer industry: "It has its place in the beer market," he says. "I don't want to sound too negative about those big companies." Plenty of craft brewers have worked at Molson, Labatt, or Anheuser-Busch InBev. The big guys know how to do consistency and quality control. However, by the late '80s, Benson was becoming aware that there were beer fans who wanted something more flavourful, more local. Big Beer was aware of it too; Benson recalls the introduction of beers that seemed like craft beers but were made by the big corporations, ones like Rickard's Red, Shock Top, and Blue Moon. Big Beer was slowly realizing that craft beer could be a threat to their market share. As Sneath put it, beer "was a $10-billion business and the Big Two [Molson and Labatt] were not known for complacency when it came to seeing their market share eroded by a bunch of rebel brewers."[29] Benson was actually part of the process of developing the "crafty" Rickard's Red for Molson. "I credit myself with naming Rickard's Red!" he laughs. Gordon Rickards was the lab manager at the time, and when they were evaluating the versions of the recipe, Benson recalls saying, "That one looks nice—it's a red. A Rickards red!" Molson gave Rickards a dollar for the use of the name. Seeing the signs that craft beer was rising in the late '80s,

Benson suggested that Molson buy Granville Island Brewing. They didn't have Benson's foresight, so they said no, and soon after merged with Carling O'Keefe, another Canadian brewing giant.

In 1989, Benson departed Molson for a job at Shaftebury as brewer and microbiologist. He remembers John Mitchell and Frank Appleton coming down to the brewery. "It was a lot of fun and a lot of learning," Benson recalls, smiling. "Paul and Tim were just kids," he says of Shaftebury founders Paul Beaton and Tim Wittig, "but it was the only real microbrewery in town!" At the same time, he was also establishing West Coast Brewing, a U-brew facility at Clark and 1st Avenue in Vancouver. But he wasn't satisfied with just two jobs: he also took a position at Newlands Systems Inc., a brewery equipment manufacturer founded by Brad McQuhae in 1990.[30] Both he and Dellow ended up there, where they had a boss who was already well established in the BC craft beer scene. While their primary work at Newlands involved setting up microbreweries, Benson recalls working with a Coors employee while he was there and tinkering with a recipe that ended up being Blue Moon. It seems that Big Beer missed out when they let Benson stray to the dark side.

Benson and Dellow's work with Newlands gave them broad experience in the craft beer industry—experience that was impossible to acquire if you were just running one brewery. Benson estimates they helped to set up about fifty to sixty microbreweries in BC and internationally. It was through their work building out breweries that they met the people who shaped the craft beer community. Via Newlands, Benson and Dellow set up Steamworks Brewing, for example, whose owners hired Shirley Warne as their first brewer. Warne had supervised a young Harley Smith when she brewed at Amsterdam Brewing in Ontario, and he went on to found Longwood Brewery in Nanaimo. When Warne started at Steamworks, she chose Conrad Gmoser as her assistant brewer. Gmoser, in turn, started up Brassneck Brewery with Nigel Springthorpe, founder of the Alibi Room.[31] Oh, what a twisted web of brewing connections Vancouver weaves! But these were the relationships that Benson and Dellow came to understand as they set up microbreweries in the early 1990s. Benson has fond memories of this time: "It was a good community back then because all the people who were in the industry were all fanatical passionate brewers who really knew their stuff."

Benson and Dellow knew their stuff too, after years of working for Molson, Shaftebury, and Newlands. They were better prepared than most to start up their own brewery. While their first instinct was to find a location on the island, fortuitously a building in the Mount Pleasant area became available. They needed to do a lot of work on the old BDH Chemicals warehouse on East 4th to make it suitable for brewing, but the price was right and it was fairly central—even if the spot was a bit sketchy (a common issue for breweries back in the day). In the '90s, the Mount Pleasant/Brewery Creek area wasn't as, well, pleasant as it later became: "It was a nasty, nasty neighbourhood," said Benson in an interview for the BC Ale Trail, remembering that they'd often find used needles in their back alley.[32] With Benson stepping over used needles and Iain Hill ducking flying chicken parts while walking to his shift at Shaftebury, it's lucky that so many brewers stuck with the job.

Times were tough for craft brewery start-ups in the '90s, particularly in the area served by R&B. There were only sixteen craft breweries in BC at the time because the broader beer-drinking public just wasn't quite ready for craft yet—at least, not at the scale needed to grow the industry. "It was really hard to sell [our] beer east of Boundary in the late '90s and early 2000s," Benson remembers. "The larger breweries controlled everything. All the taps were taken. The customer knowledge wasn't there." The tap monopoly by the big breweries was a death knell for those with a microbrewery licence at this time, since under that licence they could only sell to restaurants and pubs; nothing could be sold out of the brewery itself, to individual customers. Benson and Dellow knew they faced an uphill battle, but they were aided by the breweries who had come before, even if they weren't quite "craft" anymore—Granville Island, Shaftebury, and Vernon's Okanagan Spring. These beers began the process of consumer education, slowly shifting palates and changing expectations of what beer could be.

Rick Dellow and John Mitchell at R&B Brewing. (Photo courtesy of Mirella Amato)

Their money meant more public exposure for these beers, which in turn meant more awareness of beer options apart from Molson and Labatt. So despite the negative publicity attached to the "corporatization" of these breweries, Benson believes they did a lot of good for the craft beer industry in Vancouver.

R&B's draft business plan shows their ambition and how they saw themselves overcoming the potential obstacles to their success.[33] The early planning they did, around 1995, identifies their niche in relation to two of the larger breweries mentioned above: Granville Island and Shaftebury, both of whose beers were by then being manufactured outside of Vancouver. According to the draft documents, "this leaves a niche for R&B to become 'Vancouver's Microbrewery.'"[34] They intended for their brewery to convey a "cool, funky, individualistic attitude" while also being a "professional small business which is very much involved in the local community." Their goal was to secure taps at 1.5 percent of licensed establishments in Vancouver and its surrounding municipalities, and with this in place, to begin seeing actual profits beginning in year two. The estimated start-up capital in these early planning stages was $381,309. Their planning documents are stored with a mishmash of articles and clippings from other breweries—sources of inspiration and excitement.

Despite the "cool, funky, individualistic attitude" they wanted their brewery to embody, Benson and Dellow planned to brew traditional beers. An early ad prototype describes the beers as follows: "All R&B beers are brewed by Rick and Barry in our traditional English brewery using only the finest ingredients." Before "R&B" became official, they played with the idea of using a more historically inflected name for their business. The archival files contain Benson and Dellow's notes about nineteenth-century breweries in both Vancouver and Victoria, and draft applications to the Ministry of Finance and Corporations, Registrar of Companies list their rejected names: The Vancouver Brewery, The Vancouver Microbrewery, The Vancouver Brewhouse, Brewery Creek Brewing Co., and Brewers Creek Malting and Brewing Co. Too many of these were too close to the name of a local U-brew company, so they ended up taking an entirely different approach to the name and overall brand. R&B seemed a natural choice: after all, it was just Rick and Barry starting it up, and Rick was their first brewer (they later hired many more well-known local brewers). Notes on their planning documents show how excited the partners were about their new project; they had all sorts of ideas for how to boost the profile of craft beer in the city, including beer dinners, spent grain products, an R&B cookbook, a cooking-with-beer newspaper column, and more.

Benson and Dellow made good on those plans. They started off small, brewing only two beers in the first few months after they opened in August of 1997. The Raven Cream Ale and the Red Devil Pale Ale were the only two beers they made that year; three batches of Red Devil and two of the Raven in August and September, according to their October 1997 newsletter. In the spring of 1998, they introduced their Sun God Wheat Ale, which would end up winning numerous awards over the years. The press release for Sun God reveals that R&B was pushing back a bit against stereotypes about microbreweries: "Sun God belies the idea that Cottage breweries can only produce dark, full-flavoured beer." The beer's light citrusy quality made it perfect for patio drinking—a crushable summer beer. During spring and summer of that year, they also offered flavour training and brewing courses for local beer fans. R&B brews were on tap in thirty-five restaurants, and at the 1998 World Beer Cup in Rio de Janeiro, their Raven Cream Ale won silver in the English-Style Mild Ale category. The Raven, which was modelled after the Shaftebury Cream Ale, would end up being one of their best-selling core beers, and remains popular to this day. They were off to a great start.

Their second year of business was also when they ventured into cask-conditioned beers—a highly unusual style at the time. According to the BC Ale Trail, "R&B Brewing was one of the first breweries to provide cask-conditioned beer to local restaurants on a regular basis."[35] They hosted a Christmas event that year that boasted the introduction of cask beer to the city. Invitations were extended to various members of the media and the brewing community, exhorting

An early sketch of the Raven Cream Ale logo. (Photo courtesy of SFU Archives, BC Beer History Archive, R&B Brewing fonds (F-330)

them to "join us for the ceremonial tapping of Vancouver's first cask-conditioned beer. Cask-conditioned beers, unique to the UK, have never before been available in Vancouver." On December 11 at 7:00 PM at Fogg N' Suds' Cambie and Broadway location, they would "tap a cask of Old Nick Winter Ale...the beer will be served in the most traditional style by means of a tap hammered in to the cask...A beer in the tradition of a Scottish Wee Heavy, Old Nick is deceptively smooth, a rich and warming strong ale (7.8 percent ABV) which responds well to this method of serving dating back to the middle ages." R&B later organized regular cask nights at the Whip restaurant nearby, and they were the first to put in a cask beer engine

A draft sketch of the Auld Nick cask ale label. (Photo courtesy of SFU Archives, BC Beer History Archive, R&B Brewing fonds (F-330)

at the Irish Heather pub in Gastown, which ordered two R&B kegs a week.[36]

These cask nights, R&B's first two core English beers, and their initial hopes for a historical name might suggest that R&B aspired from the start to be a traditional brewery. In 2011, beer writer Jon Stott thought as much: "With two exceptions, the beers are in the British tradition."[37] However, in their early planning, R&B anticipated diverting somewhat from that strictly traditional track. Their planned core lineup offered a range of more conventional styles: an amber, a red, and a hefeweizen, which on opening day translated into the Raven Cream (a dark mild), the Red Devil (an amber-ish pale ale), and the Sun God Wheat Ale. However, they also had a series of seasonal beers planned that included British styles but also some unusual choices for the '90s: a lemon lager, a porter, a Kölsch, a bitter, a Belgian-style fruit ale, and a Weissenberry, which was "a classic blend of wheat beer and local seasonal berries."[38] Their quirky beer styles continue today under R&B's ownership by Howe Sound (see below), with things like the Dill Pickle Gose, a popular "weird beer" for Vancouver drinkers that won first place in the Specialty Beer category at the 2023 BC Beer Awards.

The attitude to which they aspired in their draft business plan documents was an important part of how they ended up running the business. Benson has been part of pop-punk and jazz bands for years,[39] and he brought that energy to R&B, a brewery that followed a "rock 'n' roll ethos. The brewery was wired with giant speakers; whoever got to brew got to choose the music."[40] As early as 2000 they were seen as cutting-edge and important members of the East Van community; they were invited, for example, to sponsor "Get Lit!," a poetry-slam event at the Alibi Room[41] featuring award-winning spoken-word poets like Shane Koyczan. By 2007, their sales were growing by 25 percent a year and they had realized that their power as a brewery came not just from quality beer and customer service, but from "being in tune with the city and being very local."[42] Many in Vancouver's Ultimate Frisbee community in the late 1990s and early 2000s drank R&B beer and the brewery would sponsor their games. Marc Roberts, who now owns Back Country Brewing, and Nick Menzies, the GM of Tap & Barrel on Granville Island, both have good memories of filling empty milk jugs with beer at R&B and taking them to share after practice with the team.[43] Despite its traditional ales, R&B embodied the cutting-edge, creative part of the city.

Rapid growth posed challenges for R&B, though, just as it did for Granville Island Brewing and Shaftebury. In the 2007 article about their increasing sales, Benson and Dellow say that "they are in more danger of outgrowing their premises than becoming rich." Without the funds to significantly expand their facilities, they found it more difficult to compete with the increasing number of breweries opening up nearby. Competition for restaurant taps was ramping up, and restaurants were more likely to source beers from a variety of breweries than to devote multiple taps to just one. By 2013, breweries were opening up on-site tasting rooms, which transformed the industry. However, R&B didn't have the space or capital to create their own tasting room at that time.[44] According to a 2017 interview with Benson, "R&B couldn't logistically or financially create space for a tasting room in its building. Benson admits, delicately, that the brewery fell into 'a bit of trouble.'"[45] By 2015, they had put R&B up for sale, and Howe Sound Brewing made an offer. Howe Sound, which was established in 1996 as a brewpub in Squamish under the guidance of John Mitchell, wanted to establish some inroads for their beer in Vancouver. "We were interested in reviving and expanding R&B core brands and brewing selected Howe Sound beers locally in Vancouver," said then owner Leslie Fenn in an interview with *Vancouver Magazine*.[46] The capital available through Howe Sound allowed R&B to expand and catch up: by 2016, R&B had its own tasting room, the R&B Pizza and Ale House.[47]

After the sale, Benson remained at R&B as a sales representative and general face of the brewery. It's Benson you'll see at a beer festival, bringing R&B to the masses. And he's grown and changed along with the brewery; his favourite beer used to be Sun God Wheat Ale, one of their first brews, and it's now the Vancouver Special, a bright, hoppy West Coast IPA. But he remains enthusiastic about the brewery and the craft beer industry in general. In 2022 R&B marked its twenty-fifth anniversary, and during our conversation Benson described some of the twenty-five different beers they would be releasing in celebration—including a return of Sun God. Their average customer today has a more discerning palate than the average customer of 1997. "The education has happened!" Benson enthuses. He also credits industry growth to the education and talent he sees in brewers these days, thanks in part to new brewing programs, particularly the one at Kwantlen Polytechnic University. "About three or four of our brewers have been KPU graduates," he says. But the fact remains that these brewing programs likely wouldn't have had the momentum or political support to get off the ground were it not for the earlier years of brewing and consumer education put in by Benson and others. R&B's continued presence in the Vancouver beer scene is a testament to the passion Benson still holds for this industry and his influence on so many other brewers and brewery owners.

Shirley Warne

Shirley Warne is one of the early women in the Vancouver craft beer world, but she started in Ontario, where she got her first professional brewing jobs before moving to BC where she was hired as Steamworks' first brewer. After Steamworks, she brewed in the Maritimes, then returned to BC where she worked as a consultant for Brassneck Brewery, Bomber Brewing, and Crannog Ales before establishing Angry Hen Brewing in Kaslo.

"OLD BITCH BITTER" is one of the beer names stamped, newspaper-
-style, on the back wall of Brassneck Brewery in Mount Pleasant,
just a couple of blocks from Main Street Brewing, which occupies
the place where Charles Doering's Vancouver Brewery stood in the
1880s. Men have dominated brewing since Doering's days,[48] but the
slightly shocking "OLD BITCH" on that wall reminds me of the asser-
tive, strong women who have brewed and sold beer for centuries.
Women who might get called a bitch. I'm sure Mary Mueller (whom
we met in Chapter 3) was called all sorts of names when she was
trying to make a profit at Columbia Brewery in the 1890s and 1900s.

"Yeah, that was originally Shirley's," Nigel Springthorpe,
co-founder of Brassneck, confirms when I inquire about Old
Bitch Bitter. Shirley Warne is a woman with a lengthy brewing
resumé from coast to coast. When she helped Conrad Gmoser and
Springthorpe set up Brassneck around 2013, she brewed her English
bitter recipe for them, which she unabashedly named Old Bitch.
It was one of Brassneck's very first brews. Warne recalls brewing
the same beer out of her Vancouver apartment with her twin sister
Pat in the 1990s. Both were skilled homebrewers, and their bootleg
beer sales were well known to neighbours, who would sometimes
come knocking to see what they could buy.[49] Warne also ended up
brewing Old Bitch at her own Angry Hen Brewing, one of the few BC
breweries owned and operated by women. Brassneck's description
of their version of Old Bitch captures Warne's take on the stereo-
type: "A traditional English Bitter brewed by ever-so-slightly jaded
25-year veteran of the BC brewing scene, Shirley Warne. Don't mess
with an Old Bitch."[50] Warne recalls one Angry Hen patron who
was offended by the beer's name and stomped up to the counter to
demand an explanation. "Well, I made the beer," Warne remembers
saying, "and I'm an old bitch! I should be able to name my beer
what I want!" As one of the few women in Vancouver craft brewing
during the 1990s and 2000s,[51] and an openly gay woman at that,
she quickly became used to dealing with others' responses while
staying focused on her own goals.

Warne grew up with beer. Homebrewing parents meant that she was familiar with the brewing process during her childhood living in Medicine Hat. She went on to homebrew while she attended university, but she wanted more.[52] Through a friend, she met Paul Hoyne (eventual co-founder of Lighthouse Brewing in Victoria and brother to Sean Hoyne of Hoyne Brewing), who got her in the door at Ontario's Conners Brewery. She moved from apprenticing in the cellar to working in the brewhouse, but swiftly realized that the monotony of production brewing wasn't for her—nor was the sexism to which she was regularly subjected by upper-level management. While her co-workers were great, the men in the company's upper echelons regularly sexually harassed the young brewer-in-training, first in the cellar, then in the brewhouse. She knew she wanted to be a brewer—but not there. "When I heard there was an opening at the Amsterdam Brew Pub, I went in and asked for an interview with Joel Manning," she says. "After a bit I asked to taste his beer, and it was so delicious I told him outright that I wanted the job."[53]

Brewing at Amsterdam and then its sibling brewpub, the Rotterdam, helped Warne develop her brewing skills and build valuable friendships—some of which would continue into her BC brewing career. She helped mentor both Tony Dewald and Harley Smith while at Amsterdam Brewing, two men who would make a splash in BC. Harley Smith ended up becoming a close friend despite an inauspicious beginning. She remembers Smith making an off-colour joke on his first day. "I jumped on him," she laughs. "I thought he looked really sloppy too. 'You're hiring *him*?' I asked Joel. But we became best friends. He's just such a great guy; he's so personable." With Smith, Manning, Dewald, and others, Warne had a solid group of colleagues and friends in the Toronto brewing scene. The camaraderie wasn't limited to working hours either, she remembers: "We got up to a lot of things in Toronto. We'd sit there, all of us, and keep drinking at The Rotterdam, then you'd ride your bike home and wonder what you did last night."

In 1991, after a few years brewing for Amsterdam, she moved to Vancouver to join her sister Pat. They took up homebrewing again,

Shirley Warne at the Rotterdam Brewpub in 1989, photographed by her sister Janis. (Photo courtesy of Shirley Warne.)

but this time Warne had more experience under her belt. Using supplies from Dan's Homebrew Shop (one of the only places to serve the home-brewing community back then), she started making beer that was far better than the stuff she and her sister cooked up in university. The twins brewed "Old Bitch Bitter" and other beers from their apartment and hosted parties during which neighbours would both drink and purchase their homebrew. Sometimes they'd come knocking at the sisters' door late at night, hoping that more beer was available for purchase. Warne's beer was so good, in fact, that it helped her get her first Vancouver brewing job a few years later, in 1995. By this time Warne had been exploring Vancouver's beer scene, looking for opportunities and chatting with brewers, such as Wittig and Beaton at Shaftebury. Dan Small of Dan's Homebrew Shop passed on Warne's name to lawyer Eli Gershkovitch and architect Sören Rasmussen when they came by the shop to inquire about any talented local homebrewers. Gershkovitch and Rasmussen had recently joined forces to transform The Quarterdeck, a shop in Gastown whose beautiful spiral staircase caught their eye, into a brewpub. To do that, though, they needed a good brewer.

Upon Dan's recommendation, Gershkovitch and Rasmussen invited Warne for an interview. She showed up with a six-pack of her homebrew, and when they had a taste of that, they hired her immediately. Warne's unique approach to making and naming beer was evident even at this early stage in her career. The *Sun*'s coverage of Steamworks' opening describes how they were tasting a test batch of Warne's newest beer, called "Rastabolter." According to the paper's account, "there's apparently an Australian brew known as dog-bolter. [Warne's] is a cat-bolter, named after a friend's departed feline."[54] Another *Sun* article describing the new brewpub seems a bit perplexed by the combination of Warne's job title and her gender, referring to her as "the brew-Ms" instead of "brewmaster."[55]

Warne began brewing while Steamworks was still under construction. In an interview with *What's Brewing*, she recalls "brewing with a shroud of plastic around the brewhouse. It was 'steamy' alright." One of the carpenters working on the job site while she brewed was Conrad Gmoser, a young assistant to Rasmussen who was making some extra cash in construction on the side.[56] Warne recalls that they quickly became friends and within a year he was working as her assistant brewer; he took over as head brewer when she left in 2000. "I was totally confident in him," Warne says. "He was already a brilliant brewer by then."[57] Gmoser would go on to lead Steamworks' brewing program until he opened his own brewery—Brassneck Brewing in Mount Pleasant, which he established in 2013 with Nigel Springthorpe and the help of Warne.

Warne demonstrated her brewing and business credentials repeatedly over the years, not just at Steamworks but later as a consultant to help other breweries establish themselves. These breweries included Crannog, Brassneck, and Bomber, but she also was the brewer for Ridge Brew House in Osoyoos, a job that required her to fly to the Okanagan from Vancouver whenever she needed to start a new brew.[58] This brewing gig didn't leave a lot of room for creativity; at the time, Warne said that "most of the customers are older drinkers who have fixed tastes...they want something that is a crossover, not too different from familiar tastes."[59] She wanted her own brewery.

Easier said than done. Warne recalls multiple failed attempts to establish a brewery in the Vancouver area and her eventual feeling of defeat at being let down at every turn. "It was disheartening," she says. "I knew I had good equipment and could produce top-quality beer,

Angry Hen's opening day, when friendships were formed. (Photo courtesy of Shirley Warne)

but I could not find anyone willing to back me. Potential investors disregarded my expert opinions and often seemed to actively look for reasons to dismiss my knowledge...I realized that my professional experience and expertise was not valued in the same way as a man's."[60]

Warne then cites other beer industry women who have inspired her, namely Rosa Merckx, the first female brewmaster in Belgium, and BC's own Nancy More, who has worked for decades in the beer industry and established Kwantlen's brewing certification program. Warne knows better than most what it took for women like Merckx and More to establish their names in brewing. During our conversation, she recalls how frustrating it was to not be taken seriously by investors when she wanted to make her mark in this industry.

Despite the friends she made in the tight-knit Vancouver beer community at the time, Warne was ultimately unsuccessful in finding investors, so she packed up and headed east. It was in the village of Kaslo that she started her own brewery—an ambition shared by nineteenth-century Vancouver brewer Robert Reisterer. As Chapter 2 discusses, Reisterer tried his hand at running a Vancouver brewery in the 1890s, but repeatedly expressed his desire to relocate his business to Kaslo—and he finally did (although he ended up relocating again to Nelson). Like Reisterer, Warne felt that Vancouver had little to offer her career-wise. She fell in love with Kaslo, a small community just an hour from Nelson, before she opened Angry Hen in 2017. The village's picturesque location between imposing mountains and one of BC's largest lakes, its gold-rush-style high street, and its intimate community all made it feel like the perfect place to set up her brewery.

In December 2017, shortly before Christmas, Warne was ready to open her doors. A few weeks before, Conrad Gmoser and Jeff Leake, her old friends and mentees from Brassneck, had travelled nine hours to Kaslo to help Warne with her first brews on her new system to prepare for opening day. When they departed, she was left to do her first solo brew—and it didn't quite work out as planned. She forgot to sanitize a tank in the middle of the process, resulting in the beer acquiring an extra level of bitterness due to increased contact with hops. She named the beer "Freak Out" in honour of the madness. "There are still people who ask for it!" she laughs. It was on the board for Angry Hen's opening day, along with their Christmas Ale, East Meets West IPA, a pale ale, a Helles, and a Kölsch. A local couple were so eager to try the beer that they were knocking at the door while the paper was still covering the windows. Warne decided to tear the paper down and open up to welcome Jolayne and Brenda in—and she and her wife are still friends with them to this day.

Left and right: Warne's brewery Angry Hen is a community hub in the village of Kaslo.

Middle: Shirley Warne in her brewhouse at Angry Hen in 2023. (Photos by Noëlle Phillips)

Angry Hen is now an integral part of its community, and is often referred to as "Kaslo's Living Room." Vancouver beer drinkers are lucky when one of Angry Hen's beer runs comes through town—it's their chance to try Warne's legendary beer once again. As of spring 2024, the brewery is struggling in the wake of the government's COVID loans coming due, but the community has rallied to support it.

Gary Lohin

Gary Lohin began his career in brewing in the late '80s with Whistler Brewing before moving on to Okanagan Spring Brewery in the early '90s. By the mid-'90s, he was brewing for Sailor Hagar's Brewpub. He eventually opened his own brewery, Central City Brewing, with Darryll Frost, who had been the chef at Yaletown Brewing and a colleague of brewmaster Iain Hill.

Tall and powerful-looking, with deep-set eyes, a strong chin, and blond hair, Gary Lohin could pass for a Viking (and he *did* make one of the first Scandinavian beers in BC while brewing for Sailor Hagar's Brewpub). I imagine he could be very intimidating if he wanted to be. However, he has a warm, kind demeanour that immediately puts others at ease. In my many interviews with Vancouver brewers, almost all of them recommended I also interview Lohin—the brewmaster who put Surrey beer on the map but also helped shift beer tastes and marketing in Vancouver.

Like many other early craft brewers, Lohin started by homebrewing in university. His parents bought him a homebrew kit for his birthday, "with a can of malt and a plastic bucket and spoons and stuff," that allowed him to make a batch of Cooper's Real Ale.[61] Lohin was very pleased with the results and was inspired to brew more. It was a cheap and easy way to make decent, drinkable beer—a priority for many university students. He began to be a regular patron of a homebrew shop on Kingsway near Joyce, and he ended up joining the homebrew club that the shop owner ran. It wasn't long before he was winning awards for his creations, despite the limited ingredients accessible in the 1980s (the variety of malts available could be counted on one hand, with fingers to spare: pale, amber, and dark). He brewed with friends like Bill Herdman, an old high school buddy and the future founder of Squamish's Tall Ship Ales. Herdman would become one of the style pioneers in BC, making things like hoppy IPAs well before the public was ready for them. His avant-garde style may have been one point of contention between him and David Bruce-Thomas, owner of Horseshoe Bay Brewing Company, when Herdman brewed for him in the early '90s.[62] However, as home-brew buddies, Herdman and Lohin could be as creative as they wished. They even brewed all the beer for Lohin's wedding in 1987.

Lohin soon began bartending at Sailor Hagar's, first a bar, then a brewpub in North Vancouver that was an early supporter of craft beer. He recalls how Okanagan Spring was a game-changer for the local beer industry; their pale ale was one of the first craft beers to take over taps previously dedicated to Big Beer. "It was groundbreaking," he says. "Okanagan Spring Pale Ale was in all the pubs serving Labatt or Molson or whatever. Their pale ale was this amber colour and people really liked it. If you went into any dive bar, you'd see that one tap was Okanagan Spring and everything else was the same [i.e., macro beer]. This really opened the door for guys like Granville Island and Shaftebury." While he bartended, Lohin was paying attention to these new craft beers that were starting to take up taps: the Granville Islands, Shafteburys, and OK Spring. They tasted pretty good—he remembers thinking that the OK Spring Pale Ale tasted like the pale ale he made himself. If they could make beer and sell it, why couldn't he? When Whistler Brewing, which was poured at Sailor Hagar's, came by the brewpub to look for people interested in brewing for them, Lohin stepped forward.

This was in 1989, shortly after Gerry Hieter (future founder of the Great Canadian Beer Festival in Victoria, and then Lighthouse Brewing) had established Whistler Brewing and then was compelled to give the reins to an investor.[63] Chapter 7 briefly discusses Hieter's conundrum with his new brewery, but there are connections here to Lohin's career. Hieter, then manager of Whistler's Longhorn Pub, along with four friends wanted to start a Whistler brewery. He drew up a business plan around 1987 and had Herman Hoerterer, a brewer from Okanagan Spring, lined up to brew for them once they actually opened. But funding was short and in that first year, Hieter and his partners hadn't yet brewed their first batch and were struggling. In 1989, when investor Rob Mingay offered to fund the brewery in exchange for control over the business, Hieter reluctantly accepted the deal. He sold the name "Whistler Brewing" to Mingay for one dollar. Mingay became the president and Hieter was the general manager (sometimes also referred to in the papers as VP), a position that he kept for only a couple more years before he resigned out of frustration. "Mingay was originally regarded as our savior," Hieter remembers, "but he eventually became my personal nightmare."[64] In Hieter's recollection, Mingay didn't want Hoerterer to be the brewer because he had too much experience. Instead, he wanted a newbie, someone who could be taught a controlled, systemized form of brewing—a kind of brewing that allowed very little creative flexibility. Mingay decided that Doug Nicholson, one of Hieter's initial partners and not a professional brewer, would be trained up to brew instead. Thilo Bucholz, a traditional Austrian brewer, trained Nicholson in the summer of 1989 and their first beer was released around Thanksgiving of that year.

Mingay also tried to expand too quickly, attempting to establish a market in Japan before solidifying the brewery's consumer base in BC. Hieter observed Mingay rapidly promoting and firing staff and using the brewery's money to cover his own expenses—renting a house and buying a vehicle. Hieter finally resigned around 1990, and two of his partners were fired a year later. However, it wasn't long before the board of investors fired Mingay and another investor took control. After an amalgamation with Coquihalla Brewing Co., Whistler Brewing was eventually purchased by Calgary's Big Rock Brewery and its brewhouse was shut down.[65]

But Lohin had escaped before all this messiness; he started at Whistler around 1989 and wasn't there for long. He learned a lot on the job, however; without any formal brewing education, he trained under Bucholz and learned some traditional brewing techniques.

In 1991, he was offered the position of head brewer at Okanagan Spring in Vernon and he took it. He brewed there for several years until 1994, when he received a call from Sailor Hagar's, asking him to come back. This ended up being a transformative opportunity, and one that took him on a very different path than he might have travelled at Whistler Brewing under Mingay and his successors. Sailor Hagar's owner had seen the successful recent openings of Yaletown and Steamworks, and was planning to turn the bar into a brewpub. Lohin remembers being a bit nervous at the prospect of this new position. All the responsibility for the beer would be on his shoulders—a big difference from his role brewing for Whistler or Okanagan Spring. But he wasn't one to run from a challenge, and the upside of this responsibility was his own creative freedom: "That's when I first got to brew what I wanted. I liked hops and had fun playing with IPAS and an ESB," he says, remembering the excitement of this new opportunity.[66] Sailor Hagar's turned out to have a significant influence on the development of craft beer culture—and customers' craft beer palates—in Vancouver. Beer writer Stuart Derdeyn describes Hagar's role in the Vancouver beer world at this time as "really essential."[67] And Lohin was a huge part of its success.

The new Sailor Hagar's brewpub opened in April 1994 with a 10 hL system and Lohin as brewmaster. "I remember christening the mash run by turning it into a hot tub for an evening, complete with scotch and cigars," Lohin recalls.[68] After their hot-tub party, Lohin got to work making a lineup of European-style beers for Sailor Hagar's five beer engines. He started with an English pale ale, a honey lager (using a recipe from Papazian's *Joy of Homebrewing*), an ESB, a Scandinavian lager, and a nut-brown ale.[69] As the brewpub began to draw more beer-curious customers, he would get creative with something as simple as a pale ale, offering drinkers pales made from different English base malts (like Maris Otter, Golden Promise, and Pipkin) and having them taste the beers side by side. "People were amazed at the differences!" he says.[70]

Lohin has good memories of brewing at Sailor Hagar's. As a

working father, he was able to bring his children to the brewhouse and they would play on their skateboards or with their toys while he was brewing. In the heat of summer, he'd strip down to just shorts and gumboots on a brew day—something that wouldn't happen nowadays. He recalls friends Ed Bennett and Skip Madsen of Bellingham's Boundary Bay Brewing coming up to visit him at the brewpub. Time would fly by when they'd sit in the brewhouse after work, pouring beer right from the tanks. It wasn't uncommon for them to be there until the wee hours of the morning. Occasionally he'd help out other brewers, like Conrad Gmoser at Steamworks, who needed "a bit of yeast from time to time." Lohin's deal with Gmoser was yeast for a bottle of single malt, which Gmoser happily provided.[71] There were also big names who came to try Lohin's beer at Sailor Hagar's, Lohin says. One was Michael Jackson, the famous beer writer. Lohin remembers him arriving tipsy, drinking more beer, and eating a steak. Dick Cantwell, beer writer and founder of Elysian Brewing, was another friend who'd pop by Sailor Hagar's to share a beer with Lohin.

Craft beer is very much a local industry, but the best craft brewers seek a global beer education—discovering and tasting beers from around the world. Lohin would travel to Washington and Oregon, sometimes with his family, to try new beers and attend beer festivals (back when beer festivals were a lot more niche than they are now). His beer palate was influenced by the beers being produced in these areas, and he brought some of those flavours to BC. In later years, while at Central City, he travelled to Europe as well, guest-brewing and learning about new beers. In the Czech Republic, he found European beers that were emulating Pacific Northwest beers. "We were influenced by Europe in the beginning, then it reversed!" Lohin says. He remembers meeting the original founder and brewer of what later became Hoegaarden, Pierre Celis, at a beer conference in Oregon and quizzing him about how he made his famous witbier. Celis shared how much orange and coriander he used per litre, and Lohin adapted his own recipe accordingly, eager to serve a Belgian classic to his BC customers.

This witbier became a turning point moment for Lohin, as well as for Sailor Hagar's customers. He was proud of this new beer, which was cloudy and with characteristically Belgian spiced citrus notes, and excited to put it on tap. However, to his dismay, servers kept bringing the wit back, saying customers were complaining that it wasn't made correctly. The haziness was a hurdle for a city of drinkers brought up on macro beer ads that falsely linked clarity and quality. Through multiple conversations with customers and servers, Lohin began a process of beer education. And it worked! When Lohin used finings in one batch of his wit to make it clear, he had customers send it back: "A witbier should be cloudy," they'd say. Lohin laughs, remembering thinking he couldn't win. But he knew that the second example meant that customers had actually learned about that style and were prepared for more.

Expanding customers' beer knowledge gave Lohin more room for creativity in his brewing at Hagar's. They started playing with IPAS in 1994 and 1995. At the time, this style was still fairly avant-garde; Tall Ship Ales in Squamish was really the only other brewery doing them. Lohin made several versions of a Bengal IPA for Hagar's, and a Jewel in the Crown IPA, but didn't develop them further because he wasn't interested in seeming competitive with Tall Ship. IPAS weren't Hagar's niche. By 1996 he was making bottle-conditioned Scotch ales, which were unusual for the time. As with the Belgian wit, he made sure to educate drinkers about what to expect. In an interview from this time, he recommended that customers store these ales long-term (again, unheard of for BC beer at this time), explaining that sherry-like qualities would develop over

Left: Sailor Hagar's Bengal IPA, from Lohin's collection.

Right: Sailor Hagar's Wee Heavy Scottish Ale, from Lohin's collection. (Photos by Noëlle Phillips)

a decade of cellaring.[72] These intense Scotch ales and their success set the foundation for one of Lohin's most famous and best-loved beers: the Thor's Hammer barley wine. It was 1998 when he brewed his first batch of Thor's Hammer at Hagar's, averting potential confusion among customers by explaining that there were no grapes despite the name: the grain bill was 100 percent barley, and the port and currant flavours came from the yeast.[73]

Most people know of Thor's Hammer not through Sailor Hagar's but through Central City, the Surrey brewpub, later craft brewery, for which Lohin is perhaps best known. Darryll Frost, the executive chef at Mark James's Yaletown Brewing, wanted James to open a brewpub in Surrey. When James wasn't interested, Frost did it himself, in partnership with Lohin. They opened their doors in 2003 in the Surrey Central Mall with a brewpub licence. By this time, brewpubs were allowed to distribute, a legislative change that was accomplished in 2000 due to the efforts of Paul Hadfield, founder of Spinnakers. Without this change, BC IPAS might never have taken off in the way they did.

Tall Ship was brewing really interesting, adventurous, and niche IPAS in the 1990s, but most beer drinkers weren't quite ready for those. Bill Herdman was ahead of his time. However, by the mid-2000s, with cask nights and other "real ale" events starting up at places like R&B, Dix, and Whip and an increasingly beer-savvy customer base thanks

Left: Sailor Hagar's version of Thor's Hammer, from Lohin's collection.

Right: Central City's version of Thor's Hammer, from Lohin's collection. (Photos by Noëlle Phillips)

to brewpubs like Sailor Hagar's, an IPA was no longer such a wild idea. The early IPA experiments Lohin did at Hagar's—the Jewel in the Crown and the Bengal—had honed his skills for brewing an IPA at Central City that would appeal to the craft beer drinker of the new millennium. The quality of the IPA combined with unique branding ended up making Central City famous. I'm referring, of course, to the Red Racer IPA, with the famous vintage-style image of a redhead on a bike with her skirt blowing up in the wind to show her stockings and garter belt.

Red Racer IPA didn't start out this way though. Lohin recalls that the original lineup of Central City beers included a red ale, a pale ale, a wit, an IPA, and an ESB. The images on each can were different, but all portrayed scenes from New West or Surrey history. The Boomer's Red Ale, for example, had a man riding a log down a river. The Springboard Lager depicted loggers taking down a tree. The Red Racer Pale Ale had a pin-up style woman riding a bicycle, an image inspired by an anonymous painting that Frost had seen in a restaurant. "We thought it was a fun picture," says Lohin. "A little racy, but fun." The Liquor Distribution Branch, which approved all beer branding and marketing, challenged Lohin and Frost, claiming that the picture was too sexualized for inclusion on their beer cans. The brewery owners' counter-argument was that the LDB allowed Old Milwaukee in its stores—a beer whose branding used a similarly racy pin-up image. LDB let it go, and the stylized pin-up Red Racer bicycling girl was born. She first appeared on cans of the Red Racer Pale Ale. It also felt fitting because of Lohin's own love of cycling and his warm memories of his childhood "red racer" wagon. To this day, the tasting room at Central City is full of cycling paraphernalia.

When the beers hit the shelves at liquor stores, Lohin noticed that the pale ale was easily outselling the rest. Red Racer seemed to appeal to customers. By 2005, they had rebranded all the beers as Red Racer; it became their central marketing strategy. Sales increased across the board, but especially for the IPA. It seemed that people were now ready for the balanced bitterness of a good IPA, a style that is still at the top of many BC beer drinkers' list of favourite tipples. Just three years later, in 2008, Lohin's 8.5 percent ABV Imperial IPA won Best Beer in BC according to Vancouver's chapter of CAMRA (the Campaign for Real Ale).[74] In 2010, the Red Racer IPA was included in BeerAdvocate's elite list of top ten IPAs,[75] and Central City was named the best brewery in Canada by the Canadian Brewing Awards.[76] Lohin's ability to combine brilliant marketing with adventurous brewing and a good sense of timing managed to move the BC beer world into new territory: it was time for the IPA to step into the spotlight, and Red Racer helped that happen. Central City expanded and opened new lines of production, eventually including whisky and non-alcoholic beers. The large Central City brewhouse now contract brews and packages for other companies and manages a huge barrel-aging program, as well as keeps up its own line of beers. It's an impressive set-up, and one that was ultimately enabled by Lohin's early inventiveness at just the right time in BC beer history.

Left: Two cans of the original Central City beers, from Lohin's collection.

Middle: Gary Lohin in the Central City brewhouse with some vintage beers from Sailor Hagar's.

Right: The Central City brewhouse, 2022. (Photos by Noëlle Phillips)

Tony Dewald

Tony Dewald learned to brew at Amsterdam Brewing in Toronto (where he met Shirley Warne) before moving to BC and being hired at Mark James's Dix Brewpub, where he organized popular cask nights that involved many other local brewmasters and breweries. He later worked for Dead Frog Brewery in Langley, consulted for Old Abbey Ales in Abbotsford, and then was hired as brewmaster for Trading Post Brewing in Langley.

Tony Dewald thinks of his love affair with beer as beginning in Belgium, almost by accident. It was 1988 and he was touring in Europe with his band, Deja Voodoo.[77] He was the drummer and threw all his energy into each show, winding up drenched and thirsty at the end of each hot summer night's performance. He remembers walking off the stage in Brussels and someone handing him a beer. But this wasn't a Molson or a Bud—it was a Belgian framboise. He was blown away. "I didn't know beer could taste like that!" he recalls. Back in Canada, he met Joel Manning, the brewmaster at Amsterdam Brewing, while doing a show in Toronto. Manning invited him to come over after the performance and learn how to brew. Dewald shrugged it off at the time, but a little while later, when the band had broken up and he was at a loose end, he took Manning up on his offer. He ended up working at Amsterdam for seven years, where he got to know some famous BC brewers including Shirley Warne and Harley Smith, then at Brasseurs RJ in Quebec, where he learned about Belgian brewing techniques and bottle-conditioning. When it became clear that he wouldn't advance at Brasseurs, in 2000 he decided to pack up his brewing stuff and head west, just as Warne and Smith had done.

It was Iain Hill who really helped Dewald get his foot in the door of BC's craft brewing scene. Hill and his wife Christine were about to have their first child, so Hill trained Dewald on the Yaletown system and eventually moved him around to all the Mark James Group brewpubs. Dewald also jumped in at Storm, working part-time under James Walton, whom he still calls one of the best people in the industry. He was at Storm from 2002 to 2005 and participated in "all the

Storm craziness. It was so much fun!" he laughs. "We were making lambic, which was so unusual back then. Anything was possible. I had such a good time there." In between shifts at Storm, he was brewing mainly at Dix, where he helped to establish their monthly cask nights together with Lundy Dale and the Vancouver chapter of CAMRA. The cask nights went quickly from fifteen to twenty people per event to over fifty, thanks both to CAMRA's improved communications and to the variety of beer on offer. John Mitchell would often stop by, thermometer in his pocket, for some pints of cask ale and some conversation—these evenings were how Dewald got to know him. The cask nights would feature a different guest cask each time, showcasing the skills of Vancouver's brewers and providing a hub around which the newly forming craft beer community could bond.

During these events Dewald tapped his own casks as well as the guest casks, of course. He was most famous for his IPAs, which he would sometimes make explosively hoppy—overloading the cask with hops to explore all possible flavours. "Sometimes the hops obliterated all other flavours," he admits, laughing. His IPA experiments were

Tony Dewald and other Vancouver brewers outside Dix. (Photo courtesy of Brian K. Smith)

Tony Dewald and Dix bar manager Mark Andrewsky carrying a cask on a bier for Vancouver Craft Beer Week in 2010. (Photo courtesy of Brian K. Smith)

driven by his relationship with an American couple, Adam and Gillian Gile, who loved California's hugely hoppy IPAs. The Giles would make suggestions for each brew, and he'd give it a shot. There was always a new version of his Dix IPA, and it almost always ended up being popular. In his IPA endeavours he was following in the footsteps of brewers he admired, men like Bill Herdman back in the '90s ("his IPAs were so balanced") and Gary Lohin with his more recent Red Racer IPA ("he's a magnificent brewer who towers over the crowd"). Dewald has only good things to say about his fellow brewers. "I respect them all!" he enthuses.

Dewald ended up brewing at all of Mark James's brewpubs, although Dix was always his main position. When he moved to Aldergrove around 2007, however, the commute into Vancouver became arduous, so he took a brewing job first at Big Ridge in Surrey and then at Dead Frog in Langley. Neither job suited him—he didn't feel a connection. After a few years' break working in the wine industry, for Lotusland Vineyards, Dewald returned to brewing. Another short stint at Dead Frog was interrupted by a call from Don Piccolo and John Ohler, a close friend of John Mitchell and formerly the chef at Howe Sound Brewing. Piccolo wanted to set up a brewery in Abbotsford with Ohler's help, and Ohler in turn knew that Dewald was a person with the brewing expertise needed. And this is how Old Abbey Ales was born. It wasn't too long before Ohler was recommending Dewald again, this time to Paul Verhoeff, co-founder of a new brewery in Langley—the Trading Post. Dewald joined Trading Post as their brewmaster, and it was here that he found his true brewing home. His love for Langley, its citizens, and the hyperlocal beer they brew at Trading Post is clear in how he talks about his job, his workplace, and his colleagues.[78]

Dewald's creations have won numerous awards, but awards aren't what he values. His favourite beers are the ones with which he has the best memories: the Spirit of Dixmas ale that he brews each year with Brassneck, the hoppy IPAs he made with the Giles, or just a crushable, quality lager that he can drink all evening over conversation with friends. Dewald isn't into fancy beers; he sees the industry now as backing away from novelty beers and returning to many of the classic styles, like nut browns, pale ales, and stouts. He might be right; the winner of the best beer in Canada at the 2023 Canada Beer Cup was the Basal Brown Ale by Deadfall Brewing in Prince George. One avenue for innovation and creativity that he sees in craft beer's future is in (surprise!) hops: "We never thought hops like Citra would come out! In the '90s, only Saaz and Perle were available. Citra had so much flavour. Who knows what kind of hops we'll end up developing down the road?"

Early in 2023, Dewald and his wife Andra were both diagnosed with cancer. The craft beer community rallied around the couple, offering support in all possible forms. Later that year, Dewald was selected as the first winner of the annual John Mitchell Lifetime Achievement Award for Brewing Excellence. The Barley Merchant taphouse in Langley

In October 2023, Vancouver's craft beer community gathered at the Barley Merchant in Langley, one of the best taphouses in BC, to celebrate Tony Dewald winning the first John Mitchell Lifetime Achievement Award for Brewing Excellence. (Photo courtesy of Brian K. Smith)

was packed for the event, with long-time craft beer luminaries like James Walton, Iain Hill, Harley Smith, Brad McQuhae, Ken Beattie, and many others joining to honour Dewald's life and achievements. Smith, his old colleague at Amsterdam Brewing, accepted the award on his behalf since he was too ill to attend. Many glasses were raised in his honour, however, and cheers went up for him. It's clear that the craft beer community respects Dewald as much as he respects them.

Lundy Dale

Dale isn't a brewer, but she's had a significant influence on the craft brewing industry in Vancouver. From working at liquor stores to R&B Brewing to founding the Vancouver chapters of CAMRA and the Pink Boots Society, Lundy Dale has been a voice for women in BC craft brewing since the '90s and is still active in the industry today.

When I began chatting to local brewers and beer writers when my first (academic) book about craft beer was published, a common question was, "Oh, have you talked to Lundy yet?" I hadn't at that point—but I knew of her. She's never worked as a brewer or owned a brewery, but for decades, Lundy Dale has had her finger on the pulse of BC craft beer. When people think "women in beer" in this province, they think of Dale. She's done pretty much everything in the craft beer industry except actually run a brewery or work as a brewmaster—although she does brew her own beer. During our interview, we chatted about our respective fresh-hop homebrewing efforts and she shared that she'd recently made a one-gallon batch of fresh-hop IPA with spruce-tip-infused Centennial hops from Northwest Hop Farms.[79]

"I don't know when that switch [for craft beer] actually turned on," she muses, thinking back. Granville Island Brewing may have been her "gateway" beer, as it was for so many other Vancouver craft beer fans; she remembers that her neighbour, who would teach her to knit, was a huge Granville Island fan. They'd knit together and drink the beer. Shortly after that, Dale's expat British friends urged her to join them at local beer festivals, like the Vancouver Brewers Association festival and the Great Canadian Beer Festival in Victoria. These experiences opened her eyes not just to the kind of beer she could be drinking ("Wow, this is amazing stuff!" she remembers thinking) but also the kind of community craft beer could provide. She loved talking to the brewers in their booths; they were artists with a passion for what they were making. She was so inspired that she joined the Victoria branch of CAMRA in 1999.

In the early 2000s Dale was working at the private liquor store Firefly (a prime craft beer resource), participating in beer events when she could, and wondering why Vancouver didn't have its own branch of CAMRA yet. She saw the people coming into her store and leaving with craft beer—the interest was here! She approached John Rowling, the head of CAMRA Victoria, about her plans and asked for permission to start a separate group, which he was happy to give. He did let her know, however, that a CAMRA chapter in Vancouver actually *had* started years before, but the now-forgotten members were smuggling hops across the border and stealing the group's money. "We decided to be legit—start new!" she says.

They had their first meeting in January 2003 at Dix, the Mark James brewpub whose cask nights became craft beer legend and whose brewmaster Tony Dewald could blow up your taste buds with a crazily hoppy cask IPA. Dewald was already running his monthly cask nights, so Dale asked if they could have CAMRA Vancouver meetings there on the same evenings and host guest casks from Vancouver brewers. The first cask was R&B's Red Devil cask ale, and the second was from Conrad Gmoser, brewing under the supervision of Shirley Warne. He showed up with Warne and her sister. The third meeting hosted a cask from Backwoods Brewing, later Dead Frog, who brought their nut-brown ale. CAMRA membership was small at the beginning— maybe fifteen people, Dale recalls. However, once CAMRA became involved in festivals and established partnerships with liquor stores like Brewery Creek and Firefly, membership grew quickly.

The Vancouver craft beer community found a home at Dix. From left to right: Tony Dewald, Lundy Dale, Rick Dellow, and Barry Benson. (Photo courtesy of Paul Morris)

Around this time, Dale was realizing that despite how much she loved and knew craft beer, she wasn't being respected for her exper-tise by her liquor store colleagues or the public shopping at Firefly (brewers and brewery owners, however, were a different story). She was a short, pretty blonde—and those characteristics apparently meant she couldn't possibly be a beer nerd. "People looked at me and said, 'How do you know anything about beer?'" she recalls. "It was so frustrating." She decided to do something about it: she studied for and passed the Cicerone exam, earning the title of Certified Cicerone. In the beer world, a Cicerone is like a sommelier—an expert in beer styles, production, and service. The Cicerone exam is notoriously difficult, and it took Dale three tries to pass, but pass she did (and she passed before her male liquor store colleagues, it should be noted). "I had no idea it would be as hard as it was. But it was worth it," she says. To study for the test, she started hosting beer classes at Firefly, planning the topics around the things she needed to know for the exam. Many of her students signed up for multiple sessions, eager to know more about beer and brewing, and Dale was able to clear two hurdles: recruiting people into the craft beer world and preparing herself for the arduous challenge of the Cicerone examinations.

This was around 2003, and Dale had been working at R&B Brewing on a casual basis for a while. She did everything from cleaning tanks to helping with their finnicky bottling machine (lovingly nicknamed Frankenstein) and doing general brewhouse chores. Alyson Tomlin, who later founded Riot Brewing, was R&B's brewer at the time and Dale was encouraged to see another woman in the industry. With her varied skills—from cleaning to tasting—Dale was eventually hired full-time at R&B, and she loved it: "It's great being in a small brewery where you can get your hands on everything!" With her tasting skills and beer knowledge, Dale was a valuable resource for Barry Benson and Rick Dellow as they developed events and played with new beer styles. However, Dale felt that they loved tradition so much that they were resistant to change—to pushing style boundaries. "Talk to any of their brewers, they'll tell you the same," she says. "We all *loved* the guys [Rick and Barry], but they wouldn't let us try different yeasts, different malts, different hops. They wanted the established recipes." The Dark Star Oatmeal Stout, the Red Devil Pale Ale, the Raven Cream Ale, the Sun God Wheat Ale, and the Hoppelganger IPA were their core beers for a long time (and the IPA was the most edgy and daring). Occasionally, Dale recalls, they'd follow the brewer's intuition and release a more experimental, adventurous seasonal. She remembers one brewer, Todd Graham, who was also a chef and created recipes that were what she calls "food-centric." There was one award-winning cucumber mint IPA that she loved: "All you could smell was cucumber and fresh mint when you stepped into the brewery." Graham's "Chef Series" beers were truly memorable.

From Dale's perspective, the financial difficulties R&B fell into in the early 2010s were at least partially related to the brewery's tendency to cling to old habits. R&B felt comfortable where it was and didn't feel the need to adjust when other breweries started opening. However, in the fast-paced craft beer climate of the early 2010s, where innovation sold and nearby breweries were experimenting with odd new styles, sticking with just the traditional wasn't workable. Without the tasting room legislation that was rumoured in 2012 and took effect in 2013, this may not have mattered quite so much to R&B—but it *did* take effect (see Chapter 10 for more on that). Breweries opened at a rapid rate in 2012 and 2013 because they knew they'd be able to have a tasting room and sell beer on site. It meant more customer demand for greater variety; breweries sell a limited number of styles in kegs to restaurants or in six-packs, but if people are visiting the brewery and can have a flight, they'll be looking for more kinds of beer. In 2013 R&B was brewing a limited number of styles, didn't have the capital or space to create a tasting room, and was now competing with 33 Acres, Main Street, and Brassneck. They were in a difficult position.

The purchase of R&B by Howe Sound, discussed earlier, ended up being the best possible outcome given the situation, according to Dale. Unlike other brewery takeovers, such as Granville Island's, Whistler's, and Shaftebury's, this one didn't end up either destroying or changing the brand's reputation. Howe Sound's owners at the time, Dave and Leslie Fenn, were committed to keeping the spirit and brand of R&B, while extending the brewery's beer offerings and funding the expansion of the brewery and construction of a tasting room. Benson stayed on and remains involved, and the brewery itself maintained its spot as a hub of Vancouver craft beer. Their tasting room is funky, eclectic, and comfortable. The food is excellent, as is the beer—but now they have things like the award-winning Dill Pickle Gose, a Lemongrass Saison, and fun seasonals like the Porch Ornament Pumpkin Ale as well as their core lineup.

R&B's difficulties began after Dale returned to Vancouver following a few years working in Alberta. In addition to her involvement with R&B, Dale had other connections and commitments during this time. After jumping back into CAMRA activities upon her return in 2008, she realized that she was tired of being the only woman doing everything, tired of feeling like she was the only woman who liked beer. She began reaching out to other women interested in craft beer: "Why don't we start having meet-ups? Beer dinners? Start connecting." The Pink Boots Society had officially started up back east, so after communicating with that chapter's president, Dale started a west coast chapter. This was initially called Pink Boots Vancouver, but because of the small pool of women involved, Dale eventually succeeded in calling it Pink Boots BC. They had maybe twelve women across the province at first, including Rebecca Kneen from Crannog Ales and Claire Wilson from Dogwood Brewing, but the group grew quickly. At every brewery she visited, every festival, and every cask event she'd attend, Dale would find the women—she would seek them out and make an effort to recognize them. Pink Boots kept growing. Soon Dale was writing a series for *What's Brewing* magazine about women in the craft beer industry. "These women feel like my kids," she laughs. "The women are wonderful. It's such a great community."

Lundy Dale receives the Legend Award at the 2018 BC Beer Awards. (Photo courtesy of Charles Zuckermann)

As if this weren't enough, in 2011 Dale also established October as BC Craft Beer Month (a provincially endorsed designation) and works to promote that each year. She's the head judge at the BC Fest of Ale and is regularly asked to judge beer competitions. She takes on part-time positions in various beer-related spaces, even though she thinks she should probably slow down. And although she and other women are often overshadowed by the brighter profiles of the men in craft beer, in 2018 Dale was honoured with the inaugural Legend Award at the BC Beer Awards, a tribute to "those who have gone above and beyond for beer over their lives."[80] It was a well-deserved award—and Dale is tirelessly continuing her beer advocacy to this day, continuing to be a "mother" to all the up-and-coming women working in craft beer and struggling for recognition and respect.

Mark James

Not a brewmaster but a businessman, Mark James's brewpubs and brewery launched the careers of many brewers and increased the public appetite for good craft beer. He opened five brewpubs in the 1990s, then eventually his own brewery, Red Truck Beer Company, in the mid-2000s. Red Truck is a staple Vancouver brewery to this day.

Red Truck Beer Company. (Photo courtesy of Red Truck)

Mark James's name is well known around Vancouver, but his face is perhaps less so. James is a quiet, private person and it's difficult to find information about the man himself versus his business, the Mark James Group (MJG). I was grateful when he agreed to an interview. In person, he is calm and soft-spoken, but with a low-key intensity and focus that reveal something of how he achieved so much success in the brewing industry. James is justifiably proud of the influence he's had on BC craft beer, with his founding of five brewpubs and one large brewery—Red Truck Beer Company. During our interview, we sat in a meeting room with a row of beer taps at one end and a window at the other giving a glimpse of the large brewhouse factory floor that pumps out beer twenty-four hours a day, seven days a week.

One thing James wanted to clarify shortly into our interview was the nature of his company and what it's done over the years. Some think of MJG as a giant corporate behemoth, taking over breweries and brew-pubs and turning them into chains. One reason for this misperception is likely the similar-sounding name of the Mark Anthony Group (MAG), a much larger company that buys up and rebrands beverage businesses. MAG's brands have included White Claw, Mike's Hard Lemonade, Mark Anthony Wine & Spirits, Bearface Whisky, Glendalough Distillery, and the wineries Checkmate, Mission Hill, Road 13, and others. MAG was also the owner of Stanley Park "Brewery," which isn't a brewery at all (although there is now a brewpub) but instead a brand whose beer was produced by MAG's Turning Point Brewery in Delta. In 2015, MAG divested its ready-to-drink and beer products to Anheuser-Busch InBev (a.k.a. Budweiser) via Labatt, which AB InBev also owns.[81] This means, in other words, that Budweiser owns Stanley Park Brewing, and they bought it from the Mark Anthony Group.

This rapid-fire summary should show that the Mark James Group is very different from the Mark Anthony Group, despite the similarities in the name.[82] MJG is defined in various places as "a collection" of brewing and distilling companies. Mark James himself says that these different businesses have the same owner but MJG is not a "company" in a formal sense.[83] All the beer businesses included under MJG were started by MJG and were or are local contributors to the Vancouver craft beer industry. So despite the current size of Red Truck's brewery, which far exceeds the majority of BC breweries in both production levels and space, the Mark James breweries and brewpubs were and are still very much about BC craft beer. It's just that their corporate head is a savvy businessman rather than a brewmaster.

James got his start not in beer, but in clothing. He was on the front edge of fashion in 1970s Vancouver when he brought major brands like Hermès into his shop. His eponymously named clothing store in Kitsilano was beside his restaurant, which he switched from fine dining to pizza and beer when he realized where the profit was. And it was the beer that seemed underserved in Vancouver, yet with lots of potential. According to Frank Appleton's recollection, James had calculated that 40 percent of his restaurant's profits came from beer sales.[84] He started to look into the possibility of a restaurant specializing in both beer and food—a brewpub, in other words. Travelling down to Portland, he visited various breweries and brewpubs to see how they were run. He noted the community vibe, the camaraderie of the patrons, and how beer brought people together. His next step was a visit to Victoria, where he'd heard a new brewpub was being built by the same guy who'd made a success out of Horseshoe Bay Brewery and Shaftebury. Frank Appleton was helping to set up Swan's Brewing in Victoria, and one day he saw a young man in a suit beckon him over. It was Mark James, and he (along with his father and the architect he'd hired) was interested in Appleton's help in converting the Yaletown warehouse they'd purchased into a brewpub. Over beers, they came to an agreement. Appleton recalls that this meeting "would lead to my designing the first of four pub brewery operations for the Mark James Group. The Group's Yaletown Brewing Company would be the first brewpub in Vancouver."[85] The others built by MJG would be Big Ridge, Dix, Avalon (later Taylor's Crossing), and Whistler.

MJG had an expansive enough budget to allow for the earthquake-proofing updates required on the building and the proper equipment for the space, which meant that the skills of the brewer—Iain Hill, whose story is told earlier in this chapter—could be put to optimum use. Hill was hired on the recommendation of Appleton, and ended up spearheading the brewing program at all of the MJG brewpubs, through training brewers and brewing himself. Unlike Rob Mingay, whose interference in Whistler Brewing spelled its decline, Mark James seems to be the kind of boss who hires experts and mostly lets them get on with it rather than micromanaging. Frank Appleton said as much in his memoir: "Mark James stayed in the background during the building of Yaletown Brewing, but he was always there when a decision or cheque was needed. Just before we opened…he told me, 'You know, Frank, what I thought might be a problem, something I was out of my depth with, was brewing the beer. Would it really be first-class? But it was not a problem at all. You took care of everything!'"[86] Hill stayed on with MJG for nearly two decades before opening his own brewery, and in doing so he fulfilled what James had hoped for these brewpubs. They shifted the public perception of and appetite for craft beer, and they also provided spaces for brewers to share information and hone their craft. It was at an MJG brewpub, Dix, that the first CAMRA meetings took place and cask nights were hosted. It was in the MJG brewhouses that legendary brewers like Dave Varga (of 33 Acres and most recently Shaketown) and Tony Dewald began establishing their reputations.

The MJG brewpubs all opened between the mid-1990s and mid-2000s, but by 2010 the brewpub craze was fading—and the brewery boom was about to begin. "Brewpubs are gone," James states matter-of-factly during our conversation. "The consumer wants selection. Whether it's brewed on site or not, it doesn't matter." The rise of Vancouver taphouses like the Alibi Room and St. Augustine's reinforces James's view. These taprooms are where craft beer drinkers go to find a good range of taps—they won't seek out a brewpub anymore. But in the 1990s and early 2000s, with no brewery tasting rooms and no taprooms outside of Fogg N' Suds (which was often half full of imports), the brewpubs were a place you could go to sit down and sample a few local beers.

Sensing the brewpub boom was dying down, James declined the suggestion by Darryll Frost, his chef at Yaletown, that he should open a brewpub in Surrey. Instead, he started looking into running a brewery. His Taylor's Crossing Brewpub (formerly Avalon) in North Vancouver, with brewer Dave Varga, who later would work for 33 Acres and Shaketown, was making more beer than it could sell on its 18 hL system. To deal with the excess, James loaded kegs into his beloved 1946 red Dodge truck for delivery and established a brand to sell them under: Red Truck Beer Company. This was around 2005, and their first customer was the Vancouver Canadians; the little red truck would deliver beer to Nat Bailey Stadium.[87] In Varga's recollection, once the Canadians advanced from single-A to triple-A, they started looking for more money—and that was when Red Truck expanded its distribution to pubs and restaurants. Red Truck soon became popular and was sold on tap across the Lower Mainland (delivered by the red truck, at least at first). MJG was protective of its new brand: shortly after Red Truck was born, Phillips Brewing in Victoria named one of their beers Blue Truck (after the old blue truck that Matt Phillips used for deliveries), and MJG "protested that the name was in conflict with theirs and advised that Phillips should stop using it."[88] And that's how Phillips's famous Blue Buck Ale came to be.

With the success of the Red Truck brand, James decided he needed to set up an actual brewery, and he was determined it would be in Vancouver. An initial deal on a Terminal Avenue property fell through and it took two more years to find the site where the Red Truck brewery and Truck Stop Diner ended up being built: a two-acre site not far from Mount Pleasant, the seawall, and downtown. In addition, it has historical resonance; this site was that of Lion Brewery, "where Brewery Creek once drained into False Creek."[89] A large site with easy pedestrian access was important to James; he wanted the brewery to be part of the fabric of the community, a place to eat, drink, and listen to music. To begin the construction of the brewery once the site was acquired, MJG held a celebratory event in which a red truck was

This aerial shot of an event at Red Truck gives a sense of the brewery's size. It hosts live music throughout the summer; there's plenty of space for people to gather for entertainment, food, and of course beer. (Photo courtesy of Red Truck)

dropped from a crane.[90] It was the equivalent of smashing a bottle of champagne on a ship's hull as it was launched.

The Red Truck brewery is impressively large, certainly larger than any other craft brewery in Vancouver. "You'll never see a facility of this size built in Vancouver again," James says as we walk around the factory. With forty years of experience in Vancouver development, he should know. The brewhouse is designed to produce 100,000 hL per year, but they produce well under that amount—not even 50,000 hL per year. Their lineup of beers is consistent in quality, presentation, and branding, which isn't surprising given the brewery's quality control systems. James hired specialists from Molson to handle QC and sanitation procedures. The brewery's engineers are from Molson as well. MJG did consumer studies before launching the brewery and found that the smaller the brewery, the lower the quality control. They wanted something different for theirs.

Red Truck is sometimes seen as "not craft" because of its size, its ownership by what seems like a big corporation (an inaccurate perception), and the supposed lack of variety in its beers when one compares it with edgier breweries. However, by all standards of the industry, Red Truck is a craft brewery. James isn't interested in pursuing new beer fads or avant-garde experimental beers. Many breweries do that, and do it well, but it's not his goal. He wants to produce well-made, conventional styles with a consistent quality. It seems to work—Red Truck has won numerous awards for its core brands, and it's affordable when compared with the high prices other breweries are forced to attach to their more expensively produced styles. Due to its rigorous quality control, you're unlikely to find off-flavours in Red Truck beer. The overall branding is based on nostalgia—a nostalgia evoked by the 1940s red truck—and simplicity. For those who are overwhelmed by the explosion in craft beer styles and options, Red Truck offers a simpler, more approachable version of craft beer. James is passionate about keeping the warmth and nostalgia in the

The craft beer community in Vancouver is close-knit. Here, some pioneers in the industry gather to celebrate one of their own—Tony Dewald—at an event in 2023. From left to right: Gary Lohin, James Walton, Iain Hill, and Brad McQuhae. A photo of Dewald is behind them. (Photo courtesy of Brian K. Smith and *What's Brewing*)

branding. Red Truck feels like an old-fashioned beer brand rather than a cutting-edge one—and it's supposed to.

◆

Vancouver's era of brewpubs and its rock-star, second-generation brewmasters set the tone for what Vancouver craft beer could be. The city's beer legends, most of whom are still in the industry today, established themselves during this decade—the mid-1990s to the mid-2000s. But the actual number of craft breweries in Vancouver remained low until about 2013, when there was an explosion of growth. The next chapter explains why. Get ready for the Vancouver craft beer boom!

CHAPTER 10
BREAKING DOWN BUREAUCRACY: THE CRAFT BEER BOOM POST-2012

In 2012, Vancouver's beer scene looked very different than it would a couple of years later. At that time, there were about nine craft breweries in the city, and business was going fairly well for them. These breweries included Dockside Brewing Co., Coal Harbour Brewing, Parallel 49 Brewing, Powell Street Craft Brewery, Red Truck Beer Co. (which was brewed in the shuttered Taylor's Crossing Brewpub), and of course Storm, R&B, and brewpubs like Yaletown and Steamworks. Between 2013 and 2015, however, there was an explosion of new breweries, including Brassneck, Main Street, 33 Acres, Bomber, Dogwood, Off the Rail, Postmark, Strange Fellows, and Callister. And that was just in Vancouver proper. In neighbouring cities appeared breweries like Deep Cove, Green Leaf, Hearthstone, Four Winds, Moody Ales, Steel & Oak, Dageraad, Twin Sails, Yellow Dog, and more. Although craft breweries continued to open at a rapid pace in 2016 and later, many of Vancouver's beloved and famed craft breweries appeared during that 2013–2015 window. But why? What happened to change the industry so quickly and drastically? This chapter will explore the reasons for the post-2012 craft beer boom and share some stories from the breweries that were founded during this time.

LIQUOR AND THE LAW: THE SQUEAKY WHEEL GETS MORE BEER

Why the beer boom? In one word: legislation (not the most exciting answer, but still a powerful one). This isn't new, of course; changes to BC's antiquated liquor legislation have enabled the success of craft breweries since the early 1980s. This was when John Mitchell lobbied for the government to allow his pub to brew its own beer, and Mitch Taylor successfully advocated for changes in the old, nonsensical excise law that had required brewers to produce and sell at separate locations.[1] In the 1990s, Mark James worked hard to get permission for his Yaletown Brewing to serve alcoholic drinks on an outdoor patio—an application that was eventually approved by City Council but was a point of contention with the Vancouver Police Department. Around 2000, after Paul Hadfield's ongoing lobbying, the BC Supreme Court took his side and the provincial government amended its liquor laws to allow brewpubs to sell their beer not just in the pub, but in liquor stores and licensed establishments such as restaurants. "This decision is good news for consumers," said Ian Waddell, the minister of Small Business, Tourism and Culture at that time. "They will have an increased selection of premium B.C.-crafted beers."[2] In 2000, there were eighteen brewpubs in BC and these were brewing 1.2 million litres of beer per year, which amounted to 0.5 percent of provincial beer consumption. It was an important moment for moving craft beer further into market visibility.

Legislation is constantly on the mind of craft brewers in BC, a province known for making it difficult for responsible drinkers to enjoy their beverages and for producers to make and sell them. BC's draconian alcohol laws, which until relatively recently forbade liquor stores from opening on Sundays and did not allow patrons to order a drink if they didn't also order food, have long reinforced Vancouver's regrettable reputation as a staid, boring city.[3] I interviewed many brewers and brewery owners for this book, and I asked all of them what events, policies, or legislation they thought had had the greatest impact on the craft beer industry in Vancouver. Many acknowledged the earlier legal changes referred to above, but all of them highlighted one legislative shift: the provincial lounge endorsement that was passed in 2012 and came into effect in March 2013. It's due to this change that craft breweries' share of the BC beer market was 9 percent in 2009 but 19 percent by 2013 (and 30 percent by 2021).[4] The effect of this endorsement cannot be overstated.

Up until 2013, breweries couldn't sell beer out of the brewery itself, other than small samples of up to 12.7 ounces; most of their revenue needed to be generated through wholesale (getting their beer on tap at restaurants and pubs). Breweries pre-2012 were in a similar situation to Columbia, Red Cross, and D&M in the 1890s, which were discussed in Part I—prevented from selling their beer directly to drinkers on site. Since front-of-house sales are the most cost-effective way for breweries to sell their beer, this law put breweries at an economic disadvantage. It also revealed the province's imbalanced approach to the alcohol industry, since the government *did* give permission to wineries to have tasting rooms and sell glasses and bottles of wine to patrons for consumption on site. The government's responses to two letters from William Spat, secretary of the yet-to-be-opened Skeena Brewing in 2011 and 2012, reveal how the impetus for legislative change happened.[5] We don't have Spat's original letters, but can infer that he was asking for a lounge endorsement on his brewery application, in the manner permitted to wineries. Solicitor General Shirley Bond's response to the 2011 letter suggests that brewers were starting to make a stink about the lounge laws: "Until recently, government had not received any requests from the brewing and distilling industry for these types of endorsements. However, based on recent requests, my staff is presently reviewing this matter. If a decision is made to proceed then it is likely that consultation with the industry will be necessary." The April 10, 2012, response to his second letter, this time from Assistant Deputy Minister and Liquor Control and Licensing Branch General Manager Karen Ayers, makes it clear that the consultation was indeed going to happen—and soon. Parallel 49 Brewing was another brewery pushing the government to allow the lounges, and there were likely more.[6]

Just one month later, in May 2012, the government surveyed BC's distillers and brewers for their thoughts on the matter and noted "widespread support" for a change. They describe how much of the feedback from breweries cited a number of innovative craft beer business models present throughout the Pacific Northwest and California—places where the craft brewing industry has blossomed in particularly innovative ways and has been enthusiastically supported by local governments. These cities are quickly becoming destination areas for beer enthusiast tourism, and breweries are able to distinguish themselves not only by their products but by the experience they provide visitors.[7]

The new changes to BC's laws put breweries and distilleries on par with wineries in this respect. The province's edited documents, released to me through a Freedom of Information request, reveal the differences. The former wording described a "Winery licence" and associated "Winery lounge endorsement" under the various liquor licence categories; this licence "allows patrons to purchase and consume wine manufactured and bottled in BC by the glass or bottle in a designated lounge area." The revised wording includes breweries and distilleries, and changes "Winery licence" and "winery lounge endorsement" to "Manufacturer licence" and "manufacturer lounge endorsement." According to the new licensing wording, "a lounge endorsement allows patrons to purchase and consume the manufacturer's liquor in a designated lounge area...on the manufacturing site."[8] In other words, the new legislation allowed breweries to have tasting rooms where they could sell their beer in higher quantities directly to consumers. Such a shift also enabled a more cohesive brewery culture to emerge, as breweries developed their own spaces for sharing food and drink.

GETTING THE CITY OF VANCOUVER ON BOARD

As the Liquor Control Branch regulations make clear, the relevant local government must approve the lounge endorsement before a brewery can open a tasting room in that city. In April 2013, just weeks after the province put the new legislation into effect, Vancouver City Councillor George Affleck took the first step toward making this change happen in Vancouver. "Having been to Portland and experiencing the [beer] scene there," Affleck said in an interview, "I think we can do something special... I think Vancouver could be a real destination. People tour around to drink craft beer like other people go on cruise ships."[9] Later that month, he put forward a Council motion titled "Enabling the Micro-Brewery and Distillery Industry."[10] The motion highlighted the importance of BC's tourism sector, referred to the new manufacturer lounge endorsement, and directed staff to "report back to Council on the required changes to the relevant regulations within the City of Vancouver that would permit micro-breweries, wineries, and distilleries on industrial land to sample and sell craft beer and spirits produced onsite, thus being consistent with provincial liquor policy." That staff report, which considered the zoning issues, industrial land use, and alignment with provincial liquor policy, was submitted to Council on June 13, 2013. City staff indicated that they consulted with the local brewing and distilling industry and found them "generally supportive of the proposed changes." The report emphasized that the changes would support local breweries while not negatively affecting neighbouring properties.

The last step in getting the City's approval and assessing public appetite for the changes was a public hearing, which was held on July 9, 2013. Letters of support from the expected sources were submitted, including a letter from CAMRA and a joint submission sent by Conrad Gmoser on behalf of "Vancouver's Craft Brewers." This group, which included the old-guard craft breweries as well as some brand-new ones,[11] praised Vancouver as "home to an enthusiastic and educated population of craft beer drinkers who share a particular love for locally produced beer. Brewery lounges in Vancouver will encourage...brewery tourism." There was also Campaign for Culture, which emphasized the need for sensible liquor laws. However, many other voices came out of the woodwork in support of the changes. Chad McCarthy, a Certified Cicerone, Beer Judge Certification Program beer judge, and homebrewer, drew attention to how craft breweries can "revitaliz[e] urban industrial zones challenged by the perennial flight of businesses to less expensive lands in the suburbs." Other letter writers referred to the beer culture they knew from other areas, such as Portland or Germany, and expressed hope that Vancouver would follow suit. Elizabeth Coish emphasized that breweries are a valuable alternative to bars and clubs. Many submissions referred to the province's moralizing prohibitionist leanings and draconian, outdated liquor laws. Eric Edington-Hryb seemed baffled that this was even a question: "I don't understand why there is even (apparently) a debate on the subject; why should breweries not be allowed to sell their own products for immediate consumption? The craft beer movement in Vancouver and in BC is still in its adolescence and could use your support." Many letter writers expected that brewery lounges could help rehabilitate Vancouver's reputation as "No Fun City."

All told, the public hearing received 832 emails and letters in support of the changes and 70 against (and many of those against were only against because they felt there were still too many restric-

Mayor Gregor Robertson taps the first cask at Vancouver Craft Beer Week in 2010. (Photo courtesy of *What's Brewing*)

tions). Council passed the resolution unanimously. This wasn't much of a surprise; the City was led by Gregor Robertson, a mayor known to be a craft beer fan and supporter of the industry. In fact, he'd tapped the first cask in the inaugural Vancouver Craft Beer Week back in 2010.

One year later, in June 2014, Vancouver city staff provided Council with an update on what had happened during the first year of brewery lounges being permitted. All feedback was positive—no concerns were identified. In that first year, five breweries received approval for a lounge and more were underway. Some of the breweries that had opened in late 2012 or early 2013 in anticipation of this new law (including Brassneck, Main Street, and Bomber) were among the first to have a lounge.[12] The immediate success of this legislative change was followed up by a full-scale provincial Liquor Policy Review in 2013 under John Yap and the BC Liberal Party, during which the growing craft beer industry was consulted on what changes needed to happen to bring BC's liquor laws up to date. The city's craft brewers provided recommendations that were incorporated into the final report, changes such as legal parity for all liquor, allowing liquor to be sold at farmers' markets, draft beer serving sizes, the LDB craft beer listings, and minors in licensed establishments.[13] Some of the seventy-six recommendations were put into effect; others remain untouched. Ken Beattie, head of the BC Craft Brewers Guild, asserts that the power of the recommendations was diluted by slow government action until David Eby of the NDP took over. When Eby formed the Business Technical Advisory Panel headed by Mark Hicken, Beattie says, it got all people in the alcohol industry talking and working together. Twenty-four specific recommendations were put forward. As I write this, there's still work to be done, but more cross-industry conversations are happening: beer, wine, distilling, liquor stores, restaurants, and rural agency stores all need to be part of the discussions.[14]

STORIES OF START-UPS: THE BREWERIES OF THE CRAFT BEER BOOM

With the passing of the lounge endorsement, Vancouver quickly became a craft beer destination, with iconic craft breweries sprouting up in the old neighbourhoods where nineteenth-century breweries like City Brewery, Vancouver Brewery, and Columbia Brewery once stood. Breweries that were founded during the craft beer wave of 2012–2014 include Strange Fellows, Parallel 49, Bomber, and Powell—plus more. In 2015, Off the Rail and Dogwood opened; Off the Rail was the brainchild of Steve Forsyth, owner of the Railway Club restaurant, which hosted craft beer taps long before it was trendy. Dogwood is Vancouver's first organic brewery, owned and run by brewer Claire Wilson. In that same year, Julia Hanlon became Steamworks' head brewer, succeeding Conrad Gmoser. As the craft beer boom spread, women were finding more opportunities.

The remainder of this chapter highlights some of the key breweries that opened in Vancouver during this two-to-three-year boom, breweries that significantly influenced the culture of craft beer in Vancouver. Because there isn't sufficient space in here to tell the story of each Vancouver brewery that was established in this time, I've selected those whose names were mentioned by almost every person I interviewed for this book. When I asked people what modern breweries were the most important to the growth of craft beer in the city, these were the "beer boom" breweries whose names occurred most frequently: Brassneck, Main Street, Strange Fellows, Parallel 49, and Callister.[15] I was also interested in which non-Vancouver breweries had an influence on Vancouver beer. No one can deny that some breweries outside Vancouver's boundaries established themselves as innovators and taste-shifters. These breweries helped to refine and raise customer expectations in the heart of Vancouver's beer scene and across the Lower Mainland. Dageraad and Four Winds are two good examples; both were frequently mentioned in interviews as important breweries that opened during the boom. Their presence influenced consumer habits and boosted the ability of Vancouver breweries to push style boundaries themselves.

The breweries established in 2012–2015 were a new kind of trailblazer: they weren't in the same situation as Granville Island or Shaftebury, nor were they an R&B or a Storm, but they were nevertheless key players in advancing Vancouver craft beer to the next level—a level that couldn't have been imagined by brewery start-ups in the '80s.

It seems appropriate that the new Mount Pleasant breweries, which include Main Street Brewing, Brassneck around the corner, and 33 Acres a couple of blocks away, were among the first to acquire lounge licences and the first to start transforming the craft brewery experience into what it has become today. After all, Mount Pleasant was where most Vancouver beer got its start. Brewery Creek ran from Tea Swamp down through Mount Pleasant 150 years ago, providing energy to breweries along its banks. The building that now houses Main Street Brewing was originally the property of Charles Doering's Vancouver Brewery, which opened in the 1880s. Although the current building wasn't used to brew beer, it does sit on the site of the original brewery and functioned as the brewery garage for several years.

Like Vancouver Brewery, Main Street was established by a savvy businessman—or, rather, two businessmen. Ironically, one of those owners, Nigel Pike, also is a co-owner of the Cascade Room, which shares a name with Vancouver Breweries' famous Cascade beer. His business partner Cam Forsyth formerly owned Vancouver's Portland Craft. They both knew the industry. Given the history of the building and the neighbourhood, it seemed that a brewery was a good business option. "We wanted to bring a brewery back to the neighbourhood that was all about breweries," says Pike.[16] Before the brewery's physical location actually opened, they were contract brewing with Russell Brewing in Surrey and getting their name out into the Vancouver beer market. They decided to start with a pilsner—something with a North American flair, though, rather than a hoppy European style. An approachable and flavourful single beer was their initial goal, but they quickly realized they needed more than one style. With Russell getting their beer out the door and with their own business connections, they were able to get Main Street beer on tap at restaurants long before they actually opened the brewery.[17] This gave them momentum by the time the brewery opened.

And they needed momentum. Before the lounge legislation passed, there were vocal opponents to the idea of having a brewery in this neighbourhood. One email from a Vancouver constituent in February 2012, in response to a development proposal for a multi-use facility in the area, voices the disgust some had for Pike and Forsyth's plans:

> Do you remember the District condo development, here, also in Mount Pleasant, land of many promises re maintaining the creatives still hanging around, albeit barely these days? Because when the District promised to keep the heritage garage on 7th Avenue as an artist/community ammenity [sic], the city allowed the developer to add an extra story onto the building. [. . .] Well then! Check out the plans for that heritage building now, because it is to become a restaurant/brewery, wheeeee! no mention of ah, community and such [. . .] seeing as absolutely *no one* in the actual Mount Pleasant artist and otherwise community... wants a bloody restaurant/brewery on the site! That is a retail and commercial space, it is not what was promised at all. you gave them permission contingent on an ammenity, so how in the hell does this rate as an ammenity?? That someone is going to make money off a bunch of drunks and well-off diners???[18]

Just a year later, Vancouver citizens would express their full-throated approval for brewery lounges across the city, but this letter writer viewed breweries as a place for "drunks," as if a brewery were equivalent to a bar. The lounge endorsement ultimately helped to educate the public about what brewery spaces really are. It's very unusual to see loutish drunkenness in a craft brewery; you're far more likely to see people slowly enjoying a flight, families having an afternoon break, or dog walkers stopping by for a pint. The first Vancouver brewery lounges began changing public perceptions of beer and beer culture.

When Main Street officially opened its doors after years of contract brewing, during the 2014 Vancouver Craft Beer Week, it was to a warm reception by locals. "We were running out of beer straight away," Pike remembers. "We needed more tanks!" Main Street has continued to foster its positive reputation in its neighbourhood and the craft beer community, with innovative brews (including a cask series) by brewmaster Azlan Graves and support for various causes, such as autism and gender equity.

Main Street's current head brewer, Azlan Graves. (Photo courtesy of Main Street Brewing)

Just down the block, near Main and 6th, Brassneck Brewery was opening its doors as well. This was exactly what Forsyth and Pike were counting on—fellow breweries opening up in the same neighbourhood and creating opportunities for brewery tourism in Mount Pleasant. 33 Acres Brewing just across Main Street was also joining the party. According to Nigel Springthorpe, co-owner of Brassneck, his brewery was the very first in BC to receive the lounge endorsement licence, just a month after they opened. 33 Acres and Main Street received their licences shortly afterwards, creating a small "brewery block" in Mount Pleasant (R&B was in the area as well, although they didn't have a tasting room at this stage). Like Forsyth and Pike, Springthorpe and his business partner Conrad Gmoser, formerly of Steamworks Brewing, wanted Brassneck to be in close proximity to other breweries for this very purpose: cultivating a sense of community. "Physical location is important," says Springthorpe. "This kind of place is here to serve the neighbourhood. Lots of similar businesses around, lots of people walking by."[19] Local patrons have always been the focus of Brassneck, which didn't can its beer at all until 2017 and even now doesn't distribute as widely as many others.

Nigel Springthorpe in the Brassneck tasting room. (Photo by Noëlle Phillips)

Brassneck's tasting room—the first brewery lounge in Vancouver—is striking: walls made of pieces of wood fitted together like a strange jigsaw puzzle, plants sitting on the shelves, high tables and chairs, and a cozy front window that gives a view of Main Street's passersby. The names of their beers are all stamped on a wall near the back.

Springthorpe credits the taproom's personality to woodworker Joseph Holmes-Peters, a much-loved figure in the community. Springthorpe first met Holmes-Peters at a coffee shop where they got to talking about music. He bumped into him again months later, and Holmes-Peters said, "Hold on! I have something for you." He went out to his truck and brought Springthorpe some mixed CDs he'd created for him after their first conversation. "That's the kind of guy he was," recalls Springthorpe. When Holmes-Peters designed the tasting room, he sourced all the wood from Craigslist and milled it himself. Every day for five months he spent time putting each piece of wood in place. No designer was involved—just Holmes-Peters's instinct. Brassneck remains one of the warmest and most unique tasting rooms I've visited.

Left: The author and some fellow craft beer fans in the Brassneck tasting room.

Right: Brassneck's wall of beer names. (Photos by Noëlle Phillips)

Brassneck is an iconic Vancouver brewery, but it was built on the shoulders of giants. You could think of it as the love child of the Alibi Room, Dix, and Steamworks. "Brassneck is a physical manifestation of a lot of work at the Alibi," said Springthorpe in a 2013 interview.[20] He'd gone from employee to owner of the Alibi Room in 2006, and quickly transformed what had been a restaurant into Vancouver's first craft beer taproom, hosting forty-five taps in a century-old building that had originally been a church. St. Augustine's followed shortly afterwards, but at the time this range of local beers was unheard of. Springthorpe was on the edge of a movement—more people were becoming interested in craft beer. Bottle shops were opening, like Six Acres in Gastown, and exposing consumers to an unimagined variety of beer styles. Springthorpe had slowly been converted to craft beer in the early 2000s when he began tasting imports. He remembers how the Brooklyn Brewery beers on offer at the Brewery Creek Liquor Store sparked his passion for beer. "They had a pre-prohibition super-hoppy lager," Springthorpe remembers. "I was blown away that a beer like that existed." Alibi was the first place in Vancouver to put Brooklyn Brewery on tap. But it wasn't just imports at Alibi—Springthorpe's other priority was giving the stage to Vancouver's talented brewers. The first thing he would list on the beer menu would be the brewer's name. "I wanted to highlight who was behind the beer," he says. He hired servers who knew beer, he provided the correct glassware, and he refused to install TVs. The Alibi Room was a haven for beer fans.

When he'd been running the Alibi Room for about four years, Springthorpe started to think more seriously about starting his own brewery. This is where Dix and Steamworks come in. With his father-in-law's help, he purchased the brewing system from Dix, the famous Mark James brewpub where Iain Hill and Tony Dewald had brewed and whose regular cask nights turned Vancouver's craft beer drinkers into a craft beer community. He then invited a friend over for a chat. Springthorpe had met Conrad Gmoser at Steamworks and they clicked immediately. "When I invited him over, I had no idea where he was at career-wise or finance-wise," Springthorpe recalls. "I just knew he was somebody I could see myself being in business with. And he was a really respected and experienced brewer with a good reputation among his peers." While sitting in his kitchen with Gmoser, Springthorpe asked him if he wanted to start up a brewery. Gmoser immediately agreed, and the rest is history.

Springthorpe recognizes that timing contributed to his brewery's success. The new lounge endorsement was in place and the real estate market hadn't exploded yet. What he calls the "heyday" of 2013 is over, however, and people interested in opening a brewery now probably have to look outside Vancouver's borders. Rental costs and tax rates have become prohibitively high, and making a name for yourself in Vancouver's crowded craft beer market is increasingly difficult. "I wouldn't like to be opening a new brewery now unless I was Superflux,"

Springthorpe laughs, referring to the popularity and success that brewery has experienced since opening (more on Superflux's success in the next chapter). Like many other brewery owners I interviewed, Springthorpe admires Superflux. However, he doesn't want Brassneck to *be* Superflux; Brassneck is its own thing. He's proud of the consistency, variety, and quality the brewery has shown over the first decade of its existence. In 2022, Justin McElroy created a detailed tiered (pulling no punches!) review of all breweries in southwest BC, and Brassneck made it into not just the top ten, but the actual number one spot.[21]

Gmoser wasn't the only long-time Vancouver brewmaster itching to start his own brewery around this time. In 2014 Iain Hill (formerly of Shaftebury and the Mark James brewpubs) and his business partner Aaron Jonckheere opened Strange Fellows Brewing, which included a forty-three-seat tasting room. If you're coming down Clark Drive you can't miss it: the Strange Fellows sign sits at an angle, perched high over the sidewalk, weird and very visible to all passing cars and pedestrians. The tasting room's interior is fittingly strange, with animal masks up on the walls and all the S's on their menu board reversed. Large glass windows give tasting room patrons a view into the brewhouse. This was an important part of their plan from the beginning, according to Jonckheere's brewery blog: "When you are sitting in our tasting room, you will quite literally be 10 feet away from the brewhouse. Want to watch Iain add hops to a brew, just sit back enjoy your beer and watch from your perch."[22] Strange Fellows is definitely a must-visit for any East Van brewery crawl.

Hill and Jonckheere knew that East Van was the place for their new brewery. "It's grassroots, down to earth, more affordable, more accessible. You have creative people here," says Hill. "If you're in downtown Vancouver and you open a bar or brewery, you need to charge a lot for what you're doing. You don't have the opportunities that we have over here to play around and be unsuccessful. You have to get everyone in, you have to pump out vodka soda."[23] He chose to take the plunge into brewery ownership when people were more willing to try new flavours and styles—when the customer education was already well underway. When they opened, they weren't restricted to offering a lager and a pale; they started from day one with a barrel-aging program and a range of Belgian beers, like saisons, wits, golden strongs, and oud bruins—a throwback to Hill's Yaletown Brewing days.[24]

In his blog documenting the brewery start-up process, Jonckheere lists the different roles you need to fulfill if you want to own and run a brewery (and don't have the capital to hire staff yet): salesperson, janitor, accounting, digger, marketing, steelworker, decision maker, painter, social media, psychologist, human resources, bathroom cleaner, copywriter, phone hanger-upper, retain manager, mechanic, delivery person, and production (a.k.a. brewing).[25] The list is somewhat tongue-in-cheek, but there's no doubt that running a brewery is a far more overwhelming task than just brewing for one. Hill found this out first-hand, as he moved from brewmaster to brewmaster/owner/everything else. He tries to stay involved in most aspects of the brewery, and although he's predominantly a beer maker he also has a

One of Strange Fellows' unique beer labels, this one featuring John Barleycorn, a character from brewing folklore. (Photo courtesy of Strange Fellows)

The author and Iain Hill (costumed to participate in his brewery's hauntings) at Strange Fellows' Dead Fellows Haunted Brewhouse in October 2023. (Photo by Noëlle Phillips)

passion for beer marketing. "Stories are so important—they're what make people want to try the beer," he says. "A story can bring people together to share something. We like creating these stories."[26] Hill's wife Christine, who has been with him on his beer journey since he was a homebrewer, creates many of the Strange Fellows stories through the drawings and descriptions the brewery uses on their labels, many of which are based on mythological or folkloric figures. It's part of Strange Fellows', well, strangeness. "I've always wanted to create," Hill says. "I like being a craftsman. But I'm not even that anymore—I'm an entrepreneur, which is fine, but different."[27] He confided that since he's become a brewery owner he feels he's lost some of his enthusiasm, "even though people think I'm still very enthusiastic." Hill has a vibrant energy about him, something that must go into the innovative beers he makes and the events his brewery hosts. Around Halloween in 2023, for example, Strange Fellows was the first BC brewery (that I know of) to turn their whole facility into an extensive haunted house—the "Dead Fellows Haunted Brewhouse." Drag shows, painting classes, tastings—it all happens at Strange Fellows, and the beers never get boring.

Parallel 49 Brewing is northeast from Strange Fellows, not far from the industrial area of the harbour and just a block or two from where Columbia Brewery stood over a century ago. With its large distribution network and successful tasting lounge, Parallel 49 has spread the reputation of BC craft beer farther than perhaps any other craft brewery. Other brewers have credited it with making craft beer more accessible to people in the early 2010s.[28] Unlike Strange Fellows, however, it didn't come about as a brewmaster's passion project. Instead, it was a collaborative effort by six men in the food and beverage industry: friends Anthony Frustagli, Nick Paladino, and Mike Sleeman began the process, and invited Scott Venema, Michael Tod, and Graham With to join them. Although Frustagli, Paladino, and Sleeman already owned the St. Augustine's brewhouse and knew the craft beer industry, they weren't brewers themselves, nor were Tod and Venema. It was really only Graham With, their chosen brewmaster, who had hands-on experience with brewing. The partners flew with With, a chemical engineer and a skilled homebrewer, to China to purchase brand-new brewhouse equipment and they got brewing by early 2012. From the very beginning With was a creative and prolific head brewer, producing a wide variety of styles and flavours. Many of their early beers, first brewed in 2012 or 2013, remain core offerings to this day. For example, one of their first hoppy beers, brewed in 2013, is still poured every day at P49. It's now called Filthy Dirty IPA, but its original name was Lord of the Hops—until the Tolkien estate decided to come after them for copyright infringement.[29]

With had no formal brewing education, but his science background combined with years of award-winning homebrewing made him a hit. Even after joining Parallel 49, he kept his ties to the homebrewing community and his reputation for both skill and generosity. Ben Coli, owner of Dageraad Brewing, recalls how With opened Parallel 49 as the drop point for homebrewing competitions for years and helped homebrewers purchase malt, hops, and yeast for discounted prices. He was equally generous with fellow craft breweries. This set the tone for the industry, according to Coli: "I've found that Vancouver breweries have always been really collegial and helpful. The tone that Graham set in Parallel 49 helped establish that."[30] From the beginning, With wanted to honour BC's craft brewery community and its history. In 2013 he was approached by the Vancouver Craft Beer Week organizers to create a collab beer for the VCBW. In creating this collab, With wanted to give kudos to James Walton by re-creating Red Sky Altbier, the first beer brewed at Storm and one of the first craft beers With ever tried.[31] Generations of craft brewers lovingly riffing on one another's work—it's what Vancouver craft beer seems to be about! With's award-winning beers and his generosity with others testified to his place in this new generation of brewers, and was certainly key to Parallel 49's early success. They had a good range of styles, fun cartoonish branding, and one of the most popular tasting rooms in the city.

But it was also via Parallel 49 and its employees that movements for equity in the craft brewing world became more widely visible. Unrest was evident as soon as 2014, when workers at P49 attempted to unionize. "We were in a constant struggle with our owners and our management because we had grown to a size where they were businessmen and they sat in our office all day and they never saw what was happening on the production floor," said one worker who supported the unionizing. This person also indicated that wages were also a problem, since P49 employees were paid "well below" the average wage earned at other BC craft breweries.[32] The vote was unsuccessful, however, and there was "speculation that the drive had been undermined by behind-the-scenes managerial (owner) influence."[33] Several employees who were against unionizing expressed concern that such an action would "take the craft out of craft brewing" and that the reps from the larger union body (Brewery Winery & Distillery Workers Union Local 300) didn't understand the ethos and value of craft beer.[34] Resistance to unionizing may have been due to employees' own investment in what craft beer meant rather than allegiance to the brewery's owners, but of course this remains speculation. What is certainly true is that employee dissatisfaction at P49 remained high, despite meetings in 2014 during which P49's management acknowledged mistakes they had made. In 2018, the employees attempted to unionize again, this time under the Service Employees International Union Local 2, the union under which Granville Island and Okanagan Spring workers were included. The

315

effort failed, and one of the P49 workers spearheading this union drive was fired without cause shortly afterwards.[35] There were complaints that P49 was a "revolving door" employer, "especially for service and support workers."[36]

It wasn't until 2020 that true change started to happen at Parallel 49. During that summer, the brewery's front-of-house staff started the @NotOurP49 Instagram account, which featured employees of P49 as well as those of St. Augustine's, which is under the same ownership group. The posts that began flooding this account "featured the stories of dozens of former workers, stories attesting to rampant sexism, racism, favouritism, homophobia, and retaliation at both businesses."[37] This reckoning, which shook BC craft beer, has been seen as the predecessor to a much bigger version of craft beer's #MeToo movement, which happened in May 2021 when Brienne Allan (@ratmagnet on Instagram) shared a story of sexism in her beer workplace and invited others to do the same.[38] What followed was an explosion of stories from across the craft beer world that peeled away the shiny, happy surface of craft beer culture. This exposure was needed before change could happen—and it is a slow process.[39]

Back to Parallel 49. On July 24, 2020—just a week after the @NotOurP49 account opened—Parallel 49 posted a public statement on its own Instagram account in response. This post thanked employees and the community "for keeping us accountable" and asserted that the brewery would take full responsibility for its actions and take concrete steps to improve, starting with hiring an HR consulting agency, Neutral Zone, which had already conducted a workplace climate assessment. Neutral Zone's statement, quoted in P49's Instagram post, diplomatically downplayed the accusations posted in the @NotOurP49 account, stating that in initial interviews with staff, "most have neither observed nor experienced the type of misconduct alleged on social media." Neutral Zone did acknowledge, however, that some employees "expressed concerns regarding various managerial practices, policies and procedures, and communication breakdowns."

While P49 continued to work with Neutral Zone, their most pronounced change came after they hired Ren Navarro, founder of Beer.Diversity (now B.Diversity.Group), as a consultant. As of the time of writing, she continues to work with P49. Navarro has been a tireless advocate for equity and diversity in the craft beer industry and has no qualms about calling out toxicity when she sees it. The diversity she wants to see in the industry is "not just about People of Colour: it's also about women, Indigenous groups, LGBTQ+, immigrants, people with disabilities, older folks: we need to think about *all* beer consumers, and what they look like, and reflect that in the industry itself."[40] Under Navarro's guidance, clear steps were taken to improve the workplace culture, the management style, and the brewery's involvement with local organizations supporting racial and gender justice and equity.

The @NotOurP49 movement of July 2020 emerged out of widespread and long-term unhappiness among P49 employees, which had already been witnessed by the previous two attempts to unionize. A third attempt was happening in late 2019—but this time, they were unionizing just for themselves, rather than joining a larger union body. This shift seemed to change things, because in February 2021, 98 percent of Parallel 49's employees voted in favour of establishing their own Employees Association—a body that is a legally recognized union, but which only serves the employees of Parallel 49.[41] The brewery's website enthusiastically announced the union's formation on February 25, 2021, emphasizing that "ownership was aware and supportive" of Parallel 49 staff's goal to create an Employees Association.[42] While the brewery has not made an official statement to this effect, it seems likely that the workplace changes made in response to the employee outcry in 2020 increased the owners' awareness of systemic problems and their willingness to support the formation of the Employees Association. The establishment of the EA and the changes made through Parallel 49's partnership with Ren Navarro have changed what could have been a deeply damaging trajectory for the brewery—a trajectory that would further harm not only the brewery's employees and its reputation, but the Vancouver craft beer community more generally. The Parallel 49 situation forced other breweries to acknowledge and address inequities and harassment in their own businesses. P49 may have been a very public test case, but versions of its dysfunction were (and are) present elsewhere. Many local craft beer insiders remain vigilant and vocal, advocating for inclusivity in craft beer spaces and spending their money at the breweries whose ethics match their own. And in Vancouver, there are many to choose from.

The final "beer boom" brewery I want to acknowledge here is one that had a deep influence on craft beer's success in Vancouver, but maintained a low profile: Callister Brewing. When they opened Callister in 2015, founders Chris Lay and Diana McKenzie (both homebrewers) were motivated by a desire to establish community connections and produce local products in an environmentally sustainable way.[43] They decided to start the country's first collaborative brewery, which would allow would-be brewers to lease space, brew, and sell their beer—all in the Callister facility. It was an idea first generated during a party hosted by a Vancouver homebrewing club, the VanBrewers. Lay described their idea to *The Province* shortly before opening: "We just got really excited about this idea: Wouldn't it be great if we could not only make our own beer but offer our space to other breweries who normally don't have access to this sort of thing?"[44] The idea was that brewers could come in to brew and sell under the Callister liquor licence, resulting in a wide variety of rotating beer taps in the Callister tasting room. Out of Callister's five fermentation tanks, two were devoted to Callister beer and the remaining three would be distributed among the other brewers. Each brewer would be responsible for selling their own beer and taking a weekly shift in the tasting room. "It was a very flexible, collaborative arrangement," says McKenzie.[45]

The first person to come on board was Adam Chatburn, former president of the Vancouver chapter of CAMRA, who wanted to brew cask ales, followed by Brewery Creek portfolio manager (and Canada's

The Callister tap list in their tasting room, February 2022. (Photo by Noëlle Phillips)

first Cicerone), Chester Carey, who produced Belgian-style beers. Chatburn's and Carey's respective breweries, Real Cask and Brewery Creek Brewing, never became widely known in the city, although there's a niche following detectable on Untappd. However, that wasn't always the case for Callister's visiting brewers. The popular brewery Boombox got their start at Callister before moving over to Parallel 49. Adam Henderson and Matt Kohlen began their brewery, Machine Ales, in Callister's facility soon after it opened. No one's heard of Machine Ales now, but if you drink BC craft beer you are likely familiar with the brewery that Machine Ales became in 2020: Superflux Beer Company. Check out the final chapter of this book for the story of Superflux, the brewery that beat the pandemic.

As this book was being completed, Callister announced that it would be closing its doors on December 31, 2023, after nearly a decade of operation. The Vancouver craft beer community rallied around to support Callister in its last days, with many beer fans paying one last visit in December. Social media saw an influx of Callister hashtags as drinkers paid their tributes. @one.hoppy.brewd expressed the feelings of many when he described Callister as "an early leader in BC's craft beer scene…providing a safe nest for countless amazing brewers/breweries over the years."[46] Callister was indeed a home—a safe space—for brewers who couldn't otherwise brew their beer. Its support of the craft beer community has been invaluable.

Chris and Diana of Callister Brewing in the tasting room. (Photo courtesy of Brian K. Smith)

BREWERIES BEYOND THE BORDER

The 2012–2015 beer boom didn't just hit Vancouver, of course. The lounge endorsement was quickly passed in various other municipalities, opening opportunities for craft breweries across the province, including breweries just outside the borders of Vancouver proper whose ethos and products raised the bar for BC craft beer and certainly influenced Vancouver's breweries. Across the board, my interviewees were fairly consistent about which "beer boom" Lower Mainland breweries were key to the Vancouver scene: Dageraad, a brewery that went niche, and Four Winds, a brewery that did it all. The "borderland breweries" of nineteenth-century Vancouver—Columbia and Stanley Park—occupied the edges of both the city and the law; in contrast, these new borderland breweries, sitting not far outside Vancouver's borders in Delta and Burnaby, established new expectations, styles, and standards that inspired breweries in Vancouver proper.

"We're one of the most nerd-forward breweries in the province," Ben Coli, founder of Burnaby's Dageraad Brewing, tells me.[47] He's nerdy and proud of it, but it's taken years of work to become the kind of beer nerd who can run Dageraad. Coli first realized he liked craft beer while living in Alberta as a twentysomething in the late 1990s. Big Rock and Wild Rose piqued his interest in beer—an interest he pursued while travelling in Europe. "I was blown away by cask bitter," he remembers. "The world was bigger." He had to give up the travel bug temporarily when he finished university and settled down into a suit-and-tie job, but he realized that this wasn't how he wanted to live. Travelling beckoned again. Visits to Germany, the Czech Republic, and Belgium provided him with years' worth of beer education. Adam Henderson, now of Superflux but back then a beer reporter, connected Coli to Belgian brewers—open, welcoming folks who let Coli pick their brains and sip their ales.

By the mid-2000s Coli had moved to Vancouver and started home-brewing on an old system he found on Craigslist. He had a group of several friends who would brew with him, but eventually they all dropped off and only Coli was left, brewing alone. "Sometimes I would brew two batches a day, standing on my front porch!" he laughs. His newfound passion took him to brewing school (Brewlab in the UK), where he realized he could probably brew better beer than they could. When he couldn't find a job in the beer industry back in Vancouver, he scraped together the funds to open a tiny brewery in an industrial area. "I just wanted to hang out in an industrial lot and make Belgian beers and bottle-condition them," he says. Beer appreciation classes with his homebrewing friend Mitch Warner further inspired Coli to pursue his dream—and to find some support. "I knew I needed a giant beer nerd to help me out with this [opening a brewery]," Coli laughs. He asked Warner if he wanted to join him in starting up this little brewery he had planned. Within a couple of days, Warner was on board. The two styles they had on opening day were based on beers Coli had made countless times while homebrewing: the amber and the blonde (the latter became Dageraad's famous Belgian table beer, Burnabarian). The tasting room wasn't a priority for the first while because Coli and Warner were just nerding out over the beer. Setting up a tasting lounge felt like a much lower priority—although now, Coli acknowledges that he should have done it sooner.

Dageraad soon made its name with Belgian-style beers, brewing almost exclusively to this niche. Coli loves the flexibility and breadth of Belgian brewing—there's room to play, room to be creative. "We brew our Belgian beers more to spirit rather than to style," he explains. "There's no point in copying someone else's work." The crisp, dry Randonneur Saison, the lightly spiced Dageraad Blonde, the barrel-aged mix-fermentation Entropy Series, the fig-infused dubbel... Dageraad's beers are immediately recognizable and always unique. Coli freely admits that the small-batch experiments and the odd, unconventional (for the Pacific Northwest) styles mean that margins are often tight and profits are fleeting. He would agree with what Mark James told me: you shouldn't get into craft beer if you want to make money. Get into it because you love the beer.

And Coli really does love it. Dageraad has earned its place in the BC craft beer world because of Coli's focus and specialization, and he now is in a position to expand his style repertoire. "We live our lives with our nose in our glasses, pulling the beers apart," laughs Coli. "We started with a Belgian focus but we're secure enough now that we're branching out." They began experimenting with IPAs, not a style that they usually produce. "They're not Belgian IPAs, but they're Dageraad IPAs," says Coli. "They're fermentation focused." It was only in 2022 that Dageraad finally made a lager, a style that most breweries start with. Dageraad's commitment to Belgian styles and its role in bringing important Belgian beers, like Cantillon, to taps in BC has made

good Belgian beer accessible and approachable to local craft beer drinkers. And in doing so, it has established a new level of consumer knowledge that has enabled other breweries to experiment with Belgian styles themselves. As Joe Wiebe puts it, Dageraad has ushered in a "new dawn for BC brewing," a nod to the meaning of the Flemish *dageraad*: "daybreak."[48]

Dageraad's tasting room in Burnaby. This brewery has given Belgian styles a strong platform in the Vancouver region. (Photo courtesy of Dageraad Brewing)

Across the Lower Mainland from Dageraad sits a clean, bright, unassuming little brewery called Four Winds, established by four members of the Mills family. Brent Mills recalls making a batch of homebrew with his dad Greg around 2005, after a road trip to Maine during which Greg had discovered the wonders of craft beer.[49] They were pitching the yeast and caught one another's eye. Brent blurted out, "Let's open a brewery one day!" Greg seemed into it. It would take a while, but he made good on his promise. After about three years of learning to brew at R&B Brewing and doing a road trip with Greg to a craft brewers' conference (complete with plenty of brewery stops) to learn about the industry, Brent felt confident enough to take the plunge.[50] In 2013, he left his position as production manager at R&B to partner with Greg and his brothers Sean and Adam to open Four Winds Brewing on a little industrial lot in Delta. Construction, brewing, customer service—it was all done by the four of them. It was a risky move: Brent left R&B and his brothers left their work at the family business, Mills Paints. They were striking out with something new—and they met with immediate success after their opening in June of that year. Brent told me that he was inspired early on by Granville Island Brewing, then later by Driftwood, a brewery whose vibe and general strategy he aspired to emulate with Four Winds. Joe Wiebe made just that comparison in his book *Craft Beer Revolution*: "Four Winds Brewing...very quickly became the darling of the craft beer scene. Before too long, it was being mentioned in the same breath as Driftwood as every beer geek's favourite brewery."[51] High praise indeed!

Left: The author enjoying a flight in the relaxing Four Winds tasting room.

Right: The tap list at the Four Winds tasting room in 2022. (Photos by Noëlle Phillips)

Four Winds opened with a lineup of what Brent calls "approach-able beers": an IPA, a pilsner, a pale ale, a porter...and a saison. Including the saison in their core beers back in 2013 marked them out as a brewery on the leading edge of a trend. A month after Four

Winds opened, reporter Randy Shore claimed that "this summer [2013] marks the true arrival of saison in BC."[52] Four Winds rode the saison wave from the start, offering something new and interesting in their core lineup to generate customer engagement. They were also doing some unusual stuff in their seasonal lines, producing some Belgian styles like their Triplicity Tripel and using wild yeast—Brettanomyces—in some of their saisons and in their now-famous Juxtapose Brett IPA. A barrel-aging program was established early on to create interesting sour blends. These choices were daring enough to be interesting but not reckless. A little bit of Brett goes a long way. And their strategy paid off; they began winning medals in short order, including People's Choice at the 2014 BC Beer Awards (for their Sovereign Super Saison) and Brewery of the Year at the 2015 Canadian Brewing Awards. Their experiments with older European styles and mixed fermentation continued into 2016, at which time they were producing about twenty limited releases per year and selling it all.[53]

Four Winds also set itself apart through its packaging, something that can be as important as the beer itself when it comes to getting customer buy-in. "Our idea was to elevate beer, to make it more exciting, more elegant," says Brent. "But it also needed to be approachable." Rather than a six-pack of cans, they started using a four-pack of small, pretty bottles. "I wanted people to see our beer as something elevated, something you could open in a nice restaurant and enjoy with good food," says Brent, whose previous life as a chef has doubtless influenced his decisions as a brewer. And a beer brewed by Four Winds is indeed elevated. Beer may have the reputation of being a simple, down-home drink that doesn't require much taste discernment, but they make a version that takes you on a tour of your own palate. Their Nectarous Dry-Hopped Sour, for example, has been described as a "gateway beer for all those wine drinkers in your life who don't think they like beer."[54] In an early interview, Brent expressed hope that Four Winds would stand out in a crowded beer market because of their "attention to detail and goal of artistic expression."[55]

The admiration Four Winds receives from other brewers is a tribute to everything it's doing right. Adam Henderson, owner of Superflux, told me that he thinks Four Winds is the best brewery in BC. "They make a little bit of everything and they do it very well," he says.[56] Four Winds has a winning combination of consistently high-quality beer, elegant branding, and an instinct about what styles will have longevity. Their experimental beers are wisely developed rather than wild cards (although a wild-card beer is fun now and then).

Four Winds also has a quiet sense of security in the kind of brewery it wants to be. The last point is harder to articulate concretely, but I think it comes from the stability of the family that runs it. The Mills brothers and their father have a special bond, honoured in 2020 when Greg passed and Adam, Sean and Brent brewed a special beer in his name: Greg West Coast IPA, which has become one of their more popular beers. His obituary described Greg as "endlessly proud" of Four Winds, so this seems a fitting tribute.[57] A brewery that grew organically in this way, out of a mutual love of brewing and deep family connections, is more likely to resonate with both customers and employees than one started simply as a profit-making venture. Working as brewmaster and businessman with his brothers, Brent Mills's little Delta brewery modelled for Vancouver what consistent, beautiful, elevated beer could look like. It was a revelation that made Four Winds stand out among the flood of new breweries at the time.

CHAPTER II

CONCLUSION: PANDEMIC PIVOTS AND THE FUTURE OF VANCOUVER CRAFT BEER

Beer is resilient. When the world shut down in March 2020, BC's craft breweries felt the pain but they didn't collapse under the pressure. Instead, throughout 2020 and 2021 they adjusted their footing and stood stronger—after some painful lessons in growth and adaptation.

This positive slant isn't intended to minimize the drastic changes that occurred and the challenges the industry faced at the outset of the pandemic. All beer events were cancelled; tasting rooms were closed (and when they opened they had strict capacity limits); many breweries lost restaurant accounts; most front-of-house staff lost their jobs. Ryan Parfitt, co-owner and brewmaster at Luppolo Brewing Company, saw an 85 percent decrease in his business income virtually overnight.[1] Ben Coli of Dageraad recalls that they lost every single draft account.[2] Without restaurants or taprooms, the breweries' only option was to sell beer via retail or through liquor stores, which naturally resulted in a huge profit loss. Some beer festivals—important events for growing the craft beer community—recovered after the initial crisis and went back to normal, but others did not. A notable example is the Vancouver Craft Beer Week, which was sold in 2021 to Feaster, a Vancouver event planning company. Feaster's first VCBW in 2022 had big expectations but was a public relations nightmare.[3] The 2023 event saw improvement, but the damage 2022 did to the VCBW's reputation remained. Many beer fans and brewers feel that this beloved local festival, originally helmed by Leah Henegan, Paul Kamon, Tyler Olson, and Chris Bjerrisgaard (now of Small Gods Brewing on Vancouver Island), no longer has the same intimacy and value to the industry that it once did.

HOW VANCOUVER BEER MADE IT THROUGH

We all recall the fear and uncertainty of the beginning of the pandemic. However, we should also recognize that the craft beer industry survived it—and in some areas, even thrived afterwards—at least for a while. Breweries immediately banded together and took action once the lockdown began. Ken Beattie, executive director of the BC Craft Brewers Guild, was on the phone every week with Dr. Bonnie Henry, the provincial health officer whose press conferences drew panicked attention and sometimes furor for months throughout 2020. On Thursdays at 11:00 AM, Beattie would be on the phone to hear what would be announced in that day's 3:00 PM press conference—and how the news would affect BC's breweries. "It was collaborative, transparent," says Beattie. "It gave the industry time to react."[4]

And the craft breweries reacted promptly, adjusting their business models in real time in order to meet customer needs and avoid falling into insolvency. They began delivering their beer to customers' doorsteps, using either their own staff or a co-op effort like the BeerVan, an idea that "went from non-existent to operational within a week," according to reporter Stuart Derdeyn.[5] This delivery service, which was limited to Vancouver and nearby municipalities, started as a collaboration between Faculty Brewing, Dickie's Ginger Beer, Luppolo Brewing, Slow Hand Brewing, and Temporal Artisan Ales. More beverage businesses joined later on: the Hypha Project,

Dominion Cider, Powell Brewery, Oddity Kombucha, and Brassneck Brewery. For those who weren't in the delivery area, almost all breweries offered reasonable prices on delivery, and the breweries that had limited or no packaged sales (i.e., bottled or canned beer), such as Storm, set up packaging lines. When tasting rooms were open again, breweries could apply for outdoor patios via a Temporary Expanded Service Area permit (TESA). Beattie recalls the incredibly fast turnaround of TESA applications; breweries were receiving permission within days of submitting their applications, thanks to the government's choice to fast-track the process. People were able to sit down and enjoy a beer again. "This was the best example of industry and the government working together for the common good of the public," says Beattie.[6]

Zoom beer-tasting sessions hosted by BC craft beer experts such as writer Joe Wiebe and Certified Cicerone Matthew Poirier and fun collab creations between breweries became the new ways to connect. One memorable collaboration was the two imperial stouts made by Steel & Oak Brewing in New Westminster and Dageraad Brewing in Burnaby—for one another. The two breweries both opened in 2014 and had long enjoyed a "BFF" relationship. Without being able to work together on a brew in person, they found an alternative method of collaboration: they both made the imperial stout but added their unique spin. Steel & Oak's version had Haitian cacao nibs and toasted almonds, while Dageraad's included Tasmanian cacao nibs and miso. Each can of "Steel & Oak Loves Dageraad" and "Dageraad Loves Steel & Oak" pictured half of a broken heart, a shape that matched the broken heart on the other brewery's can. They called the stouts "A Love Letter from

Erika van Veenen (@beermecanada on Instagram) shows the Dageraad/Steel & Oak collaboration beers before tasting them. (Photo courtesy of Erika van Veenen)

Isolation." I remember that both beers were excellent, but the sentiment behind them was even sweeter.

While the pandemic saw the closure of some legendary BC brewpubs, like Red Racer Taphouse in Vancouver (formerly Dix Brewpub, where CAMRA and cask nights got their start) and Surrey's Central City Taphouse, surprisingly few breweries closed down in the immediate aftermath of the pandemic.[7] The pivot to increased canning and flexible delivery options (enabled by new policies and legislation[8]), combined with people being home and rethinking their life choices, meant that an interest in craft beer actually seemed to increase. In an interview with Ken Beattie, Joe Wiebe reflects on why the statistics didn't show a slowdown in the industry:

> I kind of expected that in 2021, we'd see fewer breweries opening because if you're starting a brewery, it takes you a year or two to put it together, maybe longer. So the pandemic hits and you were thinking of opening a brewery and then you're like, no, I'm going to put the brakes on. But it's not slowing down at all. And it seems to me—and tell me what you think—that there's also this flipside for a lot of people: their lives were changed by the pandemic. What I hear from a lot of the people opening breweries now is: I always wanted to open a brewery, then I lost my job or something changed or I had to move or whatever. So the pandemic almost forced them to follow their dream, right?[9]

Brewery openings in BC during the pandemic were commensurate in number with brewery openings in other years: the average has been about twenty-two per year since 2013, and in 2020 there were twenty.[10] But there were three Lower Mainland breweries that opened between 2020 and 2021 whose strategies, products, and presence have had an outsize influence on the craft beer landscape here. While only one of these breweries is within the Vancouver city limits, all three have set new expectations for what the Vancouver craft beer world can and should be. This concluding chapter of Vancouver's craft beer story, told in the midst of the action and without the benefit of hindsight, provides a brief glimpse into these three recently opened breweries whose perseverance paid off: Locality Brewing, Barnside Brewing Co., and Superflux Beer Company.

THE FARM BREWERIES OF 2020–2021: LOCALITY BREWING AND BARNSIDE BREWING CO.

Crannog Ales in Sorrento was the first farm brewery to open in BC over two decades ago, but Locality (in Langley) and Barnside (in Delta) were the first to open in the greater Vancouver area—and they managed to do it during a pandemic. Drive just forty-five minutes or so from the busy streets of downtown Vancouver and you'll arrive at fields, hop bines, and fresh beer.[11] Farm breweries are the newest addition to the hundred-mile-diet and "eat local" movements, with their focus on making as many of their beer's ingredients as possible on site. You could say they're the craftiest of all the craft breweries, and they've set a new standard when it comes to local beer. Their presence, even at a distance, influences the practices of other breweries. Once a few breweries are using, for example, locally grown barley, customers start seeking that out. Using locally harvested malt is increasingly popular among the urban breweries; farm-based breweries are advocating for its use and consumers are increasingly demanding it. Many Island breweries are already buying their malt locally, and now Lower Mainland breweries and the BC Craft Brewers Guild are making noise about getting a craft malthouse here on the mainland.[12] Barnside and Locality have made these issues much more visible to the average Vancouver craft beer consumer.

Locality is on a large piece of farmland long owned by the MacInnes family, parents of Mel MacInnes (the current co-owner).[13] MacInnes and her husband Andy Hamer had always wanted to use the land for something community-oriented, a place where friends and family could meet, and were inspired to start a farm-based brewery there after a trip to Australia. A 150-year-old church in Melbourne had been converted to a brewery, and the couple loved how welcoming and family-friendly it was. They started planning their own brewery in 2016, planting hops and barley and setting up beehives on the MacInnes farm.

Knowing that Iain Hill (see Chapters 9 and 10) was a craft beer insider with a wealth of experience, they brought him out to the farm for a walk 'n' talk about setting up a farm-based brewery—a place where they would grow and process all their own ingredients, as well as brew the beer. Hamer recalls that Hill was straightforward about the reality they were facing: "What you're trying to do, it's not easy!" Hamer's plans seemed unattainable to a person who knew from painful experience what it took to set up just a brewery—farm not included. "Iain thought we were trying to do too many things— hops, barley, malting, brewing. He was right!" Hamer laughs. "If we'd known up front what he knew, we probably wouldn't have done it." They had to reap their first barley harvest by hand—with an actual

Locality co-owner Andy Hamer (right) harvesting hops at Locality. (Photo courtesy of Ivan Eytzen)

Locality's owners, Melanie MacInnes and Andy Hamer. (Photo by Noëlle Phillips)

scythe. And it's not just barley they harvest; they also have hops, hazelnuts, apples, and berries. They malt their own grain in a tiny malthouse (with hopes to produce specialty malt for sale to other breweries eventually), and their small brewhouse is expertly run by another Vancouver beer import: Karen Cheshire, a brewer who earned her stripes at Steamworks, and who now makes an impressively wide range of beers for Locality. They opened their doors in August 2021, in the middle of the pandemic.

Because Locality isn't structured for a tasting room, the pandemic spacing regulations didn't affect them very much. Drinkers get their beer from their small front-of-house area, then wander out to sit at the picnic tables or chairs overlooking the pond. Dogs and kids are welcome, and Hamer or a staff member will come out to start one of the firepits if you're feeling chilly. The Locality vibe is very different from any other brewery; it's a step away from the Lower Mainland rush, a chance to breathe. If you visit, dress for the weather and prepare for good beer—award-winning beer. Locality won Gold for its Smoked Doppelbock in the 2023 Canada Beer Cup and an honourable mention at the 2023 Canadian Brewing Awards for its Owl Train Vanilla Porter. In 2022, the brewery was named Innovator of the Year by the BC Beer Awards. Its Grainstorm collab beers with Beer Farmers and Barnside have been sell-out successes. Impressively, Locality is the only brewery in the Lower Mainland that does it all: grows *and* malts its own barley, grows its own hops, grows its own adjuncts, and brews its own beer. It's putting the Vancouver region on the craft beer map.

Barnside, as the other Lower Mainland farm brewery, is helping to do the same. Barnside is unable to malt its own barley, but it does the rest: growing the grain and hops, brewing the beer, cultivating its own yeast. Like Locality, Barnside is a family affair: four families who owned property in the agricultural area of Delta joined together on this venture. Back in 2015, around the same time Locality began its planning, Ken Malenstyn, Sean Buhr, Brent and Shelley Harris, and David Terpsma began chatting about starting a brewery in the spot where they'd all grown up together, playing in tree forts and on hay bales.[14] And it wouldn't just be a brewery; they'd make their own ingredients right there. "I was considering putting in hops," said Malenstyn, who is now the chair of the BC Hop Growers Association. "Brent mentioned he was growing some malting barley, and Sean and Dave did some homebrewing using that malting barley and it was pretty good beer. So we said, 'Wow, we might be onto something!'"[15] There were reams of red tape to slash through, but by 2018 they had started a barrel-aging program and by January 2020 they had opened their doors.

Unfortunately, two months later the doors were closed again when the pandemic lockdowns began in March 2020. In June, Glen Hutton came knocking.[16] Hutton, owner of Fuggles and Warlock Craftworks in Richmond, had known two of the owners, Malenstyn and Buhr, since 2014. Tension and dysfunction at Fuggles, in addition to plans for expansion that Hutton felt were too fast and too corporate, meant that he was ready to leave. He resigned in May, then a few weeks later reached out to his friends at Barnside, hoping to find a new position in the brewing business. His marketing expertise was just what Barnside needed—a new brewery, a pandemic, and lots of new restrictions meant that they needed new sales strategies. Hutton got to work, and a six-month contract turned into ten months, which turned into two years. He is currently sales manager at Barnside and clearly loves his job.

While chatting with Hutton over a beer at White Rock Beach Beer (White Rock's first craft brewery, and a cozy community hub that has a special place in Hutton's heart—and mine), I asked him what it was like starting at Barnside shortly after the pandemic hit. I was surprised at his answer. "COVID was brilliant for Barnside," Hutton said. Not brilliant because of the stress and uncertainty, but because of the way the pandemic forced the brewery to develop a deeply local strategy. They quickly brought in a canning line and opened off-sales during the pandemic, then focused on their neighbours and surrounding businesses. Their beers were named after nearby areas of Delta and Ladner—recognizable landmarks for Barnside's neighbours. They made connections with all the nearby stores and restaurants. "You have to have your own community," Hutton insists, referring to how breweries make themselves relevant and sustainable. For Barnside, these carefully cultivated local connections translated into a loyal customer base and restaurants and pubs that were happy to put some Barnside beer on tap. Hutton left Fuggles for Barnside because

The Barnside tasting room. (Photo by Noëlle Phillips)

he wasn't feeling what he thought was the most valuable thing about craft beer: community. "I came to Barnside because of the people, because of the philosophy," he says.

In a recent interview, Malenstyn concurs: "The more you can support locally, the more you keep your local community vibrant and your local economy vibrant."[17] Barnside's local efforts—its on-site production of all its own ingredients, its outdoor

beer-pairing dinners, comedy nights, puppy adoption events, and presence at farmers' markets, harvest festivals, and neighbourhood pubs—have transformed it from a local hub to a provincial destination. In October 2023, Barnside won the BC Ale Trail Best Brewery Experience Award, a prestigious honour that signals the affection BC craft beer drinkers have for this little farm brewery.

One of the "Dinner under the Bines" events that Barnside held, in which local dishes are paired with Barnside beers, all served under the hop bines. (Photo by Noëlle Phillips)

SUPERFLUX BEER COMPANY

"I wouldn't like to be opening a brewery now unless I was Superflux," says Nigel Springthorpe, wryly. Superflux was frequently mentioned by other brewers when I asked what new brewery was making the biggest splash in Vancouver. As the owner of Brassneck, Springthorpe knows what it takes to make a brewery successful, especially since the pandemic; starting a brewery in 2020 or later is a different game than starting one in 2013. He explains that Superflux has been good at understanding beer trends in other cities and bringing them to Vancouver. "They're very innovative and relentless," he says, "always on top of the next cool hops, the new trends in IPA styles. They've carved a specific niche for themselves."[18] It certainly seems that Superflux's strong focus on full-bodied, tropical hazy IPAs contributed to an explosion of this style's popularity in the Vancouver scene.[19] As Rob Mangelsdorf, a Cicerone and beer judge, put it in a Superflux review, "it always boggles my mind how much fruit flavour Superflux crams into its beers without adding any actual fruit." The judicious use of a variety of bittering and aromatic hops creates this effect and produces an impressively well-balanced beer, according to Mangelsdorf.[20] These hop-forward fruity beers appeal both to experienced craft beer drinkers, and to people who don't usually drink beer at all.[21] Mitch Taylor, original founder of Granville Island Brewing, has told me that Superflux is one of his favourite BC breweries. Craft beer drinkers across Canada know of Superflux—even those who are only dimly aware of what is going on in BC beer.[22]

Back in 2015, when Adam Henderson and Matt Kohlen were dreaming up brewery possibilities, the IPA selection in BC breweries wasn't nearly as extensive as it is now. Henderson, a former beer importer and well-travelled beer nerd, found that the interesting IPAs he was seeing in other countries didn't have much of a presence in Vancouver, so this was the style he embraced when he and Kohlen made their brewing dreams a reality.[23] The two homebrewers began their official brewing career in 2015 by leasing space at Callister Brewing, the collaborative brewing space discussed in the previous chapter. They got their start by using Callister's equipment and licence to brew and sell their own beer. After their time at Callister, they went on to do the same thing at Dogwood and Strathcona. Using a shared space and brewing small five-hundred-litre batches allowed the pair to experiment with recipes (and profit margins) before taking the plunge into full brewery ownership.

Unlike Barnside, which focuses on the hyperlocal, Superflux was intentionally non-local from the start—at least in its name and branding. When Henderson and Kohlen started brewing at Callister, their company was called Machine Ales. Henderson recalls that he liked that name because it didn't seem like a brewery name and it wasn't tied to a specific area. "There are lots of breweries named after bridges, rivers, parts of town," he says. "We wanted a brand that transcended the pure locality of beer. It was more about us doing our thing than just being the brewery closest to you."[24] However, it ended up being impossible to trademark Machine Ales, so they went back to the drawing board. The name Superflux was generated through the same impulse: to find a name unattached to anything else. "'Superflux' didn't mean anything to us," Henderson laughs. "It just seemed a little out of left field. The idea is that people can make the word mean something—mean whatever they want." The Superflux labels, produced by Kohlen, are similarly distanced from any specific imagery or allusions. He discussed an early version of one of their first beer labels, Colour & Shape, in a 2017 interview:

> It kind of reminds me of an ice cream parlour or diner from the '50s: bold, clean, soft, minimal and a little retro... You'll notice all of our can art has a consistent theme in blending unique colour palettes with basic shapes.[25]

The Superflux branding is, indeed, instantly recognizable. It has a vaguely retro look but it doesn't take you back to any specific place or

The clean lines and bright colours of the Superflux labels are immediately recognizable. (Photo courtesy of Superflux Beer Company)

era. Their labels are just…well, colours and shapes. They're visually soothing with an understated elegance. The focus on shapes over text and the clean layers of colour are minimalism at its best, and a far cry from some of the busier beer labels out there.

Superflux's ability to combine a minimalist elegance with light-hearted simplicity in its branding demonstrates the brewery's maturity and self-assurance even in its very early stages. This confidence in their identity—they weren't going to chase after every style or trend—is communicated in their brewing too. They were going to make mostly IPAS—and lots of them. The consistency of their beer and the quality of their branding gave Superflux a reputation well before 2020; their beer was popular before they even had a building. By the time they actually had a brewery, Vancouverites had been talking about it for months. When they opened their doors on August 15, 2020, craft beer fans lined up down the block to get inside and check out their streamlined, low-lit tasting room. The space feels a bit like a nice hotel bar rather than an East Van brewery.

Superflux's tasting room is streamlined and minimalist. (Photo courtesy of Superflux Beer Company)

The Superflux tasting room. (Photo courtesy of Superflux Beer Company)

The clean aesthetic of Superflux's branding and tasting room echoes the shifting demographics of craft beer in Vancouver. It's no longer just bearded, plaid-clad homebrewers or university students who are into craft beer. As Henderson acknowledges, the industry is getting more sophisticated and progressive in terms of its attitude to food and drink. Sho Ogawa, brewmaster at Mountainview Brewing in Hope, points to Superflux as one of the breweries shifting Vancouver beer in a new stylistic direction, creating seasonal styles (their fruit-forward hoppy hazies and decadent dessert stouts) that then become codified in the local industry. Could this shift be connected to the demographic change in craft beer drinkers and brewers? An academic before he was a brewer—he has his PhD in media studies—Ogawa takes a very thoughtful approach to analyzing these aspects of the industry, and his observations helped me refine and expand my own. Craft beer isn't the underclass anymore. Breweries like Superflux and Four Winds, with their homebrewing roots and collaborative spirit, have already taken steps to transform craft beer from a quirky hobby to a sophisticated drink. Others are following in their footsteps. Beer has become a way of signalling good taste—or even class.[26]

Craft beer in Vancouver now pairs with a cocktail dress or your favourite old pair of jeans. From elegant tasting rooms to rustic barns or pond-side picnic tables, the "pandemic breweries" in this region reflect something of the shifting craft beer consumer here. On the one hand, the Vancouver craft beer drinker wants a connection to the local, to nature, to the earth. They're looking for farm-to-table beer to sip after a hike. On the other, they value the increased sophistication of the city's beer offerings. They enjoy dressing in a nice outfit to enjoy a quality beer during cocktail hour. And with the range of breweries currently active in the Vancouver region, they can go from farm-style to fancy in the same day.

A BUBBLE BURSTING?

I struggle with knowing how to end a book about a local industry whose story is still being told. I'm in the middle of it—I don't have the perspective offered by time and distance. In trying to tell the story of craft beer in Vancouver, I know that I've had to leave out the experiences of many breweries and brewers, people and businesses who deserve to have their story told. I haven't been able to explore the local beer events as thoroughly as some might like. Happily, the industry has become so densely packed with talent that my strategy of going deep with a few rather than broad and shallow with all means that there's still plenty of scope for another book or two. For those who want a quick outline of the post-1980 history of BC brewing, featuring many Vancouver breweries and touching on a few folks I haven't discussed in detail, I recommend the stories of BC craft beer history compiled by *What's Brewing* magazine in their thirtieth anniversary issue, published on June 1, 2020—shortly into lockdown.[27] Pandemics certainly seem to inspire reflection.

As I conclude this book, it is early 2024. The Vancouver craft beer world remains vibrant, but it is also drifting close to its own edge. Unlike in the glory days of the 2010s, the market saturation in the

Vancouver craft beer industry now is at a tipping point, more so than it was during the pandemic. In 2022 and 2023, multiple breweries in or near Vancouver closed, most with little to no warning: Andina, Big Ridge, Deep Cove, Green Leaf, Bakery, Studio, Callister. In response to some very dire predictions about the industry, long-time craft beer insider Joe Wiebe offers a thoughtful reframing of this tough time. He suggests that this retraction in the craft beer world is to be expected (it's inevitable in any industry), and such dips have been a repeated pattern over the province's forty years of craft brewing. I agree. The pandemic came with offers of hefty loans to craft brewers, and this funding, combined with the "buy at home" mandates of quarantine, may have extended the business lives of breweries that would otherwise have had to close their doors. The province's demand to repay those pandemic loans now places a heavy burden on breweries already pressured by narrow profit margins and a crowded market.

What feels like the industry crashing, says Wiebe, is in reality more like a natural shrinking and stabilizing. It feels more catastrophic because of the decade-plus of heightened success and rapid growth the industry has experienced. Of course, Wiebe emphasizes, this perspective doesn't alleviate the real pain felt by the brewery owners who simply cannot keep their businesses going now that pandemic loans are coming due. These are livelihoods at risk, and macroeconomic explanations cannot make that feel any better. In this post-pandemic environment, the return to "normalcy" is coming at a high cost for many. "What I heard from a lot of breweries was that the government offered them these loans and they felt they had to take them," Wiebe says. "Now they're facing the deadlines to repay these loans, or they're being pressured by landlords who aren't giving them a break. It's really rough, even if it's not uncommon in an industry like this."[28]

Jorden Foss, co-founder of Steel & Oak Brewing in New Westminster, published a similarly candid editorial in *The Georgia Straight*. He points out that overall reduction in drinking and sharp inflationary pressures on consumers make the craft beer industry a particularly tenuous place to work at the moment. However, that doesn't mean craft beer is dead; it just means that priorities must shift:

> *Our perspective on what makes a craft brewery successful needs to change from volume sold to community impact. Getting people together in a space that's important to the neighbourhood to enjoy a beer you lovingly created—that's the good stuff... If you think about what made you love craft beer... it was likely being able to connect with those who make it. To feel the passion behind it. To learn that the reason why it tastes better than mass-produced versions is because actual people were involved. That's why we did it too: to connect with you. To let you know why we're so proud.*[29]

Many breweries have taken this direction with their business, including Vancouver's newest brewery, Brewing August, which focuses exclusively on local customers and local distribution—community impact, in other words.[30] Good beer spaces are made by supporting the local community, and if the community supports those spaces in turn, they'll be able to continue making that good beer.

There will still be a painful tightening of the industry though. Whether this is a bubble on the verge of bursting or the natural ebb and flow, it's clear that the craft beer boom can't continue at the same pace as it has since 2012. "The post-2012 growth isn't realistic for the long term," says Wiebe, "especially when you compare it to the rate of growth before 2012." BC has the most breweries per capita in all of Canada and purchases the most craft beer, but it drinks the least of it.[31] Where does this leave the hundreds of craft brewers trying to make a living here? The presence of a "brewers row" or "brewery blocks" in various municipalities seems to have helped sustain growth over the past ten years; such clusters of breweries now exist in Port Moody, North Vancouver, White Rock, and Langley. The "brewers rows" are a boon because the density tends to increase traffic to all of the breweries there. However, the drive to follow trends and recruit more beer drinkers won't keep the existing craft beer community—the people who are the regular, long-term brewery customers. In the view of many long-time beer industry advocates with whom I've spoken, the constant pursuit of the newest thing in beer won't expand the industry. It may be time to consider stabilization rather than growth.

Some of that stabilization can be achieved through taking what benefits we can from Big Beer—the Molsons and the Budweisers. As earlier chapters of this book have shown, many craft beer advocates and educators entered craft via corporate beer: Ken Beattie (Craft Brewers Guild), Julia Hanlon (Steamworks), Barry Benson and Rick Dellow (R&B), Nancy More (KPU brewing program), most of Red Truck's quality control staff and several brewers, and even the legendary Frank Appleton, who worked for Carling O'Keefe before his homebrew manifesto inspired craft brewers everywhere. The skills gained in brewing for the big corporations can only help boost the viability and quality of craft beer.

Another path forward to strengthen and sustain the industry may be a return to simpler styles. The pandemic already forced some movement in this direction. With narrower profit margins, there's less room for risky choices. Tony Dewald, long-time Vancouver brewer, affirms that there's saturation in the market and shakes his head at the trend-chasing he sees some breweries trying. "Novelty is a short-sighted strategy," he says. "Novelty beers won't be consumed regularly—they won't sustain the industry. Breweries need to make beer people can drink over a whole evening. Novelty won't convert other beer drinkers." His priority at Trading Post has always been quality and consistency (although he certainly had his novelty phase with some of his early experimental cask IPAs—so full of hops they were green—at Dix back in the day).[32] Joe Wiebe is of the same mind: many breweries start out by trying to grab attention with unique and oddball styles, he says, "but often the really good breweries settle into specializing in specific beers—and these are often more traditional styles. These breweries are often the ones that last. They have staying power."[33] Perhaps the industry is already moving in that direction; after all, the winner of the 2023 Canada Beer Cup was a simple, traditional style: an American-style brown ale made by one of BC's newer breweries—Deadfall Brewing in Prince George.

But beyond styles and brewery locations is the craft beer ethos itself, which Jorden Foss's editorial expressed so eloquently. Vancouver craft beer was, in many ways, built on ethics of care, quality, and community. These are the features that should set apart independent breweries from macro breweries. The Vancouver craft breweries of the late nineteenth century were all eventually swallowed up by larger brewing corporations, and the early breweries of Vancouver's craft beer revolution were as well—Horseshoe Bay, Granville Island, and Shaftebury. But despite a few buyouts here and there, most of the major Vancouver craft breweries that started up since 1990 have managed to maintain their independence, creativity, and relevance. They still embody the ethic of craft. Like their nineteenth-century counterparts, Vancouver's twenty-first-century breweries offer not just refreshment, but cultural value. Nostalgia for the homeland was evoked in the German lagers and English ales made by Vancouver's very first brewers. Modern Vancouver craft breweries are doing something quite different; they're offering connection—connection to a beer community, to the local land, to the family making the beer, to the people walking through the neighbourhood. This connection might be experienced in the tasting room itself, at a festival or cask event, or even online, in the beer nerd communities that have formed on Facebook and Instagram. "No Fun Vancouver" can feel isolating and lonely to many. However, Vancouver's craft beer culture connects people within the city and draws people from without. And this culture is the product of not just the expensive newest breweries on the block, but the perseverance and hard work of hundreds of people over the decades. From German immigrants making memories of their home to urban hippies finding art in a science, Vancouver craft beer is an integral part of the city's story and a reflection of all of us: the people who brew and drink it. We *are* Vancouver's craft beer culture.

ACKNOWLEDGEMENTS

Conducting the research for this book has been an intellectual and gustatory pleasure. My thanks go out to the numerous brewery owners and industry advocates who gave their time to me (and often shared their beer as well), telling their stories and answering all my questions. These include but aren't limited to Nigel Springthorpe, Shirley Warne, Ben Coli, Adam Henderson, Adam Mills, Mark James, Iain Hill, Andy Hamer, Glen Hutton, Gerry Hieter, Lundy Dale, Ken Beattie, Kristy Isaak, Leah Henegan, Nigel Pike, James Walton, Gary Lohin, Tony Dewald, Paul Hadfield, Barry Benson, Diana McKenzie, David Bruce-Thomas, Nancy More, Ryan Scholz, Dave Varga, Tim Wittig, Vern Lambourne, and Stuart Derdeyn.

Special appreciation goes to those to whom I turned many times with my questions, often asking for assistance in finding resources. These include Melanie Hardbattle and Richard Dancy of the SFU Archives, whose work on BC craft beer archival materials has been invaluable; Mitch Taylor, founder of Granville Island Brewing, whose generosity and encouragement have always been heartening; Bill Wilson, bottle collector and historian who graciously and promptly responded to all my questions and even sent a personal signed note with my copy of his book, *Beer Barons of BC*; and Joe Wiebe, celebrated beer author and advocate, who has helped me make many important connections in this industry. I am also deeply grateful to both Mirella Amato, another award-winning beer author and beer judge, and to John Ohler, former chef of Howe Sound Brewpub and close friend of John Mitchell, for providing me such valuable insight into Mitchell and allowing me to use their photographs. My thanks go out to John Mitchell's wife Jenny as well, who kindly allowed me to interview her in her home about her late husband's legacy. Those who shared family files with me deserve special acknowledgment. Dennis Mutter, great-great-grandson of Charles Doering, and Hugh Greer, great-grandson of John Dyke, both allowed me access to personal letters and photographs from their family records. These enabled me to shed more light on and humanize these important figures in Vancouver's early brewing industry.

Archivists at the City of Vancouver Archives and Royal BC Archives—thank you! You make this kind of research possible.

My thanks to my employer, Douglas College, for granting me funding through an Education Leave that allowed me to write the majority of this book.

And finally, I deeply appreciate my husband and our two teenagers, who watched me write this book while working full time (and who had to deal with my exhaustion and tight schedule). My gratitude is especially owed to my husband Rich—my beer-tasting partner and always my biggest supporter.

VANCOUVER BREWERIES: 1886-1957

Brewery Name	Alternative Name (if brewery was renamed, merged, or bought out)	Address	Years Active
Canadian Brewing and Malting		11th and Yew	1908–1918
Cedar Cottage Brewery			1898/1900 –1903
City Brewery	Red Cross Brewery	Seaton St.	1887–1888
Columbia Brewery		Powell St. at Wall and Victoria	1888–1912
Lion Brewery	Lansdowne Brewery (1906)	286 Front St.	1896–1907(?)
Mainland Brewery			1888–1893(?)
North Arm Brewery	Reywood/Raywood Brewery		1890(?)–1908(?)

(This chart does not include the brewery corporations that held individual breweries, such as BC Breweries or Coast Breweries)

Owner(s)	Employees	Employee Position
Henry Reifel		
George Raywood John Benson		
Jan A. Rekab John Williams		
Joseph Kappler Andrew and Mary Mueller	August Rushman Emil Gerhauser Fritz/Fred Reimer Fritz Herzberg J. Muller Herbst/Dutch Bill Robert Dawson	Brewer Labourer Labourer
Robert Reisterer	August Zoellmer Julius Reisterer C. Reisterer	Brewer
George Raywood Charles Thorson	Charles Thorson B.L. Wood	Brewer Brewer

Brewery Name	Alternative Name (if brewery was renamed, merged, or bought out)	Address	Years Active
Red Cross Brewery	City Brewery	Seaton St. near Burrard	1890–1902
Red Star Brewery		11th and Main St. (then Westminster Ave.)	1889–1891
San Francisco Brewery		11th and Main St.	1888–1889
Stadler Brewery		286 Front St. (1st) at Scotia	1898–1900
Stanley Park Brewery	Royal Brewing Co.		1896–1909
Vancouver Breweries	(this brewery was a merger of D&M and Red Cross)	Scotia St. and 7th Ave., then 11th and Yew	1902–1957
Vancouver Brewery	Doering & Marstrand Brewing Co. (after 1892)	Scotia St. and 7th Ave.	1888–1902

Owner(s)	Employees	Employee Position
John Williams E.E. Barker W.A. Anderson(?)	Ehler Henry Traeger Christopher Holmes A. Lambert Charles Sands William Whittmayr	Brewer Brewer Carpenter Cellarman Bookkeeper Brewer, 1890 Engineer, 1896 Teamster
	Fenwick Schulte Frank Brusatore H.J. Walton Otto Deckart	 Clerk Bottle-washer
	Theodore Dobzinsky John Edgar John Gilman H.T. Twiss W.A. Anderson	 Teamster Bookkeeper
Jacob DeWitt	Eugene DeWitt	Sales
Henry and Jack Reifel, Charles Miller		
August Stadler	H.E. Neibergal	
Frank Foubert John Benson	Thomas Towler John Dyke	Driver Brewer
Charles Doering, John Williams Henry Reifel		
Charles Doering (primary founder) with Louis Blum (1887–1888); with August Schwan (1890–1892); with Otto Marstrand (1892–1906)	John Reinhardt Hermann Joseph Lanky George Boye Joseph Kappler E.N. Chaumette R. Hall Curry Charles Dolman Charles Shulte Charles Thorson Richard Asbeck William Schlectinger	Brewer Master brewer Labourer Brewer Engineer Teamster Stable hand Brewer Brewer Brewer

LOWER MAINLAND CRAFT BREWERIES: 1982-2024

Brewery or Brewpub (breweries in Vancouver city limits are in bold)	Municipality	Opening Date
3 Dogs Brewing	White Rock	2017
33 Acres Brewing Co.	**Vancouver**	**2013**
Andina Brewing Co.	**Vancouver**	**2017**
Another Beer Co.	New Westminster	2019
Avalon Brewing / Taylor's Crossing Brewpub	North Vancouver	2004
The Bakery Brewing	Port Moody	2019
Barnside Brewing Co.	Ladner	2020
Beere Brewing Co.	North Vancouver	2017
Big Ridge Brewing	Surrey	1999
Big River Brewpub / Be Right Back Brewing Co.	Richmond	1997
Black Kettle Brewing	North Vancouver	2014
Bomber Brewing	**Vancouver**	**2014**
Boombox Brewing Co.	**Vancouver (no fixed location—contract brewed)**	**2016**
Brassneck Brewery	**Vancouver**	**2013**
Brave Brewing	Port Moody	2022
Brewing August	**Vancouver**	**2022**
Bridge Brewing Co.	North Vancouver	2012
Bryant Brewery	Maple Ridge	1983
Callister Brewing Co.	**Vancouver**	**2012**
Camp Beer Co.	Langley	2019
Central City Brewers & Distillers	Surrey	2003
Coal Harbour Brewing	**Vancouver**	**2010**
Container Brewing	**Vancouver**	**2019**
CowDog Brewing Co.	**Vancouver**	**2024**

Brewery or Brewpub (breweries in Vancouver city limits are in bold)	Municipality	Opening Date
Dageraad Brewing	Burnaby	2014
Dead Frog Brewery (formerly Backwoods Brewing)	Langley	1998; renamed 2006
Deep Cove Brewers and Distillers	North Vancouver	2013
Dix BBQ & Brewery	**Vancouver**	**1998**
Doan Craft Brewing Co.	**Vancouver**	**2015**
Dockside Brewing Co.	**Vancouver**	**1997**
Dogwood Brewing	**Vancouver**	**2015**
East Van Brewing Co.	**Vancouver**	**2017**
Electric Bicycle Brewery	**Vancouver**	**2018**
Faculty Brewing Co.	**Vancouver**	**2016**
Farm Country Brewing Inc.	Langley	2019
Farmhouse Brewing Co.	Chilliwack	2020
Field House Brewing Co.	Chilliwack	2016
Five Roads Brewing Co.	Langley	2019
Foamers' Folly Brewing Co.	Pitt Meadows	2015
Four Winds Brewing Co.	Delta	2014
Fuggles and Warlock / Fuggles Beer	Richmond	2015
Granville Island Brewing	**Vancouver**	**1984**
Green Leaf Brewing	North Vancouver	2013
Hearthstone Brewing	North Vancouver	2014
Horseshoe Bay Brewery	West Vancouver	1982
Horseshoe Bay Brewing Company	West Vancouver	1988
House of Funk Brewing Co.	North Vancouver	2019
Locality Brewing	Langley	2021
Loudmouth Brewing	Abbotsford	2018
Luppolo Brewing Co.	**Vancouver**	**2016**
Main Street Brewing Co.	**Vancouver**	**2014**
Maple Meadows Brewing	Maple Ridge	2015
Mariner Brewing Co.	Coquitlam	2017
Mission Springs Brewery	Mission	1996
Moody Ales & Co.	Port Moody	2014
Mountain Ale Co.	Surrey	1983
Northpaw Brew Co.	Port Coquitlam	2018

Brewery or Brewpub (breweries in Vancouver city limits are in bold)	Municipality	Opening Date
Off the Rail Brewing	**Vancouver**	**2015**
Old Abbey Ales	Abbotsford	2015
Old Yale Brewing	Chilliwack	2000
Parallel 49 Brewing	**Vancouver**	**2012**
The Parkside Brewery	Port Moody	2016
Postmark Brewing (then Settlement Brewing, then Van Urban Beer Co.)	**Vancouver**	**2014**
Powell Brewery	**Vancouver**	**2012**
R&B Brewing	**Vancouver**	**1997**
Ravens Brewing Company	Abbotsford	2014
Red Truck Beer	**Vancouver**	**2005**
Ridge Brewing Company	Maple Ridge	2015
Russell Brewing Company	Surrey	1995
Sailor Hagar's Brewpub	North Vancouver	1994
Shaftebury Brewing	**Vancouver**	**1987**
Shaketown Brewing Co.	North Vancouver	2022
Slow Hand Brewing	**Vancouver**	**2019**
Smugglers Trail Caskworks	Langley	2017
Steamworks Brewing	**Vancouver**	**1995**
Steel & Oak Brewing Co.	New Westminster	2014
Steel Toad Brewing	**Vancouver**	**2014**
Steveston Brewing Co.	Richmond	1986
Storm Brewing Ltd.	**Vancouver**	**1994**
Strange Fellows Brewing	**Vancouver**	**2014**
Studio Brewing	Burnaby	2021
Superflux Beer Company	**Vancouver**	**2020**
Surlie Brewing	Abbotsford	2014
Tinhouse Brewing Co.	Port Coquitlam	2019
Trading Post Brewing	Fort Langley	2016
Twin Sails Brewing	Port Moody	2015
WayBack Brewing	Surrey	2023
White Rock Beach Beer Company	White Rock	2014
Wildeye Brewing	North Vancouver	2019
Yaletown Brewing	**Vancouver**	**1994**
Yellow Dog Brewing Co.	Port Moody	2014

NOTES

INTRODUCTION

1 The brewing was relocated to the new plant at 11th Street by then.

2 See Nils Fredrickson's survey of the Vancouver Breweries buildings for his full description (see Bibliography).

3 See Appendix 1.

4 Matthews, *Early Vancouver*, 5:21.

5 Jesse Donaldson, "The Rise and Fall (and Rise) of Brewery Creek," *Vancouver Is Awesome,* September 30, 2015, https://www.vancouverisawesome.com /courier-archive/living/the-rise-and-fall-and-rise-of-brewery-creek-3019116.

6 Macdonald, *Vancouver: A Visual History,* viii.

7 Stuart Derdeyn, "History of BC Beer Is Long and Colourful," *The Province*, April 12, 1998.

8 Wiebe, *Craft Beer Revolution*, 103.

9 For more on this history, I recommend Judith Bennett, *Ale, Beer, and Brewsters in England: Women's Work in a Changing World, 1300–1600* (New York: Oxford University Press, 1999), and David M. Perry, "What Google Bros Have in Common with Medieval Beer Bros," *Pacific Magazine*, August 22, 2017, https://psmag.com/social-justice/alewives-and-google-bros.

10 Wiebe, *Craft Beer Revolution*, 8.

11 "What Is Craft?," *Canadian Craft Brewers Association,* https://ccba-ambc.org/about/.

CHAPTER 1

1 "City Went Skyward in a Sweeping, Fiery Blaze," *The Province*, May 21, 1936.

2 According to a photo preserved in the New Westminster Archives (Item IHP7776), the earliest saloon to open in New Westminster was The Retreat in Sapperton (now 129 East Columbia Street) around 1861. However, Gassy Jack himself owned the earliest version of the Globe Saloon in New Westminster, which opened shortly after The Retreat—from 1862 until he moved it to Gastown in 1867. See John Mackie, "This Week in History: 1867 Gassy Jack Deighton Moves to the Future Vancouver," *Vancouver Sun*, September 29, 2017.

3 Glenn Tkach, "The Hastings Mill," Forbidden Vancouver Walking Tours, https://forbiddenvancouver.ca/the-hastings-mill/.

4 The history of Gassy Jack isn't central to the history of Vancouver brewing, but it is important to acknowledge how problematic he was behind the jolly facade that history has given us. In February 2022, his statue in Gastown was toppled after years of activists calling for its removal. Both archival and oral histories reveal that John Deighton took a twelve-year-old Indigenous girl, Quahail-Ya, as his second wife, with some testifying that she ran away from him at the age of fifteen.

5 McDonald, *Making Vancouver*, 13.

6 "The Vancouver Daily World: Illustrated Souvenir Publication. The Financial, Professional, Manufacturing, Commercial, Railroad and Shipping Interests of Vancouver, B.C.," pamphlets, BC Historical Books ([Vancouver]: [McLagan & Co.], [1891?]), doi:http://dx.doi.org/10.14288/1.0222268.

7 Macdonald, *Vancouver: A Visual History*, 20.

8 Ibid., 22.

9 Macdonald, *Vancouver: A Visual History*, 22; Smith, *Vancouver Is Ashes*, 21.

10 Macdonald, *Vancouver: A Visual History*, 24.

11 There is much of this history that I cannot explore in this small book—particularly the histories of First Nations peoples and the role of the CPR in land development. For much more thorough treatment of the early years of Vancouver, I refer readers to Bruce Macdonald's *Vancouver: A Visual History*, Robert McDonald's *Making Vancouver,* and Norbert MacDonald, "The Canadian Pacific Railway and Vancouver's Development to 1900," BC *Studies*, no. 35, 1977, 1–33.

12 "City Went Skyward."

13 Smith, *Vancouver Is Ashes*, 22.

14 Ibid.

15 Ibid.

16 Ibid., 8.

17 Ibid., 20.

18 Quoted in Smith, *Vancouver Is Ashes,* 109.

19 Ibid., 72.

20 Ibid., 110.

21 Draper, *Vancouver City Directory, 1888*, vi

22 *Vancouver Daily Province*, May 21, 1936, 9.

23 Hamilton, *Sobering Dilemma*, 36.

24 This information was obtained from the permit record books housed in the City of Vancouver Archives. See also Robert Campbell's work on saloon culture in *Demon Rum or Easy Money.*

25 "Discriminatory BC Laws," BC *Redress*, https://bcredress.ca/wp-content/uploads/2021/06/discriminatory_legislation_in_bc_1872_1948-reformatted.pdf, last updated May 2022.

26 Hamilton, *Sobering Dilemma*, 34.

CHAPTER 2

1 McDonald, *Making Vancouver*, 33.

2 See Chapter 5.

3 I'm aware that "craft" is our modern term for small, independent brewing, and wasn't used at the time. I'm using it here for convenience and to mark the difference between these small breweries and the larger consolidated corporations that gradually came to dominate the industry.

4 It is possible that he was living elsewhere in adulthood, but I could find no evidence for it. Numerous records attest to Doering being born in Leipzig but none were available showing his residency anywhere else in Germany.

5 Dennis Mutter files. Dennis Mutter is Charles Doering's great-great-grandson and he allowed me to consult his family documents relating to Doering.

6 Poling, *Germany's Urban Frontiers*, 19–21.

7 Ibid., 33.

8 Evans, "The Vancouver Island Brewing Industry," 19.

9 The timing is uncertain. Doering was naturalized as a British subject in Canada in 1890, which meant that he had been living in Canada for at least six years (since 1884). He lived in Victoria before moving to Vancouver, and I could find no record of him living elsewhere in Canada. Vancouver newspaper articles from 1890 and 1891 state that he first lived in Denver after leaving Germany when he was twenty-two. Evidence from "British Columbia Naturalization Records, 1859–1926" in Familysearch.org indicates that he lived in San Francisco. Obituaries of his business partner Benjamin/Bernard Wrede confirm that he lived there and then travelled to British Columbia with Doering in approximately 1881. However, Bill Wilson states that Doering arrived in Victoria in 1879. See also: *Victoria Daily Times*, July 8, 1897, and Wilson, *Beer Barons of BC*, 7. Wilson's source for the 1879 date is *Vancouver Voters 1886: A Biographical Dictionary*, published in 1994 by Peter Claydon, Valerie Melanson, and members of the British Columbia Genealogical Society.

10 This information about how Nelson and Doering met was obtained from Brian Vanvliet's article in the September 1985 edition of the Fraser Valley Bottles and Collectables Club Newsletter. I was unable to independently verify all of the information in Mr. Vanvliet's article, although his extensive binder of notes corroborates some of it. He was unable to recall the exact sources he had used.

11 *The Victoria Daily Times*, January 15, 1887.

12 Newspaper ads from throughout 1887 describe the saloon in these terms and identify Doering and White as the new proprietors.

13 *The Victoria Daily Times*, December 13, 1886. When there was some uncertainty as to who won the contest, Doering's opponent, a William Snyder, tore up his shot card so that accurate measurements could not be taken. The article gives the crowd's final consensus that Doering had won the match.

14 *The Victoria Daily Times*, January 15, 1887.

15 *The Daily Colonist*, September 7, 1887.

16 *The Victoria Daily Times*, July 18, 1897.

17 Wilson, *Beer Barons of BC*, 7.

18 What was then Seaton Street is now the section of Hastings west of Burrard. See Lazarus, "The Life and Death of Seaton Street."

19 *Daily News Advertiser*, August 17, 1904. According to this story, Kappler "came to Vancouver in 1886, before the great fire, and built the first brewery here on the site of the present establishment of the Vancouver Breweries Limited on Mount Pleasant. Mr. Charles Doering later bought out Mr. Kappler and he [Kappler] then established the Columbia Brewery."

20 City of Vancouver Archives, COV-S383.

21 *Vancouver Daily World*, September 29, 1888.

22 Sources conflict regarding when John Williams bought City Brewery and renamed it Red Cross. The Watsons' *Pioneer Breweries of British Columbia* gives 1892 as the year and Hagelund's *House of Suds* claims 1888. Sneath's *Brewed in Canada* claims that Rekab founded City Brewery in 1887 and John Williams purchased it in 1888 (57), then, confusingly, later claims that Williams *founded* City Brewery in 1887 and changed its name to Red Cross in 1891 (358). Wilson's *Beer Barons of BC* (possibly the most reliable source of all of these) gives 1887 as the year Rekab opened City Brewery and 1888 as the year Williams bought it. He also records Red Cross as first being in existence in 1890 (57). Newspaper accounts confirm that by 1889 John Williams owned the brewery, but it was still called City Brewery and not Red Cross (*Vancouver Daily World*, April 4, 1889).

23 *Daily News Advertiser*, July 8, 1900.

24 The record of his request is in the City Council minutes from November 21, 1887. This information is recorded in Greg Evans's notes from these minutes, housed in Simon Fraser University Archives, BC Beer History Archive, F216-3-5-0-8, Greg Evans fonds.

25 This advertisement occurs multiple times throughout 1890 in Victoria and Vancouver newspapers.

26 A record of Clara, her father Alois, and her sibling immigrating in 1885 is found in the following source: Passenger Lists of Vessels Arriving at New York, New York, 1820–1897 (National Archives Microfilm Publication M237, roll 484); Records of the US Customs Service, Record Group 36.

27 *Vancouver Daily World*, February 21, 1893.

28 *Vancouver Weekly World*, September 28, 1893.

29 Clara's father Alois, having fallen ill with dropsy, tragically took his own life at what is described as his son-in-law's house in Vancouver, where he was living at the time (*Nanaimo Daily News*, June 15, 1894).

30 Sneath, *Brewed in Canada*, 358.

31 *Vancouver Daily World*, September 5, 1894.

32 Bex Dawkes, "Nelson Brewing: 30 Years of Craft Beer," BC *Ale Trail Blog*, May 14, 2023, https://bcaletrail.ca/nelson-brewing-30-years-of-craft-beer/; Sneath, *Brewed in Canada*, 362, 368; Wilson, *Beer Barons of BC*, 49.

33 Evans, "The Vancouver Island Brewing Industry," 43.

34 Ibid., 30.

35 Julius Reisterer and C. Reisterer are both recorded as employees in 1892. It is possible that the C. Reisterer was his wife Clara, since other breweries (such as Columbia) did record female employees or co-owners this way, but we just cannot know for sure. See Simon Fraser University Archives, F316-3-5-0-8, Greg Evans fonds.

36 *Vancouver Daily World*, May 1, 1893.

37 See Chapter 5.

38 *Victoria Daily Times*, September 15, 1888.

39 Carr, "Metchosin Petunias."

40 *The Province*, May 20, 1904.

41 *Vancouver Semi-Weekly World*, July 14, 1899.

42 Mackinnon, "New Evidence," 121.

43 *Daily News Advertiser*, March 21, 1902.

44 *Daily News Advertiser*, August 4, 1906

45 *Weekly News-Advertiser*, October 10, 1888.

46 Simon Fraser University Archives, BC Beer History Archive, F216-3-5-0-7, Greg Evans fonds.

47 *Weekly News-Advertiser*, October 2, 1889.

48 Ibid.

49 Kheraj, *Inventing Stanley Park*, 135.

50 *The Province*, October 24, 1900.

51 *Daily News Advertiser*, August 18, 1904.

52 According to the archival information summarized on the Changing Vancouver website, Doering owned each of these one at a time. See: https://changing vancouver.wordpress.com/2013/12/.

53 *Vancouver Daily World*, January 6, 1890.

54 *Vancouver Daily World*, January 6, 1890.

55 *Weekly News-Advertiser*, March 23, 1892; January 20, 1892.

56 *Daily News Advertiser*, July 27, 1892.

57 Later in the summer, the papers reported that Williams's sister-in-law Miss Brown came to take her nephew and niece (his children) to England. It is not clear whether those two children included the infant.

58 *Weekly News-Advertiser*, April 8, 1891; *Daily News Advertiser*, September 27, 1891.

59 BC Archives Genealogical Records, reg. no. 1893-09-116129, microfilm no. B13810; *Daily News Advertiser*, March 28, 1893.

60 *Vancouver Daily World*, July 13, 1894.

61 *Vancouver Daily World*, July 14, 1897.

62 *Weekly News-Advertiser*, February 11, 1891; *Vancouver Daily World*, August 2, 1906.

63 *The Province*, April 1, 1902.

64 Evans, "The Vancouver Island Brewing Industry," 57–58.

65 *Daily News Advertiser*, October 12, 1899.

66 Wilson, *Beer Barons of BC*, 8.

67 *The Province*, February 17, 1900.

68 The September 14, 1946, interview with Mrs. Williams was given by City Archivist J.S. Matthews and housed in the Vancouver City Archives.

69 Complaints about this issue first start to surface in newspaper accounts from March of 1899, and occur for several years following.

70 For the next one to two years, there were still advertisements in local papers referring to specific beers by one of the two breweries, as if they had not amalgamated. It is not clear why this was done. One explanation may be that the April 1900 date is incorrect, and the amalgamation occurred later. Another may be that Doering and Williams still wanted to use the power of their respective brands, at least until their new joint flagship beer was released (see below).

71 Wilson, *Beer Barons of BC,* 8; "Cascade Beer Was Sampled," *The Province*, June 24, 1902.

72 City Archivist J.S. Matthews recorded this conversation for the City of Vancouver Archives, where it is now housed: AM 54 S23, Box 505-E-03 fld 147.

73 Bartlett, "Real Wages," 39.

74 *Vancouver Daily World*, June 11, 1902.

75 *The Province*, May 29, 1902.

76 *The Province*, June 24, 1902.

CHAPTER 3

1 Admittedly, the current Stanley Park Brewing is not a craft/independent brewery and only some of their brewing is done on site—they produce their packaged beer at the Labatt plant in Delta, BC. See Rob Mangelsdorf, "Stanley Park Brewing Restaurant and Brewpub to Open July 29," *The Growler,* July 16, 2019, https://bc. thegrowler.ca/news/stanley-park-brewing-restaurant-and-brewpub-to-open -july-29/. The recently opened Brewing August, near Granville Island, is as equally far west as the Stanley Park Brewpub, although it is not near the original city settlement the way Parallel 49 and Stanley Park are.

2 Due to the inconsistency of naming in the newspapers, it is possible that Fred Millar was in fact the person elsewhere identified as Andrew Mueller, co-proprietor of the brewery and husband of Mary Mueller. However, I cannot confirm this. It may also be that this Millar is the same as the Mueller who stabbed Kappler in a fight (see note 36). Regardless, it seems that Columbia was full of excitement.

3 Accounts of the event as summarized and quoted in this paragraph and the following paragraph were provided in the August 19 and August 20, 1889, issues of the *Vancouver Daily World.*

4 *Vancouver Daily World,* August 20, 1889.

5 *Weekly News-Advertiser,* August 28, 1889.

6 *Vancouver Daily World,* August 27, 1889.

7 *Vancouver Daily World,* September 18, 1889.

8 The 1888 Vancouver city directory lists Kappler as a brewer for Vancouver Brewery.

9 This brewery is a bit of a mystery, and the sources aren't very consistent. San Francisco Brewery doesn't even make it into Sneath's otherwise very detailed chronological history of Canadian breweries in his book *Brewed in Canada.* The Watsons' *Pioneer Breweries of British Columbia* gives it a single line (the address and date of opening, which they suggest was 1889), and Hagelund's *House of Suds* refers to a rumour about a San Francisco Brewery that was built on 12th Avenue (not 11th) but alleges there are no records that substantiate it. Bill Wilson's *Beer Barons of BC* and a 2008 report prepared by Donald Luxton and Associates for the City of Vancouver both indicate that the Reifels opened San Francisco Brewery for a brief time in 1888, but that the same location became Red Star Brewery from 1889 to 1891.

10 *Vancouver Daily World,* August 20, 1889.

11 *Vancouver Daily World,* August 19, 1889.

12 *Vancouver Daily World,* June 4, 1892.

13 *Vancouver Daily World,* December 14, 1891.

14 *Vancouver Weekly World,* August 25, 1892.

15 Watson, *Pioneer Breweries,* 11.

16 Lani Russwurm, "Squatting in Early Vancouver Part 1: Tar Flat," https://forbidden vancouver.ca/blog/tar-flat/.

17 *The Province,* April 19, 1902.

18 *The Globe,* April 28, 1898.

19 "Mueller" is spelled inconsistently in the public records (Mueller, Muller, Miller), and the first name of Mary's husband is also inconsistently reported (Andrew, Alois, Joseph), so there is uncertainty about whether the various "Millers" and "Muellers" referred to in relation to Columbia are part of Mary and Andrew's family.

20 *Daily News Advertiser,* April 28, 1893.

21 Simson's account is recorded in the City of Vancouver Archives, AM54-S23-2--, Box 504-G-02 fld 181.

22 It may also have been that Mary was functionally the proprietor/manager while they were still alive, since earlier stories occasionally refer to her as managing the brewery. While Kappler died in 1904, the date of Mr. Mueller's death is uncertain, partly because his first name is different across different newspapers and public records.

23 *The Province*, August 3, 1903. Gordon responded by turning on Mr. Mueller and knocking him over, for which he received a ten-dollar fine in court. *The Province* has a lengthy addendum to this story, which relates how a large man entered the court and paid Gordon's fine for him, then got into an altercation outside the courtroom. It concludes with the following mysterious account of the actions of Gordon's defender: "In the corridor there was the sound of a struggle, and then something like the side of a house began to bump down the stairs. The final crash raised the dust in the courtroom. Downstairs a man on the sidewalk started, turned and asked the maker of faces: 'What was that that dropped?' 'Me,' was the answer and the man walked off."

24 *The Province*, November 9, 1905; *Daily News Advertiser*, November 10, 1905. One of the papers lists Mary as the proprietor of the brewery: *Vancouver Daily World*, November 9, 1905.

25 *The Province*, July 25, 1901.

26 The account that follows of Mary Mueller and Dutch Bill is taken (in quotation and summary) from the following newspaper accounts: *Vancouver Daily World*, March 31, 1891; April 2, 1891; June 6, 1891. *Daily News Advertiser*, April 3 and 5, 1891; May 1891.

27 Some newspaper accounts refer to him as Dutch Bill (real name William H. Viannen), while others call him, confusingly, "Herbst." The *Daily News Advertiser* says that he was called by both names. All accounts are referring to the same incident, although some of them suggest that Herbst/Bill was a former employee of the brewery. Regardless of the confusing reporting about the victim, Mary Mueller's actions are clearly described.

28 Patricia Mary Johnson, "John Foster McCreight: First Premier of British Columbia" (master of arts thesis, University of British Columbia, 1947), 68.

29 *Daily News Advertiser*, May 10, 1891.

30 The following account is taken from the *Vancouver Daily World*, July 9, 1891.

31 *Vancouver Daily World*, February 25, 1891; April 7, 1891.

32 There is no other mention of an Emil Miller at the brewery, although there are several Millers/Millars and one Emil Gerhauser, who was the main brewer. This may be another instance of the reporter mixing up names.

33 *Daily News Advertiser*, September 5, 1903.

34 Just a few months earlier, in February of 1891, the *Vancouver Daily World* reported that the Vancouver Institute's February 7 discussion on "Different Methods of Regulating the Liquor Traffic" would include Balfour-Ker speaking on non-prohibition.

35 V*ancouver Daily World*, February 8, 1896.

36 *Vancouver Daily World*, May 6, 1896. This story refers to Joseph Mueller as stabbing Kappler, but specifies that Mueller had been in business with Kappler for years. Another story describes Mary as married to Joseph Mueller, so it seems

that sometimes Andrew was referred to as Joseph, or simply that the papers made this error on occasion.

37 *Vancouver Daily World*, May 14 and 15, 1896.

38 *Vancouver Daily World*, September 21, 1900.

39 *Vancouver Daily World*, May 9, 1902.

40 *Vancouver Daily Province*, February 5, 1904; January 21, 1904.

41 See, for example, Green's *Vancouver City Directory, 1899–1900*, which features ads for Columbia Brewery and Stanley Park Brewery on nearly every second page.

42 Michael Stein, "A Lager Darkly: In Search of Culmbacher, One of America's Great, Extinct Beers," *Good Beer Hunting*, March 16, 2021, https://www.goodbeer hunting.com/blog/2021/3/16/dark-lager-hunting-in-search-of-culmbacher -one-of-americas-great-extinct-beers.

43 "The Vancouver Daily World," 12.

44 The following information is taken from Mary's court testimony as recorded word for word in the *Weekly News-Advertiser* of September 23, 1896, and the newspaper coverage of the case in the *Daily World* of September 16 and 17, 1896.

45 Sneath, *Brewed in Canada*, 60.

46 *Vancouver Daily World*, January 31, 1899.

47 *The Province*, August 16, 1904.

48 Ibid.

49 *The Province,* April 15, 1905.

50 *Vancouver Daily World*, June 13, 1907.

51 Wilson, *Beer Barons of BC,* 58.

52 The legalese here gets complicated, but the core issue at stake is the extent of federal versus provincial jurisdiction when it comes to regulating the production and sale of alcohol. The Dominion Inland Revenue Act—a federal law—could license brewers to make beer and carry on trade as a brewer. However, a provincial licence was still required for the sale of alcohol. The Supreme Court case of the King vs. Neiderstadt in 1905 involved a situation similar to that of Mary Mueller. Neiderstadt, a BC brewer, contested that he could sell his product in amounts smaller than two gallons (i.e., sell it retail) because he had a Dominion licence. The court disagreed, stating, "A brewer may properly be convicted under a provincial license law for selling liquor with a provincial license, although he holds a license under the Dominion Inland Revenue Act to carry on the trade or business of a brewer. *Semble,* the license under the Inland Revenue Act applies only as a permit to manufacture as regards the excise duties." W.J. Tremeear, ed., *Canadian Criminal Cases Annotated* (Toronto: Canada Law Book Company, R.R. Cromarty, 1906), 10:292.

53 *The Province*, December 29, 1906.

54 The account of this party is given in the *Daily News Advertiser,* August 20, 1907.

55 *Daily News Advertiser*, June 7, 1907.

56 *The Province*, November 3, 1908.

57 *Vancouver Daily World*, April 17, 1908.

58 *Vancouver Daily World*, February 16, 1910.

59 *The Vancouver Sun*, December 30, 1950.

CHAPTER 4

1 Wilson, *Beer Barons of* BC, 14; *Vancouver Daily World*, April 18, 1891; 1901 Census of Canada. Province: BC. District: 1/Burrard. S. District: D. Subdivision: 2 in Vancouver City, page 3. The May 19, 1891, issue of the *Vancouver Daily World* records the Finance Committee's recommendation of where to direct Foubert's fine (to R.E. Gosnell, the census commissioner who would eventually become BC's first archivist and librarian).

2 Wilson, *Beer Barons of* BC, 14; *Vancouver Daily World*, January 4, 1890; "Frank Foubert: A Business History," Holedown Newsletter, Fraser Valley Bottles and Collectibles Club, August 1986; *Daily News Advertiser*, September 10, 1892.

3 See, for example, the advertisement from *Daily News Advertiser*, September 10, 1892.

4 Adam Chatburn, "Stanley Park Brewing," *What's Brewing*, January 2018, https://www.whatsbrewing.ca/2018/01/stanley-park-brewing-part1/.

5 Siebel, *One Hundred Years of Brewing*, 295. It's not clear how accurate this estimate was.

6 *Vancouver Daily World*, July 2, 1895.

7 Wilson, *Beer Barons of* BC, 15; *Vancouver Semi-Weekly World*, June 23, 1896.

8 Wilson, *Beer Barons of* BC, 15.

9 The personal recollections about John Dyke and his family have been sourced from these family documents, many of which have no titles, and therefore are not cited formally.

10 The couple had ten children, but only eight survived past infancy. The eldest child died at the age of two months, and another child was stillborn several years later.

11 In city directories until about 1911 or 1912 he is listed as "Brewer," but there is no record of whether he was actually employed anywhere. It is certain that by 1914 he was working at the sawmill; a newspaper story from that year reports on an accident he experienced in which he lost part of his hand.

12 The BC Geographical Names database explains the peak's origin story, referring to Phyllis by her married name of Beltz: https://apps.gov.bc.ca/pub/bcgnws/names/39314.html.

13 Quoted in James Wood, "Social Club or Martial Pursuit? The BC Militia before the First World War," BC *Studies*, no. 173 (2012): 56.

14 McDonald, *Making Vancouver*, 202.

15 *The Province*, May 18, 1898.

16 *Daily News Advertiser*, May 9, 1899.

17 Matthews, *Early Vancouver*, 1:40.

18 Wood, "Social Club or Martial Pursuit?," 50–51.

19 T.O. Townley, "A Pre-war Sketch of the Militia of Vancouver," *The Duke* 2, no. 19 (September 2019): 77, https://bcregimentmedia.storage.googleapis.com/wp-content/uploads/2019/09/19081709/The-Duke-September-2019-Reduced-PDF.pdf.

20 The following quotations and information about the battle are taken from the July 3, 1899, edition of *The Province*.

21 Quoted in the *Daily News Advertiser,* November 30, 1899.

22 *The Province,* September 26, 1900.

23 *Vancouver Semi-Weekly World,* July 17, 1896. It is not clear whether Miller was present to inspect every brewery that opened or if he attended Foubert's opening week as a special favour.

24 The R.E. Green city directory of 1899–1900 records a W.B. McKinnon who was a civil and mining engineer, and newspaper accounts of the time refer to a William B. McKinnon who ran the Alhambra Hotel. Either of these McKinnons is a possible candidate for the man who was a Royal shareholder. Bill Wilson's book indicates that McKinnon gave his professional identity as "Gentleman" on the incorporation documents, leaving us none the wiser as to his identity.

25 Wilson, *Beer Barons of BC*, 15–16.

26 *Vancouver News-Herald,* March 27, 1952; see also the entry for R.L. Leigh-Spencer on the *WestEndVancouver* blog: https://westendvancouver.wordpress.com /biographies-a-m/biographies-l/leigh-spencer-rosa-leigh-1857-1937/.

27 Wilson, *Beer Barons of BC*, 15–16.

28 *The Province,* May 16, 1902.

29 *The Province,* April 7, 1903.

30 Wilson, *Beer Barons of BC*, 16.

31 See Chapter 5 for an outline of what happened with these smaller and less influential breweries.

32 Taken from the description in the Cedar Cottage fonds at the City of Vancouver Archives.

33 Wilson, *Beer Barons of BC*, 16. Files MSS 54, vol. 15, no. 326, City of Vancouver Archives.

34 See Wilson, *Beer Barons of BC*, 18, for a discussion of when Dyke stopped brewing. Apparently Dyke was still listed in directories as being a brewer until 1912, but there is no indication that he was actually working as a brewer after 1903 or 1904.

35 *Vancouver Sun,* October 22, 1914.

36 *The Province,* May 11 and 12, 1903.

37 Wilson, *Beer Barons of BC*, 17; *Daily News Advertiser,* August 14, 1906; *The Province,* March 19, 1906.

38 Wilson, *Beer Barons of BC*, 18; *Vancouver Daily World,* April 7, 1908.

39 *The Province,* March 1, 1910.

CHAPTER 5

1 See Chapter 1 of Robert Campbell's *Demon Rum or Easy Money* for a high-level overview of how prohibition came to be enacted in British Columbia. See Douglas Hamilton's *Sobering Dilemma* for a more thorough exploration of prohibition's causes and consequences.

2 Most of the basic information provided here involving dates and names (some of which is contested among the sources) is from the following sources: Bill Wilson's extensive listing of breweries in *Beer Barons of BC*, the *Mount Pleasant Historical Themes* document from the City of Vancouver, and George and Ilene Watson's *Pioneer Breweries of British Columbia*. Additional sources are cited in endnotes.

3 *The Province*, June 16, 1902.

4 *Weekly News-Advertiser*, July 1, 1891, and October 21, 1891.

5 See, for example, *Vancouver Daily World*, October 26, 1901, and *Vancouver Semi-Weekly World*, July 3, 1903.

6 *Daily News Advertiser*, December 13, 1907.

7 *Daily News Advertiser*, July 20, 1890; *Vancouver Daily World*, July 29, 1890.

8 *The Province*, September 30, 1903.

9 Sneath, *Brewed in Canada*, 95–100.

10 *Victoria Daily Times*, February 16, 1909; *Evening Post*, April 5, 1909.

11 Evans, "The Vancouver Island Brewing Industry," 170, 203–5.

12 The liquor licence register shows brewery wholesale licence fees to be $125 in 1906 and $250 in 1909, so the amounts Royal refers to in its appeals must be a combination of different licensing costs.

13 *Vancouver Daily World*, April 18, 1906.

14 *Vancouver Daily World*, February 29, 1912.

15 This letter is included in the BC Archives, PR-0873, Hat Creek Ranch fonds. It refers to potential actions taken by Victoria-Phoenix Brewing and Vancouver Breweries and suggests that "your company [likely a brewery] will no doubt do the same." This indicates that the addressee isn't the owner of either of those breweries, so Doering is ruled out. It could possibly be Reifel, although information from the letter written the following day (see note 22 below) might make that less likely.

16 *The Province*, July 29, 1907; *The Nicola Herald*, August 2, 1907.

17 This is the brick building at Scotia and 6th—it's beside Main Street Brewing on Scotia.

18 *Evening Post*, June 12, 1909.

19 *The Province*, November 30, 1910; Wilson, *Beer Barons of BC*, 59; Watson, *Pioneer Breweries*, 58–59.

20 Wilson, *Beer Barons of BC*, 59.

21 This means something equivalent to "drag" or a downer.

22 BC Archives, PR-0873, Hat Creek Ranch fonds.

23 https://www.bankofcanada.ca/rates/related/inflation-calculator/.

24 *Saturday Sunset,* September 21, 1912.

25 *The Province,* February 15, 1913.

26 UBC refers to Union Brewing Company, not University of British Columbia— although this was a point of confusion at the time.

27 Appleton, "Underground Brewmaster," 86.

28 Wilson, *Beer Barons of BC,* 59.

29 *National Post,* September 1916.

30 Printed in the *Victoria Daily Times,* August 23, 1916.

31 Some letters about this legal action are preserved in the BC Archives, Hat Creek Ranch fonds, but I have not found much secondary source material that discusses these documents or the court case. I have thus far been unable to find actual court records of the case, although they may exist.

32 Sneath, *Brewed in Canada,* 204, 388, 391.

33 The entire MOA is preserved in the BC Archives, Labatt Breweries of British Columbia fonds, MS-1883.1.13 (1911).

34 *Consolidations in Canadian Industry and Commerce, January 1, 1900, to December 31, 1933.* https://qspace.library.queensu.ca/bitstream/handle/1974/12012 /consolidationsin00slsn.pdf?sequence=1&isAllowed=y.

35 Sneath, *Brewed in Canada,* 96.

36 See Campbell, *Demon Rum,* 65, and BC Archives, Labatt Breweries of British Columbia fonds, MS-1883.1.3.

37 *The Province,* October 26, 1926. I could not find his first name, but according to the Brewers Journal Directory of 1918, R. Samet was at one point president of the California Brewers Association and vice-president of the Brewers Protective Association of San Francisco.

38 Campbell, *Demon Rum,* 64–66.

39 "United States v. Pacific Forwarding Co. Ltd. et al.," *vLex,* no. 20884, District Court, W.D. Washington, N.D., October 26, 1934, https://case-law.vlex.com/vid /united-states-v-pacific-890475038.

40 Campbell, *Demon Rum,* 65.

41 And they are! There are several histories that explore corporate beer in the twentieth century, including Merrill Denison's *The Barley and the Stream: The Molson Story* (1955), Matthew Bellamy's *Brewed in the North: A History of Labatt's* (2019), Maureen Ogle's *Ambitious Brew: The Story of American Beer* (2007), Paul Brent's *Lager Heads: Labatt and Molson Face Off for Canada's Beer Money* (2004), and William Knoedelseder's *Bitter Brew: The Rise and Fall of Anheuser-Bush and America's Kings of Beer* (2014).

CHAPTER 6

1 Thomas Hopkins, "24 Million Cans of Beer on the Wall," *Maclean's,* October 2, 1978; Tony Eberts, "$50 Million Loss to B.C. Economy in Beer Strike," *The Province,* September 8, 1978.

2 Sneath, *Brewed in Canada*, 204.

3 Appleton, *Brewing Revolution*, 33.

4 Appleton, "Underground Brewmaster," 84.

5 Appleton, "Underground Brewmaster," 86.

6 Interview with Jenny Mitchell, August 10, 2021; John Mitchell Foundation /
What's Brewing, "In Memoriam: John Mitchell, Canada's Original Craft
Brewer," *What's Brewing*, June 17, 2019, https://www.whatsbrewing.ca/news
/john-mitchell-in-memoriam/.

7 Appleton, *Brewing Revolution*, 58–59; interview with Jenny Mitchell, August 10,
2021; "Who Really Came First?," *Beerology*, 2009, https://beerology.ca/articles
/who-really-came-first%E2%80%A6/.

8 In some accounts it appears that the Troller sold Carling, not Molson. It is not clear
whether the Troller changed suppliers, but I have taken this detail about Molson
from Jenny Mitchell's recollections.

9 The information in this paragraph was largely gathered from my interviews with
Jenny Mitchell and John Ohler, and corroborated by contemporary newspaper
accounts.

10 Quoted in Appleton, *Brewing Revolution*, 52.

11 Ibid., 53.

12 According to Appleton's book, he drafted the entire proposal himself while John
and Jenny toured around the Kootenays. However, John Mitchell later contested
various elements of Appleton's account. It seems likely that they both contributed
in some way.

13 Quoted in Appleton, *Brewing Revolution*, 55.

14 Sneath, *Brewed in Canada*, 215.

15 Linda Diebel, "Legislature Antics Rival Kindergarten," *The Vancouver Sun*, April
30, 1980.

16 Denny Boyd, "Some Flickers of Fun amid the Gloom," *The Vancouver Sun*,
February 10, 1982.

17 Tony Wanless, "Cheap Beer—or More Froth?," *The Province*, March 15, 1981.

18 Quoted in Appleton, *Brewing Revolution*, 59.

19 Interview with Jenny Mitchell, August 10, 2021. See also Appleton, *Brewing
Revolution*, 59–60.

20 Bonni Raines Kettner, "'No Collusion' on Beer Hikes," *The Province*, October 1,
1981.

21 From John Ohler's collection of John Mitchell documents.

22 From John Ohler's collection.

23 Appleton, *Brewing Revolution*, 60, 186.

24 Minutes of the Special Meeting of the Council of the Corporation of the District
of West Vancouver, February 15, 1982.

25 Appleton, *Brewing Revolution*, 74–75.

26 Al Sheehan, "Home-Brewed Ale a Sellout for Pub," *The Vancouver Sun,* July 17, 1982.

27 Bruce McLean, "'Bayle' Brew a Winner," *The Province,* July 4, 1982.

28 Interview with Paul Hadfield, January 12, 2022; interview with Jenny Mitchell, August 10, 2021; Kim Lawton, "Hops among Friends: Paul Hadfield of Spinnakers," BC *Ale Trail Blog,* December 1, 2017, https://bcaletrail.ca/hops -among-friends-paul-hadfield-spinnakers/; Appleton, *Brewing Revolution,* 77–85; Sneath, *Brewed in Canada,* 216.

29 From John Ohler's collection.

30 A shorter version of this account, which is drawn from my interviews with David Bruce-Thomas, was published in a summer 2023 post on the BC *Ale Trail.* My interview with David took place in April 2023.

31 There is an occasional mention in articles from *What's Brewing,* but the accounts of the post-Mitchell Horseshoe Bay Brewing still seem largely unknown.

32 Sneath, *Brewed in Canada,* 216, 426.

33 This summary of Wilson and Patrick's motivations was taken from my interview with David Bruce-Thomas, in April 2023. Bruce-Thomas worked for Wilson and Patrick during this time.

34 Dave Smith, "Bill Herdman: A Brewer's Tale," *What's Brewing,* January 1, 2016, https://www.whatsbrewing.ca/2016/01/bill-herdman/.

35 Interview with John Ohler, July 23, 2021; "Uncorking a Legend: Discovering the John Mitchell Story," *Beer Me BC,* July 7, 2019, https://beermebc.com/2019/07/07 /john-mitchell/.

36 Interview with John Ohler, July 23, 2021.

37 Interview with Iain Hill, June 8, 2021.

38 "John Mitchell Raises Toast to BC's Craft Breweries in Parting Message," What's Brewing BC, YouTube, June 17, 2019, https://www.youtube.com /watch?v=oG4VHnGZ4co.

39 The information from the previous two paragraphs was gathered from my inter- view with Sean Hoyne on November 30, 2022, and Appleton, *Brewing Revolution,* 126–27.

40 Interview with John Ohler, July 23, 2021.

41 Ibid.

42 Dave Smith, "In Memoriam: Frank Appleton: Brewer. Writer. Gentle Man," *What's Brewing,* April 29, 2021, https://www.whatsbrewing.ca/2021/04 /frank-appleton/.

CHAPTER 7

1 Matt Meuse, "How Granville Island Changed the Course of Vancouver Urban Design History," CBC, March 12, 2017.

2 There is uncertainty about which brewery was actually the first. Granville Island is often claimed to be the first, but Bryant Brewery of Maple Ridge and Mountain

Ale Co. of Surrey both technically opened before Granville Island. However, these were both very short-lived and relatively unknown. It is certainly true that Granville Island was very early on the craft beer scene and had a huge influence on the development of the BC brewing industry.

3 Taylor, *Making Way,* 7–16.

4 Ibid., 75.

5 Ibid., 97.

6 Interview with Mitch Taylor, September 21, 2022.

7 Taylor, *Making Way,* 76.

8 The two previous quotations were from *The Province,* May 23, 1973, and *The Vancouver Sun,* August 24, 1973.

9 Sneath, *Brewed in Canada,* 218.

10 Taylor, *Making Way,* 101.

11 October 1988 speech given at the Resources for Business Growth Conference, from Mitch Taylor's private files (these files are now housed in the Simon Fraser University Archives, BC Beer History Archive, Mitch Taylor fonds, but were not when I initially consulted them).

12 Taylor, *Making Way,* 175.

13 Interview with Mitch Taylor, September 21, 2022; Mitch Taylor files.

14 Interview with Mitch Taylor, September 21, 2022; Taylor, *Making Way,* 177–78.

15 Interview with Mitch Taylor, September 21, 2022.

16 Taylor, *Making Way,* 178.

17 Ibid., 179.

18 Email from Mitch Taylor, October 22, 2023.

19 Sneath, *Brewed in Canada,* 218; email from Mitch Taylor, October 22, 2023.

20 Taylor, *Making Way,* 177.

21 Anne Tempelman-Kluit, "Brewing up a Fresh, New Lager," *The Globe and Mail,* June 27, 1984, SB5.

22 These UBC analyses are preserved in Mitch Taylor's files.

23 2014, Taylor's speech for the Granville Island Brewing thirtieth anniversary celebration, Mitch Taylor files.

24 Pete McMartin, "What's Brewing on the Island," *The Vancouver Sun,* June 20, 1984.

25 Unless otherwise cited, information about Whistler Brewing is taken from my interview with Gerry Hieter on December 2, 2022, and follow-up email correspondence.

26 In Sneath's account, Mingay wrote the business plan and brought it to a Vancouver stockbroker to see if it would be an investment possibility. However, in his interview with me, Gerry Hieter indicated that he filed the business name, wrote the business plan, and established the company before Mingay was on the scene at all. His account is supported by contemporary accounts: a *Vancouver Sun* article of July 8, 1988, by Rodd Nutt ("Third Exposition Expects First Profit") describes

Hieter as the president of Whistler Brewing Co. and seeking investors. Another *Sun* article written a year later, on July 20, 1989 ("Whistler Brew Market Bound"), describes Hieter as the *vice*-president and Whistler Brewing as supported by nine investors who provided $1.25 million in start-up capital. Sneath is correct, however, in his summary of how Mingay funded the brewery via a venture capital corporation. See Sneath, *Brewed in Canada*, 250.

27 The organizational chart and job descriptions are part of Mitch Taylor's files.

28 Email from Mitch Taylor, December 6, 2022.

29 Tony Eberts, "Beer's to You," *The Province*, June 29, 1984.

30 Ibid.

31 McMartin, "What's Brewing on the Island"; Damian Inwood, "The Best Beer in British Columbia," *The Province*, October 13, 1985.

32 Dave Smith, "Bill Herdman: A Brewer's Tale," *What's Brewing*, January 1, 2016, https://www.whatsbrewing.ca/2016/01/bill-herdman/.

33 Interview with Gary Lohin, November 25, 2022.

34 Ray Chatelin, "Cheers! Fine Brew, Good News," *The Province*, August 3, 1984; Jon Ferry, "Kitsilano Goes Trendy," *The Province*, February 17, 1985; Gordon Keast, "White Collar Brew: Quenching a Thirst for Premium Brew," *Andras Dances North Light*, September 1988. See Chapter 8 for the story of Shaftebury Brewing.

35 Quoted in Ben Tierney, "Competition Is Brewing in BC's Beer Industry," *Montreal Gazette*, July 20, 1985.

36 Interview with Mitch Taylor, September 21, 2022.

37 Ibid.

38 Mitch Taylor files, including a 1987 Management Information Systems study on GIB that was drafted by SFU. Taylor's files are now housed in the Simon Fraser University Archives, BC Beer History Archive, Mitch Taylor fonds.

39 Tierney, "Competition Is Brewing."

40 Interview with Mitch Taylor, September 21, 2022; Taylor, *Making Way*, 259.

41 David Baines, "Brewer States Case," *The Province*, September 13, 1985.

42 Sneath, *Brewed in Canada*, 220.

43 Ibid.

44 *The Province*, June 26, 1985.

45 Joe Dizney, "Fatal Attraction: When Big Business Comes Courting, Small-Business Owners Can't Resist," *Wall Street Journal*, date unknown (photocopied article found in Mitch Taylor files).

46 Taylor, *Making Way*, 259.

47 Noel, *Barrel-Aged Stout and Selling Out*, 145–47.

48 Appleton, *Brewing Revolution*, 195.

49 Taylor, *Making Way*, 261.

50 Ibid.

51 Dizney, "Fatal Attraction."

52 Interview with Mitch Taylor, September 21, 2022.

53 Dizney, "Fatal Attraction."

54 Taylor, *Making Way*, 262.

55 Eve Lazarus, "Granville Island Brewing Renaming Beer Brands," *Marketing Magazine* 102, no. 21 (1997): 4.

56 Malcolm Parry, "Money and Other Scents at Women of Distinction," *The Vancouver Sun*, May 17, 1997, D9.

57 Stuart Derdeyn, "Uncapping New Look: Granville Island Brewing Offers New Tastes, Ideas," *The Province*, May 25, 1997, B33.

58 Eve Lazarus, "Granville at New Stage in 'Beer Life,'" *Marketing Magazine* 107, no. 25 (2002): 4.

59 Brian Morton, "Granville Island Brewery's Focus Helps It Remain Strong," *The Vancouver Sun*, May 6, 2009.

60 Larry Pynn, "'Mass-Market Lagers' Win in Hop-Sided Olympics Beer War," *The Vancouver Sun*, February 5, 2010.

61 Interview with Gerry Hieter, December 2, 2022. In 2019, however, when the Victoria Beer Society took over the GCBF, Granville Island Brewing was not grandfathered in because it did not meet the criteria for a craft brewery.

62 Jan Zeschky, "Granville Island's Mocha Porter Full of Alluring Subtlety," *The Province*, December 11, 2016.

63 Randy Shore, "Craft Movement Has Started Beer Renaissance in Canada," *The Vancouver Sun*, April 5, 2016; Carolyn Ali, "New Brewmaster Kevin Emms Starts at Granville Island Brewing," *The Georgia Straight*, June 1, 2015, https://www.straight.com/food/461881/new-brewmaster-kevin-emms-starts-granville-island-brewing.

64 World Brand Design Society, "Brandopus's Redesign of Granville Island Brewing Invites You to Discover What's 'Just around the corner,'" September 13, 2022, https://worldbranddesign.com/brandopuss-redesign-of-granville-island-brewing-invites-you-to-discover-whats-just-around-the-corner/#:~:text=At%20Granville%20Island%2C%20adventure%20is,each%20brew%20to%20come%20through.

65 Gerry Hieter, "What Was Brewin' in the '80s," *What's Brewing*, Summer 2020, https://issuu.com/whatsbrewing/docs/2020-02/11.

66 In the summer of 2023, the taproom employees of Granville Island Brewing went on strike. An agreement was settled upon in mid-August, but the strike was very visible in the Granville Island area and drew attention to the non-craft and highly corporate ownership structure of the current Granville Island Brewing.

CHAPTER 8

1 Noëlle Phillips, "A Perfect Pairing: Craft Beer and Ultimate Frisbee," *The Growler*, October 22, 2022, https://bc.thegrowler.ca /features/a-perfect-pairing-craft-beer-and-ultimate-frisbee/.

2 Quotations from Ralph Berezan are taken from my interview with him on October 3, 2023.

3 Glen Schaefer, "New Brew Making Friends," *The Vancouver Sun,* August 25, 1983.

4 Bob Chamberlain, "Charlie's Wish Comes True," *The Province,* August 25, 1983.

5 Damian Inwood, "The Best Beer in British Columbia," *The Province,* October 13, 1985.

6 Chamberlain's article also cites this line as their slogan.

7 Len Grant, "Beer Revolution," *The Province,* August 4, 1985.

8 Gerry Hieter, "What Was Brewin' in the '80s," *What's Brewing*, Summer 2020, https://issuu.com/whatsbrewing/docs/2020-02/11; Ian Austin, "Two Brothers Hop out of Suds," *The Province,* March 10, 1986.

9 Simon Fraser University Archives, BC Beer History Archive, F-330, R&B Brewing fonds, Box 27687, 2023-012, 157-3-6.

10 Email from Mitch Taylor, October 12, 2023.

11 Appleton, *Brewing Revolution*, 36.

12 Gordon Keast, "White Collar Brew: Quenching a Thirst for Premium Brew," *Andras Dances North Light,* September 1988; Brian Lewis, "Steveston Takes Cap off Brewing Attraction," *The Province,* July 20, 1986.

13 "Beer Firm Falls Flat, Receivers Take Over," *The Province,* July 10, 1989.

14 Inwood, "The Best Beer in British Columbia."

15 Appleton, *Brewing Revolution*, 194.

16 Unless otherwise cited, the information provided about Shaftebury in the following pages is taken from my interview with Tim Wittig on September 29, 2022.

17 Simon Fraser University Archives, BC Beer History Archive, R&B fonds, F-330 157-3-6, Box 27687.

18 From Shaftebury's draft business plan in Simon Fraser University Archives, BC Beer History Archive, R&B fonds, F-330 157-3-6, Box 27687.

19 Jean Kavanagh, "Bureau Gets Its Own Santa," *The Province,* November 12, 1993; Shawn Conner, "Empty Stocking Fund: Lower Mainland Christmas Bureau Welcomes Big, New Headquarters as Holiday Campaign Kicks off," *The Province,* November 22, 2022. Back issues of the Jewish Museum and Archives of BC *Chronicle* (jewishmuseum.ca) reveal that when the museum launched a major donation campaign in 2016, Leon Menkis signed up at the donor level of Sustainer, meaning he was giving $5,000–$14,999 per year for at least the next several years (the final year I could find him listed as a donor was 2019, three years before his death).

20 Simon Fraser University Archives, BC Beer History Archive, R&B fonds, F-330 157-3-6, Box 27687.

21 Wittig emphasized to me that what was later named the Shaftebury Coastal Cream Ale was *not* an ale, but a Sleeman's lager (since Sleeman acquired Shaftebury).

22 Noëlle Phillips, "Why Bitter Is an Under-Appreciated Beer Style," *The Growler,* June 2, 2022, https://bc.thegrowler.ca/beer/why-bitter-is-an-under-appreciated -beer-style-plus-10-brewed-in-b-c-bitters-to-try/.

23 Jackson, *Beer Companion*, 69.

24 Wiebe, *Craft Beer Revolution*, 168.

25 See Chapter 6.

26 Interview with James Walton, July 12, 2022.

27 Chuck Davis, "A 'New' Way to New West and Other Lucky Discoveries," *The Province,* December 23, 1990.

28 Stuart Derdeyn, "Pumping Up Brand Loyalty," *The Province,* June 21, 1998; Mark Wilson, "Shaftebury Sells Brand Names," *The Province,* January 20, 1999.

29 Stuart Derdeyn, "Rumors Flowed Like Ale at Victoria Fest," *The Province,* November 22, 1998.

30 "Sleeman's Brews Deal to Acquire Shaftebury," *The Vancouver Sun,* January 15, 1999.

31 Appleton, *Brewing Revolution,*194. In my interview with him, Tim Wittig also expressed his awareness of this.

32 Bruce Constantineau, "Bigger Bats Taking Over Some Small Breweries," *The Vancouver Sun,* May 1, 1999.

33 Stuart Derdeyn, "Sleeman's Takes Over Shaftebury," *The Province,* January 17, 1999.

34 Interview with Ken Beattie, August 25, 2022.

CHAPTER 9

1 Interview with Stuart Derdeyn, October 4, 2023.

2 Noëlle Phillips, "A Perfect Pairing," *The Growler,* October 21, 2022, https://bc .thegrowler.ca/features/a-perfect-pairing-craft-beer-and-ultimate-frisbee/.

3 "The Class of '94: A Brave New Wave in BC Brewing," *What's Brewing,* July 9, 2020, https://www.whatsbrewing.ca/2020/07/class-of-1994/.

4 Wiebe, *Craft Beer Revolution*, 102.

5 See Chapter 10.

6 Interview with Tony Dewald, May 30, 2023.

7 This practice, according to Dageraad founder Ben Coli, "turned brewers into celebrities!" (interview with Ben Coli, November 25, 2022).

8 Unless otherwise cited, information in this section is taken from my interview with Iain Hill on June 8, 2021.

9 J. Random, "What's Bruin: The Career of Iain Hill," *What's Brewing,* September 13, 2018, https://www.whatsbrewing.ca/2018/09/whats-bruin-the-career-of-iain-hill/, and interview with Iain Hill.

10 Including the brewpubs started by Mark James, such as Dix, Big Ridge, and Avalon, and others like Steamworks. All of these were started in the 1990s.

11 Random, "What's Bruin."

12 Ibid.

13 Appleton, *Brewing Revolution*, 133–34.

14 Random, "What's Bruin."

15 Stuart Derdeyn, "Real-Ale Campaigners Make Difference at Fest," *The Province*, November 23, 1997.

16 The moniker is one that multiple people have used over the years, including Joe Wiebe in his book *Craft Beer Revolution* (141), the intro to Storm at www.vancouverbrewerytours.com, and reporter Mia Stainsby in a September 2015 feature for the *Vancouver Sun*. Indeed, Walton himself welcomes the nickname: "I think I call myself 'mad scientist' just because I like how it sounds. I kind of identify with [animated character] Rick Sanchez. He's a mad scientist that's always drunk." (Transcript from interview recorded by Rewild Films for *Trek* magazine, "Craft Beer Revolutionist," February 20, 2019, https://magazine.alumni. ubc.ca/2019/winter-2019/features/craft-beer-revolutionist.)

17 Unless otherwise cited, information about James Walton is taken from my interview with him on July 12, 2022.

18 Mia Stainsby, "James Walton, a Cutting Edge Brewer," *The Vancouver Sun*, September 25, 2015, https://vancouversun.com/news/staff-blogs /james-walton-a-cutting-edge-brewer.

19 Ibid.

20 Many craft beer drinkers agreed at the time that the Alexander Keith's IPA did not meet the style guidelines for an IPA. See: Mike Doherty, "Canadians' Love Affair with India Pale Ale," *Maclean's*, August 5, 2011, https://macleans.ca/society/life /canadians-love-affair-with-india-pale-ale/.

21 Wiebe, *Craft Beer Revolution*, 141.

22 "The Class of '94: A Brave New Wave in BC Brewing," *What's Brewing*, July 9, 2020, https://www.whatsbrewing.ca/2020/07/class-of-1994/.

23 Wiebe, *Craft Beer Revolution*,142.

24 Interview with Tony Dewald, May 30, 2023.

25 Ibid.

26 This GCBF 2003 program is preserved in Simon Fraser University Archives, BC Beer History Archive, F-330 R&B Brewing fonds, Box 27561 148-2-2.

27 Unless otherwise cited, information in this section was obtained from Barry Benson during my interview with him on February 16, 2022.

28 Stott, *Beer Quest West*, 148.

29 Sneath, *Brewed in Canada*, 286–87.

30 As Chapters 6 and 8 discuss, McQuhae was one of the first brewers at Spinnakers and John Mitchell's partner in helping get Shaftebury off the ground.

31 Lundy Dale, "Shirley Warne's Legendary Life in Brewing," *What's Brewing*, July 15, 2020, https://www.whatsbrewing.ca/2020/07/shirley-warne/.

32 Matt Carter, "R&B Brewing Wins 2021 BC Ale Trail Best Brewery Experience Award," BC *Ale Trail Blog*, October 7, 2021, https://bcaletrail.ca/best-brewery -experience-2021/.

33 Information relating to R&B's pre-opening business planning is taken from materials available in Simon Fraser University Archives, BC Beer History Archive, Box 27559, Accession 2023-003, F-330.

34 The draft business plan's survey of other breweries does include Storm, but it is presented as not much of a threat because of the used equipment and the overall loose style of running a business that Walton had. Storm's longevity likely took many customers and colleagues from the 1990s by surprise.

35 "R&B Brewing," BC Ale Trail brewery listings, https://bcaletrail.ca/breweries /rb-brewing-co/.

36 Benson recalls this to be around 2006 but was unable to confirm the exact date.

37 Stott, *Beer Quest West*, 149.

38 Simon Fraser University Archives, BC Beer History Archive, R&B fonds, Box 27559, F-330. In a conversation with me on October 21, 2023, Benson laughed when recalling these beer plans, saying that no one in the '90s was looking for styles like that. He was right, but R&B's rock 'n' roll ethos could not be stopped!

39 His bands included the Spores in the 1980s, the Aging Youth Gang from the '90s until now, and the Jazzholes for the past ten years.

40 Carter, "R&B Brewing Wins 2021 BC Ale Trail Best Brewery Experience Award."

41 At this time, the Alibi Room was a beer hangout but not the craft beer mecca that Nigel Springthorpe turned it into a few years later.

42 Michael Kane, "'Passion for Beer' at Heart of East Vancouver Brewery," *The Vancouver Sun,* September 19, 2007.

43 Phillips, "A Perfect Pairing."

44 Appleton, *Brewing Revolution*, 187–88.

45 Ryan Ingram, "BC's Legacy Craft-Beer Brands Change with the Times," *Vancouver Is Awesome,* March 29, 2017, https://www.vancouverisawesome.com/courier -archive/living/bcs-legacy-craft-beer-brands-change-with-the-times-3049177.

46 Jennifer Elliott, "Howe Sound Buys R&B Brewing," *Vancouver Magazine,* April 15, 2015, https://www.vanmag.com/drink/bars-and-lounges /howe-sound-buys-rb-brewing/.

47 Carter, "R&B Brewing Wins 2021 BC Ale Trail Best Brewery Experience Award."

48 For much of the Middle Ages, however, brewing was an industry dominated by women. See Noëlle Phillips, *Craft Brew Culture and Modern Medievalism: Brewing Dissent* (Leeds: Arc Humanities Press, 2019); Judith Bennett, *Ale, Beer, and Brewsters in England: Women's Work in a Changing World, 1300–1600* (New York: Oxford University Press, 1999); and Tara Nurin, *A Woman's Place Is in the Brewhouse: A Forgotten History of Alewives, Brewsters, Witches, and CEOs* (Chicago: Chicago Review Press, 2021).

49 Unless otherwise cited, information about Shirley Warne is taken from my

interview with her on November 14, 2023, in Kaslo, British Columbia.

50 Brassneck website, https://brassneck.ca/old-bitch/.

51 Credit here to the other women from this era, such as Alyson Tomlin, brewer for R&B, and Lundy Dale, a Cicerone who founded CAMRA Vancouver and much more. As far as I can tell, however, Shirley Warne was the only woman from this time period who actually owned and ran a craft brewery.

52 Jurgen Gothe, "A Bright New Scene Brewing," *The Vancouver Sun*, Saturday Review, August 26, 1995.

53 Dale, "Shirley Warne's Legendary Life in Brewing."

54 Gothe, "A Bright New Scene Brewing," 42.

55 Mia Stainsby, "Pub the Place to Let Off Steam in Gastown," *The Vancouver Sun*, August 24, 1995, 39.

56 Stott, *Beer Quest West*, 91; Dale, "Shirley Warne's Legendary Life in Brewing."

57 Dale, "Shirley Warne's Legendary Life in Brewing."

58 Stott, *Beer Quest West*, 91.

59 Ibid.

60 Dale, "Shirley Warne's Legendary Life in Brewing."

61 Unless otherwise cited, quotations and other information about Lohin's life and career are taken from my interview with him on November 25, 2022.

62 See Chapter 6 for more on this.

63 The exact timing of Lohin's employment at Whistler Brewing is remembered slightly differently by Lohin and Hieter, who didn't know one another at the time. I have attempted to confirm accuracy as much as possible. It is clear, however, that Hieter was largely pushed out (if he hadn't formally resigned) by the time Lohin was working there.

64 Email from Gerry Hieter, October 28, 2023; interview with Gerry Hieter, December 2, 2022.

65 Interview with Gerry Hieter, December 2, 2022. As the Whistler Brewing discussion in Chapter 7 explains, later newspaper accounts and Sneath's book *Brewed in Canada* both erroneously describe the relationship of Mingay to Whistler Brewing, claiming that he started the brewery and wrote up the business plan, and that Gerry was "Jenny." It appears that these accounts, which are belied by earlier newspaper articles about Hieter and Whistler Brewing from the late 1980s, were based upon 1990s interviews with Mingay and little other information.

66 Stott, *Beer Quest West*, 129.

67 Interview with Stuart Derdeyn, October 4, 2023.

68 Gary Lohin, "The Class of '94: Sailor Hagar's Heyday," *What's Brewing*, June 25, 2020, https://www.whatsbrewing.ca/2020/06/gary-lohin-sailor-hagars/.

69 Alan Daniels, "Brew-ha-ha in North Shore Pub," *The Vancouver Sun*, May 3, 1994.

70 Lohin, "The Class of '94."

71 Ibid.

72 Stuart Derdeyn, "'Wee Heavy' Sends You to the Highlands," *The Province*, December 15, 1996.

73 Stuart Derdeyn, "Barley Wines Are Really BIG Beers and Not Wine at All," *The Province*, December 14, 1995.

74 Michael Kane, "Cheers to Surrey, the City That Has the Best Beer," *The Vancouver Sun*, January 29, 2008.

75 Randy Shore, "Central City's Gary Lohin Is a Rising Star in the Beer World," *The Vancouver Sun*, April 29, 2010.

76 Randy Shore, "Brewmaster Pushes Frontiers of Flavour," *The Vancouver Sun*, April 13, 2011.

77 Unless otherwise cited, information about Dewald's life and career is taken from my interview with him on May 30, 2023.

78 Mallory O'Neill, "Tony Dewald: Scholar, Drummer, Brewmaster," *What's Brewing*, February 5, 2016, https://www.whatsbrewing.ca/2016/02/trading-post/.

79 Unless otherwise cited, all information about Lundy Dale's life and career is taken from my interview with her on October 26, 2023.

80 Rebecca Whyman, "2018 BC Beer Awards: Honouring a Legend and Some Newcomers," BC *Ale Trail Blog*, October 21, 2018, https://bcaletrail.ca/2018-bc-beer-awards-honouring-a-legend-and-some-newcomers/.

81 "The Mark Anthony Group Announces Divestiture of the Company's Ready-to-Drink Cider and Craft Beer Brands in Canada," *Cision News*, November 10, 2015, https://www.newswire.ca/news-releases/the-mark-anthony-group-announces-divestiture-of-the-companys-ready-to-drink-cider-and-craft-beer-brands-in-canada-545110962.html.

82 This is anecdotal evidence, but I've noted this mix-up between Mark Anthony and Mark James in various conversations with BC craft beer drinkers. In this Reddit thread from 2016, two different posters make the same mistake: https://www.reddit.com/r/vancouver/comments/5ecghm/new_to_the_city_and_really_want_to_get_into_the/?rdt=46909.

83 He also clarified that the brewpubs in Yaletown and Whistler now have their own ownership group, of which he is a part.

84 Appleton, *Brewing Revolution*, 131.

85 Ibid., 132.

86 Ibid., 135.

87 Charlie Smith, "Mark James Highlights History of Brewery Creek at Launch of Red Truck Brewery and Truck Stop Diner," *The Georgia Straight*, June 3, 2015, https://www.straight.com/news/465056/mark-james-highlights-history-brewery-creek-launch-red-truck-brewery-and-truck-stop.

88 Stott, *Beer Quest West*, 205.

89 Wiebe, *Craft Beer Revolution*, 125.

90 Ibid., 136.

CHAPTER 10

1 See Chapter 7.

2 https://archive.news.gov.bc.ca/releases/archive/pre2001/2000/3414.asp.

3 "No Fun City" is a common moniker used to describe Vancouver.

4 Frank Luba, "Something Big Is Brewing in East Van," *The Province*, March 7, 2014.

5 The government's responses to these letters were included in FOI Request Response PSS-2022-23239.

6 Interview with Ken Beattie, August 25, 2022; Frank Luba, "Zoning Bylaws Put a Stopper to New Provincial Liquor Rules," *The Province*, February 22, 2013.

7 BC Government FOI Request Response PSS-2022-23239, "July 2012 Liquor Control and Licensing Branch Consultation Document."

8 BC Government FOI Request Response D11654815A_Response_Package_JAG-2014-01536, "Edited Report: Local Government and First Nations Roles and Responsibilities in Liquor Licensing Process."

9 Randy Shore, "Vancouver May Allow Lounges in Breweries," *The Vancouver Sun*, April 24, 2013.

10 All Vancouver City Council and public hearing minutes and information is taken from the City of Vancouver's archived minutes and agendas, found here: https://covapp.vancouver.ca/councilMeetingPublic/CouncilMeetings.aspx.

11 The signees were 33 Acres, Powell Street, Bomber, R&B, Brassneck, Red Truck, Coal Harbour, Storm, Main Street, and Parallel 49.

12 The change didn't take effect until March 1, 2013, but newspaper articles from earlier that year indicate that breweries knew it was about to happen. Tasting rooms were being planned well ahead of time.

13 BC Government FOI Request Response D11654815A_Response_Package_JAG-2014-01536, letter from Adam Chatburn of CAMRA for use in a government meeting on September 24, 2012.

14 Interview with Ken Beattie, August 25, 2022.

15 Perhaps a future book will offer a deep dive into all of the Vancouver beer boom breweries—not just these four, but other important breweries, including 33 Acres, Bomber, Powell, and more.

16 Unless otherwise cited, information and quotations about Main Street are taken from my interview with Pike and Forsyth on July 15, 2021.

17 This is a proven strategy used by other breweries, such as Superflux and Brewing August, that want a head start before investing their money in a permanent brewery location.

18 Elizabeth Fischer, letter to Council, February 2012, https://council.vancouver.ca/20120227/documents/item6othercommentsRedacted.pdf.

19 Unless otherwise cited, information about Brassneck Brewing and the Alibi Room is taken from my interview with Nigel Springthorpe on October 20, 2022.

20 Nikki Bayley, "Nigel Springthorpe of the Alibi Room on Fifteen Years behind the Bar," *Eater,* October 29, 2013, https://vancouver.eater.com/2013/10/29/6343911 /nigel-springthorpe-of-the-alibi-room-on-fifteen-years-behind-the-bar.

21 Justin McElroy, "The 10 Best Breweries in Southwest British Columbia," June 27, 2022, https://justinmcelroy.com/2022/06/27/the-10-best-breweries-in-southwest -british-columbia/.

22 https://imstartingacraftbrewery.com/tag/aaron-jonckheere/page/4/.

23 Interview with Iain Hill, June 8, 2021.

24 Wiebe, *Craft Beer Revolution*, 143.

25 https://imstartingacraftbrewery.com/tag/aaron-jonckheere/page/4/.

26 Interview with Iain Hill, June 8, 2021.

27 Ibid.

28 Interview with Ben Coli, November 25, 2022.

29 Wiebe, *Craft Beer Revolution*, 127.

30 Interview with Ben Coli, November 25, 2022.

31 Randy Shore, "Nine-Day Festival 'Hopping' with Fun," *The Vancouver Sun,* April 25, 2013.

32 Jesara Sinclair, "Parallel 49 Craft Brewery Union Vote Result of 'Growing Pains,'" CBC, December 15, 2014, https://www.cbc.ca/news/canada/british-columbia /parallel-49-craft-brewery-union-vote-result-of-growing-pains-1.2872594.

33 Anderson, "Craft Capitalism," 166.

34 Sinclair, "Parallel 49 Craft Brewery Union Vote."

35 Anderson, "Craft Capitalism," 166.

36 Ibid., 169.

37 Ibid., 122

38 Charlie Smith, "The Beer Issue: US Craft Brewer Brienne Allan Generates Onslaught of Whistle-Blowing about Sexism," *The Georgia Straight,* June 2, 2021, https://www.straight.com/food/beer-issue-us-craft-brewer-brienne-allan -generates-onslaught-of-whistle-blowing-about-sexism.

39 This topic deserves its own book.

40 Navarro, "Afterword," 391.

41 See the Parallel 49 EA website at https://p49eaonline.ca/ and Parallel 49's announcement of this change here: https://parallel49brewing.com/articles/7.

42 https://parallel49brewing.com/articles/7.

43 Wiebe, *Craft Beer Revolution,* 112; Callister Brewing website, https://callisterbrewing.com.

44 Jan Zeschky, "Startup Brewers Find Shared Home at Callister," *The Province*, July 10, 2015.

45 Interview with Diana McKenzie, November 2, 2023.

46 Instagram post, December 25, 2023.

47 Unless otherwise cited, all information about Dageraad and Ben Coli is taken from my interview with him on November 25, 2022.

48 Wiebe, *Craft Beer Revolution*, 158.

49 Unless otherwise cited, information about Four Winds is taken from my interview with Brent Mills on October 1, 2021.

50 Meagan Albrechtson, "Four Winds Brewing Company: A Brewing Brood," *Montecristo Magazine,* May 15, 2015, https://montecristomagazine.com /food-and-drink/four-winds-brewing-company.

51 Wiebe, *Craft Beer Revolution*, 160.

52 Randy Shore, "Drinkable Belgian Makes a Splash in the Marketplace," *The Vancouver Sun,* July 10, 2013.

53 Robin Brunet, "Sudsy Soothsayers," *The Province,* May 31, 2016.

54 Carlos Mendes, "Six Minutes with Brent Mills, Co-Founder and Brewmaster at Delta's Four Winds," *Scout Magazine,* April 3, 2017, https://scoutmagazine .ca/2017/04/03/drinker-six-minutes-with-brent-mills-co-founder-brewmaster -at-deltas-four-winds/.

55 *Pint Sighs Blog,* "An Interview with Four Winds Brewing Co.," May 17, 2013, https://pintsighs.blogspot.com/2013/05/an-interview-with-four-winds-brewing -co.html.

56 Interview with Adam Henderson, July 23, 2021.

57 *The Vancouver Sun,* May 28, 2020.

CHAPTER 11

1 Stuart Derdeyn, "Call the BeerVan," *The Vancouver Sun,* April 30, 2020.

2 Interview with Ben Coli, November 25, 2022.

3 "Vancouver Craft Beer Week Festival Criticized for Long Lineups," *Canadian Beer News,* July 12, 2022, https://www.canadianbeernews.com/2022/07/12/vancouver -craft-beer-week-festival-criticized-for-long-line-ups-high-cost-and-other-issues/.

4 Interview with Ken Beattie, August 25, 2022.

5 Derdeyn, "Call the BeerVan."

6 Interview with Ken Beattie, August 25, 2022.

7 Joe Wiebe, "2020: A Year for Beer Like No Other," *BC Ale Trail Blog,* December 31, 2020, https://bcaletrail.ca/2020-a-year-for-beer-like-no-other/.

8 According to Beattie, for example, during the pandemic the province "temporarily allowed direct delivery from third party warehouses by the brewers directly to consumers." See Wiebe, "2020: A Year for Beer Like No Other."

9 Joe Wiebe, "The Road Ahead," *The Growler,* September 17, 2021, https:// bc.thegrowler.ca/features/the-road-ahead/.

10 Wiebe, "2020: A Year for Beer Like No Other."

11 To be dubbed a farm brewery, according to the 2015 revision of the Agricultural Land Reserve Regulations, at least 50 percent of the brewery's raw ingredients must be grown on site. A 2017 amendment allowed breweries to obtain up to half their ingredients from other farms in the province if they cannot meet the

50 percent requirement. For a summary of this issue, see Matt Cavers, "Farmers First," *The Growler,* June 25, 2021, https://bc.thegrowler.ca/features/farmers-first/.

12 Noëlle Phillips, "Malting: BC's Hidden Beer Industry," *The Growler,* May 26, 2023, https://bc.thegrowler.ca/features/malting-b-c-s-hidden-beer-industry/.

13 Unless otherwise cited, information about Locality is taken from my interview with Andy Hamer on July 29, 2021.

14 Matt Carter, "Barnside Brewing Wins the 2023 BC Ale Trail Best Brewery Experience Award," BC *Ale Trail Blog,* October 26, 2023, https://bcaletrail .ca/2023-barnside-best-brewery-experience-award/.

15 Ian Jacques, "Something Brewing on the Farm," *Delta Optimist,* January 30, 2020, https://www.delta-optimist.com/local-business/something-brewing-on-the -farm-3115852.

16 Unless otherwise cited, information about Hutton and his work at Barnside is taken from my interview with him on November 9, 2021.

17 Carter, "Barnside Brewing Wins the 2023 BC Ale Trail Best Brewery Experience Award."

18 Interview with Nigel Springthorpe, October 20, 2022.

19 Interview with Sho Ogawa, December 4, 2022; interview with Iain Hill, June 8, 2021. Superflux now makes beers other than hazy IPAs, but hazies remain their core style.

20 Rob Mangelsdorf, "Drink This: All Together by Superflux," *The Growler,* April 30, 2020, https://bc.thegrowler.ca/beer/beer-reviews/drink-this-all-together-by -superflux/.

21 "We love that Superflux makes beers that even non-beer people will love!" enthuses Helen Siwak in a *Medium* essay on the brewery. See Helen Siwak, "Why YVR's Newest Brewery Is Pretty Superflux'ing Great," *Medium,* November 3, 2020, https://medium.com/ecolux-lifestyle-co/vancouvers-newest-brewery-is-pretty -superflux-ing-great-ecolux-lifestyle-c0c49f557e0.

22 This is, admittedly, an anecdotal conclusion based upon discussions in some craft beer groups on Facebook, but it remains true that Superflux's name is widely recognized among beer drinkers.

23 The Casca blog, https://casca.com/blogs/news/superflux-beer.

24 Interview with Adam Henderson, July 23, 2021.

25 Thalia Stopa, "What's the Deal with Superflux Beer Company's Awesome Branding?," *Scout Vancouver*, October 26, 2017, https://scoutmagazine .ca/2017/10/26/whats-the-deal-with-superflux-beer-companys-awesome -branding/.

26 Wilson and Stone, *Beer and Society,* 44.

27 The whole issue can be found here: https://issuu.com/whatsbrewing/docs/2020 -02/11.

28 Interview with Joe Wiebe, January 11, 2024.

29 Jorden Foss, "Why BC Craft Breweries Are Having Such a Hard Time Right Now," *The Georgia Straight,* April 27, 2024.

30 Noëlle Phillips, "The Breweries of Kitsilano: From Big Beer to the Craft Community," BC *Ale Trail Blog,* May 1, 2024, https://bcaletrail.ca/the -breweries-of-kitsilano/.

31 Zach Clarke, "Craft Beer Sales Continue to Rise," BCIT *News,* October 12, 2023, https://bcitnews.com/2023/10/12/craft-beer-sales-continue-to-rise-despite -b-c-drinking-less-beer-every-year/.

32 Interview with Tony Dewald, May 30, 2023.

33 Interview with Joe Wiebe, January 11, 2024.

BIBLIOGRAPHY

ARCHIVES CONSULTED

Simon Fraser University Archives
City of Vancouver Archives
Royal BC Museum and Archives
Personal files from Mitch Taylor, Hugh Greer, Dennis Mutter, and John Ohler

PRIMARY SOURCES

Periodicals (contemporary and historical):
  The BC Ale Trail Blog
  The British Colonist
  The Daily Colonist
  Daily News Advertiser
  The Georgia Straight
  The Globe and Mail
  The Growler: BC's Craft Beer Guide
  The Montreal Gazette
  The Province / Vancouver Daily Province
  Scout Vancouver
  The Times Colonist
  Vancouver Is Awesome
  The Vancouver Daily World
  The Vancouver Semi-Weekly World
  The Vancouver Sun
  The Victoria Daily Times
  Weekly News-Advertiser
  What's Brewing
Draper, Thomas (compiler). *Vancouver City Directory, 1888.* Victoria: R.T. Williams, 1888.
Green, R.E. (compiler). *Vancouver City Directory, 1899–1900.* Vancouver, 1900.

Henderson's British Columbia Gazeteer and Directory for 1890. Victoria: Henderson, 1890.

Matthews, Major James Skitt. *Early Vancouver*. Vols. 1–5. Vancouver: City of Vancouver, 2011.

Siebel, J.E. *One Hundred Years of Brewing*. Chicago: H.S. Rich & Co., 1901.

Vancouver City Directory, 1896. Vancouver: Hodgson & Co., 1896.

"The Vancouver Daily World: Illustrated Souvenir Publication. The Financial, Professional, Manufacturing, Commercial, Railroad and Shipping Interests of Vancouver, B.C." Pamphlets. BC Historical Books. [Vancouver]: [McLagan & Co.], [1891?]. doi:http://dx.doi.org/10.14288/1.0222268.

SECONDARY SOURCES

Anderson, Benjamin. "Craft Capitalism: Labour and the Narratives of Artisanal Production." PhD diss., Simon Fraser University, 2022.

Appleton, Frank. *Brewing Revolution: Pioneering the Craft Beer Movement*. Madeira Park, BC: Harbour Publishing, 2016.

Appleton, Frank. "The Underground Brewmaster." *Harrowsmith*, May/June 1978, 84–97.

Bartlett, Eleanor. "Real Wages and the Standard of Living in Vancouver, 1901–1929." *BC Studies* 51 (1981): 3–61.

Campbell, Robert. *Demon Rum or Easy Money: Government Control of Liquor in British Columbia from Prohibition to Privatization*. Ottawa: Carleton University Press, 1991.

Canadian Craft Brewers Association. "Who We Are: Promoting and Protecting Independent Craft." Canadian Craft Brewers Association. Last accessed December 28, 2023. https://ccba-ambc.org/about/.

Carr, Emily. "Metchosin Petunias." In *This and That: The Lost Stories of Emily Carr*, edited by Ann-Lee Switzer. Victoria: TouchWood Editions, 2007.

Coutts, Ian. *Brew North: How Canadians Made Beer and Beer Made Canada*. Vancouver: Greystone Books, 2010.

Derdeyn, Stuart. "History of BC Beer Is Long and Colourful," *The Province*, April 12, 1998, B14.

Donaldson, Jesse. "The Rise and Fall (and Rise) of Brewery Creek." *Vancouver Is Awesome*, September 30, 2015. https://www.vancouverisawesome.com/courier-archive/living/the-rise-and-fall-and-rise-of-brewery-creek-3019116.

Evans, Greg. "The Vancouver Island Brewing Industry: 1858–1917." Master's thesis, University of Victoria, 1991.

Fredrickson, Nils. "The Doering and Marstrand Vancouver Breweries: 263 East 7th Avenue and 280 East 6th Avenue, at Scotia." History 205, University of British Columbia, taught by Diane Newell, December 5, 1986.

Hagelund, William. *House of Suds: A History of Brewing in Western Canada*. Surrey, BC: Hancock House Publishers, 2003.

Hamilton, Douglas. *Sobering Dilemma: A History of Prohibition in British Columbia.* Vancouver: Ronsdale Press, 2004.

Jackson, Michael. *Michael Jackson's Beer Companion.* London: Mitchell Beazley, 1994.

Kheraj, Sean. *Inventing Stanley Park: An Environmental History.* Vancouver: UBC Press, 2013.

Lazarus, Eve. "The Life and Death of Seaton Street." https://evelazarus.com/the-life-and-death-of-seaton-street/.

Mackinnon, Mary. "New Evidence on Canadian Wage Rates, 1900–1930." *The Canadian Journal of Economics* 29, no. 1 (1996): 114–31.

Macdonald, Bruce. *Vancouver: A Visual History.* Vancouver: Talon Books, 1992.

McDonald, Robert A.J. *Making Vancouver: Class, Status, and Social Boundaries, 1863–1913.* Vancouver: UBC Press, 1996.

Mount Pleasant Historical Themes. City of Vancouver. May 2008. Accessed January 4, 2024. https://vancouver.ca/files/cov/mount-pleasant-historical-themes.pdf.

Navarro, Ren. "Afterword." In *Beer and Brewing in Medieval Culture and Contemporary Medievalism,* edited by John Geck, Rosemary O'Neill, and Noëlle Phillips, 389–95. Cham, Switzerland: Palgrave MacMillan, 2022.

Noel, Josh. *Barrel-Aged Stout and Selling Out: Goose Island, Anheuser-Busch, and How Craft Beer Became Big Business.* Chicago: Chicago Review Press, 2018.

Poling, Kristin. *Germany's Urban Frontiers.* Pittsburgh: University of Pittsburgh Press, 2020.

Smith, Lisa Anne. *Vancouver Is Ashes: The Great Fire of 1886.* Vancouver: Ronsdale Press, 2014.

Sneath, Allen Winn. *Brewed in Canada: The Untold Story of Canada's 300-Year-Old Brewing Industry.* Toronto: Dundurn Press, 2001.

Stott, Jon C. *Beer Quest West: The Craft Breweries of Alberta and British Columbia.* Victoria: TouchWood Editions, 2011.

Taylor, Mitch. *Making Way: A Memoir.* Mitch Taylor, 2021.

Tkach, Glenn. "The Hastings Mill—Visit the Site of Vancouver's First Settlement." Forbidden Vancouver Walking Tours. https://forbiddenvancouver.ca/the-hastings-mill/. Last accessed December 28, 2023.

Watson, George and Ilene. *Pioneer Breweries of British Columbia: A Look at BC Breweries from a Collector's Point of View.* Westward Collector Publishing, 1974.

Wiebe, Joe. *Craft Beer Revolution.* Madeira Park: Douglas & McIntyre, 2015.

Wilson, Bill. *Beer Barons of BC: Featuring the Secrets of the Stanley Park Brewery.* Lantzville, BC: Tamahi Publications, 2011.

Wilson, Eli Revelle Yano, and Asa Stone. *Beer and Society: How We Make Beer and Beer Makes Us.* Lanham, MD: Lexington Books, 2022.

INDEX

Photo by J. Nordstrom.

NOËLLE PHILLIPS is the author of *Craft Beer Culture and Modern Medievalism* and co-editor of the collection *Beer and Brewing in Medieval Culture and Contemporary Medievalisms*. She is a regular contributor to *The Growler,* BC's craft beer magazine, and the BC Ale Trail blog. She teaches in the English Department at Douglas College.